THE HOTEL AND RESTAURANT BUSINESS

THIRD EDITION

DONALD E. LUNDBERG
Chairman, Department of
Hotel and Restaurant Management
California State Polytechnic University
Pomona

CBI

CBI Publishing Company, Inc.
51 Sleeper Street
Boston, Massachusetts 02210

Library of Congress Cataloging in Publication Data

Lundberg, Donald E
    The hotel and restaurant business.

    Bibliography.
    Includes index.
    1. Hotels, taverns, etc.   2. Restaurants, lunch
rooms, etc.   I. Title.
TX911.L785   1979   338.4′7′6479   79–207
ISBN 0-8436-2142-7
ISBN 0-8436-2175-3 pbk.

Cover/Jacket Design—Baldwin Design
Place Setting Photograph—George Perkins
Hotel—Waldorf-Astoria, New York City
Flatware—Courtesy of The Ritz Carlton, Boston
Linen and Dishes—Courtesy of The Hilton Inn at Logan Airport

CONTENTS

INTRODUCTION

What is the field of hotel and restaurant administration? It is an area of work and study that applies principles and information from a number of disciplines to the problems of selling food, beverages, and lodging to persons away from home. It includes a number of practices and techniques, which have been developed, mostly from experience, for accomplishing these purposes.

A closely related extension of the field of serving the public is the area covered by foodservice in institutions: food served in schools, colleges, hospitals, and nursing homes. The management of city and country clubs also is within the purview of the broader field of hotel and restaurant management.

The field of restaurant and hotel management is interdisciplinary. It draws upon economics, psychology, management, food technology, food chemistry, microbiology, physics, engineering, architecture, accounting, marketing, and law. From these disciplines are formulated approaches, systems, and analytical tools designed to make lodging and foodservice satisfying emotional experiences for people when they are away from home.

Much of hotel and restaurant keeping is an art and will remain so in the future. The relations with people—guests, patrons, employees, purveyors, and the community at large—are closer and often more sensitive than in most fields. The retailer is concerned with customer relations but he does not have his customer eating, drinking, and often sleeping under the same roof.

The hotel and restaurant keeper or club manager often deals with his clients under stress conditions. A patron or guest may be exhilarated, and at his best as a person. He may be depressed, drunk, or expressing his latent feelings of deficiency in many ways.

THE ART IS COMPLEX

Systems and practices make the job of hotel and restaurant keeping much simpler but the human element is difficult to systematize. Sinclair Lewis, who worked in a hotel for a number of years and knew the business well, expressed some of the complexities of the hotel business when he had one of his characters, a traveling salesman, tell the hero of the story in *Work of Art:*[1]

"Look here, son! Somebody been ribbing you about hotelkeeping not being a dignified and highfalutin' line of business? You tell 'em to go soak their head! Dignified! Why, say, fellow was telling me, he was a college professor or something, I met him on a train, and he showed me where in the olden days surgeons were barbers, too, and folks didn't think much of them. They about ranked with the third assistant hired girl. But now, good Lord, when a surgeon agrees to cut you up, you'd think he was the King of France! Hotelkeeping—well, up till now it hasn't been so good because the hotels—taverns they used to call 'em, and inns,

---

1. Sinclair Lewis, *Work of Art* (New York, NY: Doubleday, 1934). Reprinted with permission.

and so on—and they weren't so good. But that's all changing. I tell you, way I figure it, some day there's going to be even bigger and sweller hotels than the Waldorf, and then, as the hotels get bigger, the hotelmen are going to be more important. Lots of swagger folks will get sick of housekeeping and go live in hotels. It will be one of the most important lines of business in the country, with some of the biggest folks in it.

"And as for the usefulness of hotels, well, say, it takes a traveling man to appreciate a hotel—come in all tired and wet and sick of day coaches and cinders, and get a good hot cup o' coffee like Mother Weagle makes, and a good clean bed like here—thought you might have some of the mattresses made of straight-grained pine, next time, and not all this knotty stuff. But I'm just joking. Nothing you could do more important—or interesting—meet all kinds of people, and see 'em with their shirts off, you might say; see the Senator soused and the up-state banker meeting a peacherino. And you belong to the hotel; you've got the start. Nobody, hardly ever, learned hotelkeeping right down to the ground unless he was born under the kitchen sink and did his teething on a file of overdue bills! Go to it, boy! You've got to learn a lot. You'll have to get into a lot bigger hotels than this—say, like in Bridgeport—biggest city of its size in the U.S.A.! You'll have to learn accounting and purchasing; not just run out and pick up a beefsteak, like you do here, but deal with big supply houses for maybe a thousand knives and forks, a hundred turkeys, five kegs of oysters—how to bargain and how to stand in with 'em. You'll have to learn manners—learn to be poker-faced with guys that would take advantage of you. Now, of course, you're only a kid, but even so, you're too dog-gone open-hearted; I can tell right away when you're pleased or kind of hurt. You'll have to know all about china and silver and glass and linen and brocade and the best woods for flooring and furniture. A hotel manager has to be a combination of a hausfrau, a chef, a bar-room bouncer, a doctor for emergencies, a wet nurse, a lawyer that knows more about the rights and wrongs of guests and how far he dast go in holding the baggage of skippers than Old Man Supreme P. Court himself, an upholsterer, a walking directory that knows right offhand, without looking it up, just where the Hardshell Baptist Church is and what time the marriage license bureau opens and what time the local starts for Hick Junction. He's got to be a certified public accountant, a professor of languages, a quick-action laundryman, a plumber, a heating engineer, a carpenter, a swell speechmaker, an authority on the importance of every tinhorn state senator or one-night stand lecturer that blows in and expects to have the red carpet already hauled out for him, a fly cop that can tell from looking at a girl's ears whether she's sure-enough married to the guy or not, a money-lender—only he doesn't get any interest or have any security. He's got to dress better'n a Twenty-third Street actor, even if he's only got a thin dime in his pocket. He's got to be able just from hearing a cow's moo to tell whether she'll make good steaks. He's got to know more about wine and cigars than the fellows that make 'em—they can fool around and try experiments, but he's got to sell 'em. And all the time he's got to be a diplomat that would make Thomas F. Bayard look like John L. Sullivan on a spree. He's got to set a table like a Vanderbilt and yet watch the pennies like a Jew peddler. If you can do all this, you'll have a good time. Go to it, Cap'n. Well, I think I'll go in and feed."

Sinclair Lewis overstated some aspects of hotelkeeping and tended to give the impression that a hotel man must be a slave to his job and master of everything to be successful. It is true that most people do not have the temperament to stand the pace, sometimes the intensity, and very often the long hours required of the successful hotel manager or restaurateur. This is changing; now there are many management positions in the field which require only forty hours a week of work when the manager has the necessary skills and organizational ability.

On the other hand, many people are so constructed that they revel in long hours of work, finding it not work but "great fun" much of the time. Generally speaking, however, the hotel or restaurant manager should have a high level of energy and be able to live with long hours and a multitude of demands on his nervous system.

DIVERSE PERSONALITY REQUIREMENTS

Studies have shown that the successful entrepreneur who starts his own business may be quite a different personality than the success-

Figure 0-1 *The Feathers Hotel of Ludlow, Shropshire, England. The hotel first opened for business in 1600.*

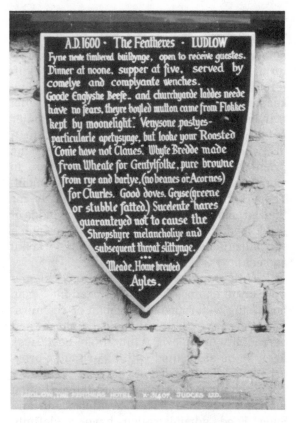

Figure 0-2 *This welcoming sign lists a most appetizing bill of fare, as well as an unusual invitation—"Tyne name timbered buildyne, open to receive guestes. Dinner at noone, supper at five, served by comely and complyent wenches."*

ful professional manager. In many cases, the entrepreneur becomes a successful business-man, not because he has particular gifts not possessed by the bureaucrat or because he is more daring, but because he does not fit into a bureaucratic system. In other instances, the entrepreneur is not content to be a part of a larger organization or he may be strongly motivated for money and feel that his opportunities will be greater if he goes into business for himself.

A greater range of skills and knowledge is usually required of the independent operator than of the person who is part of a chain organization. The stresses are usually also greater for the independent operator who often stakes all he has on the business venture for the possibility of greater financial return. It is not unusual to find an independent restaurant operator making considerably more money than the president of a large chain organization. On the other hand, the independent usually does not have the perquisites and prestige which go with the corporate office.

The owner of a hotel or restaurant is usually profit-minded and thus his concern with profit dominates his thinking until he retires or sells the business. The professional manager has somewhat different motivations. After about the age of forty, the professional manager tends to settle down into a particular area of hotel or restaurant management. He thinks of himself as a club manager, resort manager, a chain commercial house manager, a manager of a luxury restaurant, a quantity food producer, or whatever niche he fills.

MANAGING THE LARGE HOTEL

The 400 or so managers of the really large hotels throughout the country tend to be a fraternity among themselves. They march to a different drummer than the hundreds of innkeepers of the Holiday Inns. The large hotel manager usually starts his career in a major hotel whether as a recent college graduate, a dishwasher, or front desk clerk. Rarely is the progression of jobs from motelkeeper to medium-sized hotel to large hotel management. These hotelmen may be known primarily for their promotional skill or for their knowledge of good food, because there is need for much specialization in the field of large hotel management.

With the growth of the large hotel and restaurant chains, there is less need for "mein host," the well-rounded hotelman or restaurateur, the suave conversationalist, diplomat and personality in his own right. "Mein host" was likely to be associated with a particular property over a long period of years.

Such an association is more the exception than the rule today. The Sheraton chain and Saga Food administration have a definite policy of shifting managers every year or so. Such a policy, it is believed, prevents the manager from getting into a rut, offering him fresh challenges in a new scene of activity at regular intervals.

Other personality types needed in foodservice/lodging are the comptroller/accountant, the personnel, and clerical types. Each of these personalities tends to have certain values and to be motivated in a particular way. The accountant personality places much value on precision, on order, often tending to be compulsive about the need for a structured environment. He is likely to place excessive value on rules, procedures, control, and restraints. Cashiers are likely to have similar personalities. Every organization has need for a few such people.

"Personnel" is another staff job that requires the helpful, but not necessarily the managerial, type of personality. The employee in personnel is likely to be highly intelligent and people-oriented, rather than profit-oriented as the manager must be. He is usually not willing to take great risks and has less confidence in his own worth than the typical manager-entrepreneur is inclined to have.

The independent operator is thrown upon his own resources, experience, and judgment while the manager in the chain organization is likely to be guided by a detailed policy manual. The chain or franchise manager makes few of the policy level decisions, almost no financial, merchandising, or basic economic decisions. He works within the policy framework laid down by top management or the franchisor.

The innkeeper in a Holiday Inn unit or a Howard Johnson Motor Lodge unit is primarily concerned with day-to-day operations, especially those relating to his employees. He engages in little competitive buying and is not concerned with site, decor, or even menu planning decisions to any extent. What he can and cannot do is carefully spelled out in manuals or in discussions with his area supervisor. His salary reflects these limited responsibilities. The franchise holder's position is similar to the chain manager; but since he has risked some of his own capital, his rewards are usually greater. He also must conform to franchise policy. Variations between independent ownership and professional management exist. Some companies give their unit managers partial membership and require only limited investment from them.

TraveLodge, a large motel company, with headquarters in San Diego, offers still another arrangement between company and operator, a partnership. Under this plan usually a husband and wife who want to enter the motel business invest one-half the cost of the motel. TraveLodge then helps them select a site and construct the motel. The couple receives a salary for managing the motel. The husband runs the front-of-the-house; the wife is usually the housekeeper. Profits from the operation are divided 50–50 between the company and the couple.

Glamor Assignments

Whether or not a job is glamorous depends upon the individual viewing it, especially his social aspirations, the level of excitement he enjoys, and his values. What could be more glamorous than being a manager of a luxurious resort hotel in the Caribbean? For many people the job holds no glamor at all; for others, it is the ultimate glamor.

Many people would find the job of foodservice director for a college foodservice to be

Table 0-1 Comparative Requirements, Advantages, and Disadvantages for a Manager of a Hotel, Restaurant, or Club

Manager	Hotel/Motel	Restaurant	Club
People Relations	Supervisor/owner Department Heads Large numbers of employees Guest Relations Public Relations	Patron Relations Employee Relations: high turnover large percent teenagers and women	Chairman of House Committee Member Relations Department Heads Employee Public Relations
Time Demands	High (can be seasonal)	Very High (weekends highest; can be seasonal)	Moderate High on weekends and during club events (can be seasonal)
Energy Level Required	High	Very High	Moderate
Personal Qualities	Determination/Confidence Personal organization Cost Consciousness Imagination	Determination/Perseverance Personal organization Cost Consciousness	Affability Personal organization Good taste
Special Skills	People Skills (leadership) Marketing Food and Beverage (F&B) Front Desk Accounting	People Skills (drive) Food and Beverage Financial (if owner)	Social Poise Diplomacy/Tact Good taste Food and Beverage
Toughest Problems	Owner/Supervision relations Marketing Department Head Relations Employee Relations Food and Beverage	Cost Controls Employee Relations Maintenance of Food and Beverage Standards	Board Relations Member Relations Department Head Relations Financial
Advantages	Status Several fringe benefits for owner or manager Social/Cultural opportunities Sports in a resort	Large profits possible on investment	Comfortable life Low stress Sports availability
Disadvantages	Can feel imprisoned Can be stressful Nontenured	Less social/cultural time Constant attention required High risk of owner High tension for some Odd & long hours Nontenured if not owner	500 bosses Unconventional hours of work Nontenured

demanding, exacting, and monotonous. Others are thrilled at the challenges offered by the students, the excitement of being in authority over perhaps hundreds of employees, the novelty of continually searching for new ways to prepare and present food, control costs, and satisfy thousands of student patrons.

The introspective person, who places high value upon time to reflect and to withdraw from business life, is usually not happy in a hotel or restaurant job. Characteristically, the person who is stimulated by working for and with people and who enjoys a relatively exciting atmosphere gets "the hotel or food business in his blood."

For the average employee in the business, wages are relatively low, but the intrinsic rewards from the job are such that he would not trade for a job on an assembly line, for example, with twice the pay. For those whose egos are enhanced by rubbing shoulders with persons of fame and fortune, life in a better class hotel or motel can be thrilling. As is true in any field, when a person gains competence and knowledge he becomes more secure and confident.

Many of the careerists in hotel and restaurant management might have been just as satisfied in other fields. However, once they have started in the hotel and restaurant field, they feel comfortable in it, build friendships, attend meetings and conventions for the fraternity, and are hesitant to try another field.

Entertainment usually centers around banqueting, and this is another "reward" for being in the field. A special loyalty is likely to develop in their field, compounded of their emotional reactions—both favorable and unfavorable. This peculiar loyalty is not found in many other fields; the community of feeling that develops is unusual.

Nearly every manager in a foodservice/lodging operation receives his meals at no cost, at least while he is on the job. In some jobs, such as front desk responsibilities in a hotel, a uniform-type of coat is provided. The managers of most hotels are granted, or take, the privilege of not paying for their drinks. In some of the larger operations an entertainment account is set up for the manager which may run into several hundred dollars a month.

In resort properties, as well as in many other hotels and motels, managers are ex-

pected to live on the premises and are given complete maintenance, that is, food, beverages, and rooms for themselves and their families. This practice has declined considerably in the last twenty years, many managers preferring to live away from the hotel or motel. A similar circumstance exists in country clubs.

The ready availability of food and beverages has its liabilities. There is the tendency to overeat and to drink too much coffee. The manager of a resort hotel must be continually on his guard to avoid visiting the bar too frequently with his guests. They assume that he is as free to drink as they, forgetting that they are on vacation.

The Hazards of Management

Some managers are thrust into their positions before they have been tempered with experience and their new power "goes to their heads." Finding that they are now the center of attention, at least of their employees, some managers are carried away with their importance. Suddenly, a manager, even though only moderately attractive in appearance, finds he has great appeal to women who are interested in the advantages of associating with people of influence.

Ready access to cash is also a temptation which has been the downfall of some managers. As the old saying goes, "fast women, slow race horses, and alcohol" are ever-present temptations. The long hours and consequent stresses which are almost inevitable at times in the business weaken the defenses against such pursuits.

A well-organized personality and efficient planning can make the life of an innkeeper or restaurant keeper fairly routine and can keep stress at a minimum. However, generally speaking, the field is not one in which to grow old gracefully.

Managers in this field are much more mobile than in most fields, and necessarily so. The assistant manager or manager usually has to move on if he wants to move up, to acquire more responsibility and income.

Long Work Hours

Long hours and work during the evenings and weekends are the rule rather than the exception in the hotel and restaurant business. This looms as a disadvantage to the person who prizes a weekend of leisure, long hours with the family, or a routine that fits in with the habits of his neighbors. To many people, the unusual hours are no handicap at all. To many, the excitement of the job more than compensates for what might be considered disadvantages by others.

In taking over a new position, it is not unusual for a manager to stay on the job sixty or seventy hours a week; in larger hotels the manager may not leave the property for days at a time. In the seasonal resort the first few weeks of opening the property are particularly exhausting. All time and effort must be focused on the problem of getting the hotel open in time, usually with a large number of inexperienced personnel.

Strangely enough, many hotel and restaurant managers speak with pride of the excessive number of hours they work, perhaps considering it evidence of their stamina. Unfortunately, they often see the long hours as a model for others to follow and justify it in terms of economic necessity.

The work week, however, is getting shorter in hotels and restaurants, and for everyone. It has been found repeatedly that reducing a work week from fifty to forty-four hours, or from forty-eight hours to forty hours, increases the efficiency per hour worked. In most cases total productivity has not been markedly reduced.

For the average manager, efficiency drops after forty-four or forty-eight hours of work a week. His decision-making ability suffers with the longer hours. The person who works extremely long hours is handicapping the enterprise. The forty-hour week is becoming standard in hospital, industrial, and school foodservice.

The manager of a hotel or restaurant usually works with a large percentage of employees who are relatively unskilled, uneducated, and disadvantaged. For well over a hundred years a large portion of the employees in hotels and restaurants in the East have been recent immigrants; in the last few years the majority have been from Puerto Rico and Cuba.

In New York City over 40 percent of the employees in the industry are Spanish-speaking. The southern kitchen is typically manned by black men and women. In the Southeast the majority of employees are black or Mexican-American; in the Southeast the kitchen staff will most likely be Hispanic.

At one time the better kitchens around New York City were almost completely French, but few Frenchmen are coming to this country now. In the 1960s, many of the food and beverage directors of New York City hotels were of Hungarian extraction. Working with newly arrived or disadvantaged groups can be a challenge and a problem.

According to results of the Wonderlic Personnel Test, the average waitress, cook, baker, and maid scores well below the high school level of intelligence, although there are exceptions to this statement. It should be pointed out that academic intelligence as such is not as important in the jobs mentioned as is emotional stability, personal organization, energy, and tact. Even so, the hotel and restaurant manager should realize that, by and large, he is working with employees who require more training and supervision than is true in many other fields.

The status of the manager varies widely depending upon the status of the establishment he manages and his own personal wealth and education. Ellsworth Statler, the famous hotelman, envisaged the hotelman as being an owner-manager, a pillar of the community. Some hotelmen have achieved such status and others, though not owners, have acquired much prestige and recognition.

Generally speaking, the managers of the larger, more luxurious establishments have the most status while the small restaurant operator, even though he may have an income superior to the morning-coated hotel manager, has little status. The owner of a roadside diner may have an income in excess of $50,000 while the manager of a large city hotel may be in about the same income bracket. The status gulf is considerable.

Restaurant operators are particularly sensitive concerning status and with good reason. In large sections of this country restaurant keeping has not been held in high repute. A few restaurant chains existed before the turn of the century, but the rapid chain growth took place after World War II. Before then most of the restaurants were relatively small and many were family enterprises, often operated by immigrants. The Greek family restaurant was a standard in the Midwest in the 1930s.

Club management as a recognized field of work is also of recent origin; as late as 1912 the steward of the Harvard club insisted upon a contract in which he was named as manager, not steward.

Despite the sacredness of our belief in democracy, there have always been elements of the master-servant relationship between those who own and those who do not, between those with status and those who lack it. This goes back to our colonial period and is still very much present in the East and South.

It was not so long ago in some parts of the country that respectable families would not allow their daughters to work in hotels or restaurants. Fortunately, such attitudes have almost disappeared. Summer work in hotels and restaurants for college students apparently has never carried any stigma.

The range and style of operation within the hotel and restaurant arena is tremendous. It is not realistic to think that a "hotelman" or a "restauranteur" can step in and manage well any hostelry or foodservice operation. The skills and social poise needed to manage an elite club are fairly rare. The person who might be highly successful in such a club might not do well at all as a director of a college foodservice.

The manager of the Waldorf-Astoria in New York City must necessarily rely on his department heads who are specialists in their own right. Such a manager is primarily an administrator and coordinator. He does not need to be particularly knowledgeable in any one of the specialties found within the hotel. This same manager might not do well at all as a country innkeeper with no expert department heads to call upon.

Manager Needs "Nuts and Bolts"

Oddly enough, the manager of the small operation must know more "nuts and bolts" than the manager of the large operation. Similarly, the owner-operator of a highly successful restaurant may find himself unable to work within the confines of an organization of which he is not the boss.

Many restaurants are the reflection of the personalities of the owners, while the personalities of some chain enterprises are the result of the thinking of a number of specialists—site experts, food specialists, architects, decorators, and financial planners.

In some cases presidents of large and successful hotel operations have been failures when they struck out on their own as owners. Ralph Hitz, the well-known hotel operator of the 1930s, was able to make impressive profits when he operated for other owners. According to his son, Ralph Hitz, Jr., he was never able to make a profit in the hotels he owned himself. He seemed to cast aside caution when it came to investing his own money in a property or in an idea.

It is only necessary to attend a meeting of a group of hotelmen, to observe their dress and manner, and then compare them with a group of motel owner-operators to see that their motivation is different. Restaurant owners also tend to differ from professional restaurant managers.

Hotel managers, characteristically, are not owners and, as might be expected, place high value on maintaining friendships with the accounting firms and with individuals who can help them into better positions. The investor is usually keenly interested in improving his operation to increase profits, the professional manager much less so.

This book is an attempt to present an overall view of the hotel and restaurant business. The view is necessarily selective. Only enough background information is given to provide a feeling for the place of the inn, and later the hotel and restaurant, in history. When possible, the emphasis is on interpretation rather than fact.

IT'S A PEOPLE BUSINESS

All business reflects people, but the hotel and restaurant business is primarily a people business. It is especially important to look at the men who have shaped this business. We can learn from their experiences. Unfortunately, we can learn little from their mistakes because successful men usually succeed in hiding most of their weaknesses and mistakes.

The reader should get a feel for the history of the industry and an understanding of the scope and variety of technology, skill, and temperament which can be put to use in hotel and restaurant management. He should also get an idea of the vast opportunities which await the energetic and the capable who pursue foodservice/lodging careers.

A major appeal of the entire hospitality field, that may explain at least in part why people in it say "it gets in your blood," is the sociability factor. It is hard to be lonely working face to face with customers. Add to this the fact that much of the personal interaction takes place in pleasant surroundings, much of it with people who are enjoying themselves, and it becomes clear that loneliness, that bugaboo of a competitive society, is less likely to be around in the hotel and restaurant business.

THE ROUND PEG IN THE ROUND HOLE

The skills and personality traits that make for success in the hotel have much in common with those needed to do well in the restaurant business. The club field also requires qualities in common with those of the hotel and restaurant fields. Condominium management, cruise ship "hotel" operations, and attractions management are not far away in requiring similar qualities.

Table 0–1 (p. 5) is intended to be informative and provocative. It compares the demands placed on the manager of the hotel, restaurant, and club, and suggests some of the advantages and disadvantages of each field. All of the hospitality fields place an emphasis on people relations, and some are more demanding than others in time and energy. Personal qualities required in each field are somewhat different, as are the special skills needed.

The accountant/auditor personality, for example, is supposed to be of a separate mold, suspicious, trained to be withholding. In a facetious note Albert Hubbard, writing in 1922 described the auditor as ". . . . a man passed middle life, tall, spare, wrinkled, intelligent, cold, passive, noncommittal, with eyes like a codfish, polite in contact but at the same time unresponsive, cool, calm, and as damnably composed as a concrete post or a plaster-of-

paris cast: a human petrification with a heart of feldspar and without charm of the friendly germ; minus bowels, passion or a sense of humor. Happily they never reproduce, and all of them finally go to hell."[2]

UNIVERSITY EDUCATION FOR THE HOTEL AND RESTAURANT BUSINESS

Until the 1920s, education for the hotel manager was largely through experience. Most managers, like the managers of other enterprises at that time, did not have the advantage of a university education. The American Hotel Association was responsible for initiating a program of instruction for hotel management at the college level.

Frank Dudley, who became president of the American Hotel Association in 1917 when it became a truly national trade association, was president of the United Hotel Corporation, a company which was building hotels in the cities. J. Leslie Kincaid, chairman of the board of the American Hotels Corporation, was interested in building hotels in smaller communities. As their hotels grew in number, each man became painfully aware of the shortage of trained managers and department heads.

Maitre d's and chefs had been coming from Switzerland and France, but the demand exceeded the supply. Hotel managers, trained in the European tradition, did not understand the American commercial and family hotel. Dudley, as president of the AHMA, appointed Lucius Boomer, president of the Waldorf-Astoria, to chair an Education Committee to study educational needs.

First Courses at Cornell

One of the committee's recommendations was to establish a School of Hotel Management at Cornell University, Ithaca, N. Y. The late Howard B. Meek, who had taught a course in resort management at Boston University beginning in 1918, was appointed to head the school which was started in 1922. Financial support, pledged by AHMA members, did not materialize; Ellsworth Statler then stepped in

2. Quoted in *Cornell Hotel and Restaurant Administration Quarterly*, May 1977, page 4.

to underwrite $70,000 of the association's indebtedness, if the other members would pay off the remaining $30,000 of their debt.

Statler, who did not favor college education for hotel managers, visited Cornell in 1925 as a personal favor to an old friend. At one of the classes on the first day of his visit, he was asked to say a few words and dropped this bomb, "Boys, you're wasting your time here. You don't have to learn this stuff to be a hotelman. When I have an engineering problem, I hire an engineer. I don't know a damn thing about the British thermal units, and there's no reason for you to, either. Go on home and get a job."[3]

By the end of his second day on the campus, however, Statler had changed his mind and at a banquet, marking the end of the two-day "Hotel Ezra Cornell," he was asked to speak again. His second speech was as startling as the first: "I am converted. Meek can have any damn thing he wants." The words were prophetic. In his will, he left 10,000 shares of Statler common stock (then worth $10 a share) to set up a Statler Foundation. By 1975, the Cornell Hotel School had received more than $10 million for the construction of teaching facilities, faculty salaries, research projects, and student scholarships. Since then, additional millions have been given the school by the foundation.

The Cornell Hotel School under Professor Meek, and later Robert Beck, became the best-known of the hotel schools. Its Statler Hall, completed in 1950, pointed the way for hotel training facilities. With Statler Foundation sponsorship, a number of research projects were begun at Cornell in the early 1960s.

A number of other universities ventured into hotel management education, with varying degrees of enthusiasm and persistence. In 1928, Michigan State University started a hotel program under Bernard "Bunny" Proulx. Later, the school was headed by such well-known administrators as Leslie Scott and Donald Greenaway.

The M.S. and Ph.D. degrees were offered at Cornell, beginning in 1927, but were open only to those who completed the undergraduate

program there. An active Master of Business Administration program with a hotel and restaurant major was offered at Michigan State in 1962. In the latter 1930s, the University of Massachusetts, Pennsylvania State University, the University of New Hampshire, and Washington State University began hotel programs. After World War II, Florida State University and Denver University undertook similar programs of study.

Programs Begun at Other Universities

More recently, programs have begun at the University of Hawaii and University of Las Vegas Nevada. Two universities in Britain, Strathclyde in Glasgow and Surrey in Guildford, also established four-year degree programs in hotel administration. Three more universities added programs in 1969: the University of Houston, Stout State University in Wisconsin, and the University of Guelph, the first such university program in Canada. In 1972, the first classes in hotel, food, and travel services began at Florida International University in Miami. In 1973, California, the largest state in tourism, got its first four-year degree program at California State Polytechnic University, Pomona.

A directory of baccalaureate programs in hotel, restaurant, and institutional management in the United States, published in 1977, listed 71 institutions offering such programs.[4] More than 100 junior and community colleges offer programs in hotel and food management, two of the more prominent being the City College of San Francisco and Paul Smith College in upstate New York.

As a new discipline, hotel management has received only sporadic support from university and college administrators. Most of the programs have too few faculty members and insufficient financial support. Several universities have started programs only to allow them to lapse. The curricula in most of the four-year schools include blocks of instruction in food preparation and service, accounting, hotel engineering, management, finance, marketing, and business law; these are in addition to the usual university-required blocks in the basic

---

3. Floyd Miller, *Statler, America's Extraordinary Hotelman* (Ithaca, N.Y.: The Statler Foundation, 1968).

4. National Restaurant Association, 1977.

sciences, humanities, mathematics, and English. More recently, courses involving data processing have been added.

Hotel and restaurant management is an eclectic discipline drawing upon numerous other disciplines, especially economics, nutrition, psychology, marketing, engineering, insurance and real estate, law, accounting, statistics, and data processing.

Closely related to the general business field, many of the skills useful in hotel and restaurant management are transferable to any management field. Signal evidence of the transferability of hotel management skills to another field was seen in the career of Edward Carlson who grew up in the hotel business and became president of Western International Hotels, then president of United Airlines of which Western International is a subsidiary. Mr. Carlson did an outstanding job of management in both presidential positions.

For a person to be successful in any business requires that he/she has highly developed skills in time management, social management, money management, and strategic planning. These are transferable skills, useful in a bureaucracy as well as in a business enterprise. The hotel and restaurant manager requires some numerical skills such as those in accounting, statistics, and data processing. Business law, insurance and real estate, and marketing principles are invaluable, and most programs in hotel and restaurant management require that those majoring in the field take these subjects in the school of business. But hotel and restaurant management requires specific technical skills as well: professional background knowledge, some understanding of nutrition, a great deal of skill in food preparation and service, particular skills in food and beverage cost controls, knowledge of wines and spirits, specialized information about hotel management, restaurant management, travel management, and property management. The manager must also take marketing principles and adapt them to the specialized hotel and restaurant field.

In looking at the four-year degree program as offered in most universities in the U.S., one finds that the programs can be broken down into three parts: two years are devoted to general education as required by the university at large, one year of business subjects offered by the school of business, and one year of specialized hotel and restaurant courses.

It took almost 50 years for university administration and the field itself to recognize hotel management as a separate discipline, one complicated enough and broad enough to be offered at the university undergraduate and graduate level. In 1969, about 700 degrees were granted to students completing the 4-year courses; about 35 graduate degrees were granted. The numbers involved have increased sharply since then. Graduates of these programs are expected to number around 4,000 a year by 1980, one-third of them women.

THE CERTIFIED HOTEL ADMINISTRATOR

The American Hotel and Motel Association has established a certificate program, Certified Hotel Administrator (CHA). Details are handled by the Educational Institute of the American Hotel and Motel Association headquartered at East Lansing, Michigan. Among the qualifications for the certificate is work experience of at least three years in a staff operational or educational phase of the lodging industry, completion of ten courses in the Institute's Diploma Program, or passing of the Educational Institute's Diploma Challenge Examination. In addition the candidate must complete five other Educational Institute courses. Other individuals who, because of their leadership positions in the industry, feel they qualify for the certificate may take a comprehensive examination without completing the formal Institute courses.

GROWTH OF SERVICES
RELATED TO HOSPITALITY BUSINESS

Forecasts bode well for the hospitality business: more spending in hotels, restaurants, and for travel; more hospitality employment; more hospitality managers.

Economists divide the economy into four sectors or types of activities: primary (extractive), secondary (industrial), tertiary (services to primary and secondary), and quaternary (services for their own sake). The primary sector comprises agriculture, forestry, fisheries, and mining. The secondary sector involves contract construction and manufacturing, where-as services deals with transportation, communication and public utilities, wholesale and retail trade, finance, insurance and real estate, and services in government. As an economy develops it moves from the primary sector (largely agriculture) to the other phases. As industrialization increases and moves through a postindustrial era, the primary and secondary sectors become relatively small compared with the third and fourth sectors.

In the United States, for example, services by 1972 accounted for 67.5 percent of the employment and 56.4 percent of the gross national product. It is estimated that services will climb to 71 percent of employment by 1985 and constitute almost 60 percent of the G.N.P.[5]

5. Kahn, Brown, and Martel, *The Next 200 Years* (New York, NY: Morrow & Co., 1976 p. 52).

Questions

1 The hotel and restaurant business is fast becoming a science. What parts are likely to remain an art?

2 Name at least three personality requirements of a successful hotel or restaurant manager.

3 In what way does the large chain partially eliminate the need for "mein host?"

4 Owning and operating a hotel or restaurant calls for several skills not required of the nonowner-manager. Name three of them.

5 It is often said that the hotel and restaurant business gets into your blood. Analyze the statement and name the factors that could make this true.

6 What are some of the temptations for a hotel or restaurant manager that can lead to failure?

7 What qualities would be necessary to manage an elite country club well that would not be necessary in a small hotel?

8 Who would need more detailed technical knowledge—the manager of a 150-room hotel or a manager of a 500-room hotel?

9 The qualities of affability and good taste would probably be more important in which of these operations: a private club, a restaurant, or a medium-sized hotel?

10 Tight cost controls are probably more important for which of these: hotel, restaurant, or club?

11 If you are seeking high status, you would probably aim towards managing which of these: large hotel, prestige restaurant, or country club?

12 Which of these operations would probably demand the least personal energy: country club, large hotel, or highly successful restaurant?

13 Which of these would require the most personal time: highly successful restaurant, hotel, or club?

14 The financial return would probably be greatest in which of these: hotel, a highly successful restaurant, or a name club?

THE EARLY INN/TAVERN

ONE

The Innkeeper has been around for centuries. Necessarily so, because he satisfies basic needs, the need to eat, drink, and sleep. He is one of society's escape valves. He offers (1) a respite from ceaseless competition; (2) the pleasures of the table and the bed; (3) a sanctuary for the weary; and (4) titillation for the bored or frustrated.

Reference to tavern keeping was made as early as about 1700 B.C. in the code of Hammurabi. The death penalty could be imposed for merely watering the beer. The Greek tavern keeper, like his modern day counterpart, offered food, drink, and sometimes a bed. The taverns of ancient Athens served both domestic and imported wine. The food served was likely to be based on the Mediterranean triad of grain, olive oil, and wine.

There might have been cheese (made from goat's milk), barley bread, cabbage, peas, broad beans, and lentils. Figs and olives were available. Cheese cakes, honey buns, cakes of sesame seed were favored.

If there was meat, it was usually goat, pork, or lamb. A banquet might include thrushes, finches, and hares. Stuffed paunch of ass was considered a delicacy in Athens. There might also have been sausages and hog puddings. Fish and eel were common.

Coriander was the most popular seasoning; but cumin, fennel, and mint were also used.

AFTER THE SACRIFICE, A FEAST; AFTER THE FEAST, DRINKING

For a very practical reason, the tavern might be located close by a temple. From the temple the sacrificed animals were taken to the tavern and eaten (after the sacrifice, a feast; after the feast, drinking). Each guest lay on a couch with a cushion or bolster under the left arm.

Flute girls were called upon to exercise their talents during the meal. At some of the taverns there might be a small stage for theatrical entertainment. When the meal was finished it was the Athenean custom to pour three libations: one to the gods, one to the departed heroes, and one to Zeus. Garlands were handed out and, on occasion, perfumes. Then the drinking began. Some taverns had cubicles into which the worshipers of Aphrodite might retire.[1]

In Egypt, during the same as well as earlier periods, the menu was based on bread, birds, beef, fish, and fruit. Roast goose was a particular favorite. The poor ate mainly dried fish and whatever bread they could afford. At a banquet, the guests wore wigs, and they might also have a small cone of ointment placed on their heads, which melted and ran down over wigs or hair. The serving girls and the guests were provided collars of flowers.

By the time Rome had conquered the then known world, inns and taverns were well established. An accurate picture of what they were like can be seen at Pompeii and at Herculaneum, small resort towns in southern Italy that had the misfortune to be located near Mt. Vesuvius. In A.D. 79, the mountain erupted as a volcano. Ashes, lava, and hot mud smothered these towns, preserving them for modern times.

---

1. William Younger, *Gods, Men, and Wine* (London, England: The Wine and Food Society, 1966).

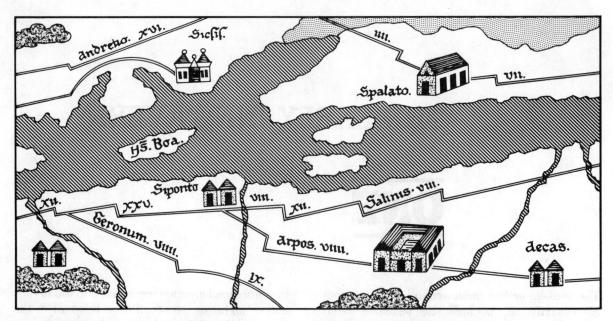

A segment of a military road map of the Roman Empire in the time of Emperor Theodosius Magnus (347–395 A.D.). The symbols on the map indicate types of accommodation:

 1. the simplest roadside accommodations suitable only for rest

 2. better accommodations than the places uninhabited

 3. better quarters for larger units but no service (no live-in slaves or local vassals)

 4. good shelter, a place for longer rest, recuperation, and refurbishing of supplies.

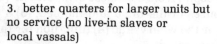

Figure 1–1 Artist's rendering of a military road map of the Roman Empire at the time of Emperor Theodosius Magnus (347–395 AD). The symbols indicate types of accomodation.
Source: Map privately printed in Vienna in 1753. Used here courtesy of Chef Louis Szathmary, The Bakery, Chicago, Illinois.

A segment of a military road map of the Roman Empire in the time of Emperor Theodosius Magnus (347–395 A.D.) is a kind of mobile tour guide of the time. The symbols on the map indicate the kind of accommodation:

1 The simplest roadside accommodations suitable only for rest;

2 Better accommodations than the places uninhabited;

3 Better quarters for larger units but no service (no live-in slaves and local vassals);

4 Good shelter, a place for longer rest, recuperation and refurbishing of supplies.

The traveler can wander about Pompeii and see the hospiteum, the caupona, the popina, thermopoliums, and the tabernas. They are much as they were, even the graffito "Serena hates Isadore," on a wall in the town.[2] The caupona and hospiteums were inns or hotels providing lodging and, in some cases, a basic menu of wine, bread, and meat.

The reputations of the operators, the caupones or innkeepers, were even worse than those of the tavern keepers. Apart from being accused of fraudulent or immoral dealings, the female caupones occasionally achieved a reputation for sorcery. Nearly every block of houses had its own bar, in much the same way that we find cafes in every downtown block of

2. Howard Luxton, *Pompeii and Herculaneum* (London, England: Spring Books, 1966).

American cities. In Pompeii alone, a relatively small town in its day, 118 bars or restaurant bars are identifiable.

The thermopoliums, the snack bars of the day, sold wine from a "hot drink and food counter," which faced on the street. Pottery jars were set into a marble counter and held snacks such as olives, dried vegetables, and probably pickle appetizers. Some of the counters were fitted with a small furnace used to heat water for the caldum, a hot drink made of wine and boiling water. Some thermopoliums had a room behind the counter which served as a dining area. The popina, predecessor of our modern restaurant, sold hot restaurant food only. Thermopoliums sold only snacks.

Tabernas, forerunners of the bar of modern times, might also sell food and offer such attractions as gambling and prostitutes (not too different from some bars and B-girls of today). In Rome, taverns were identifiable by their pillars, "girt with chained flagons," and the fact that red, thyme-flavored sausages were hung around the walls. Floors were bright with mosaics and the walls were enlivened by paintings, similar to the decor found in the trattorias of modern Italy.

In the country were rustic pubs where the owner might grow his own grapes and make his own wine. Small dried cheeses hanging in rush baskets were also available.

With the decline of the Roman Empire, in about 500 A.D., several hundred years passed during which the inn was largely lost to civilization. Travel was infrequent and trade largely at a standstill. Since there were few travelers, there was little need for innkeeping.

CHURCH HAVEN FOR TRAVELERS

The church came to be dominant and the only recognized authority from one country to another. Monasteries and other religious houses took in travelers (donations welcomed). Hospices, a form of inn, were operated by religious orders; guest houses were also maintained by some of these orders.

One such religious order, the Knights of St. John of Jerusalem, was founded in 1048 when a hospital was erected in Jerusalem to care for pilgrims making the visit to that city. Later it became a military and religious order of considerable power and was given the responsibility by the Pope of protecting pilgrims to and from Jerusalem.

Many cathedrals and monasteries made guests welcome, the rich and noble sitting with the head prelate, the poor being housed in separate quarters. There were no room rates. Often the monastery porter, whose primary function was that of gatekeeper, also managed the guest house. It might be said that the church operated the first hotel chain.

The Crusades, beginning in 1095 and lasting over the next 200 years, encompassed a great social revolution, creating trade that led to the rise of a middle class. Indirectly, it revived innkeeping. Northern Italy was the first to feel the effects of the renaissance brought on by the Crusades. Innkeeping there became a solid business and guilds of innkeepers flourished, making regulations for themselves and for their guests.

In Florence, Italy, for example, there were enough innkeepers by the year 1282 to form a guild, a mutual-benefit society. The guild innkeepers of Florence controlled business to the extent that all strangers to the city were interviewed at the gates by city officials who directed them to officers of the guild. These, in turn, assigned foreigners to designated inns; natives of Tuscany, the local province, were assigned to other hostelries.

THE OLD ENGLISH INN

The early English inn followed in the tradition of the ale house or ghildhus of Saxon England where people gathered to socialize and to express themselves. An evergreen bush attached to a pole was understood by everyone to mean that ale could be had inside. (The custom is still observed in some Austrian villages. A green bough or twig signifies that apple wine is available and for sale in the wine cellar.)

It was in an inn over a glass of ale, according to one commentator, that the rudiments of self-government were evolved; there, also, much of what meager pleasures were to be had could be found. By the thirteenth century, the inn had special significance, at least for one Walter de Map who said, "Die I must, but let me die drinking in an inn..."

Though each parish had its ale house, those that rented rooms were few as late as in 1400. Inns were found in the larger towns and

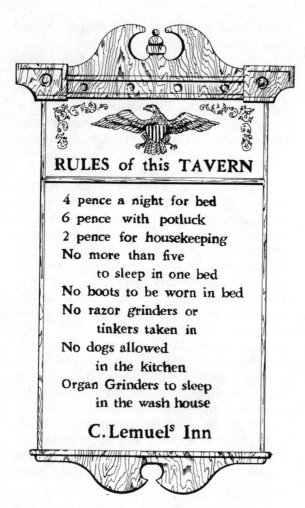

RULES of this TAVERN

4 pence a night for bed
6 pence with potluck
2 pence for housekeeping
No more than five
   to sleep in one bed
No boots to be worn in bed
No razor grinders or
   tinkers taken in
No dogs allowed
   in the kitchen
Organ Grinders to sleep
   in the wash house

C. Lemuel's Inn

Figure 1–2   A sign for a local tavern of the Tudor period (1485–1603).

at the crossroads and ferries. Buildings were often little more than shelters with a minimum of furnishings. Rushes thrown on an earthen or stone floor acted as a carpet and made a convenient place to throw bones or other food remnants. A main room with mattresses placed along the walls for guests to sleep on was the extent of the appointments. Meals were an individual matter as most guests brought their own.

By the fifteenth century, some of the inns had twenty or thirty rooms. The George Inn, one of the better known, had a wine cellar, a buttery or pantry, kitchen, and rooms for the host and for the hostler, the caretaker of the horses. The rooms or chambers were named after well-known people, cities, or for prominent offices; they included the Earl's chamber,

Oxford chamber, the Squire's chamber, London chamber, and the Fitzwarren chamber.

During the Tudor period (1485–1603), and for some time thereafter, the courtyards of some of the inns were used by traveling troupes of players. They declaimed to the audience who sat in the surrounding galleries of the courtyard.

The inns or taverns were identified by simple signs. This was necessary because of the number of people who could not read, though they could say, "Meet me at the sign of the Bull." There were many Lions, Golden Fleeces, White Harts, Black Swans, Dolphins, and similar signs.

In the later 1700s some of the names were changed to include the word, "Arms": the King's Arms or Dorset Arms. Display of a lord's arms at an inn often meant that the inn was in the territory of a particular noble family and was under its protection. Some heraldic signs were related to the original ownership of the land on which the inn stood. Or a servant-turned-innkeeper might use the arms (or badge) of his former master.

Some early inns had open galleries which were approached by outside staircases. With time the galleries were enclosed as a protection against weather. In the courtyards were boxes or stalls, harness and hostler's rooms. A mounting block in one corner allowed the more portly customer to climb aboard his horse. At the larger inns, above the stables, were quarters for the postboys, the boys who carried the mail.

Many old inns had a garden and bowling green and some had brew houses for making beer. A long room or assembly room contained a fireplace at one end and was the function room for banquets and dances. A partial census of 1577 counted 14,202 alehouses, 1,631 inns and 329 taverns in England and Wales.[3]

Inns Helped by Henry VIII

Without intending to do so, Henry VIII fostered the growth of innkeeping by suppressing the monasteries in 1539. They had played a major role in travel, maintaining the principal roads

---

3. Michael Brander, *The Life and Sport of the Inn* (New York, NY: St. Martin's Press, 1973).

for pilgrims to the larger cathedrals. Hostels had been established adjacent to an abbey or monastery where pilgrims could stay for two days, accommodated and fed according to their rank. When church lands were given away or sold, the church's function as host to the traveler disappeared.

Another factor that favored the development of inns was the fact that long before a national postal system was established, selected innkeepers were forced to retain stables and horses to meet the demands of the royal post.

The first stagecoaches in England, first mentioned in 1635, were huge, lumbering vehicles, joyless for the riders, especially since travel began early in the morning, usually before sunup, and lasted until late at night.

Later stagecoaches improved, had springs, seats for four inside, eight or ten on top. Outside passengers were treated as a superior race of Spartans, says one historian, while the interior seats were left for "anaemic spinsters and querulous invalids."

Menus in the early English inn relied heavily on meat and ale; the vegetables eaten were relatively few. The vegetables we are fond of today were not eaten because they were not available until the sixteenth century. Tomatoes, sweet and white potatoes, pumpkin and squash, string beans, kidney beans, lima beans, peppers, cocoa, tapioca, corn, cranberries, blueberries, and strawberries are all products of the New World. Potatoes were not known to Europe until Pizarro found them in Peru and Chile.

Figure 1-3   The Swan, Lavenham, England. This half-timbered inn grew from three houses built in 1425. In its early day, it had stabling for fifty horses. Here, traveling apothecaries invited sufferers of diverse diseases to come to the Inn to be cured. In 1607, John Girling, the innkeeper, issued a trader's token—a sure sign of a good reputation.
Source: Courtesy of Trust House, Limited.

In the middle 1600s some inns even issued unofficial coins which the innkeepers, men of repute, guaranteed to redeem in coin of the realm. The fact that an innkeeper issued such tokens meant that the inn was of considerable importance at the time.

The English Inn was headquarters for a variety of sports, both indoors and outdoors. A variety of dart and dice games and dominoes going by such odd names as Hazard, Strutt, Shove-groat, as well as billiards and bagatelle were played; cockfighting was common, both indoors and out. The bloodthirsty could enjoy bull and bear baiting—putting dogs on the animals—and throwing at cocks. Those who liked the active sports used the inns as headquarters for fishing, shooting, coursing, hunting, and falconry. Dogfights and prizefighting practiced on rough grounds were popular. Of course the main pastime was drinking beer, ale and wine, and later gin.

Old Inns Still Operate

English common law early declared the inn to be a public house and imposed social responsibilities for the well-being of travelers upon the innkeeper. The innkeeper had not only the right to receive travelers, but the duty as well. He was required to receive all travelers who presented themselves in reasonable condition and were willing to pay a reasonable price for accommodations.

Some 200 of the old coaching and posting inns, together with some hotels, are operating today in England and Wales as part of the Trust Houses, Limited. Some of these date back more than 400 years.

The Trust Houses began in 1903 under a group that wished to prevent the old inns from becoming merely local taverns. The majority of these old inns are now managed by husband and wife teams, much as they were originally. The standard of cleanliness, the quality of food and service are excellent. Rates are quite low compared with the usual city hotel rate. Trust Houses, Limited, has become the largest hotel company in Great Britain and in 1966 reached a partnership agreement with TraveLodge, Australia, Limited.

The image we are likely to have of the old English inn is that of the coaching inn, which flourished during the eighteenth and early nineteenth centuries. The coaching era in Great Britain began in earnest in 1784 when Parliament commissioned government mail delivery by coach. Until then mail had been carried by postboys riding horseback over the poor roads of the time.

Mail coaches soon made their appearance and were easily identified by scarlet wheels and underbody with the upper part of the coach painted black. At one time there were fifty-nine of the large mail coaches, each pulled by four horses, in England and Wales, sixteen more in Scotland, and twenty-nine in Ireland. Attesting to the size of the operation, more than 30,000 men and 150,000 horses were employed primarily in moving the mail.

The mail coaches carried a maximum of seven passengers: four inside, three up in front with the coachman; only the guard rode in the rear. At the height of the coaching era, seventeen mail coaches assembled each evening at the General Post Office in London. Nine others left inns in Piccadilly and the West End of London each day of the week.

The traveler paid a little more for riding in the mail coach with its security and the limitation on the number of passengers. Private stagecoach companies had their own coaches and took as many passengers as could be squeezed in on top of the coach. Sometimes as many as thirteen people rode in and on a coach, four inside, four up front, and five in back, with luggage piled on the roof.

A traveler with the money and the desire for prestige and privacy could ride a post chaise. This was drawn by two horses, one of which was ridden by a youngster called a postboy. Although costs for such elegant travel were twice as much as for the usual tallyho, many people used the post chaises. A nationwide posting system was established with many inns used exclusively as posting inns.

Speeding the Stagecoach

Speed was the challenge and the coach company that could cut travel time got the business. The mails averaged about ten miles per hour and the stages or inns where the horses were changed were ten miles apart. Competition to decrease travel time was fierce. One way was to cut the time required to change horses and this was finally reduced to forty-

Figure 1-4 *The Black Swan Hotel, Helmsley, North of York, England. This inn has been added to and renovated many times in 400 years. The rough stone walls are more than two feet thick. For many years the Earl of Feversham held his annual Rent Dinner here, entertaining over seventy tenents. Venison from the Earl's deer park has been served here at least once a week in season. Source: Courtesy of Trust House, Limited.*

five seconds. In 1830, the Birmingham Independent Tallyho averaged 14-1/2 miles per hour on the trip from London to Birmingham.

The coachmen were the athletic heroes of the day, many of them driving four horses and averaging sixty miles a day, three stages out and three stages back. Young gentlemen often bribed the coachmen to let them take the reins. So intense was the interest in driving that a few noblemen set up their own stagecoach companies to insure their participation in the sport of driving.

The country inns were largely dependent upon the travel habits of their customers, and a large part of their business came from providing horses for the coaches. Several inns maintained as many as 50 horses, while the Bow and Mouth in London kept 400 horses. However, travel was still slow and it required something like 34 stages and 42 hours to cover 400 miles.

Figure 1–5 Table setting of an early American tavern (Ordinary at the Hall Tavern, Charlemont, Massachusetts, 1700). Note the use of the wooden serving ware and the horn drinking cups. Dinner was served family style. In some taverns along the Eastern seaboard, the menu was fairly long. At the more primitive inland taverns, the menu might include corn (in some form), bread, bacon, and whiskey. Source: Courtesy of the Heritage Foundation. Photograph by Samuel Chamberlain.

When the railroad appeared in 1825 in England, most people were not aware of its implications for innkeeping; the innkeepers were no exception. Travel time from London to Bath, a distance of 110 miles, was reduced from the 11 hours required by coach to only 2.5 hours by steam locomotive. The choice of travel was obvious.

In 1838, when Parliament permitted carrying of mail by railroad, the coaching era was over. It was not until the 1900s, when the country inns were rediscovered by cyclists and then later by motorists, that the beautiful inns of the countryside of England, Wales, and Scotland returned to their former position.

THE EARLY AMERICAN TAVERN

"With a heart full of love and gratitude, I now take leave of you. I most devoutly wish that your later days may be as prosperous and happy as your former ones have been glorious and honorable." It was General George Washington saying farewell to his top-ranking officers on December 4, 1783.

Washington spoke with difficulty, "I cannot—I cannot come to each of you but shall feel obliged if each of you will come and take me by the hands."[4] The place was the old DeLancey

4. *American Heritage Book of the Revolution* (New York, NY: Simon & Schuster, 1958).

mansion, The Fraunces Tavern, at the corner of Pearl and Broad Streets in New York City. The proprietor was black, Samuel Fraunces, known as Black Sam.

The Fraunces Tavern was an appropriate place for Washington to say farewell to his officers since it had been a meeting place of the Sons of the Revolution. Samuel Fraunces, a former West Indian, was later to be voted cash grants for his services to American prisoners of war and for "other acts." When British officers occupied New York and frequented the tavern, they apparently were unaware that Fraunces' sympathies remained unchanged and that he was one of our first intelligence agents. He later became the first chief steward of the Executive Mansion, again serving Washington, this time when he was president.

Patrick Henry called the taverns of Colonial America "the cradles of liberty." In Boston, The Green Dragon and the Bunch of Grapes had been the meeting places of the Sons of Liberty during the Revolution. The Boston Tea Party was planned in The Green Dragon.

Buckman Tavern had been the rallying point for the Lexington militiamen. Catamount Tavern was where Ethan Allen and the Green Mountain Boys met to plot their strategy against the New York Staters and against Gentlemen Johnny Burgoyne. Generals Israel Putnam, Jethro Sumner, and George Weeden were former tavernkeepers. John Adams, our second President, owned and managed his own tavern between 1783 and 1789.

Coles Ordinary, First Inn in the Colonies

The first tavern in Boston, and probably the first in the Colonies, was opened by Samuel Coles in 1634 and known as Coles Ordinary. Coles, who had been a comfit-maker in England, came with the first shipload of Puritans in 1630. His place was later to be called the Ship Tavern. Coles became one of Boston's first citizens, a deacon of the First Church, a steward of Harvard University, and a leading businessman.

The ordinaries followed closely the establishment of churches. The courts at first recommended, and later required, that some kind of public house be set up in each community. Sometimes land was granted and tax exemp-

tions or other inducements were offered to encourage the keeping of an ordinary. The term comes from England where it was customary for eating places to have a daily "ordinary," a midday meal or supper, often consisting of a particular dish in which the host specialized, served at a common table at a fixed time.

The principal meal of the day was served at two o'clock in the afternoon. Guests were called together by ringing a bell in the street. Customary fare was salmon in season and veal, beef, mutton, fowl, ham, vegetables, and pudding. Each guest had a pint of madeira at his place. The carving was done at the table in the old English way, each guest helping himself to what he liked best.

The early New England taverns were under the strict guardianship of the Puritan fathers. Prices were well regulated. In 1634, when the first taverns were built, sixpence was the legal charge for a meal and a penny for a quart of ale or beer in a tavern.

If a man were clocked at his beer tankard on a weekday for more than a half hour, he was guilty of idleness and could be fined. In 1633, a Robert Coles of Boston was fined ten shillings and enjoined to stand with a white sheet of paper pinned to his back which read "Drunkard."

Happier Days with the Huguenots

Luckily for us today, the Puritans were followed by Huguenots in 1685. The Huguenots came to escape religious persecution following the revocation of the Edict of Nantes. They were everything that the Puritans were not—merry, buoyant, cheerful, music-loving. They loved dancing, theatricals, and entertainment. They even went so far as to buss their wives and other men's wives on Sunday, or any other day, for that matter.

Although French cuisine was never widely popular in the U.S., it has influenced our hotel and restaurant menus. Thomas Jefferson was especially fond of French cooking and wines and entertained (far beyond his means) as president, and later at his home, Monticello.

A well-known hostelry of the colonial period was the City Tavern. Built on the docks of New York City in 1642 by the West India Company, it was primarily for the English traveling from New England to Virginia. The Blue Anchor, on the Delaware, in what is now Philadelphia, was where William Penn first stopped on his arrival in the New World.

In Colonial Williamsburg some thirty inns, taverns, and ordinaries welcomed guests. The King's Arms in Williamsburg offered a meal of some fifteen courses. Four well-known taverns of the period have been reconstructed on their original foundations and reopened as distinctive colonial eating places: Christina Campbell's Tavern, the King's Arms Tavern, Chownings, and The Raleigh Tavern.

It was The Raleigh Tavern that Phi Beta Kappa, the honor society, was founded. The tavern's motto "Hilaritas, Sapientiae et Bonae Vitae Proles," "Jollity, the offspring of wisdom and good living" is appropriate to any good hostelry, then or now. The Williamsburg taverns have been modernized to an extent and the menus are not completely authentic pre-Revolutionary, but the overall flavor is there.

On the Bill of Fare in Early Plymouth

Meals in a colonial tavern were simple but plentiful. Here is a bill of fare from an early Plymouth, Massachusetts tavern:

A large baked Indian whortleberry pudding

A dish of saughetach (corn and peas)

A dish of clams

A dish of oysters and a dish of codfish

A haunch of venison, roasted by the first Jack brought into the Colony

A dish of sea fowl

A dish of frost-fish and eels

An applie pie

A course of cranberry tarts and cheese made in the Old Colony

Beverages flowed freely. At first the only choice was between poor beer and rum. Later, these were combined to make the most popular drink, flip. The recipe is enough to make one flip: rum, beer, cream, beaten eggs, and spices, heated by plunging a hot loggerhead into the mixture. It was said to be both food and drink, and if you had enough, it was also lodging for the night. There were also bounce and sling, punch and shrub, eggnog, and Tom and Jerry, some hot, some cold, but all basically rum.

Travel was on the rugged side. Travelers were called at 3:00 A.M. and rode until 10:00 P.M. One pair of horses usually carried the stage twelve to eighteen miles. The first regular stagecoach inn was established in 1760, between New York City and Philadelphia. Later, between Boston and Providence as many as forty coaches were on the road at one time.

In populous sections like Pennsylvania, where the 66-mile Lancaster Turnpike was located, there were sixty taverns of varying social acceptability. Wagon drivers slept on bags of hay and oats on the taproom floor. Cattle drovers stopped at drover stands, taverns which had lots into which the livestock could be turned and fed. These taverns were also known by their signboards, some of which were imaginative: "The Jolly Tar" "A man free of trouble."

The word "turnpike" came from the practice of placing a pike or staff across the toll road. One side was embedded with spikes. When the toll was paid, the pike was turned, spikes down, so the traveler could pass. The first turnpike was built between Philadelphia and Lancaster in 1792. By 1838 Pennsylvania had 2,500 miles of turnpike.

Accommodations follow travel. In the late 1820s, the state of Pennsylvania began the development of what eventually became 1,200 miles of canals. Canal taverns sprang up every 10 or 12 miles. New York State also had a fairly extensive canal system with taverns, and later hotels, edging the canals.

Old Taverns Open for Inspection

Many a New England village and town today contains a home that was previously a tavern, for most of the taverns were originally constructed as large homes and were used as homes by the tavernkeeper. The furnishings and the equipment of these old taverns is not a matter of speculation since considerable effort has been taken to preserve a few of them.

In Old Deerfield, Massachusetts, one can tour the Hall Tavern and see the long tavern table set for guests with "treen," wooden dishes, horn spoons, and cups. Pewter plates replaced the wooden ones in later Colonial America. The barroom stands ready to serve the traveler and one can almost hear the tavernkeeper call out, "mind your p's and q's" (mind your pints and quarts), to permit another round of drinks before closing time.

The family of the tavernkeeper was kept busy making souse (boiled pig's feet, ears, and skins pickled in vinegar) sausage; filling pork and corned beef barrels; preparing lard and tallows for candles; making mince, apple, and cranberry pies. If this was not enough to keep the innkeeper's wife busy, she could make clothes for her family. In the cellar were barrels of cider, vegetables in bins, seed, and the apples of the time—golden pippins, greenings, russets, seek-no-furthers, and pumpkin sweets.

The Hall Tavern was originally a home built in Charlemont, Massachusetts in 1760. The Halls took it over toward the end of the eighteenth century to serve travelers on the road which was built along the Mohawk Trail. It became the center of village activity for both travelers and villagers. Soon it was the meeting place for local gossip and the looked-for spot on the trip westward. All classes of people frequented it, from the Mayhew family of Baltimore, who arrived with their four-horse carriage complete with coachman as well as footman, to the drovers and teamsters. If the tavern beds were occupied, Mrs. Hall provided ticks filled with straw that could be spread on the ballroom floor.

Many travelers brought their saddles and harnesses indoors with them for safekeeping. The townspeople used it was a meeting place where they could hear the latest news brought over the hills by stagecoach; discuss town affairs, or just gossip, play checkers, smoke, or drink.

The ballroom, with a blazing fire at one end, was the scene of dancing to a fiddle. But never on Sunday. In fact, little if anything except churchgoing took place on Sunday and the children could scarcely wait until sunset when they could resume play. The Hall Tavern was moved from Charlemont to Old Deerfield and today contains a pewterer's shop and a wallpaper shop. These shops were originally not part of the tavern but were included in the

reconstruction since old taverns often contained little shops.

FACTORS IN THE GROWTH OF THE HOTEL AND RESTAURANT BUSINESS

Innkeeping, and later the hotel and restaurant business, has paralleled the growth of trade, travel, and industry and in modern times correlates highly with disposable income and the cost and convenience of travel. The ancient period, 500 B.C. to about 500 A.D., saw the growth of inns in Ancient Greece and in Ancient Rome, inns, snack bars, and military messes. During the medieval period, from about 500 A.D. to about 1300 A.D., trade and travel was severely limited; and much of the travel had to do with pilgrimmages, the travelers being fed and sheltered at various religious houses. The Crusades had the effect of spurring trade and travel and the Rennaissance, from about the fourteenth century in Northern Italy to the seventeenth century in England and Northern Europe, saw the rebirth of tavern and innkeeping. The suppression of the monasteries in England by Henry VIII in 1536 forced the growth of innkeeping in England.

Prior to 1775, all societies were preindustrial. In the period 1775–1875 Northwestern Europe, Japan, and North America became industrialized; and in the period 1875 to 1950 mass-consumption societies developed in those places. Beginning about 1950 there was rapid worldwide economic and population growth, and industrial societies made disposable income available for the masses to travel and to frequent hotels and restaurants.

Invention in travel modes has also been a determinant in the growth of the hotel and restaurant business. As each new form of transportation brought down the cost of travel and increased its convenience—the steamship, the railroad, and the automobile—travel became possible for other than the elite, the immigrant, and the warrior. The commercial jet airplane in 1959 ushered in the era of international travel.

The time chart on page 24 provides some perspective to the modern period of the growth and development of the hotel and the restaurant.

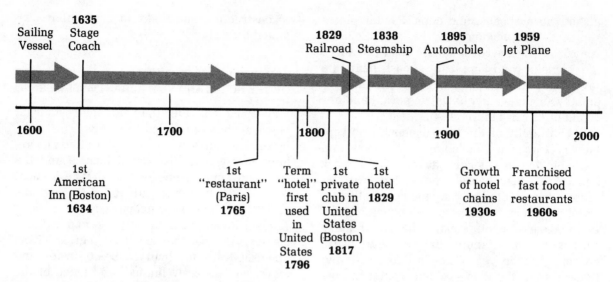

Figure 1-6   *Hotel and Restaurant Time Chart, 1600–2000* A.D.

Chronology, Hotel and Restaurant Business to 1900

ANCIENT PERIOD, 500 B.C. to 500 A.D.

Greek symposiums, Spartan and Roman military mess the forerunner of the private club.

Greek inns close to temples "after the sacrifice, a feast . . . after the feast, drinking."

In the Middle East the travelers stopped with their caravans at caravanseries and kahns, primitive types of inns.

Roman inns, caupona, and hospiteum, provided rooms, sometimes a restaurant. Served limited menu of bread, meat, and wine, perhaps figs and honey. First limited menu (not from choice but by necessity).

Popinas sold wine and restaurant food; thermopoliums, wine, and snacks; tabernas were essentially bars.

Nearly every block of houses in Roman times had its own bar.

MEDIEVAL PERIOD, 500 A.D. to 1300 A.D.

Monasteries and other religious houses took in travelers; donations welcome.

Inns were primitive. In England beer was the beverage and could be had at the sign of the bush, any green bough or bunch of leaves. (In Austrian villages today a green bough over a wine cellar means apple wine is available and for sale.)

1095, First crusade preached by Pope Urban. The crusades stimulated trade and travel.

During the period of the crusades, hospices operated by the Knights Hospitaler (founded in 1048) in Jerusalem primarily for pilgrims to and from the Holy Land.

About 1183, public cookhouses on London's river bank offered "dishes of roast, fried and boiled fish, great and small, venison and byrds."

RENAISSANCE PERIOD, 14th and 15th centuries [in Italy] and 15th and 16th centuries [Northern Europe].

In 1400, food sold at Westminster Gate in London included "bread, ale, wyne, ribs of beefe, hot peascod, hot sheppes feet, macherel and oysters."

Inns in northern Italy as trade revived.

In Tudor England (1485–1603) selected innkeepers forced to retain stables by Royal Act.

(continued)

Some innkeepers acted as unofficial postmasters and kept stables for the royal post.

1533, Catherine de Medici (from Florence) married the future Henry II (both at the ripe old age of 14) and is credited with initiating a concern with things gastronomic. Brought brigade of chefs with her.

1536, Henry VIII suppressed the monasteries, forcing the growth of inns.

Inns served meat, poultry, ale, bread. New World foods not available: turkey, cranberries, tomatoes, corn, potatoes, cocoa, coffee not yet introduced.

Mermaid Tavern, scene of the first English Club, founded by Sir Walter Raleigh; frequented by Shakespeare.

Catering established in France. There were few inns, but private homes could be rented for the occasion.

Henry III, 1574 to 1589, of France made the fork fashionable.

EARLY MODERN, 17th and 18th Century Europe

Louis de Bechamel, Marshal Mirepoix, and Cardinal Richelieu were food-minded, invented or had sauces and other culinary items named for them.

1645, First coffee house in Venice.

1650, First coffee house established at Oxford. Coffee houses reached great popularity in late 17th and early 18th centuries. More than 200 coffee houses in London by 1700.

1653-1658, Cromwell in power in England suppressed culinary and other pleasures.

1658, Stage coaches introduced in England. Gave taverns further prominence.

Louis XIV (reigned 1643-1715), the "Sun King," glutton with a tapeworm, made dining a state occasion, and focused attention on food. Hated water (did not bathe) but loved food.

1669, Coffee introduced to Paris by Turkish ambassador. Served by beautiful slave girls.

Louis XV (reigned 1715-1774) interested in love and food, in that order.

1765, The first restaurant (as distinct from an inn, tavern, or food specialty house), opened by Boulanger in Paris.

1784, Coaching era in England with first government mail routes.

About 1790, Count Rumford, born Benjamin Thompson in Woburn, Massachusetts, invented the drip coffee maker, the kitchen range, and learned much about heat transfer. Invented portable steamers for cooking army food; invented Rumford soups, boiled combinations of peas, barley, and potatoes. Added croutons. Helped make potatoes popular in Europe.

1792, Louis XVI, after being condemned to death, was able to sup on six veal cutlets, a chicken, eggs, and three glasses of wine.

In France, hotels, the residences of nobility, were made available as public houses because of the absence of their owners, some of whom lost their heads.

In England, posting and other inns plentiful, usually built around a central courtyard (unlike American taverns). Many of these English inns are still operating.

MODERN, 19th and 20th Century Europe

1800-1833, Careme fashioned "La Grande Cuisine."

1825, *La Physiologie Du Gout* published by the world's best known gourmet, Brillat-Savarin.

1825-1858, Alexis Soyer gained culinary eminence. Wrote *Gastronomic Regeneration*. Introduced steam cooking at Reform Club, London, in 1840s. Only chef to be mentioned in Britain's *Dictionary of National Biography*.

1841, Thomas Cook began the travel agency business in England.

1880-1900, Cesar Ritz enticed the elite from their homes to hotels for entertaining. Managed the Claridge, the Carlton, and the Savoy.

(continued)

1907, Ritz Development Company franchises the Ritz name to the Ritz-Carlton Hotel, New York City. Later the franchise used in Montreal, Boston, Lisbon, Barcelona.

1880–1935, Auguste Escoffier, known as "chef to kings and king of chefs," worked with Ritz, published *Le Guide Culinaire* (1907), considered by many to be the New Testament of Cookery.

INNKEEPING IN THE UNITED STATES—from Tavern to Motel

1634, Ships Tavern, Boston, opened by Samuel Cole who had arrived with the Puritans in 1630.

1642, City Tavern, New York City, built by West India Company.

1670, First coffee house in Boston, served coffee and chocolate.

American Plan in use, although not called by that term. It was similar to table d'hote, the French plan in which the traveler or guest sat with other such people, with the host at the head of the table. The meal was called the ordinary, and some of the taverns were called ordinaries.

Menu favorites: Journey cake (johnny cake) dunked in cider, suppawn (cornmeal in milk or butter), cornmeal sometimes boiled in molasses, Tipsy cake, cake with wine or liquor added.

Beverages were rum and beer and variations of the two such as flip—strong beer and rum sweetened with dried pumpkin; cherry bounce—rum and cherries sealed in a keg for at least a year, and other whimseys such as "Whistle Belley Vengeance," sour beer and molasses.

In 1775, the Green Dragon in Boston was the meeting place of American revolutionists. Patrick Henry called the taverns of colonial America "Cradles of Liberty."

Most taverns were named for their proprietors, but there were many "Red Lions," "Golden Bowls," "White Horses," and "Black Horses." After the Revolution a number quickly became "George Washington's," Washington's visage being painted over that of the British monarch, George III.

1785, Jefferson was American minister to France, which began his interest in French cookery and wines. Served French wines and crepes while President.

1790s, Term "hotel" began being used in United States.

1794, The City Hotel (first known as the Burns Coffee House), 115 Broadway, New York City (had population of 30,000).

1794, the first canal opened, a modest affair, circumnavigating the falls of the Connecticut River, South Hadley, Massachusetts.

1794, French refugee opened a restorator in Boston. Served truffles, cheese fondue, and delicious soups.

1801, Francis Union Hotel, Philadelphia. Made from the former presidential mansion and later an inn.

1801–1820, Taverns rechristened "hotels," following a surge of popularity for all things French. The tavern then became a place with emphasis on drinking.

A typical tavern of the early 1800s was a large home-style building painted white with green blinds and trim. It contained about twenty-five rooms and a combination dining room and bar.

1806, The Exchange Coffee House in Boston, 7 stories tall, contained 200 apartments. Largest building in America.

1817, Forerunner of the Somerset Club formed in Boston.

1824, The Mountain House, first of the large resort hotels in the Catskills opened, eventually had 300 rooms, accommodated 500 persons. American neo-classical architecture.

1825, First record of gas stove.

1825, Erie Canal opened, linked New York Harbor via the Hudson and Mohawk Rivers with the Great Lakes; hotels built fronting on the Canal.

1826, City Hotel of Baltimore (Barnum's) became the first "first-class" hotel; 200 apartments.

1827, Concord Coach appears; makes travel more bearable.

(continued)

1829, America's first restaurant opened, Delmonico's in New York City, served lunch, and had a lady cashier. First of more than a dozen eating establishments that brought the name "Delmonico's" to pre-eminence in the service of fine food.

In 1829, The Tremont House in Boston appeared with these firsts:
1. first bellboys (rotunda men)
2. first inside water closets
3. first hotel clerk, complete with standard smile
4. french cuisine on Yankee menu
5. first menu card in this country
6. annunciators in guest rooms
7. room keys given to the guests

Designed from cellar to eaves to be a hotel: 3 stories, 170 rooms. Building still in use.

American plan established itself during the 1830s when "Americans were churning around the West." Resembled the French "table d'hote."

Tipping had, theretofore, been considered undignified by the "help," but because of immigration of persons accustomed to receiving tips, tipping became part of the business.

1834, Boston and Worcester railroad opened.

New England-trained hotel managers were in demand in the nation.

1834, The Astor House, New York City, first palatial hotel. Rooms furnished in black walnut and Brussels carpeting.

1836, First private membership club with rooms of its own in New York City, established in the City Hotel.

1846, First centrally heated hotel, the Eastern Exchange Hotel in Boston.

1848, Safety deposit boxes provided for commercial guests by New England Hotel, Boston.

1855, Original Parker House of Boston opened, offered the "European Plan."

1856, Baking powder sold commercially.

1859, First passenger elevator ("verticle railway") in a hotel; upper rooms could have a higher rate than those on lower floors.

1868, Commercial yeast available.

1870s, Sporting country and city clubs formed in United States.

1875, The Palace Hotel, San Francisco, "World's largest hotel." Floor clerks installed.

1875, *The Hotel World*, trade magazine, started. *The Hotel Red Book* first published.

1876, Fred Harvey founded the company that in the 1880s established Harvey Houses every 100 miles along the Sante Fe Railway.

1881, Louis Sherry opened his first restaurant, developed the art of catering.

1882, Electric lights dazzled the guests of New York City's Hotel Everett.

1880 to 1890s, Resort boom in Florida, New England, Virginia, Pennsylvania, and Atlantic City. Fred Harvey and John R. Thompson, first of the large restaurant chains to develop.

1884, First co-op apartment in New York City (now Chelsea Hotel) forerunner of condominiums in this country.

1887, *Stewards Handbook and Dictionary*, Jessup Whitehead.

1887, Ponce de Leon, St. Augustine, built. First luxury hotel in Florida.

1888, Del Coronado built, first luxury resort in California.

1890s, The John R. Thompson Company operates first extensive commissary system (Chicago).

1894, *The Epicurean*, cookbook by Charles Ranhofer, chef at Delmonico's "gave away Delmonico's secrets."

Questions

1 Tavernkeeping is an old business going back as early as ____ B.C.

2 The early Greek tavern was often located near a temple for a very practical reason. What was that?

3 Fastfood services were seen in what ancient culture?

4 In Ancient Rome taverns were identifiable on the outside in that their pillars were hung with what?

5 In what way was a hospice similar to a hotel of today?

6 How would a passerby of an early English tavern know that ale was served inside?

7 The early inns and taverns of England had tavern signs, such as a white hart, a black swan, for a very good reason. What was it?

8 Besides being a place offering food and lodging, the early English inn had other functions. Can you name two or three of them?

9 Why were stagecoaches called by that name?

10 Henry VIII had an influence on the development of the early English inn. In what way?

11 In 1825 something happened in England which drastically changed the hospitality business. What was it?

12 In what way did the Huguenots leave an imprint on the hospitality business of this country?

13 The Crusades in the Renaissance had what impact on the development of the hospitality business?

14 The Roman military roads were used by the military and what other group of people during the Roman period?

THE DEVELOPING HOTEL/MOTEL

TWO

The Hotel emerged from the tavern by the simple expedient of a name change; the term tavern was changed to that of hotel. The word hotel had a more glamorous ring, since in France it was the city residence of a wealthy or prominent person, or referred to a public building such as the "hotel de ville," the town hall, or, better yet, the "Hotel de la Monnaie," the mint.

During the French Revolution, many private places in France were converted into public houses and naturally called hotels. Country houses which served as inns were known then, and are still known, by the term "auberge." Things French were popular about 1790 both because of French aid to us during the American Revolution and because the early days of the French Revolution were looked upon as a great democratic upsurge.

The term "hotel" has a common root with the words hospitality, hostelry, hospital, hospice, and host. The Spanish word, "huesped" (guest) probably goes back to the same Latin origin.

Colonial taverns and taverns-turned-hotel were originally designed as private homes where the innkeeper lived with his family. The term "hotel" was well known in America at least as early as 1791, and the city directories of the 1790s show that many a tavern became a hotel.[1]

About 1800, the terms "tavern," "hotel," and "coffee house" were being used, but by 1820 the word "hotel" was the generally accepted term. From this point on, the tavern became more of an eating and drinking place with emphasis on the drinking.

SPECIAL STATUS FOR HOTELKEEPERS IN THE UNITED STATES

From the outset in America, tavernkeeping and, later, hotelkeeping were usually in the hands of respected members of the community and enjoyed a status not found in Europe. George Washington owned several small public houses, and, later, Abraham Lincoln was part-owner of a tavern in Springfield, Illinois.

In the thirty years before the Civil War, hotelkeeping came to be referred to as a "profession." Many managers strove to be hosts rather than proprietors, which puzzled the British visitor no end. Charles A. Stetson, manager of the Astor House in New York City, put the difference like this, "A tavernkeeper knows how to get to market and how to feed so many people at a public table. A hotelkeeper is a gentleman who stands on a level with his guests."[2]

Many hotelmen were New Englanders who served their apprenticeships under older well-known hotelmen. Even in the deep South, in 1860, the managers and clerks were generally New Englanders, while the waiters and

---

1. Doris Elizabeth King, "Early Hotel Entrepreneurs and Promoters, 1793–1860," *Explanations in Entrepreneurial History* (Harvard Research Center in Entrepreneurial History, VIII, February 1956).

2. Thomas Lately, *Delmonico's, A Century of Splendor* (Boston, MA: Houghton Mifflin Co., 1967).

Figure 2–1   The Nicolett House was a structure that Minneapolis could well boast of in 1858—five floors and seventy spacious rooms. The first floor was rented to a bank and several stores, which gave the House an assured income. Ladies had a private entrance and separate "parlors." Speaking tubes led from the front desk to all floors, and bell pulls for service were in all rooms, a practice borrowed from the early inns. Cooks and porters stoked the hotel's ranges with cordwood. Three complete meals and a room cost $2.00. The building was used until 1923 when a new thirteen story Pick-Nicollett was built on the same site.
Source: Courtesy of Albert Pick Hotels.

chambermaids were usually Irish or German immigrants or free blacks.

The early hotels continued the tavern custom of serving an "ordinary," a set meal served at a given hour and at a fixed price. Hotels from the beginning were known for their good tables, or lack of them. The Astor House, the most sumptuous hotel on the American continent before about 1850, served a table d'hote meal four times daily which was included in the charge for a room—$2.00.

The cuisine, a combination of French and American cooking, was described with mixed French and American terminology on the menu as well. The menu included a wide assortment of roasted game and boiled and roasted domestic animals, as well as fish.

By 1849 the Astor House menu was written in more easily understood American terms, leaving the French menu to the Delmonico restaurants of the same city. At the Astor, engraved cards informed guests that the schedule of meals would be:

Breakfast—7:30 in Ladies' Ordinary, 8:00 in Men's Ordinary

Dinner—3:00 in Ladies' Ordinary, 3:30 in Men's Ordinary

Tea—6:00 to 9:00

Supper—9:00 to midnight[3]

The quantity of food served at the ordinaries was enormous. For breakfast there were three kinds of griddle cakes, ham and eggs, sausages, fish, chicken, beefsteak, pork, oysters, an assortment of bread and biscuits, plus coffee, tea, and chocolate. A description of the dining room of 1834 by a British visitor shows that even then we were a nation of fast eaters: "The hotels are numerous, large, and convenient . . . but the meals are taken in the public room, where fifty to one hundred persons sit down at the same time. A vast number of dishes covers the table, and the dispatch with which they are cleaned is almost incredible. From five to ten minutes for breakfast, fifteen to twenty for dinner, and ten for supper is usually sufficient. Each person, as soon as satisfied, leaves the table without regard to his neighbor; no social conversation follows."[4]

Hotels proliferated as the cities grew. New York City had only eight in 1818; by 1836 there were twenty-eight; and ten years later, in 1846, there were one hundred-eight.

THE IMPACT OF THE HOTEL ON AMERICAN CULTURE

Until recently, historians had little to say about the effect of the hotel in shaping our culture. Daniel J. Boorstin in his book, *The American National Experience,*[5] fortunately has much to say on the subject. He titles his chapter on hotels "Palaces of the Public." Williamson in his book, *The American Hotel,* calls the hotel "the most distinctively American of all our institutions."[6]

An English barrister, Alexander McKay, who traveled in this country in 1846, observed the differences between English and American hotels. He pointed out that in England hotels were regarded as purely private property, in appearance very much like the private houses that surrounded them. In America, hotels were looked upon as public concerns and even looked like public buildings. Often, they were the most impressive and grandest buildings in the town or city.

The magnificence and splendor of some of the American hotels overwhelmed some foreign visitors. A London journalist writing in 1861 said that the American hotel "is to an English hotel what an elephant is to a periwinkle. . . ." He exaggerated a bit when he praised the American hotel as being as roomy as Buckingham Palace. The American hotel was a new type of structure, indigenous to this country, and, even before the Civil War, it was being copied in Europe and elsewhere.

AMERICAN HOTELS DIFFERED FROM ENGLISH INNS

Indeed, the American hotel served a different purpose than the inn or the railroad hotel in England. The class system was not firmly rooted in the country, and the hotel was a place where all classes of people stopped and all classes of people tended to mingle, the wealthy together with the workingman or the frontiersman.

Tipping, so much a part of the hotel today, was considered un-American until the flood of Irish and German immigration appeared in the 1830s and 1840s. It did not become widespread until an even greater flood of immigration took place at the end of the century.[7]

In England, the upper-classes had enormous homes and large staffs of servants. When they traveled they were likely to stop with friends. When they entertained it was in their homes. It was not until the turn of the century that they were enticed away from their homes to dine out with Cesar Ritz and Escoffier in such places as the Savoy and the Claridge.

In America, the hotel was a place for businessmen to gather. In fact, many of the hotels were called exchange houses and operated somewhat as a stock exchange. Some secured bank privileges and issued paper currency. As late as the 1860s the Burnet House in Cincinnati issued $5 bills authenticated by its cashier, and carrying an engraved likeness of the building. In New Orleans, the lobby of the St. Charles Hotel was used for public slave auctions. Hotels were the usual meeting places of civic committees, associations of businessmen and, in the frontier communities, were the meeting places for the city council and other government agencies.

Quite logically, the promoters of the new towns recognized the values of a good hotel, and, in several instances, the hotel was built before the town even existed. As Daniel Boorstin says, the hotels were both the creature and the creator of communities, as well as symptoms of the frenetic quest for community. At Port Sheldon, Michigan, a hotel, The Ottawa House, was built at a cost of $200,000 in the

---

4. Ibid.

5. Daniel J. Boorstin, *The American National Experience* (New York, NY: Random House, 1965).

6. Jefferson Williamson, *The American Hotel: An Anecdoted History* (New York, NY: Alfred Knopf, 1930).

7. Doris Elizabeth King, *The Community Hotel* (SFA Economist, Dept. of Business Administration, Austin State College, Vol. 4, No. 2, Spring, 1960).

heart of a black pine forest. This was in 1837. By 1842, five years later, the city had failed to materialize, and the hotel was dismantled, and the four pillars which graced its front were dragged away by ox team to become part of a mansion in Grand Rapids.

Chicago, in 1835, had a population of 350 but had a brick hotel that served food with napkins and offered printed menus. By the mid-1850s, Chicago had something like 60,000 inhabitants and about 150 hotels. By 1902 there were 15,135 year-round hotels with 50 or more rooms, according to an estimate made by the editor of the *Hotel Monthly* magazine at the time.

HOTELS AND TOWNS "RUN TO THE RAILROADS"

Anthony Trollope, an English observer of the American scene in the 1860s, had this to say about hotels in isolated spots. "They are to be found in all towns, and I may almost say in all villages. In England and on the Continent we find them on the recognized routes of travel and in towns of commercial or social importance. On unfrequented roads and in villages there is usually some small house of public entertainment in which the unexpected traveler may obtain food and shelter, and in which the expected boon companions of the neighborhood smoke their nightly tipple. But in the States of America the first sign of an incipient settlement is a hotel 5 stories high, with an office, a bar, a cloakroom, 3 gentlemen's parlours, 2 ladies' parlours, a ladies' entrance, and 200 bedrooms.... When the new hotel rises up in the wilderness, it is presumed that people will come there with the expressed object of inhabiting it. The hotel itself will create a population, as the railroads do. With us, railroads run to the town; but in the States the towns run to the railroads. It is the same thing with the hotels."

The public nature of the American hotel was quite clear when Barnum's Hotel in Baltimore became involved in litigation in 1860. A Baltimore judge ruled it had to be kept open because, as a first-class hotel, it was a "public institution and a public necessity."

One of the appeals of the coffee house had been the availability of newspapers to be read by anyone at no charge. The "reading room" of some of the hotels was a leading attraction in

America before the arrival of the public library. Boston's Tremont House, for example, provided a variety of newspapers at no charge to its guests and charged a small annual fee for use of the room by local citizens.

The American did not cherish his home in the same way as did the Britisher; consequently, the Englishman, who would retire in an English inn to his private room for tea and his meal, felt very much out of place in the American hotel. According to Boorstin, "Americans lived in a new realm of uncertain boundaries, in an affable, commercial world which, strictly speaking, was neither public nor private; a world of first names, open doors, front porches, and front lawns, and naturally, too, of lunch counters, restaurants, and hotel lobbies."

Origin of the American Plan

The "American Plan," the arrangement by which one charge covers both room and meals, probably was the extension of the practice of tavern keepers of offering room and board (also beer in many taverns) for a single all inclusive price. The European Plan (first introduced in France) was first offered in the United States in the 1830's. A visiting New Englander to New York City reported three hotels in that city were operating under the new system— food, beverage, and room being priced separately.[8] The American Plan especially suited the resort where families might stay for the season, and many resorts even today operate on the American Plan.

Even in the early nineteenth century, Americans gathered to do their politicking and conventioneering. The first national nominating convention of a major party met in 1831 to name Henry Clay for president, and where did it meet? Quite naturally, in a hotel, Barnum's City Hotel in Baltimore, a six-story building with 200 apartments, reputed to be one of the best in the country. The custom of group meetings has been with us for a long time but it reached its full blossom in the 1950s, and today conventions account for over one-third of the occupancy in our hotels. In some properties, convention sales constitute 90 percent or more of the business.

8. Dorsey and Devine, *Fare Thee Well*, (New York, NY: Crown Publishers, 1964), p. 33.

Another way in which the nineteenth-century American hotelkeeper was different from his counterpart "mein host" in Europe was his self-concept and his social standing. The innkeeper in England was supposed to be a genial, deferential individual, one cut above a servant.

TAVERNKEEPER IN EARLY AMERICA

In early America, the tavernkeeper might be an officer in the local militia, own his own establishment, and be a person of some prestige. He refused to bow, even to English gentlemen. Boorstin says that some travelers from abroad were surprised and shocked by the fact that the innkeeper honored the guest with his company, rather than vice versa.

Americans have always been geographically and socially mobile, and hotels reflected and abetted mobility. Privacy, according to Boorstin, was a vice akin to pride, and the desire to be alone was a species of neglect, if not offense. A westerner might share his table and be expected to be chatty with anyone who

sat there including common soldiers, farmers, laborers, teamsters, lawyers, bankers, or generals.

SIZE AND SCOPE OF
THE INNKEEPING INDUSTRY

Gross sales of the innkeeping industry was about 14 billion dollars in 1977. Hotels accounted for 6.6 billion; motels and motor hotels about 7.4 billion dollars.[9]

The 17,525 hotels in 1974 had about 1.3 million guest rooms; the 27,625 motels and motor hotels had about 1.5 million guest rooms. An average of about 1.6 million rooms are occupied each night of the year. The rate of hotel occupancy dropped from 70 percent in 1958 to 60 percent in 1963. In 1979, occupancy ran about 68 percent.

Of the motels, about half of the business was done by motor hotels, the larger motels that combine the luxury and comfort of the hotel with the convenience of the motel.

9. *Trends in the Hotel Motel Business, 1978.* (New York, NY: Harris, Kerr, Forster & Co.)

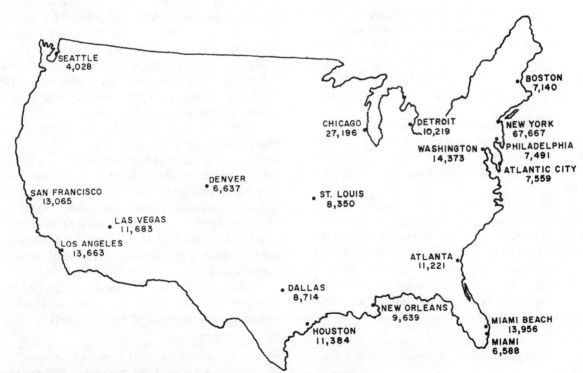

Figure 2–2   Hotel Concentration in Major Cities in the United States.

Total commercial lodging places in U.S.	45,150
Number of hotels	17,525
Number of motels and motor hotels	27,625
Gross sales (annual)	$11.1 billion
American Hotel & Motel Assn. Members	7,020 (905,894 rooms)
Number of rooms available per day	2.8 million
Average number of rooms occupied per day (annual)	1.7 million
Average percentage of hotel/motel room occupancy (annual)	61%
Average number of rooms per establishment	60.9
Average daily room rate per guest	$15.94
Average number of guests per occupied room	1.46 (45% are double-occupied)

Figure 2–3   United States Innkeeping Overview.

These new, larger motor hotels are more representative of the new lodging business than the older, smaller motel or the huge downtown hotel built in the 1920s. Motel receipts nearly doubled between 1958 and 1963 and again between 1963 and 1968. Much of the increase, however, can be attributed to inflation.

The shift in employment has been equally dramatic. In 1948 motels accounted for less than 10 percent of total industry employment. By 1975 the share was probably about one-third.[10]

For the United States as a whole, there are about 13 hotel-motel rooms with private baths per 1,000 persons. This ratio, probably the highest in the world for any large country, has remained constant since 1948 and earlier. Australia, a contrasting example, has a ratio of only 4.4 rooms with private baths per 1,000 persons.[11]

Four Major Classifications for Hotels

There are different ways of classifying hotels. According to Gerald Lattin, the four major classifications of American hotels are: (1) the commercial or transient hotel; (2) the resort hotel; (3) the residential hotel; and (4) the motel/motor hotel. Among the 17,525 hotels, approximately 75 percent are commercial, 16 percent are resort, and 9 percent are residential.[12]

The 6,060 members of the American Hotel and Motel Association (A.H. & M.A.) in 1977 classified themselves as follows:

transient hotels	5,224
all year resort hotels	364
seasonal resorts	314
residential hotels	116
condominium hotels	25

The most common transient hotel had between 76 and 200 rooms, the model resort hotel had between 76 and 125 rooms. The same was true for the residential hotel.[13]

The larger, newer motel, "the motor hotel" as it is termed, became popular in the 1950s. An industry newsletter, produced by the Helmsley-Spear Company of New York City since 1965, has published an annual census of these properties. Their definition of a motor hotel is "a property with transient lodging facilities, built or completely modernized since 1945, open more than half the year, and containing at least fifty guest units, plus adequate on-premise free parking." Motels and motor hotels numbered 27,625 in 1974.

Perhaps another useful classification is the convention hotel, the hotel that builds its occupancy around group business. Such hotels include what would ordinarily be called commercial hotels and many resort hotels as well.

Still another term frequently used is "budget motel," a property where rates may be one-third to one-half less than the usual motor hotel, usually a motel without frills and without a restaurant.

Many of the larger hostelries that carry the name motor hotel are also convention-oriented. Recognition of the convention hotel

10. Victor R. Fuchs, *The Service Economy* (National Bureau of Economic Research, Inc.: Columbia University Press, 1968).

11. *The Accountant, LKHH,* Vol. 48, No. 3, 1969.

12. Gerald W. Lattin, *Modern Hotel and Motel Management* (San Francisco, CA: W. H. Freeman & Co., 1968).

13. American Hotel and Motel Association, 1977 membership.

and motel as a separate classification was seen in 1968 when the *Hotel Red Book* first published a separate listing of properties with business meeting facilities, nearly 700 of them in the United States.

The resort hotel might also be called a vacation hotel or motel. Until about 1950, most resort hotels were seasonal, open either in the winter or summer. Many still are, but most resorts in Florida, California, Hawaii, and the Caribbean remain open the year around, with low seasons in the spring and fall.

The residential hotel is essentially an apartment building, offering maid service, a dining room, room foodservice, and possibly a cocktail lounge. Some of the better-known hotels, such as the Hotel Pierre and the Plaza in New York City, rent a large number of suites on a permanent basis which makes them at least partially residential in character. The Waldorf Towers, a part of the Waldorf-Astoria Hotel, is also residential in character.

Hotel Classification by Number of Rooms

Although the typical hotel is small, the large hotel does the lion's share of the business. The 700 properties that are included in the Harris, Kerr, Forster Annual Survey have revenue equal to more than 25 percent of the receipts of all the nation's hotels and motels. In 1962 there were 1,400 hotels operated by million dollar enterprises, of which about 1,000 were units of chain enterprises. These million dollar enterprises employed almost half of the 600,000 employees in the industry.

The average number of hotel rooms jumped from 62 rooms in 1948 to 72 rooms in 1974. From 1948 to 1974, motels and motor hotels with payrolls increased from 11,302 to 27,625; the number of motel rooms from 304,000 to about 1.5 million, an increase of close to 500 percent.

Quite naturally, the older, less well-located properties are in their declining years,

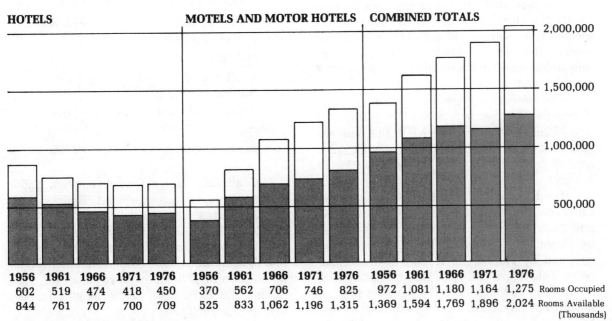

Figure 2–4 The Trend in Available Rooms and Occupancy for the Nation's Hotels and Motels.
Source: Trends in the Hotel-Motel Business, 1977. Harris, Kerr, Forster, and Company, New York City, 1977.

many of them only marginal operations. Competitive obsolescence forces hundreds of them out of business each year while the newer and brighter operations are usually quite profitable.

HOTEL CITIES

Where is the hotel business concentrated? The greatest concentration of hotel rooms is in the cities that are population and trade centers. Population alone is not a guide to the number of hotel rooms expected in a city.

Institutional cities, such as Washington, D.C., have a larger concentration of hotel rooms. Market cities, for example, New York, Los Angeles, Chicago, Atlanta, Boston, and San Francisco, require a number of hotel rooms for the large number of buyers and other businessmen visiting the cities.

Cities that are primarily industrial centers have fewer hotel rooms because their populations are stable, and there are fewer reasons for travelers to visit them. Cleveland, Pittsburgh, and Detroit are examples of such cities.

The map on the facing page shows the concentration of hotel rooms owned by AH & MA members in various cities. The number of rooms listed for each city is not the true total; only hotels listed in the *Hotel Red Book* for 1977 are included.

The *Hotel Red Book* lists only hotels and motels that are members of the American Hotel and Motel Association. The AH & MA believes that its member hotels represent about 75 percent of the first-class hotel rooms in the United States.

Total number of rooms for sale is something else. New York City, for example, in 1969 had about 116,000 guest rooms, as estimated by Stephen W. Brener based on information supplied by Harris, Kerr, Forster and Company. This figure had remained relatively constant since 1945. In 1976 the figure was even lower. Boston has a total of 10,000 rooms; Miami Beach, about 38,000 (forty-eight hotels per square mile). Las Vegas, Miami Beach, and Atlantic City are hotel centers, convention, and resort cities, with probably the highest concentration of hotel rooms per capita in the world. (Small areas such as Monaco, in Southern France, may have even higher hotel rooms resident rates.)

LEADERS IN LODGING

A few hotel chains existed before the turn of the century. The Statler chain dominated the hotel world until the 1930s when Conrad Hilton began building the Hilton chain and Ernest Henderson, the Sheraton chain. On the West Coast, headquartered in Seattle, Western International Hotels grew slowly but surely. In the 1950s, the motel chains appeared, and in the 1960s the motor hotels and motel chains surged ahead to lead in number of units. *Institutions/VF Magazine* ranks foodservice and lodging corporations according to volume of sales, in their July issue each year.

According to Service World International, June 1977, in 1977 the ten largest lodging operating companies worldwide, were:

Holiday Inns	278,000 rooms
The Sheraton Corporation	97,000
Ramada Inns	94,000
Trust Houses Forte, LTD. London	76,000
Hilton Corporation	62,820
Howard Johnson Company	59,220
Balkantourist, Sofia, Bulgaria	54,465
Day's Inn of American, Inc., Atlanta	39,000
Travel Lodge, International	32,000
Quality Inns International, Inc.	30,000

Continental Hotels Corporation had 27,540 rooms; Western International Hotels about 27,000; Hilton International about the same number; Hyatt Corporation had 24,000.

In 1975 chain-affiliated properties totaled 8,677, accounting for about 1.1 million rooms, or 41 percent of hotel/motel rooms at the time. Within the United States the lodging leaders are seen in the table.

Probably the best indicator of the concentration of the hotel business is seen in the wage and salary disbursements made by hotels and other lodging places. These figures, compiled by the U.S. Dept. of Commerce each year, show the number of millions of dollars paid to employees of hotels and other lodging places by state.

Table 2-1 Top twenty-five United States Lodging Chains

No.	Name of Chain	U.S. Properties 1977	U.S. Rooms 1977
1.	Holiday Inns, Inc.	1,518	240,639
2.	Best Western, Inc.	1,504	118,247
3.	Ramada Inns, Inc.	648	86,873
4.	Budget Motels & Hotels	1,285	80,000
5.	Sheraton Corp.	335	73,648
6.	Hilton Hotels Corp.	175	63,383
7.	Friendship Inns	1,045	62,000
8.	Howard Johnson Co.	517	58,075
9.	Days Inns of America	283	39,970
10.	TraveLodge	454	31,281
11.	Timoa Inns, Inc.	362	30,770
12.	Quality Inns	274	29,158
13.	Hyatt Hotels Corp.	52	25,100
14.	Motel 6, Inc.	239	23,589
15.	Red Carpet/Master Hosts	159	19,545
16.	Marriott Hotels	47	17,681
17.	Rodeway Inns	135	16,467
18.	Superior Motels, Inc.	300	15,000
19.	Western International	22	14,887
20.	Hotel Systems of America	68	9,500
21.	La Quinta Motor Inns	66	7,390
22.	Americana Hotels	13	7,262
23.	Dunfey Family's Hotels	24	6,870
24.	Stouffer Hotels & Inns	18	6,600
25.	Pick Hotels Corp	31	6,348
Totals		9,574	1,090,283

Note: Property and room figures are as of 9/30/77.
Source: Lodging Hospitality, December, 1977

TOP TEN "HOTEL STATES"

In 1967, the top ten "hotel states," in terms of wages and salaries (in millions of dollars) paid employees were as follows:

1	New York	320
2	California	284
3	Florida	174
4	Illinois	144
5	Texas	112
6	Pennsylvania	104
7	New Jersey	79
8	Ohio	77
9	Michigan	62

Such figures do not indicate the relative importance of the hotel business to a state. In Vermont, for example, in 1969 only $13 million was paid out to hotel and other lodging employees, but this represented a sizable percentage of all wages and salaries paid within the state. The same can be said for several other states such as New Hampshire, Arizona, Colorado, and Nevada, Georgia, a state that one would not ordinarily pick as a large hotel state, doubled its wage and salary disbursements to hotel and lodging employees in the period 1962–1967. Among the other states which have doubled, or more than doubled, such payments in that five-year period were Idaho, Nevada, and Tennessee.

ridors, eat in their dining rooms, and talk with their personnel.

THE PLAZA

A word about The Plaza. Overlooking Central Park, it has the distinction of having no name on it, the reason being that anyone who would have to identify the hotel by looking for its name should not be stopping there.

The Plaza, representing social stability, wealth, and timeless luxury, opened in 1907. Shortly thereafter, 90 percent of the hotel was taken over by permanent residents paying from $15,000 to $35,000 annually for their suites. Distinguished by its gabled, green mansard

Figure 2–7 The Plaza Hotel seen from the vantage point of the picturesque duck pond in Central Park, which is directly across from the hotel on 59th Street in New York City. Considered by many to be the queen of hotels, the Plaza displays no sign. There is a belief that if a patron does not recognize the Plaza, he should not be going to the hotel.

roof, Pulitzer Prize Memorial Fountain, and French atmosphere, it has been the scene of many a society gathering and has seen an ebb and flow in society and in its own fortunes. The top two floors were for the help who traveled with the guests—they did not require baths.

In 1943, it was losing money and Hilton picked it up for $7,400,000. Its losses were an asset to Hilton because under the tax law he could use them to offset profits earned in his other hotels. In 1953, he sold it to A. M. Sonnabend (founder of Hotel Corporation of America) for $15 million making a nice capital gains profit. At the same time, Hilton was given an operating contract for two years. The Sonnabend interests put up only $1 million in cash for the deal.

By 1961, occupancy had dropped to 60 percent, and the place began to be known as an old ladies' home. Although $12 million was needed to break even in the house, revenue was $10.4 million. Hotel Corporation of America spent $9 million in rehabilitation. By 1968, occupancy had climbed to 85 percent, average rate was $28.07, income exceeded $21 million a year, and profits were $2,131,000 before taxes.[33] In 1974, the Plaza was purchased from Sonesta International for $25 million by Western International, subsidiary of UAL.

Unlike most of the larger city hotels in the country, the Plaza is not a convention hotel. It has no coffee shop; it spends some $7,000 a year on the chocolate mints that each guest finds on his bedside table each evening. Three ice carvers are on hand to produce buffet displays and considerable labor is needed to wipe the fronds of the palms in the Palm Room. The Oak Room is considered one of the fine eating places of the city; only the St. Regis, the Pierre, and the Waldorf Towers are serious rivals for the social elite market in New York City. The Oak Room was turned into a business office during prohibition.

The New York Hilton gets on no one's "great" list, but it is certainly the world's greatest convention hotel, an engineering marvel.

GREAT ROOM SERVICE

Robert Morley, the well-known British actor, comments on his list of "great" hotels insisting that room service should be rushed to the guest room, the breakfast tray received in two minutes. The simple secret, he says, is to have a kitchen on each floor. This is no secret, but it is expensive.

Morley declares the greatest hotel in the world to be the Ritz in Paris. He loves the golden clocks that he found in each Ritz establishment. At the Ritz, the guest is a guest, and nobody forgets it for a single moment. He does not care for hotels that conserve space, likening them to batteries for hens or humans. He hates to be attacked by the fast-moving doors of the modern elevators. Too bad; slow-moving elevator doors mean slow elevators.

Morley graciously includes an American hotel, The Century Plaza of Beverly Hills, in his list of greats. Designed by Minoru Yamasaki, the hotel is part of a "city within a city—a place to work, to live, to shop, and to participate in leisure activities." The hotel has 800 rooms, including 67 suites, each with private balcony, lanai, and color TV. It has the largest hotel ballroom in the West, seating up to 3,000. Morley has one objection: he does not care for the Chinese costumes on the Chinese coolie bellboys.

The writer would include the Warwick Hotel of Houston on any list of great hotels. The owner, an oil multimillionaire, has refurbished an old hotel into something special. Among other things, he dismantled two French chateaux and installed their paneling and furnishings in his hotel. The lobby is spacious, gracious, and charming. The rooms are large and beautifully furnished. The rooftop club is reached by an outside elevator; the ride in it is an experience in itself.

Aesthetically one of the great hotels of the world is the Caneel Bay Plantation in the U.S. Virgin Islands. Mexico has Las Brisas and The Princess in Acapulco. Both are architecturally unique. Las Brisas, built up the side of a small mountain, has 200 villas with private pools. The Acapulco Princess, part of the Princess chain, headquartered in New York City, is probably the most beautiful high-rise resort ever built. With 770 rooms, it employs about 1,500 people, 70 of whom keep its magnificent landscaping and plants beautiful. Twenty flower-bedecked floors center on a breeze-swept patio. The floors are stepped to resemble a Mayan temple.

---

33. *Fortune Magazine*, September, 1969.

Many a person's secret desire is to run a small hotel like the sixteen antique-filled rooms of The Mansion in San Francisco. Robert C. Pritikin, The Mansion's owner, bought a three-story house for $100,000, and spent $45,000 on Victorian-era furnishings, Oriental rugs, and fresh flowers. Mr. Pritikin has tried to create an Edwardian fantasy world in his Queen Anne-style building, which was built by a Gold Rush millionaire. Breakfast is served in bed: coffee, orange juice, warm croissants, butter, and strawberry jam. The owner, dressed in striped trousers, greets the guest at the door and escorts them in for a glass of chablis while taped strains of Bach play in the parlor.

SOCIAL PRESTIGE DETERMINES RATING

The social prestige of the clientele of a hotel determines its overall rating. The Claridge of London gets high points for exclusivity as does the Paris Ritz and the Beverly Wilshire in Beverly Hills, California.

The posh hotel, it is reported, should be ready for any occasion. Claridge's in London has a story that one evening an elderly, titled lady marched out of the lift on her way to an important dinner, dressed only in her jewelry. She had simply forgotten to put any clothes on, a mistake that was instantly rectified by the Manager. He at once stepped forward, covered the lady with his own coat and accompanied her back into the lift as though nothing had happened.[34]

That hotel also ran into another problem when two kings arrived, both intent on staying in the Royal Suite. The solution: the Manager ordered the workmen to pull down half the ceiling in the Royal Suite, showed the unfortunate damage to the ambassadors of both countries in question, and arranged for two smaller royal suites immediately. The Claridge, incidentally, isn't much to look at from the outside but arranges for no fewer than six waiters, six chambermaids, two valets, a house porter, and three bathroom cleaners to be ready at the ring of the appropriate bell to come springing along the corridor to administer to the guest's slightest need. Even, it is said, a simple whiskey and soda arrives on a trolley covered with a white

Figure 2–8   The Waldorf-Astoria is probably the best known hotel in the world. It was completed in 1931 and carries the name of the older, now demolished Waldorf-Astoria, built in the 1890s.

linen tablecloth, together with "crisps," black and green olives, and hot salted almonds. That hotel is also one of a very few that has a number of "courier" rooms set aside for the personal servants of guests.

A good press must be maintained if a hotel is to be recognized for its name and "greatness." Certain writers or publications have to be cultivated. Lucius Beebe was well known for pontificating on matters of good food and lodging. The Sheraton-Palace of San Francisco was forever appearing in his columns as a place par excellence. Needless to say, he was well received at the Sheraton-Palace.

Other writers have their own favorites. Of course, the greater the prestige of the evalu-

34. Christopher Matthew, *A Different World* (London, England: Paddington Press, 1976.)

ator, the better for the hotel. Cesar Ritz could do no wrong after the Prince of Wales, later Edward VII, said, "Where Ritz goes, I go."

Opened in 1975, the Ritz Hotel in Chicago represents the luxury hotel in the Ritz tradition as seen in America. The hotel, reported to cost $80,000 a room (about twice the cost of the first-class urban hotel built in 1975) is located on floors eleven through thirty-one of the seventy-four story Water Tower Place on fashionable North Michigan Avenue. Like many hotels, it is part of a condominium building which also contains offices and a seven-story shopping center containing such prestigious stores as Marshall Field and Company, and Lord & Taylor.

The Chicago Ritz makes food and beverage catering, secretarial, and maid service available to condominium owners who also have access to the health club, which has a swimming pool, exercise rooms, saunas, and masseurs.

The twelfth floor is the main lobby, a three-acre, glass-walled expanse of dining rooms, bars, and a 210-foot promenade. A skylighted garden terrace is part of the hotel's showcase, and a ballroom with 400,000 gem-quality crystals adorning the ceiling is part of the foodservice.

Much larger than the Paris Ritz in France, as well as most of the other five Ritz hotels in existence around the world now, this one has 450 guest rooms and twenty apartments for permanent residents. The larger suites have two floors, connected by spiral staircases. Some have such deluxe appointments as oriental rugs and dressing rooms with mirrors on all four walls. Employees will number three for every two guests as opposed to the 2 to 3 ratio at most hotels, according to the general manager. The guests in any of the rooms may summon a waiter by pushing a bedside button, and each floor contains a food pantry.

According to a former general manager, service is elegant, "No staff member will commit the unpardonable sin of asking the guest if everything is all right." Discriminating guests who are used to excellent service will complain if they do not like the service.

Details of equipment have been carefully considered. Extra-thin china, which costs twice the price usually paid for china, is used. China teapots, especially made to be dripless, were imported. The place opened with an inventory of 25,000 bottles of French wine.

The hotel has been equipped to reduce noise. Walls of guest rooms are twice the thickness of most new hotel rooms. Air conditioning equipment has been specified with oversized fan coils.

The market for the hotel, according to the management, is the top-level corporate executive who will not mind single room rates starting at about $75 and suites that cost $450. To instill the "Ritz Mystique" in new employees, each was invited to spend a night in the hotel prior to the opening. With all of its ritzy appointments and service, the hotel got off to a shaky start, occupancy the first year running at 50 percent and a little later Cabot and Forbes, which owns 50 percent interest selling out for $2 million. Because the hotel lost about $4 million the first year, its General Manager was let go and service cut (one waiter for two floors). Marketing policy was changed to attract small groups.[35]

European hotels are likely to be rated by the national tourist office. France, for example, has 82 deluxe hotels, 311 Four Star, 1738 Three Star, 4,978 Two Star and about 10,000 One Star Hotels. Spain also has a rating system imposed by its national tourist office. In Italy the Ciga Hotels management characterize their deluxe hotels as having wide corridors, high ceilings, and spaciousness. The look is said to be luxurious: crystal chandeliers, veined marble, frescos, tapestry, silk and velvet draperies, period furniture, fine art in baroque frames. According to Ciga sales literature, little things count too—hand milled soap, fresh flowers, thick bath towels, engraved stationary, plenty of personal service, your robe laid out every night on your turned-down bed, and buttons to summon chambermaid, valet, hall porter, or waiter from stations on each floor.

The editors of the Mobil Travel Guide each year select a number of hotels, motels, and resorts to receive its 5 Star Awards each "One of the Best in the Country." In the 1977 list of resorts was the Arizona Biltmore in Phoenix, honored for eighteen consecutive years with the 5 Star designation; the Broadmoor Hotel in Colorado Springs (seventeen years); Greenbrier in White Sulphur Springs, West Virginia

---

35. Wall Street Journal, Sept. 14, 1947.

(sixteen years), and the Boca Raton Hotel and Club in Florida.

Among the city properties so honored were the Fairmont Hotel and Tower of San Francisco, the Stanford Court in the same city, and the Beverly Wilshire in Beverly Hills. Opposing the notion that only small or medium-sized hotels can achieve ratings of distinction, the Mobil Guide lists the enormous Waldorf-Astoria in New York City and the Century Plaza near Los Angeles in its top classification.

Most major cities around the world have at least one or two outstanding hotels: in Paris, The Crillon and the Ritz; in Lisbon, The Ritz; in Madrid the Ritz and The Palace; in Vienna, The Sacher and The Imperial. In New York City, the Plaza and The Pierre, chateau-like, have long enjoyed outstanding reputations.

The AAA Tour books include ratings of some 15,000 properties that are graded on a scale of one to five diamonds.

Mobil Travel Guide awards 1 to 5 Star ratings of 4,000 restaurants, 15,000 motels, 1,000 hotels, and 400 resorts.

In considering hotel glamour, it must be said that there are at least two hotel worlds. The one is the glamour hotel that covers the luxury resort hotel and the prestigious city hotel. Together, these hotels may constitute less than 20 percent of the innkeeping industry.

A good share of the spending at the prestigious city hotel is by the expense account person. The $75 single rate means little to him since he is not spending his own money. He is probably invited to a hospitality suite maintained by a company that would like to sell him something or influence him in some way. The tabs for several of his meals are picked up by somebody else, or they go on the expense account.

Then there are the people of wealth who can well afford the prestigious hotel, or the people on the way up who cannot afford to stop at other than a prestige hotel. The glamour resorts are frequented by the wealthy in season, by the not-so-wealthy out of season.

HOTELS FOR THE MAJORITY

The other 80 percent of the hotel world is prosaic; it is the one where the vast majority of people stay when they travel. The hotel is likely to be smaller, the rates may be one-half or less than those in the glamour places. The hotel can be located in just about any community.

The newer motor hotels, including Holiday Inns, Ramada Inns, Rodeway, TraveLodge, Hilton Inns, the Howard Johnson Motor Lodges, and dozens of other chain operations, are the stopping places for families of moderate income, the traveling man, the businessman, the other technical and professional people of the vast middle class.

The motor hotel or the average hotel that has been well maintained is a pleasant place in which they spend the night or several nights. One room, however, looks pretty much like another. Men who travel a great deal say that sometimes, before they are wide awake in the morning, they look around the room and wonder which city they are in.

Hotel restaurant fare is fairly standard throughout the country, the menu selected to appeal to the great American taste that thrives on meat and potatoes. No French chef in the kitchen, only the local cook who learned his trade by looking over the shoulder of the man ahead of him.

Despite all this, the "leading hotel" in town manages to convey a certain sense of excitement. It probably has a lively bar, where boy meets girl, and a certain amount of gaiety prevails. Hotels on the way out, however, are sad places, indeed, where the desperate hopes of the owners are mingled with the stoicism of the guest.

WHAT HOTEL GUESTS WANT

Ernest Dichter, the founder of Motivation Research, has a great deal to say about the way people really feel about hotels and hotel rooms.[36] Dichter, by conducting depth interviews with a number of people, reaches down into their subconscious and exposes how they really feel about things.

Hotel guests, Dichter says, want a "live-in." They want reassurance and ways of avoiding that old devil, loneliness. They want to take possession of the hotel room by inspecting, feeling, trying out the lights, and performing various rituals to reassure themselves. A call from the front desk or VIP treatment from an assistant manager goes a long way.

36. Ernest Dichter, Address before the American Hotel and Motel Association, October 20, 1967.

Once the guest is in the room he resents intrusion on his privacy, such things as the maid checking the room. The room should reflect the city where the hotel is located. Too many hotel rooms, Dichter observes, have paintings or pictures of faraway places like Paris, or Greece, or London. He wants local scenes on the walls. The traveler wants to be needed and to meet other people. Make the hotel a social center where guests can mingle and meet, satisfy the craving for companionship. The hotel should be more like a club, not just a cold empty room.

The average guest, according to Dichter, is searching for adventure and would welcome the feeling of independence derived from finding a pantry in his room where he could help himself. In Sweden some of the hotels have breakfast bars where guests help themselves, then carry their trays to their rooms or into a snack room.

He advises hotel operators to try to avoid giving the guest the feeling of being anonymous. Piles of luggage in the lobbies look as though the people are being evicted. Set up hospitality rooms such as is done by the airlines. Add Tower Suites, like the ones in the Palmer House in Chicago, where there is a small kitchen from which guests can help themselves to cookies, crackers, sandwiches, and fresh fruit with payment by the honor system. The corridors of the modern hotel, says Dichter, look very much like a cell block. To avoid this he suggests circular floors.

Whit Hobbs, speaking at the same meeting, said that the hotel guest has changed dramatically: "Guests want more. And every move is a move up . . . Out of economy and into luxury . . . Always wanting more . . . More style, more quality, more flair. More originality and surprise. Today there has to be a very personal, one-at-a-time, customized approach."

A quick survey of 200 of Hobbs' friends revealed their appraisal of the hotel today as too cold, too impersonal. And tasteless. And personality-less and sterile. Their comments include these remarks: "Sears Roebuck decor. No atmosphere. No special favors. Nobody really cares. All motels are plastic. They all look the same, tacky, tacky, tacky."

Their favorite hotels were the Plaza, the Bel Air in Beverly Hills, the Royal Orleans, the Brown Palace, the Fairmont, and the Ambassador East. As for motels, Hobbs' friend's favorite was the Mountain Shadows Motel.

When these people were asked what they would do for a guest if they were running a hotel, the list was long: a comfortable easy chair, disposable paper slippers, a really good map of the city, a good clock in the room, a radio in the bathroom, more mirrors. Larger pieces of soap, larger towels, larger towels, larger towels, longer beds, better insulation between the rooms. "You sneeze and the guy in the next room says gezundheit," was a common criticism.

NO TIPPING

Mr. Hobbs' friends hate tipping. "I dread driving up to the front door, and out comes the bucket brigade to handle the luggage: doorman to bellboy, to desk, to bellboy, to room. I hate to have to worry about it, to have change ready. Whatever it is, add it to the bill."

Another universal gripe is: "Those spooky women who knock on the door—or don't knock on it—at ungodly hours—and stick their heads in. Just checking. On what? It's none of their business."

The survey showed that nearly everyone was in favor of a buffet breakfast that "costs a buck" and is optional when you register. "There it is. To eat or not to eat. No waiting. No tipping. No fuss."

Another universal gripe was the checkout line. "Isn't there an easier, faster way of getting out of there?" In answer to the gripe, Sheraton and Hilton have arrangements by which there need be no checkout, if the guest sees an assistant manager or the credit manager some time before leaving. Oddly, only about 15 to 20 percent of the guests use this "instant checkout" service.

Mr. Hobbs' friends wanted the same kind of shoeshine service found in European hotels where the guest can place his shoes outside the door at night to be shined. In a big U.S. city, no shoes. The respondents wanted to be treated as someone special. "Don't always do it for money; sometimes do it for love." "Put a piece of chocolate on my pillow with a note that says 'sweet dreams' " (the Warwick in Houston puts the chocolate on the bedstand). They like what they find in Japan. "A small refrigerator in each room that's stocked with beer, and coke, and booze, and snacks—with the price list on the door, and I pay for what I use."

Do Hobbs' friends steal? About half of them do. "I never take anything myself, but my wife usually does." Or, "Ho hum, what's to steal?" (One reason there are no little paintings or pictures on hotel room walls is to discourage guests from taking them.) Of course, most people would be very pleased with something free like a continental breakfast, a free phone call home, a free drink, or a free paperback.

Humanize Hotels

Hobbs was more than critical of hotel advertising. The one hotel ad he liked was a tiny one in *The New Yorker* for the Ritz-Carlton: "The only things we overlook are the Charles River ... Back Bay ... and the Boston Public Garden."

Like Dichter, Hobbs wants the hotel to be a social center, a friendly informal place where good fellows get together. Where it is easy to break the ice and break the silence without embarrassment or strain. The guest has an enormous hunger for companionship. "Have a family table, or a manager's table, or a captain's table, or maybe a fractured French table, where no one including the waitress is allowed to speak English." He is all for after-dinner coffee served in front of the fire in the living room every night. The guest room key should be the key to "the club."

About half of business travelers surveyed take their wives with them on at least one business trip a year which means that the businessman-oriented property must offer amenities that appeal to women as well as men.

No-Shows and No-Go's

The staff of *The Wall Street Journal* in 1968 interviewed scores of travelers from coast to coast to learn their reactions to hotel service. The biggest complaint heard had to do with being turned away while holding confirmed reservations. A 1975 American Express survey showed that over one-quarter of their card-members had a supposedly guaranteed hotel reservation not honored. At least half said they would not stay at the hotel involved again.

Hotel managers explained that large numbers of persons making reservations are no-shows. The Regency-Hyatt House of Atlanta reported that 18 of every 100 persons making reservations there did not show up. Naturally, the hotel overbooked, and once in a while almost everyone appeared "and you're in a bucket," since hotels typically overbook 15 percent, especially if they can direct the overflow elsewhere.

One reason for going overboard is that many guests overstay their scheduled visits, meaning that patrons with reservations arriving later sometimes cannot be honored. Miami hoteliers complained that this often happened when a cold snap up north spurred patrons to linger a while longer in Florida. The hotel manager tries to ease the overstayer out, sometimes locking him out of his room.

Common Complaints

Another complaint had to do with high prices. One patron said he was charged a high price at a new hotel and found his room so small "I had to go out in the corridor to change my mind." Hotels often either tried to raise their quoted prices when conventioneers started showing up or put them in the worst rooms.

Travelers were generally displeased with slip-ups on the part of inexperienced hotel personnel. One gentleman said that telephone operators at a major hotel in Los Angeles had on three occasons told people calling for him that the hotel had never heard of him, that he was not registered. Actually, he was a convention manager of a medical organization and had been in the hotel for three days.

Complaints about banquet foodservice are common, but understandable, since many banquet waiters are moonlighters who are mailmen, taxi drivers, or policemen sent over for the evening by the union and who have little or no interest in, or knowledge of, proper table service.

A survey of travelers conducted by *Market Facts* found that though first-time guests mentioned convenience (location) as a prime reason for staying at a hotel/motel for the first time, repeat guests placed cleanliness/appearance in first place and moved service up to a strong second place. The overwhelming reason for guests going elsewhere was lack of service.

The major offender was the Don't-Give-A-Damn front office treatment. Another was inadequately made-up guest rooms.

What infuriates a number of travelers is to be moved from one room to another because of an error or deficiency in the room. James J. Kilpatrick, a syndicated newspaper columnist, reported on one of his trips to a hotel in Las Vegas—the experience proved a disaster and received a host of sympathetic reaction from readers. "A hostile desk clerk assigned my wife and me to Room 2379, which was already occupied; then to 2307, which was intolerably small; then 2361, where the television didn't work. The housekeepers' office couldn't say when the TV might be repaired—maybe today, maybe tomorrow, maybe never; and no, it wouldn't be possible to send up a spare TV set because there weren't any. An assistant manager exuded hauteur and hostility; he could not have cared less. After a modest uproar, a fourth room assignment was attempted, no. 2641; the prior guest had left it in a shambles, and by 3 o'clock in the afternoon no maid had put a hand to it. We wound up in Room 1375 and my exhausted wife turned back the bedspread to take a nap: the sheets were dirty."

The writer complained bitterly about "the snippy, snappy clerks giving the guest the kind of cold eye reserved for deadbeats and bill collectors. When he is carrying a two-pound briefcase a bellman appears as if by magic, eager to assume the dreadful burden, but on the other hand when the guest is carrying something heavy the bellman can be hard to come by. On the way to the room were dirty breakfast trays still languishing on the floors outside guest doors, another common complaint. The TV set—that indispensable friend of the lonesome traveler—is on the fritz one time in five," said Kilpatrick.

At checkout time the traveler often discovers that the cashier's window offers the least courtesy and the least efficiency in the whole establishment. According to Kilpatrick it has not occurred to the manager that as many as five or six guests might want to check out at the same hour. "The idea has not crossed his mind."

"At bottom," said Kilpatrick, "the guest wants a little tender loving care, to be treated as a guest, as a tired human being who asks little more than a clean room, a firm mattress, some ice down the hall, and a TV set that works. He wants prompt room service, cheerful telephone operators, a cashier who speeds the guest cheerfully on his way. The difference between a poor hotel/motel and a good one lies in the experience, the attitude, and the personal attention of the man or woman who runs the place. If the manager does a good job in training the maids and pays them tolerable wages, and treats them with dignity, and praises them for doing well, that manager's rooms will be comfortable rooms where the maids will have checked the light bulbs and tried the TV before they leave. If the manager insists upon friendly courtesy on the part of his desk clerks, he can get it—or he can get some new desk clerks."[37]

---

37. "Nation's Business," December, 1977.

Chronology, Hotel/Motel Keeping, 1900–1976

1904, Statler built the Inside Inn, a temporary hotel for the St. Louis World's Fair with 2,257 rooms, largest building of the time. The hamburger, as Americans know it, first served at the same fair.

1907, Buffalo Statler opened. Every room with a bath. 300 rooms, 300 baths. "A room and a bath for a dollar and a half." In 1923 name changed to Buffalo Hotel when a new Buffalo Statler was built. Some Statler firsts:

1. access plumbing shafts that served two bathrooms and ran from first floor to top floor
2. posting of room rates
3. built-in "free" radios
4. free newspaper under the door each morning
5. circulating ice water in guest rooms
6. "servidors" in doors that eliminated tipping for cleaning and pressing service
7. provided free stationery for all guests
8. mail chutes connecting all floors

(continued)

1907, The Plaza on Central Park opened for the elite. Pincushions and room telephones. 1,000 rooms.

1910, American Hotel Protective Association of the United States and Canada incorporated in Illinois. Fore-runner of the American Hotel and Motel Association.

1912, McAlpin in New York City, 1,700 rooms, twenty-five stories, "World's Largest", at that time.

1913, Miami Beach is reached by causeway from Miami.

1918, Pitco fry kettle marketed.

1919, The National Restaurant and Hotel Associations take on their present form.

Frank Lloyd Wright first to electrify a hotel kitchen. The Imperial Hotel, Tokyo.

Hotel Pennsylvania opened, 2,200 rooms, "World's largest."

1920s, The "drive-in" and "motel" appear on the edge of town.

1921, The Pig Stand, outside Dallas, one of the first drive-in restaurants.

Child's Restaurants becomes the largest restaurant chain.

1922, Cornell University offers first degree-course in hotel administration.

1925, *Hotel Management,* by Lucius Boomer. First substantial book on hotel management.

1926, First motel in San Luis Obispo, California. First fast food franchise: A & W in California.

1928, The Stevens Hotel (now The Conrad Hilton), until recently hotel with most rooms, was built. Cost $35 million.

1928, John Courtney, Cornell Hotel School student, initiated the exchange of accountancy information among fifty hotels. Picked up by Harris, Kerr, Forster and by Horwath and Horwath.

1929, Hotel New Yorker built: forty-three stories, 2,500 rooms.

1929, First airport hotels go up at Croyden, England; Templehof, Berlin; Oakland, California.

1932, The new Waldorf-Astoria opens, best-known hotel in the world and until 1967 the largest in cubic space: forty-seven stories, 2,150 rooms.

1940s, Sheraton and Hilton became major chains.

From 1942 to 1945 (World War II) number of meals eaten in restaurants climbed from 20 to 60 million per day.

1947, Intercontinental Hotels, a subsidiary of Pan American Airways, began operations in Latin America and became first large international hotel chain.

1948, Raytheon introduces the first microwave oven, Radarange.

1949, Shamrock Hotel, Houston opened. First large hotel built since early 1930s.

1949, Hilton goes international with management contract to operate the Caribe-Hilton in Puerto Rico.

1952, Holiday Inns started in Memphis. Franchising plans become popular for motels and restaurants.

1950s, Howard Johnson demonstrates profitability of large scale commissary and long distance distribution of frozen foods.

Convention business grows in importance. Many hotels become convention-oriented.

Beginning of computer applications made to hotels and restaurants.

Large hotels developed specialty restaurants, HCA, later Sheraton, Hilton, and others.

Large motor hotels built by hundreds. Older hotels razed. Number of hotels declines but number of hotel rooms remains constant.

1954, Federal tax law permits rapid depreciation that encourages hotel construction.

1959, Gas-fired convection oven introduced.

(continued)

United States Airlines begin shift to jet planes.

United States Supreme Court rules to include many hotels and restaurants under jurisdiction of National Labor Relations Board (declared to be interstate commerce).

1960s, Era of mergers and franchising.
Transportation companies enter the hotel and motel field.

Frozen entrees begin to be used in restaurants. Swing to convenience foods.

1962, Budget motel industry began with Motel 6 in Santa Barbara.

1964, Supreme Court ruling strengthens prohibition against racial discrimination in hotels and restaurants.

1967, TWA purchased Hilton International. Offers travel club plans in competition with travel agents. Forty or more other airlines enter accommodations business.

Federal minimum wage law applied to hotels, motels, resorts, and restaurants grossing $500,000 or more in sales annually.

1967, Hilton permits guest to check out when he checks in.

1967, Hotel Rossiya in Moscow opened, took over title of "world's largest hotel." 3,182 rooms accommodating 5,890 guests; can serve food to 4,500 persons simultaneously. Really three adjoining properties, each with own manager.

Food manufacturers enter the restaurant business.
    Del Monte—Service Systems
    General Foods—Burger Chef
    United Fruit—A & W Root Beer
    Ogden Corporation—ABC Consolidated
    Pillsbury—Burger King
    Pet, Inc.—Schrafft's
    General Hosts—Uncle John's

The Hyatt Regency of Atlanta opens and sets style for multistoried hotel lobbies.

1968, Twelve franchise food companies have sales exceeding $50 million. Big Boy (Marriott), Burger Chef, Burger King, Castle Franchise, Denny's, Frisch's, McDonald's, Shakey's, A & W Root Beer, Howard Johnson, ITT, International House of Pancakes, Orange Julius.

1969, About 2.5 million public guest rooms available. 270,000 public eating places.

The value of meals eaten away from home exceeds $24 billion.

Federal minimum wage law applied to hotels, motels, resorts, and restaurants grossing $250,000 or more in sales annually.

1967–1969, The number of junior colleges offering hotel and restaurant courses of study increased from forty to ninety-eight.

Hotel and restaurant stocks boom. Price/earnings ratios of 35 to 50 become common.

1969, Holiday Inns of America merge with TCO (second largest inner-city bus line and Delta Steamship Lines).Becomes the largest of the travel-accommodations conglomerates with twenty-five subsidiaries.

McDonald's initiate a 4½-day work week for all office personnel.

Travel to Caribbean exceeds 4 million tourists.

1970, Serious fall-off in hotel and luxury food business.

Puerto Rico and Virgin Islands suffer drop in tourists.

Several franchise food operations fail.

United States Airlines suffer over $100 million in losses.

1971, Edward Carlson, President, Western International Hotels, made president of United Air Lines, first hotel man to head a major airline. Demonstrated the interchangeability of hotel know-how with airline management.

(continued)

AMTRAK formed to upgrade and increase efficiency of passenger rail service.

1970s, The management contract for hotels supplants the franchise: risk free enterprising. Grew out of the lease, why lease when you can contract?

Real Estate Investment Trusts (REITS) loaned more than $1 billion for hotel and motel construction—becoming owners by default.

In the middle 1970s a revitalization of central business districts included new hotels funded in part with government money.

Hotels added facilities and services to attract pleasure travelers.

Sharp increase in consumer and employee litigation against hotels, restaurants, and travel companies.

In 1976 eighteen of twenty largest hotel chains were using data processing for at least part of their corporate accounting and reporting. Five of the eighteen relied on outside computer services, the others had their own computer installations.

Questions

1 The early hostelries of the United States were known as taverns, but later the name of many of them was changed to hotel. Can you explain how this came about?

2 Why have the larger city hotels been called the "palaces of the public?"

3 If someone says, "tipping has always been a part of American hotel and restaurant keeping," what is your reply?

4 After about 1840 and until the 1940s the best location for a downtown hotel was likely to be close to what?

5 How does the early American hotelkeeper compare in social status with the innkeeper of England?

6 Hotels can be classified in a number of ways: commercial or transient hotel, resort hotel, residential hotel, and what other major classification?

7 By all odds the largest number of any particular classification of hotels are: transient, resort, residential, or condominium?

8 Can you name two organizations that rate hotels in this country?

9 Name five major "hotel" cities.

10 Which hotel chain has the most hotel rooms?

11 Chain properties control what percentage of the total number of hotel/motel rooms in this country?

12 In the late 1940s, which hotel chain made a major commitment in Latin America and really started Americans in the international hotel business?

13 Which hotel in Puerto Rico acted as a model for large hotels in the Caribbean when it was built in 1948?

14 Numerous hotel companies operate abroad today. Why is it that U.S. companies seem to have an edge in international hotelkeeping?

15 Kemmons Wilson has had a major impact on hotelkeeping in this country by forging the Holiday Inn system. Name three factors that may account for the spectacular success of that company.

16 In observing the growth of hotels would it be safe to say that there are more hotels today than there were thirty years ago? Why or why not?

17 Which city is the biggest convention city in the world?

18 A person with the title "tours director" in a hotel does what?

19 Why is it that the major hotel chains get the lion's share of the convention business?

20 While the national occupancy may be 65 percent, does this occupancy level hold generally around the country?

21 Generally speaking, the highest hotel occupancy and the lowest occupancy are experienced in which two months?

22 Name the two international accounting firms that are the source of most of the statistics available on hotel operation.

23 Who publishes the *Red Book* and what is its purpose?

24 Several of the referral groups use an 800 number in relation to the reservation system. How does this work?

25 Travelers have complained loudly and longly about arriving at a hotel with reservations and finding no room available. Some of the major chains are now doing something about this problem. Explain.

26 Travel writers and other writers like to pick "great" hotels. What are some of the criteria used in making these nominations?

27 Name five "great" hotels in this country or abroad?

28 The "great" hotels always provide excellent room service. From the point of view of the hotelier, what is wrong with offering such splendid room service?

29 In Europe the term "deluxe hotel" is used widely. Who decides whether a hotel is in the deluxe category?

HOTEL/MOTEL FINANCES AND BUILDING

THREE

The person thinking of operating a hotel can go a number of routes if he has the knowhow and access to money. He can build or buy an existing hotel, then operate it himself. Traditionally, he could lease a hotel and pay the owner a percentage of gross sales—such as 20 to 35 percent—or make some other agreed upon financial arrangement. He can get a group of friends and form a syndicate and perhaps manage a hotel which the syndicate buys or builds. He can purchase a concession from the owner of a concession in one of the state or federal parks, or he can bid for a concession from the state or federal government directly.

With the rapid growth of condominiums, he may—with enough background and knowledge—develop a condominium, sell the units, and manage the rental pool, which he sets up for the owners, as well as manage the condominium itself. The hotel/motel business can be thought of as two separate businesses: (1) financing, building, and owning, and (2) managing and operating. The two are often quite different businesses.

The big change in operating practice that has come about since about 1970 has been management by contract. Most of the major chains are divesting themselves of ownership and seeking to manage by contract, a happy arrangement for the operator since he invests little or no money, takes few or no risks, and receives payment for his services regardless of profitability of the venture, or what happens to the economy and the value of the property itself. To get a contract usually presupposes that the manager or management firm is a well-known, established operator who will have no difficulty in performing well. It helps if the operator has already established a large referral system and has a sizable promotion and advertising program under which the unit can be managed and integrated.

FINANCIAL MANAGEMENT AND PROFITS

The greatest profit connected with the hotel business does not usually come as profit generated by the sale of food, beverages, and lodging to the general public. The great fortunes in the hotel business have come in other ways, largely as a result of looking at the hotel business as requiring as much real estate manipulation as actual innkeeping.

People build hotels for a variety of reasons: pride of ownership; profit from building; profit from promoting and financing; profit from appreciation in value of the property; to increase the value of surrounding property; and for reasons connected with reduction of income taxes. In the 1920s, many hotels were built by promoters who had no intention of operating the properties.

Today, many hotels are being built as a part of large-scale housing or entertainment complexes and as part of the rehabilitation of the downtown area of cities. The great increase in value of the Hilton and Sheraton Companies has not come from operating profits but from buying, selling, tax advantages, and in the appreciation of value of the hotels with time. Financial management is the name of the game, and it is a complex game.

Profits reported from hotel operations have always been small, ranging from 0 to about 10 percent of the income of the hotel.

If return on sales and return on investment is so low, why does anybody go into the hotel business? How is it possible that many fortunes have been made in the business?

The answer to this question varies with the economic conditions of the country, especially the price of real estate, the tax laws in effect, and the competitive advantage of particular hotels at the moment. Professor Albert Wrisley at the University of Massachusetts presents his hotel classes with a standard conundrum: how can a hotel worth $10 million break even year after year, and the owner still come up with more than $1 million gain in assets, if he sells at the end of five years?

The answer revolves around the owner's taking the maximum depreciation allowable, and the fact that, over much of U.S. history, real estate has appreciated in value. In selling, he would probably have received $10 million or more. It is quite possible, and even likely, that the hotel built in 1960 for $10 million would have been worth $15 million in 1979.

THE VIRTUES OF GOING INTO DEBT

Get rich by going into debt. This is exactly what happens if money is borrowed at reasonable rates of interest, and the value of money depreciates each year. Borrow $100,000 this year and five years later you may be paying it back with money worth $80,000. Of course, the money borrowed must be returning some income to offset the cost of the interest paid on the loan. Oddly, in our economy, the man who can owe $10 million has usually arrived. God has been on the side of the optimist over the long pull. Over the short pull, many men are wiped out.

Conrad Hilton is a good example of the optimist who, even though he lost most of the ownership of his eight hotels in Texas during the depression of the 1930s, came back strong in the late 1930s and 1940s to create a hotel empire. Ernest Henderson, in 1938, began buying hotels for a fraction of their value in cash. Before his death in 1967, he had created the largest hotel chain the world had known.

Borrow or otherwise acquire as much money as possible, buy properties with as little cash down as possible, take maximum depreciation, and when the depreciation has begun to run out, sell the property. Buy a new property, again with as little cash as possible, and repeat the cycle.

As long as there is a rising economy and the property shows some profit, the entrepreneur can pyramid his holdings spectacularly. If the economy falters or some of the properties are losers, it is quite easy for the entrepreneur to become overextended. The system can then collapse. The system has been used many times in other businesses, but it is particularly effective in the hotel business since it is as much real estate as hospitality.

The system works because people have confidence in a particular business and will buy bonds or stock in a business; the economy continues upward; real estate appreciates; and the value of the dollar depreciates.

Conrad Hilton was able to buy controlling interest in the Waldorf-Astoria, the world's best-known hotel, for $3 million in cash. Hilton himself clinched the deal with only $100,000 of his own money. The purchase, he points out in his book *Be My Guest*, did not come off as a coup d'etat, but was the result of four years of delicate negotiation, careful planning, and a lot of prayer.

METHODS OF FINANCING HOTELS

The methods of raising capital for a hotel run a fascinating gamut. Several of the first hotels built in the 1790s were put together by "tontine" associations. Early in the 1790s, a group of New York City merchants built The Tontine Coffee House. The famous City Hotel of New York was another product of the tontine, an arrangement by which the survivors among the investors inherited the interest held by the other investors. The tontine arrangement of survivor-take-all would not seem designed to promote peace and tranquility among the "partners."

As civilization spread westward, the hotel went along, sometimes even preceding the people. Real estate developers, quick to recognize the importance of a hotel for the growth of a community, often built the hotel before the community arrived. (The Gayoso Hotel in Memphis stood alone in a meadow for years.) A few other hotels never acquired a town around them and fell into decay.

The dangers of overextension of credit were experienced early. The most impressive public house erected in America between 1793 and 1825, according to historian Doris King, was the Boston Exchange Coffee House. It was a victim of poor financing.

OVERBUILDING IN THE 1920s

In the early 1920s, hotel investment looked very tempting. Room occupancy had jumped from 72 percent in 1919 to 86 percent in 1920, and up until 1927 the occupancy never dropped below the break-even point for nearly all hotels. The great boom in hotel building resulted. Chicago, for example, had 11,000 hotel rooms in 1920; by June, 1926, the figure increased to more than 22,000.

Hotels were built for a variety of reasons other than pure investment. In many towns without a first-class hotel, the hotel was an expression of civic pride and the center for community activity. In some of the larger communities, the hotel was built to boost a particular section of the city. Hotels were also built to satisfy an individual's vanity or as a monument to someone or to something.

It also became clear that a valuable piece of land could be made more valuable by the addition of a hotel. Promoters who had a considerable part in creating the boom were able to do well for themselves financially. Investment houses, too, were interested since a new hotel provided an outlet for the sale of securities. In the 1920s, much of the investing public had a mistaken notion about the value of bonds, thinking that the word "bond" denoted a sort of value which would not depreciate. Many were so eager to buy bonds that they bought first and questioned the value of the bond later.

Mr. Charles Moore, who was active at that time as a hotel promoter, relates that the total cost of financing many hotels in the 1920s averaged between 12 and 20 percent, with as much as 88 percent of the total amount borrowed for actual payments on construction. Many hotels had very little actual cash put into them by the owner up to the time the building was completed. If it was a success from the start, well and good. If not, trouble lay ahead.

The idea of buying a large mortgage, dividing it up into small pieces, then selling it to the public was sound in theory, says Mr. Moore, but many people entered the field who did not know the business and too many hotels were built.

Creating a Hotel from "Thin Air"

An example of how a hotel could be created out of thin air (with no equity capital) is based on what happened in Pittsburgh in the late 1920s when a contractor needed a job to keep his organization busy. He purchased a large lot in exchange for a second mortgage, providing an equity behind the purchase in the form of securities or services. He then created a third mortgage, for about twice his legitimate fee as a contractor, sold half of the third mortgage to subcontractors to build a hotel, and retained the other half for his fees.

An apartment house costing $1.5 million was built with not one dollar of cash invested in it except what was secured from selling first mortgage bonds to the public, bonds that sold like hot cakes the moment they were announced in the local newspapers throughout the country.

A typical hotel was financed in this period by an owner with an equity equal to about 30 to 40 percent of the total cost of the land, building, and financing expense. He applied to one of the first mortgage houses for a combined building and permanent loan. If approved, the building started at once, even though this method of financing was relatively expensive.

The interest rate varied from 5.5 to 7 percent, depending on the type of loan, the location of the property, the time, and other factors. The mortgage houses discounted the face value of the loan by 6 to 12 percent; interest during construction was paid on the entire loan from the day of the closing of the loan, even though the money was paid out to the borrower only as the hotel was built in its several stages. The mortgage house demanded that the total issue be matured within ten to twelve years.

Aftermath of Overbuilding

Hotels financed in this way made good investments as long as occupancy was high. High occupancy required the kind of monopoly in location which was hard to come by, since overbuilding was rife. If a 100-room hotel was needed in a community, local enthusiasm often forced the building of a 200-room house.

With the depression of the 1930s, occupancy dropped below 40 percent in many hostelries, and many of the hotel ventures sold for a few pennies on the dollar. It is said that over 80 percent of the country's hotels were in serious financial trouble, many of them taken over by insurance companies and other lending institutions that were forced to foreclose on their mortgages.

Many hotels, however, were successful from the day they opened, especially when they were: (1) in prime locations, (2) financed with cash, and (3) built so that the first floor of the hotel could justify a good share of the value of the land. As always, it was important to build so that not an inch of space or a single dollar was wasted.

THE RISE OF CHAINS

The debacle in hotel values in the 1930s offered a rare opportunity for a few bold entrepreneurs. The story of Sheraton Corporation of America is a case in point. In the 1930s, Ernest Henderson and Robert Moore, of Boston, secured control of three investment trusts and reinvested the money from one of them in the Hotel Continental in Cambridge, Mass. They improved the building and began merchandising the food and rooms. Out of the profits they paid off the mortgage and bought additional property.

At the time, control of hotels and office buildings was easy to get with a small amount of cash. The Park Square building in Boston, which was owned by the First National Bank of that city, had a sale price of $4 million. However, Henderson and Moore acquired control for only $125,000 in cash. The bank was persuaded to give a first mortgage of $3 million, and an individual put up $150,000 for preferred stock. The $125,000 went to buy half of the $250,000 in common stock which was created.

The process was continued by Messrs. Henderson and Moore as they took earnings from properties that they owned to acquire loans against buildings bought from banks and insurance companies. The sellers of the properties were pleased to take back second mortgages from Henderson and Moore, particularly after seeing the success these men were having with other Sheraton properties.

In Detroit, a hotel was taken over for no cash at all because the owner was impressed with what Sheraton had been able to do elsewhere. The Sheraton Corporation took a huge step forward in 1956 when it purchased twenty-two hotels from Eugene Eppley, who had acquired them all in the course of his lifetime.

Conrad Hilton had a similar experience. He purchased his first hotel in Cisco, Texas in 1919 when the owner, who was doing capacity business, preferred selling his hotel for $50,000 down and going out for oil in the area.

Following World War II, motel construction boomed, but by today's standards these motels were Mom and Pop operations of six to thirty or forty units. The money for construction came from savings, banks, and local savings and loan associations. Many were owned and operated by couples retired from a principal career, such as military or retail trade. The land and buildings were mortgaged as collateral for the construction and development loans. Few hotels were built until the middle 1950s.

From then, and especially during the 1960s, numerous large hotels were built, as were motor hotels with more than 100 units. Larger properties tended to replace smaller ones which with time became obsolete.[1] Typically, motor hotels were built on or near major highways leading to or around towns and cities, bringing obsolescence to the downtown hotel, typically an older property built in the booming 1920s.

In the late 1960s and early 1970s, several cities became overbuilt with hotels, a prime example being the Orlando area where motels and hotels were built in quantity to serve visitors to Disney World and what was expected to be the growing Orlando area.

Major hotel chains expanded rapidly in the cities, at first by constructing and operating. Later, the big chains, such as Hilton and Sheraton, shifted policy from owning to operating under management contracts. It had proved much safer and more profitable to manage than to own and operate.

Hotel construction was fostered in the late 1960s by investors who had become discouraged with the bear stock market and were

---

1. Laventhol & Horwath, *Financing the Lodging Industry: A Survey of Lender Attitudes* (Philadelphia, PA, 1975).

seeking tax-sheltered investments, investments which produced significant tax losses as a result of allowable tax deductions. The resulting tax losses were used to reduce tax liabilities which were attached to other, unrelated taxable income of the investors. Most tax-sheltered investments were made possible because of tax laws passed by Congress and were not the result of tax loopholes as many people believed. A hotel/motel business seemed an excellent medium for realizing capital gains rather than straight income.

THE REAL ESTATE INVESTMENT TRUSTS

Another major factor in the rapid hotel construction of the period came as a result of a new type of trust made possible by a law in 1968, the Real Estate Investment Trust (REIT), "a mutual fund of real estate loans." Such trusts acquired millions of dollars, which eager investors made available because of two features of the REIT:

> By law, the REIT must pass 90 percent of its earnings on to its investors (in the usual public corporation, the Board of Directors decides whether the investor gets anything at all).
>
> The trust, being a trust, was not taxed.

A number of REITs went public, attracting billions of dollars, and were able to borrow additional millions from commercial banks. As an example, a REIT with $10 million might borrow $90 million and invest $100 million in hotels and other real estate. At first, the REITs prospered mightily, loaning money to developers at rates of 15 percent and more; a few REITs had millions of dollars to invest every day, and many rushed into construction and development (C and D) loans for hotels and motels without proper investigation of the borrower's experience or a reasonable feasibility study of the site and the project.

Savings and loan associations, commercial banks, insurance companies, and mortgage bankers were guilty of the same thing, but to a lesser degree. A 1975 study of financing for the lodging industry found that twenty-four lending institutions had made $3 billion in loans and investments in the hospitality business in the previous few years.[2]

REITs had made C and D loans covering 82 properties, and, of these loans, 72 percent were "distressed," which means that the lenders were not being paid according to agreement or had foreclosed on the property. It was nothing like the conditions prevailing in the 1930s, but serious.

Overbuilding, the energy crisis which hit in late 1973, increases in construction costs, increased interest rates, and reduced demand for all sorts of real estate were principal causes of the problem faced by lenders to the hospitality business. Unemployment increased and travel—both pleasure and business—dropped. Developers, many of whom were highly leveraged and lacked backup capital, lost some or all of their equity in the hotels or motels they were constructing. Inexperienced operators failed to budget enough money to cover start-up costs, which in a major downtown convention hotel could run up to $1,500 a room before the hotel reached a break-even point in sales.

Lenders pushed up the cost of money to 15 percent and more. Overly optimistic developers paid not only record interest rates for their borrowed money, but also agreed to front end fees, charges made in addition to interest. Equity kickers were also demanded the lender receiving 1 or 2 percent of gross room receipts—this on top of the high interest rates on front end fees.

In 1975, lending institutions and borrowers were a chastened lot. Lenders were extremely cautious in loaning money, investigating borrowers very carefully, and requiring that the operator have at least five to ten years of operational experience. C and D loans were not made unless the borrower had a firm commitment for long-term financing. Many lenders would not get involved unless the borrower agreed to invest in the project and put up as collateral as much as 25 percent of the value in cash or land placed in escrow.

When a property became distressed, the lender was reluctant to foreclose because costs of the hotel and construction continue even though the construction has halted. Capital is tied up in unproductive real estate, taxes continue, and guards must be employed to protect the property. If an operating hotel is closed down, getting the traveler to come back after it opens again is difficult. Bankruptcy of the owner often means loss of liquor licenses,

2. Ibid.

which can cost thousands of dollars to acquire. The lender usually tries to reach a "workout" agreement, perhaps granting a moratorium on the repayment of interest, even advancing money to keep the property operating. In return, the borrower usually agrees to various stipulations, providing monthly financial reports and permitting frequent inspections. In some cases, management is changed and a consulting firm brought in to assist management in turning the property around.

THE BIG HOTEL INVESTORS TODAY

Three insurance companies—Prudential, Equitable Life Assurance Society of the United States, and John Hancock Mutual Life Insurance Company—had investments of over $2 billion in the lodging industry in 1976. Insurance companies invest heavily in lodging because of the ability of hotel management to change rate structures rapidly, one of the few areas of real estate which can rapidly reflect inflation. Another reason for insurance company interest in hotel investment has been the high inflation rates. Although an insurance company may get a 9 percent return on an investment, if the inflation rate is at 7 or 8 percent and corporate income taxes are 50 percent of earnings, the company actually loses in purchasing power each time it pays taxes.

WHAT IS A MOTEL WORTH?

What is a property worth? Over the years motels and hotels have been selling for between about six to nine times the average annual operating profit after taxes and insurance, before income taxes. Suppose this amount is $50,000 for a particular motel. The value of the property then would be $400,000, based on a times-earnings ratio of 8. If the motel in question sold for $400,000, the percent return on the equity investment might be arrived at as follows:

Purchase Price[3]	$400,000
Equity Investment	200,000
50% Mortgage Debt	200,000

Projected Income		50,000
Less: Interest @ 7%	$14,000	
Depreciation (Est.)	2,000	$ 30,000
Taxable Income	$16,000	$ 20,000
Income Tax—Corporate Rates		7,000
		$ 13,000
Present Return on Equity Investment		6.5%

In 1977 motels and motor hotels in California were selling for between three times and six times the gross income. The buyer tried to buy for three times the income and sell for six times that amount. Operating costs for the motel were running at about one-third of gross income, not counting the labor of Mr. and Mrs. Operator.

Because of tax considerations, sellers did not want to take more than 30 percent of the sales price as a down payment (including the first year's installment payments). If they took more the payment was considered straight income and taxed at that level. Under the 30 percent figure, income could be considered capital gain. The vast majority of motels and motor hotels in California from 1975 on were purchased by Koreans, Taiwanese, Thais, and people from India. A motel purchase presents an opportunity to become a legal resident of the United States, provided that the person invests at least $40,000, and at least one United States citizen is employed in the operation.

THE BEST USE OF LAND

Fortunes have been made by asking the simple question: "Is a property being used to its maximum advantage?" In other words, what kind of property should be built on a piece of land? Should an office building be erected, or a hotel?" In New York City, the answer has often favored the office building over the hotel. In some cases, the hotel should be razed and the land used for an office building. Some of the older motels can be better used as apartments or offices, especially those that have been bypassed by super highways.

The "best use" of some of the older resort hotels may be found by giving them to a charitable or educational institution. By giving them to such organizations, the donor has the right to value the property at its book value, or at a value established by an appraiser. The book value may be much higher than the market value. Usually the appraised value is higher than its real market value. By giving the property away, the donor is able to write off of his income taxes the full amount of the appraised value or of the book value. If he is in a high income bracket, he may be "making" money by giving away the resort. This has happened several times in the past.

Fires offer another way of getting maximum value from some hotels. A surprising number of resorts have burned that have been fully insured. The place burns; the owner is delighted; he collects much more from the insurance company than the market value of the hotel.

JUNIOR MORTGAGE BONDS AND NOTES

Junior mortgage bonds and notes, another means of financing hotels, constitute high risk financing. The seller is often offered a second mortgage provided it can be paid off over a longer period of time. Since the second mortgage has less value to the seller, he will usually increase his asking price for the hotel.

If the cash sale price of a hotel is $1 million, the seller might increase the sale price to $1.2 million or even $1.5 million. Such financing enables a chain to "own" a property with a relatively small amount of cash as down payment. More is paid in total, but payment extends over a longer period of time. If the hotel "throws off" a good profit, everyone is happy. If not, there are problems.

DEBENTURE BONDS

Debenture bonds for raising capital were widely used by Ernest Henderson in expanding the Sheraton chain. A guest in a Sheraton Hotel might find a brochure placed on his nightstand suggesting that he buy Sheraton bonds and receive 7 percent interest, an interest rate about 40 percent higher than he could get at the bank at the time.

Mr. Henderson, in his biography, states that such financing was good business. In effect, he paid about 3½ percent interest on the bonds. This was possible because interest on bonds is considered by the Internal Revenue

Service to be expense before taxes. This is in contrast to the interest paid on common and preferred stock which must come out of profit after taxes.

Sheraton employees were also encouraged to invest a portion of their income in the Sheraton Corporation by buying debenture bonds. To increase the appeal, employees could buy the bonds at a 5 percent discount, a $100 bond for $95. The bonds could be bought with cash or through payroll deductions. Interest was paid quarterly. Debenture bonds are not a loan to the company in the sense that the bondholder may think. A debenture is issued against the general credit of the company—no specific property is pledged as collateral, as is the case with corporate bonds. The bondholder is an equity participant rather than a lender, and his investment is subject to wider fluctuations in value than the usual loan.

Small entrepreneurs often offer some shares of common stock together with a bond, offerings which are misleading to the extent that the buyer thinks the debenture is a true debt and the stock a bonus. The debenture buyers may well supply the major portion of the funds for a hotel, while the promoters control the common stock with only a small amount of cash investment.

FRANCHISING AS A MEANS OF FINANCING

Franchising is also a means of financing growth, although indirect and not ordinarily thought of as a means of raising capital. The franchisor, in effect, uses the resources of each franchisee to expand the franchisor's business.

Franchising became important in the hotel and restaurant business with the growth of the Howard Johnson restaurants in the 1930s. During World War II it came almost to a halt. In the 1950s, the rapid growth of Holiday Inns of America demonstrated the advantages of franchising, and in the late 1960s franchising spread across the country. The franchise potential dealing with the movement is discussed in Chapter 4.

GOING PUBLIC

Since 1965, "going public" with a stock offering has been the favorite means of raising capital for foodservice operations and, to a cer-

Figure 3-2 The Willard Hotel of Washington, D.C., the prestige hotel of the city for many years. The hotel is now closed.

RESIDENTIAL HOTEL, AN AMERICAN DEVELOPMENT

Americans have long resided in hotels for long periods of time, much to the astonishment of Europeans. Until about 1950, there were sizable numbers of hotels known as residential hotels. These hotels often took in a few transient guests but devoted most of their attention to "permanents" who lived in suites or apartments and had access to all services offered by the hotel.

When the Plaza Hotel in New York City opened in 1907, about 88 percent of its occupancy was by permanent guests. Lucius Boomer developed the Sheraton Netherlands (no longer in existence) to combine the best features of hotel life with modern apartment house life. It provided freedom from the care or concern over food, supplies, and the hiring or supervision of servants.

A large percentage of the guests at the Hotel Pierre on Central Park in New York City are still permanents. So too are the residents of the Waldorf Towers in the present Waldorf-Astoria. Managers of residential hotels sometimes find that, even though the permanent rate is high, more profit can often be made by

renting to transients, and make some or all of the residential rooms or suites into "transients." On the other hand, transient hotels with low occupancies often become partly residential.

The large hotels of the twentieth century are towns in themselves. The Dallas Statler-Hilton Hotel has a capacity of 10,000 people; the Palmer House, 15,000 and the Conrad Hilton, 20,000. The telephone switchboard in the Conrad Hilton has more equipment than is used in a city with a 35,000 population.

William B. Tabler, architect for many Hilton Hotels, says it takes from two to five years, sometimes even ten years, to put together a large hotel. There is the matter of land acquisition, architectural planning, financing, and finally the construction of the building. Actually planning for the guest rooms is only a minor part of designing a hotel; planning the dining facilities is a particular challenge and calls for a foodservice consultant to lay out the kitchen equipment. Night clubs and ballrooms, shops, offices, laundry, valet, barber shop, beauty shop, telephone rooms, refrigeration, incineration, and boiler plants are

Figure 3-3 The Terrace Plaza was built in the 1950s and is located in Cincinnati. The hotel begins on the eighth floor; the glassed-in circle and adjoining structure on top of the hotel was one of the first glassed-in top restaurants.

part of the hotel. Some of the larger hotels have medical departments with emergency rooms, isolation rooms, and laboratories.

It is little wonder that there are such major oversights in the planning as happened at the Sheraton-Philadelphia which was planned with insufficient elevator capacity. Although elevators in the larger hotels are likely to be computer-controlled, many hotels have elevator traffic problems. These can occur in the morning, when guests all decide to get up at the same time; in the evening when there is a check-in, and later when they all decide to move from floor to floor to visit friends or the public rooms. At the New York Hilton, which has had extremely high occupany in recent years, the guest may wait twenty minutes to get on an elevator at certain times of the day.

"RULES OF THUMB" FOR HOTEL PLANNERS

Mr. Tabler, who has designed most of the newer Hilton Hotels in this country, has listed eight "rules of thumb" for planners of commercial hotels. (He does point out that there are exceptions to the "rules.")

1 The cost of construction per room should equal about $1,000 per $1 of average room rate. If the room can be sold for $15 on an average, no more than $15,000 can be spent per room. This includes the cost of the public and service areas. Per room cost in a hotel is total cost divided by the number of rooms.

2 At least 50 percent of the total space in a commercial hotel should be given over to bedrooms. It may seem strange that the hotel may have more public and service space than bedroom space but it is quite possible. Public and service space has been responsible for 60 to 65 percent of the construction cost in some hotels. In downtown areas, land costs and the cost of attendant facilities have forced the reduction of the size of the bedrooms. Bathrooms seem to be getting smaller and smaller. In some, a large person standing in a bathroom can reach from wall to wall.

Of the $10,000 per room cost of the Dallas Statler-Hilton, opened in 1959, about $3,500 was spent for the actual bedroom. The other $6,500 per room cost went for lobbies, banquet and convention rooms, restaurants, kitchens, shops, and "behind the scenes" areas. Even though most of the cost of the hotel went for public and service areas, the bedrooms accounted for a large amount of the profit. Operating profits as the percentage of gross income were: 70 percent from the bedrooms, 50 percent on beverages, 15 percent on rental areas. Believe it or not, the restaurants brought in no operating profit.

Statler, recognizing the high cost of support facilities, did not build hotels in the secondary cities that could not support a 1,000-room hotel. When he built a hotel of less than 1,000 rooms, he found that the public and service areas were proportionately higher, profits lower. Motels, built on less costly land and including less public space, can have larger bedrooms and a small swimming pool.

3 The hotel should be planned so that it can be operated with less than one employee per room. Some luxury hotels located in countries with low labor costs can have two and even three employees per room. The Savoy of London has three employees per guest room.

American hotels are making do with something like .8 of an employee per room. In other words, a 100-room hotel could employ about eighty people. The layout of the hotel, especially the kitchens and dining rooms, accounts for built-in labor costs which are likely to last the life of the building.

4 The cost of land, in most cases, should not exceed 10 percent of the building cost. Where land costs are exceedingly high, the alternative is to put more rooms one on top of each other, stretching the hotel skyward, thus reducing the per room cost of land. Mr. Tabler points out exceptions to the rule, one being the Palmer House in Chicago which has revenues of more than $1 million from ground floor shop rentals. In such a case, land costs can be more.

5 What profit should be expected from each department in a hotel? Mr. Tabler says that departmental profit should be 70 percent for rooms and 50 percent from the sale of beverages. Rentals should bring in 20 percent of the hotel's total revenue. No profit at all is expected from the sale of food. This may be the experience of hotels in general, but need not be. Hotelmen are seldom outstanding restaurateurs. The hotel restaurant has traditionally found it difficult to compete with the good restaurant which is located nearby or one that, even though it is some distance from the hotel, has acquired a culinary reputation. Some restaurant operators say that the best location for a restaurant is directly across the street from a major hotel. Specialty or theme restaurants in hotels have been much more profitable than the usual dining room or coffee shop operations. The Hotel Corporation of America opened its Rib Rooms starting in 1952 and now has one in each of the HCA Hotels. Polynesian restaurants have been favored in Hilton and Sheraton Hotels. Mr. Tabler's rule of thumb that the food contributes nothing to the profit of the hotel can be gainsaid by instances where hotel foodservices make fairly sizable profits. In some of the smaller hotels, the food and beverage operation is the major reason for the existence of the hotel, the rooms being secondary to the restaurant business.

6 The hotel must have at least 60 to 65 percent occupancy to break even financially. In designing a hotel, Mr. Tabler says, the design should allow for the reduction of operating costs when occupany drops.

7 If room rates are to differ depending on the size of the bedrooms, to qualify for a higher rate a room must be at least 20 sq. ft. larger than the room being rented at the next lowest rate. A smaller differential is not noticeable to the guest; he expects to see an appreciably larger room if he is being charged a higher rate.

8 The minimum size for a bedroom is 90 to 110 sq. ft. for a single room; 130 to 150 sq. ft. for a double room; 160 to 180 sq. ft. for a twin bedroom.

Hotel lobbies have varied in size and grandeur over the years. Few general statements can be made about them. Resort hotels are likely to have comparatively large lobbies because the lobby is the gathering point for guests. The Fontainebleau and several of the other Miami Beach hotels have high-ceilinged lobbies on a grand scale perhaps to serve as a stage setting for the hotel.

Motels tend to have lobbies only large enough in which to check guests in and out. Cesar Ritz favored the small lobby to discourage idlers; he viewed the lobby primarily as a corridor to dining room and guest rooms.

Statler, who was very cost- and space-conscious, built a tremendous lobby at the Pennsylvania Statler, perhaps because the hotel was built with Pennsylvania Railroad money and leased by him. Some of his other lobbies are also quite large and impressive.

Hilton, well known for his ability to carve revenue-producing space out of a lobby, did so by adding restaurants and bars in lobby space. In some cases he even lowered the ceiling to produce another floor above the lobby. The New York Hilton Hotel has immense lobby space but very few chairs and seems to be designed primarily to move people from floor to floor to function and dining room spaces. The Summit Hotel in New York City has a lobby so small that the front desk space is jammed with patrons during check-in and check-out times.

Resort hotels typically have had large lobbies where the guests can congregate. In Miami Beach some of the lobbies have been grand; in Las Vegas they house slot machines by the score. The Hyatt Regency lobbies, described later, are awesome in scale and appointments marking a new adventure in hotel design.

DINING ACCESS TO STREET

In hotels that were built in the 1920s, there is a trend currently to relocate dining room spaces and especially coffee shops so they have direct access to the street. The formal dining room has been out for some time; the specialty room is in. The specialty room almost always is built with access to the street, since patronage from the hotel guest alone will not make it profitable.

The cost of transforming dining rooms or other spaces into specialty rooms can be remarkably high, often costing $500,000 or more. Usually a remodeled dining room requires about six months to a year of operation before it begins to be profitable.

ALLOCATION STUDIES
GOVERN SPACE ALLOTMENT

The Sonesta Hotel's management has done a number of studies to establish criteria for the allocation of space in a hotel. In foodservice areas they allocate 18 to 20 sq. ft. per seat in a dining room, 15 sq. ft. per seat in a coffee shop, 12 to 15 sq. ft. per seat in lounges and bars, and

10 to 12 sq. ft. per seat in banquet facilities. These figures allow 25 to 33 percent of the space for free circulation of service personnel within the facility.

These studies indicate that the kitchen serving a dining room and coffee shop should be about 60 percent of the total area of the dining room and the coffee shop. This indicates that about 10 to 11 sq. ft. should be allowed per seat in these foodservice areas. If there is a coffee shop only, the kitchen should be about 45 percent of the size of the coffee shop serving area, allowing 6¾ sq. ft. per seat. Space allowed for food and beverage storage should be about half that set aside for the kitchen, or about 5 sq. ft. per seat.

Banquet kitchens, of course, are much smaller; only about one-fifth of the space of the banquet facility is needed for the banquet pantry and only about 8 percent of the banquet area is needed for banquet storage.

Space to be allocated for housekeeping and general storage gets smaller per guest room as the hotel gets larger, ranging from 8 sq. ft. per guest room in a 1,000-room hotel to 15 sq. ft. in a 100-room property. The same relationship is seen in the need for space for administration and rooms department, ranging from 3 ft. per guest room in a 1,000-room hotel up to 5 ft. per guest room in a 100-room property.

Often overlooked in planning hotel and motor hotels are the needs of the personnel for eating facilities, lockers, lounge, showers, and so on. Approximately 7 sq. ft. should be allotted per guest room in a 100-room property for employee facilities.

The location of towel racks and hooks is a part of the architect's problem. Towel hooks are placed so that the guest will use a towel an average of three times before throwing it into the hamper. Towel shelves are located so that

Figure 3–4   The Sheraton Hotel. An example of Sheraton's combination living and bedroom suite.

towels can be reached from the tub and so cuts the laundering of bath mats by half.

Designers are forever attempting to maximize a "quality experience" in a minimum of space. Once a desirable room layout has been achieved the room is then replicated tens and even hundreds of times in the same hotel or motel or in a chain of properties. The dollar savings can be considerable. Guestrooms today tend to run to a standard of about twelve feet wide and twenty-four to twenty-six feet long, including the bathroom. Designers tend to make suites two or three times larger and often plan them for two levels connected by a stairway.

Again to save space, combination sofa beds are used; in some cases the old Murphy Bed, which folded up into a wall space, has reappeared.

In 1977 The Sheraton Corporation introduced a room plan that can be used in almost

any room which, with the addition of a draw curtain and a sofa bed, changes the typical bedroom into a combination bedroom/sitting room.

Great care and attention can be devoted to the design and furnishings of a guest room, since a guest room is repeated several hundred times in a large hotel. Savings in space or cost of furnishings is also repeated. For a time, bedrooms got smaller and smaller but the trend now is toward larger and more comfortable bedrooms.

The use of double-paned glass has permitted "glass walls" to be part of the building; the Flying Carpet Motor Inn, opposite Chicago's O'Hare International Airport, and the Downtown Motor Hotel both have 90 percent of their exterior constructed of glass. The new silent and heat-resistant glass muffles up to 66 percent more of the transmitted noise than plate glass. The sound waves are con-

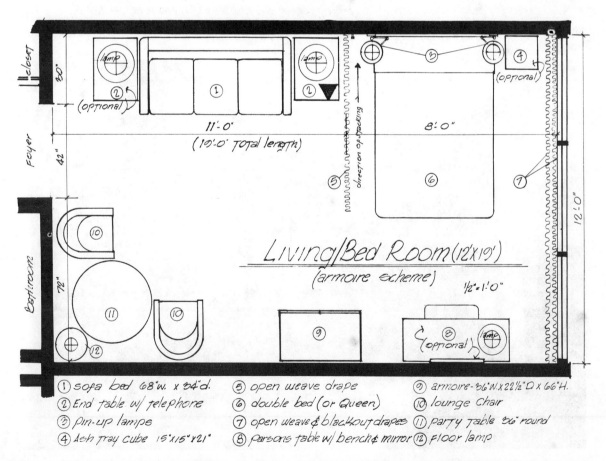

① sofa bed 68"w. x 34"d. ⑤ open weave drape ⑨ armoire-36"W.x22½"D x 66"H.
② End table w/ telephone ⑥ double bed (or Queen) ⑩ lounge chair
③ pin-up lamps ⑦ open weave ¢ blackout drapes ⑪ party table 36" round
④ Ash tray cube 15"x15"x21" ⑧ Parsons table w/ bench ¢ mirror ⑫ floor lamp

Figure 3–5 Floor Plans for a Living/Bed Room (12" x 19"). This particular plan is titled the Armoire Scheme.

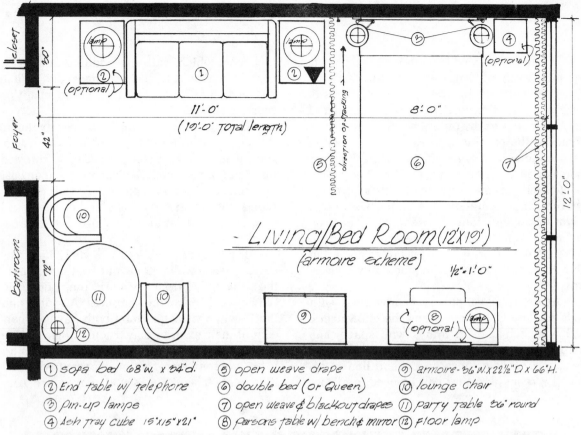

① sofa bed 68"w. x 34"d.   ⑤ open weave drape   ⑨ armoire- 36"W. x 22½"D x 66"H.
② End table w/ telephone   ⑥ double bed (or Queen)   ⑩ lounge chair
③ pin-up lamps   ⑦ open weave & blackout drapes   ⑪ party table 36" round
④ Ash tray cube 15"x15"x21"   ⑧ Parsons table w/ bench & mirror   ⑫ floor lamp

Figure 3-6   Floor Plans for a Living/Bed Room (12" x 19"). You will notice that there is no armoire.

Figure 3-7   The Master Bedroom of the "Celestial Suite" complete with Roman bath, and featured at the Astrodome Hotel. Wherelse but in Texas and at $2500 per night!

verted into heat energy by absorption into a treated inner layer between the double glazing. A self-shading glass eliminates glare and heat. Made like a miniature Venetian blind, it is composed of thousands of tiny louvers which are sealed airtight between the two panes of glass.

The new convention hotels usually include an assembly room, a banquet room, smaller meeting and private dining rooms, a registration lobby, and an exhibition hall. Dining rooms and meeting rooms should be near and on the same level as the kitchen, if possible, for reduction in wage costs. The beautiful Beverly-Hilton Hotel is built as a "Y" with three wings

emanating from a central core which houses the kitchen.

BASIC HOTEL DESIGN

Characteristically, motels and hotels have been built as horizontal slabs, rectangular-shaped buildings. In the beginning they were one or two stories high. Then with the development of structural steel and building expertise hotels shot up into the sky. In 1976 a hotel designed by John Portman as a cylinder reached seventy stories into the sky of Atlanta, soon followed by another such hotel in Detroit. The downtown

Figure 3–8   A rendering of the $100 million, 1,500-room major convention hotel and retail center in Los Angeles's Bunker Hill area. The Bonaventure Hotel appears from the corner of Figueroa and Fifth Streets. It is in the center, its five bronzed glass guest-room towers rising from an expansive podium structure. Western International Hotels manages the hotel for the owners, the Los Angeles Portman Company. Architects and Engineers: John Portman and Associates, Atlanta.

hotel in the 1920s was likely to be two to four slabs built around an open court. Later hotels took on all sorts of shapes, L-shaped, Y-shaped and finally, cylindrical. A three-sided motor hotel, the triarc, featured by the Travel Lodge Corporation, favors a view because two blocks of a motel can face an ocean or other scenic view. The elevator is located in the central core.

The hotel built in rectangular form permits orientation along an east-west axis so the rooms face south and north. Such orientation to the sun avoids facing the guest rooms to the west where the heat of the afternoon sun can drive up the cost of air conditioning in a warm climate. Balconies can be built to project four

to six feet from the guest room and provide a partial sunscreen. Vertical walls separating each unit are also helpful in excluding direct sunlight.

Most budget motels are built on the barracks plan and if in a moderate climate, can avoid the necessity of inside hallways, an added cost.

A comparison of twenty-seven highrise hotels showed that the circular form plan is the most efficient in terms of surface-to-volume ratio.[8] The guest rooms are necessarily at least partially pie-shaped. The rectangular slab

8. Clark and Benner, "Hotels and Life-Cycle Costing," *Cornell Hotel and Restaurant Administration Quarterly*, February 1977.

Figure 3–9   In the Portman view of the new inner-city, the hotel is seen as one habitat among several, an integral part of a living complex where business, entertainment, and residences come together. The cylindrical building in this picture is the hotel in a redevelopment project of downtown Atlanta.

design is more efficient than the more compact, nearly-square tower. The corners of a pure square-shaped hotel are often left void because of the difficulty in providing direct corridor access to them. The floor plans below show the circular, slab, square and a deformed-square-floor plan for hotels.[9]

To avoid a slab-sided, uninteresting exterior, the resort hotel or any hotel that commands a view is likely to have a balcony on

each guest room. The balcony adds glamor and architectural interest to the building.

Panel wall construction began in the 1950s. The *Architectural Forum* gives William Tabler credit for using the first true curtain or panel hotel wall in the Hartford Statler. The curtain wall replaces masonry, is lightweight, and has twice the insulating factor of masonry construction, a factor in reducing air conditioning requirements.

The curtain wall is also more watertight than masonry. During the 1955 hurricane, nine

---

9. Ibid.

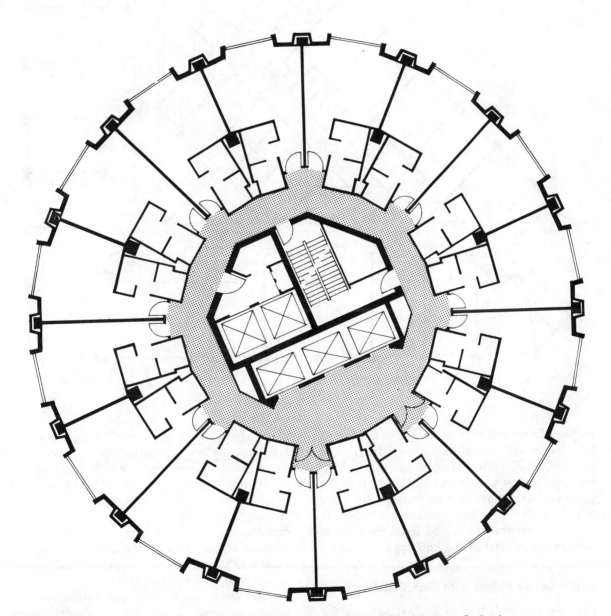

Figure 3–10   *A rendering of a circular Hotel Plan. Stouffer's Riverfront Towers, St. Louis.*

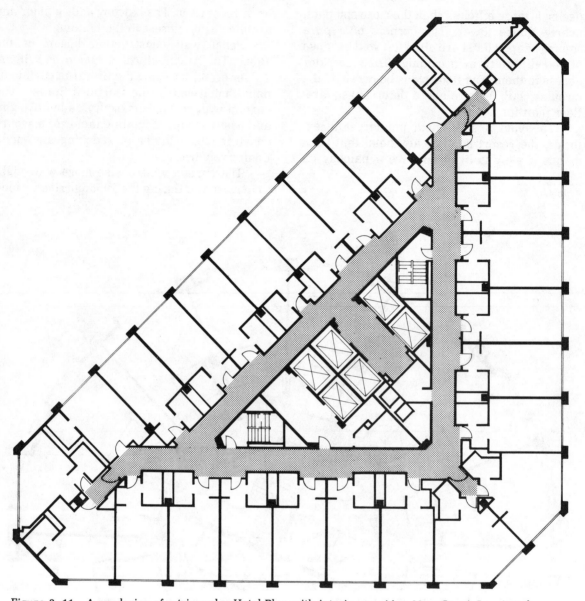

Figure 3-11   *A rendering of a triangular Hotel Plan with interior corridor. New Otani, Los Angeles.*

900 12

inches of rain fell in New York City in twenty-four hours and seventeen ceilings dropped in the New York Statler. Two weeks later about fourteen inches of rain fell on Hartford in the same period of time with no damage. By using panel walls, the heavy columns needed to support masonry are moved from the outside wall to the interior of the building.

Fewer Lobby Pillars with Slab Construction

For the Statler-Hilton in Dallas, Mr. Tabler used cantilevered flat slab construction. These slabs are raised along a central core and are held in place by a central support. This reduces the number of columns and the size of the foundation by 50 percent. No beams are required or used, less reinforcing steel needed. Another advantage in the use of the flat slab construction is the need for only half the usual number of columns in the lobby. These are columns that usually get in the way and have to be covered with expensive marble.

Some hotels are designed with a specific market in mind; it may be the upper income group, the traveling man, the conventioneer,

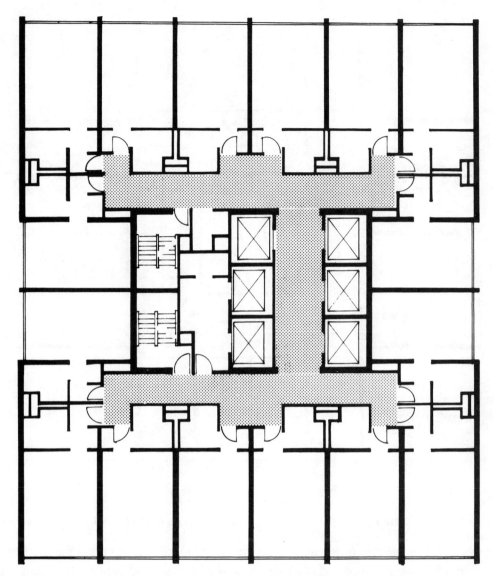

Figure 3–12 A rendering of a square Hotel Plan. Stouffer's Cincinnati Towers.

the corporate training group, the air traveler, and similar classifications. Hotel markets are not nearly so well defined as are restaurant markets. The highway hotel is probably appealing to all possible markets, anyone with the price and the inclination to stop at the hotel. The highway traveler is almost anyone with a car, although he may be a tourist or a traveling man.

A motel located in an industrial park area has probably identified its market as being largely people who have business at the park. A resort hotel, located some distance from its market, must be much more highly selective in its clientele and must design the hotel appro-

priate to that market. A hotel in the Virgin Islands, for example, necessarily caters to people in the middle and upper income brackets, at least at the height of the season. Only people in those brackets have the discretionary income and freedom to take vacations at that time.

Optimal Size?

What is the optimal size of a hotel or a motel? The answer to this question has not been definitely established. It probably is best arrived at in a series of steps. Most motel experts feel that a motel must be at least 50

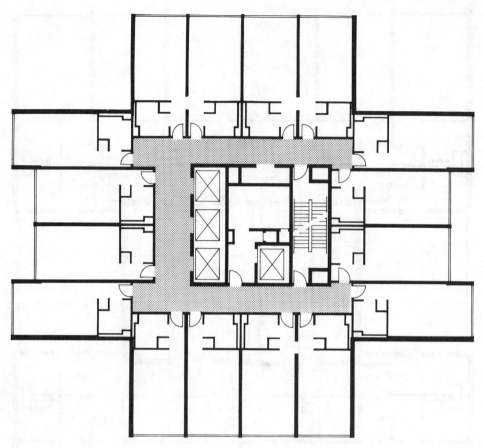

Figure 3–13 A rendering of the "deformed" square Hotel Plan. Holiday Inn, Quebec.

rooms in size to be large enough to (1) support a capable manager, and (2) produce enough profit for the motel to be of interest to a big investor or to a chain operation. A remote resort hotel probably has to have at least 150 to 200 units to stand on its own and be profitable.

If the area can support more rooms, the optimal size of the motel might jump to 100 or to 150. Motels that have 100 rooms and are doing capacity occupancy might well add another 50 rooms. The additional rooms would show a higher percentage of profit on the gross income than the rooms already in existence. The cost of labor for operating the 50 additional rooms is minimal. The only extra personnel needed in the 150-room motel would be two bellmen, one clerk, and four maids. In other words, adding 50 rooms to a 100-room motor inn increases the basic payroll costs by only $1,200 to $1,500 a month. Computed on an 85 percent room occupancy, the additional labor costs for the added 50 rooms are only 11 to 15 percent of the gross

sales. Some experts feel a 225-room hotel to be optimal.

At some size the hotel begins to take on a more impersonal character that operates against the personal service expected in a luxury hotel. It is for this reason that the deluxe hotel operator is likely to feel that if maximum personal service is to be offered, the hotel must be under 400 rooms, or perhaps even smaller.

From the point of view of maximum profit on rooms and service areas, the hotel might be any size, depending upon the market. An extremely large hotel may be needed to attract the largest conventions. From this viewpoint, anything smaller would not be efficient.

Large ballrooms may require as much as 25 percent of the ballroom space for use as a reception area, space for reception and cocktails before the meal, for use as a registration area, and for coffee service when the ballroom is used for meetings. Additional space of 10 to

15 percent of the ballroom area may be needed for furniture and equipment storage, such as tables, chairs, platforms, audio-visual equipment.

ENERGY MANAGEMENT AND DESIGN

Energy control has become one of the important control aspects of the hotel and restaurant business together with food cost control and labor cost control. Together with time management, financial management, and social management, the cost of energy has placed it among the other major aspects of management. Energy management necessitates a greater emphasis on "Present Value Analysis," looking at a capital cost from the point of view of not only its present cost but of its cost in years to come, its life cycle cost. From this viewpoint, a building costing $1 million may be a much less desirable investment than one costing $1.5 million, if the added investment will result in lower energy and maintenance costs over the life of the building.

Energy management involves the design of the building, less glass area, the use of solar screens (screens to shut out the sun when not wanted), increased insulation; perhaps even the consideration of building a hotel into the ground with clerestory windows to let the light into a central well or patio, with guest rooms facing the well.

Equipment is purchased with particular consideration for the life cycle. Controls are installed which permit energy reduction during the peak load hours when the cost of electricity is highest. For example, ice machines can be purchased that will not be operated during the 5 to 8 P.M. period when there is peak load demand on electricity. No hot water need be heated during that period either; instead it can be stored from times when energy cost is less.

The use of solar collectors to collect heat from the sun and use it in heating the water for the hotel and restaurant was beginning to get serious consideration in 1975. Several hotels, especially resort hotels, added collectors which permitted a large input of Btu's from the sun and a reduction in the amount of oil consumed.

Several hotels and motels are now using solar energy to heat water up to 140°F. and some are using solar energy for air conditioning. Frenchman's Reef, a luxury resort in St. Thomas, U.S. Virgin Islands, uses 13,200 sq. ft. of specially designed solar collectors from Northrup, Inc. The collectors track the sun across the sky and concentrate and focus the rays on copper absorption tubes. Water in the tubes is heated almost to steam and is then pumped to absorption chillers of an air conditioning system.

Most restaurant and hotels owners who have turned to solar energy are installing solar collector panels on the roof aimed at the sun so as to get maximum sunshine each day. In most systems the piping carries a liquid that is heated by the sun and then moved to a large water tank (heat exchanger) where the heat passes from the pipes into the water. (The liquid in the tubing must contain antifreeze to avoid freezing in temperate climates.) Such systems ordinarily heat the water to about 130°F. If higher temperatures are needed the water is boosted by conventional means, either by electricity or gas.

The heated water can be used in the kitchen or can be pumped by tubes to guest rooms where blowers transfer the heat from the tubes into the rooms for heating.

THE PERENNIAL PARKING PROBLEM

Automobile parking has been a problem for hotels ever since the automobile appeared in any number; however, after about 1950 many a hotel succeeded or failed, depending upon parking availability.

The Christopher Inn of Columbus, one of the most attractive, produced a novel approach to the parking problem. The first three floors of the circular inn are a ramp upon which cars can be parked. The inn begins on the fourth floor and extends up ten stories. All guest rooms have a view since they are on the outside of the circle. The rooms necessarily must be somewhat pie-shaped.

PARKING SPACE NEEDS

Speculation as regards the number of parking spaces needed in a hotel has been resolved by experience. Podd and Lesure in their book, *Planning and Operating Motels and Motor Hotels,* state the requirements as follows:

One parking space for each guest unit

One parking space for each five restaurant seats

One parking space for every three employees

Two additional parking spaces for service trucks

One unobstructed loading space

An automobile requires between 300 and 400 sq. ft. of space, including the driveway but not including the entrance way. It can be seen that parking requirements add up fast as guest rooms increase.

Since the older hotels had no provisions for parking, most of them had to make arrangements with parking garages to handle guests' automobiles.

A delay in getting a guest's car from the parking garage can sometimes last half an hour or an hour. Such delays are not calculated to soothe the guest who is in a hurry. Sheraton Hotels have instituted a policy of providing free parking for all guests at their hotels, regardless of the cost to the hotel.

Free-standing restaurants require at least one parking space for every two seats; a 100-seat restaurant will need fifty parking spaces. Some municipalities require a greater ratio of parking to seating.

HOTEL DESIGNERS

Design of the modern hotel has been greatly influenced by four men: Morris Lapidus, William Tabler, Emanuel Gran, and John Portman. Tabler did the designs of the new Statler Hotels and Mr. Gran has been the consulting architect for Hilton Hotel International. Portman is a designer/architect/developer who first teamed up with Hyatt Hotels, later with Western International Hotels.

Lapidus, originally a retail store designer, thinks of the hotel, and especially its lobby, as a stage which should connote luxury, excite-

Figure 3–14 The La Fontaine Room of the Warwick Hotel, Houston. The room is not so large that it loses its charm and feeling of intimacy. This "Top" restaurant and bar is accessible by an outside elevator.

ment, and the unexpected. The traditional Grand Hotel achieved an impression of luxury with numerous lounges, thick carpeting, dozens of service personnel, and ornate design and heavy furniture.

The new hotel and motor hotel offer a gala atmosphere that is lighthearted as well as functional. Color is important. Lighting is used for effect as well as for illumination. Lapidus reintroduced the use of hanging lighting fixtures and chandeliers.

He mixed classic design with contemporary, contrasted textures, and made wide use of columns in his lobbies. Whereas the commercial hotel lobby was getting smaller and smaller, Lapidus produced huge lobbies at the Eden Roc and the Fontainebleau in Miami Beach and the Arawak in Jamaica. He is best known for his Fontainebleau design and for the Americana of New York.

According to Lapidus, nobody wants to go to a resort. The average vacationer is not tired and he does not need a rest. He does not want peace and quiet. What he does want is a change. Most people, according to Lapidus, are too restless to spend even a week in a hotel. The average stay in a resort area is about four days. He contends that every hotel is a resort; the commercial hotel has been married to the resort hotel.

Nobody, says Lapidus, wants the "home away from home," nor do guests want to do at a hotel what they would normally do at home. Business is conducted in a holiday atmosphere which can hardly be separated from pleasure.

The huge costs of the new downtown hotels, according to Lapidus, are exaggerated. In some cases, publicly stated costs are almost double the real ones.

Confirming Lapidus's idea that the downtown hotel is a kind of a resort, the Palmer House in Chicago built a $10 million "resort within a hotel" by roofing over a twenty-four-story well at the twelfth floor. The Los Angeles Statler, designed by Tabler, introduced reflecting pools and palm trees as part of the lobby of a large downtown hotel.

SPECTACULAR DESIGN

The spectacular in hotel design in recent years has been created in the Mauna Kea, a Western International hotel in Hawaii, the Princess

Figure 3–15 The River Front Inn of St. Louis was built in 1968. An impressive part of its setting is the magnificent arch overlooking the Mississippi River. It is one of several inns operated by Stouffers, a subsidiary of Litton Industries.

Hotel in Acapulco, and in a series of John Portman hotels.

The 1970s saw a number of hotels that departed radically from the traditionally designed hotels, hotels which better fit the character of a particular location, be it New York, Denver, or Los Angeles. Instead of being built by hotelmen as in the past, the new properties are being built almost exclusively by developers. One reason has been the shortage of money and its high cost. Banks no longer would provide loans for the 60 percent mortgage money for hotel construction. In the 1970s, both banks and insurance companies required a much higher equity by the holder and in many cases demanded participation in the ownership.

In 1967, the Regency Hyatt House in Atlanta with its twenty-one-story open lobby or "atrium," established a new trend in hotel architecture. Designed by John Portman as part of a renewal project in downtown Atlanta, it paced a series of similar huge-lobbied hotels, most managed by the Hyatt Company. The Atlanta Regency was the first new hotel in

Figure 3–16   The Prudential Center of Boston has helped to change the face of the city. The center is a trade-educational-entertainment complex. At the top of the fifty-two-story Prudential building is the Top of the Hub restaurant, also operated by Stouffer's. The Sheraton-Boston Hotel, opened in 1965, was the first major hotel to be built in Boston since the 1920s. Twenty-nine stories high, it has 1,012 guest rooms and can accommodate meetings of 2,500. The complex also contains the Hynes Auditorium where trade shows and educational meetings of considerable size are held.

years to create a special atmosphere within a large downtown hotel. Probably the most spectacular is the Hyatt Regency, San Francisco. The San Francisco Hyatt with its seventeen-story lobby seems to fit San Francisco, an airy city built on hills.

The Century Plaza Hotel in Los Angeles, designed by Minoru Yamasaki, was also a landmark in hotel construction in that it created its own environment by including a handsome garden, which the lobby overlooks. Its garden restaurant, glass-walled on the garden side, contributes to the garden ambience.

Since the opening of the Atlanta Hyatt Regency, John Portman, who designed that spectacular hotel, has had the greatest impact on hotel design of any architect, possibly of any architect in history. The Regency concept, rooms surrounding an open lobby, is nothing

new. The scale, the grandeur, the multi-storied mobiles, glass-sided elevators gliding up and down the lobby, in full view to those in the lobby and in the elevators, are new.

The open lobbies, soaring to the top of the hotel, are called atriums, from the Roman patios of the same name. The lobbies, says Portman, are an explosion of space, an attempt to overcome the tight and cramped space of the central city. Forty-foot trees, lakes, open restaurants, waterfalls, "people spaces" —elevators and people moving on different balcony levels—give the atriums a "live, or kinetic, quality." Birds, trees, reflecting pools, vines trailing down from guest room balconies within the atriums, grounded and hanging sculptures, add interest and warmth. The lobbies are not only filled with guests of the hotels but have become tourist attractions in their own right.

What makes the Portman design properties in great demand around the world is that their occupancies were running near capacity in 1975, while the industry as a whole was in the low 60 percent of occupancy.

When the Atlanta Regency was being built, Portman invited the officers of the major chains to Atlanta to discuss possible management contracts. They were not impressed. Portman recalls that Conrad Hilton after looking down on the hotel construction announced, "That concrete monster will never fly." When the hotel was offered for sale, the Pritzkers, principals in Hyatt Houses, bought it. Between 1967 and 1972, several Hyatt Regency Hotels—Portman designed—were built and taken on by Hyatt in major cities, an association which helped considerably in making the Hyatt company the fastest growing large-hotel chain in the 1970s.

Unusual for an architect is the fact that Portman is also a developer, an investor in many of the properties he designs. In 1972, he severed relations with Hyatt and later moved to collaborate with Western International Hotels, subsidiary of United Airlines.

Portman is responsible for a major breakthrough in hotel design, which in effect means hotelkeeping. In the city of over 500,000, Portman sees the hotel as a part of a complex, a rearrangement of inner city living, closing the environment and air conditioning huge blocks of space.

Figure 3-17 *The President's Suite in the Warwick Hotel, Houston. Many of the furnishings were brought from chateaux in France. The Warwick is one of the luxury hotels in the United States.*

Introducing symbols of rural life into the central city, Portman rearranges space so that it surrounds large areas, producing a new geometry inside of the hotel and in its relation to the other parts of the complex which Portman envisions. Many architects have tried this in the past; Portman is doing it and, in the process, making a fortune for himself and those associated with him.

The problem with enclosing such huge spaces is the rising costs of the energy required to heat and air condition the spaces. The building codes of 1975 required that fresh air be brought in from the outside for each recirculation, air which usually must be heated or cooled at considerable cost.

Portman has the distinction of having designed the world's tallest hotel—in Atlanta the seventy-story Peachtree Center Plaza Hotel—opened in 1976 under the management of Western International. And another seventy-story Portman hotel has been opened in Detroit.

THE FUTURE OF THE SUPER HOTEL?

The massive super hotel, represented by the Bonaventure in Los Angeles, is viewed by many as the hotel of the future and has been used in futuristic films as backdrop. People seem to react strongly to these large-space lobbies, either strongly for or against. As a setting for conventions and tour groups—these are prime market targets—these glass, concrete, and steel structures with a large atrium seem to be efficient places for holding conventions and large group meetings, places for an exciting weekend and an overnight stop for the groups. The super or "mega" hotels are not on a scale to generate warmth and intimacy. Traditionalists have a difficult time identifying with the ambiance. So contrasting are the super hotels to the European personal service luxury hotel that a super hotel may be indeed uncomfortable or downright disorienting to many travelers. Buck Rogers would feel at home but maybe not Mr. and Mrs. Middle Class on a vacation.

MOTEL/MOTOR HOTEL DESIGN

Today, design of the larger motel is often indistinguishable from that of the hotel. The motor hotel makes the distinction even less easy. In the beginning, the motel was easily defined because it was a single-story, flimsily constructed building, usually erected as a separate cabin. Architecture and design were given scarcely a thought.

Later, to keep building costs at the minimum, several units were built side by side under a common roof. Some of the early units included a carport adjacent to the guest room, but it was soon realized that the automobile was hardier than the horse that had formerly required such protection. As this became clear, many of the owners of the carports got out hammer and nails and made additional rental units out of the carports.

Early Motels Mostly Owner-Designed

Most of the early motels were designed by the owners. When architects were employed, they were cautioned to keep the structure simple and inexpensive. The early motel could have passed for a long row of boxes in which the tired traveler would enjoy the reverberations of passing traffic throughout the night. Indoor plumbing came as an improvement; the hanging light bulb was changed to a lamp. Every several years progressive owners tore down existing units and replaced them with something more modern and permanent.

The first motels offered no food facilities, recognizing that business from the guests in the dining room was likely to be too small to create a profit. The guest was directed down the road to a good restaurant. Kemmons Wilson, who pioneered Holiday Inns of America, saw the necessity of a restaurant operation in the motel and, beginning in 1952, built one at each of his properties. Gradually the larger motels added food facilities.

The first motels comprised only a few units; for many years the average was less than 20 rooms. Gradually the motel grew larger, and today the usual motel built by the Holiday Inns of America exceeds 130 units.

Because Kemmons Wilson and his partner, Mr. Johnson, were building contractors, they built their Holiday Inns well and efficiently. One of the reasons for the success of Holiday Inns is the fact that the average unit cost in 1969 was $10,000 a room. Even in high-cost Chicago, Holiday Inns built a property for $12,500 a room. In the South, where construction labor is cheaper, the per unit cost may be even less. One of the secrets of keeping building costs in a motel low, according to Wilson, is to omit construction of a basement.

Motel Cost

What is the breakdown of costs in building a new motel? The motel is not likely to have the public space of the hotel and can concentrate more of the investment in bedrooms. Land cost is likely to be less because the motel is usually out of the downtown area with its high land cost. Podd and Lesure in their book, *Planning and Operating Motels and Motor Hotels,* suggest a breakdown for motel costs as follows:

Land	10 to 20 percent
Buildings	65 to 70 percent
Furnishings and	
Equipment	15 to 20 percent

Since motels are generally built on land that is not as expensive as that used by the hotel, room size is usually bigger, running as high as 20 by 20 ft. Today's motel is very likely to include a swimming pool, even though it may be miniature in size.

The rule of thumb in building a motel is to break down total cost as follows: 70 percent for construction; 15 percent for furnishings; 10 percent for land, and 5 percent for landscaping. In downtown areas land cost may go as high as 25 percent of the total investment and beach property may account for a similar percentage.

Many Motel Shapes

The characteristic motel silhouette of the past was a long line of single, one-story units stretching along the highway. The motel today comes in a variety of shapes and patterns, some exceedingly beautiful. The beach front motel is likely to be a "U," with the swimming pool in the center of the "U," and the back of the property facing the beach. The high rise motel looks very much like a hotel; it may be a hotel in everything but name.

Today the average motor hotel contains well over 100 rooms; ten years ago few motels had as many as 40 rooms. The better motels have a room size of about 14 ft. wide by at least 24 ft. long, including bathroom. Because of the cost of land and construction, most good sites require a minimum of 60 rooms for economic feasibility; for absentee management, a 100-room minimum is recommended.

In planning a motel always allow for expansion up or out, if at all possible. As for square footage, at least 650 sq. ft. are needed per room for a two-story motel; this includes the restaurant. The minimum size room averages 12 ft. by 24 ft., or 288 sq. ft. The remaining 362 sq. ft. go outside—for driveways, parking, landscaping, pool, and other facilities. A 100-unit motel then would need a minimum of 60,000 sq. ft.; 100,000 sq. ft. would permit larger rooms and a more attractive "siting." Restaurants need between 40 to 60 sq. ft. per person, including parking space and 100 ft. of frontage.

Kitchenettes should not be a part of the motel unless it is a resort motel catering to the family. Then one-third of the units might be so equipped.

As for motel restaurants, Hot Shoppes, a highly experienced restaurant chain, recommends having one parking space for every 2.5 seats in the restaurant. A 100-seat restaurant needs about forty parking spaces. Some city building codes require one parking space for every two seats.

A trend in the motor hotel is toward larger lobbies. Where prestige is important, more money must be spent on the lobby, and the lobby should be placed so it is easily seen by the traveler on the highway. Within reason, the larger the lobby, the more people respect the motel. The bigger lobby can usually be paid for by a slight increase in the room rate.

Another trend is to create "fun domes" with swimming pools, miniature golf, pool tables, table tennis, and other recreational facilities which attract the weekend guest, as well as the commercial guest. A major advantage of the motel without foodservice is the reduced need for personnel. A TraveLodge motel of 250 rooms, for example, has only fifty-

five employees, with a labor cost of less than 25 percent of total sales.

COMPUTER STANDARDIZING STRUCTURAL ELEMENTS

A novel use of the computer is being made by William W. Bond, Jr., architect and vice-president of Holiday Inns. Bond has standardized many structural elements in motels and developed optimum sizes for dining rooms and lobbies.

Much of the information is stored in a computer that is linked to a Norwegian-made drafting machine. A rough sketch is made of a proposed new inn and standard bedroom. The information is coded and placed on tape. The tape can be used to activate the drafting machine which in twenty-five minutes provides detailed plans and elevations for an inn accurate to .002 inches.[10]

Use of the computer saves a great deal on interest charges because it is so fast. Each month's delay in building an inn, in effect, raises the cost at a $1 million building site by several thousand dollars.

TraveLodge Corporation has developed an unusual floor plan for reducing costs. Its "tri-arc," 200-room lodge is in the shape of a triangle with concave sides. Because it has no front or back, it can be placed on almost any site. Each lodge requires eight to twelve months to build—about two-thirds the time needed to construct the usual 200-room hotel.

MOTEL LANDSCAPING

In the past, motel experts have recommended that motels be constructed on large plots that can be easily seen for some distance from the highway that passes the motel. The large lot was used for a swimming pool, landscaping, parking, and for possible expansion in the number of guest rooms.

The rising cost of land, however, has forced a change of design on the motel. The swimming pool is frequently located above a terrace or on the roof. Sometimes it is indoors. Landscaping at some motels is also being moved indoors with plants now placed in

10. "Reveille Sounds for the Hoteliers," *Fortune Magazine,* September 1969.

lobbies. Parking is sometimes underground or on several levels reached by a ramp.

Most motels could do with more and better landscaping. Landscaping, say the experts, should relate to the region. Trees and other plantings should come from the region to make certain they will thrive in the climate where the motel is located.

Stone walls and rambling roses, for example, are perfect for New England, enhance the appearance of the property, and fit the New England image. Trees can be used to screen streets from the buildings and to soften the hard surfaces of the buildings. A few trees, properly placed, effectively "break" or soften harsh horizontal lines of buildings and make them more inviting. Low spreading plants at the base of motel entrance signs "tie them down" to Mother Earth, helping the viewer make the transition from vertical to horizontal.

Lighting can create a romantic glow for a motel, casting shadows on walls, emphasizing beauty spots and adding color at night. A drive past Miami Beach motels after dark should convince anyone of the magic of lighting cast on palms, pools, and other plantings.

Some motels have added pieces of sculpture and reflecting pools to their entrance areas. The Cabana Motor Hotels have beautiful, landscaped grounds, including putting greens. A number of pieces of sculpture are set up in front of the motel, reminiscent of the grounds of an Italian villa.

"THE WORLD'S LARGEST"

"The world's largest" anything has a ring about it which inspires awe. Large hotels are usually among the largest buildings and, in many cases, are the largest buildings in our towns and cities. They constitute landmarks, centers of community activity, objects of civic pride. The first building in the United States to be built as a hotel, The Tontine City Tavern, created something of a sensation because it had seventy-three rooms. Built in 1794, the name was changed quickly to the City Hotel.

The most impressive public house in the period 1793 to 1818 was the Boston Exchange Coffee House. Referred to by travelers as the largest building in America, and the best hotel, it had over 200 apartments, nearly 300 rooms, "elegant" private bedrooms which were num-

bered, private drawing rooms, a billiard room, a hairdresser's room, and several "bathing" rooms. In November, 1818, the place burned to the ground.

The "biggest" title then shifted to Baltimore where, in 1826, David Barnum, who had managed the Boston Exchange Coffee House, opened the City Hotel. Also known as "Barnum's," the six-story hostelry contained "200 apartments" and was said by many to be "the best hotel in America." It was in referring to Barnum's that the term "first-class" hotel was initially used.[11]

The Tremont House of Boston appeared in 1829. Neo-classical in architecture, it set a pattern for U.S. hotels both in its style and operation. At 170 rooms, it was one of the world's largest until the Astor Hotel in New York City was built in 1834. Two stories higher, the Astor had 309 rooms and was considered a palace by then current standards. Plumbing had advanced so that water closets could be installed on upper floors instead of only on the first floor. The place was lavishly furnished to justify its leading position.

The Fifth Avenue Hotel of New York, finished in 1859, was called the first great modern hotel. It captured the "biggest" title and held on to it until the "Palace" rose in the West in San Francisco. The Palace cost $5 million, a tremendous sum for those days, and had 800 rooms. The Palace burned to the ground following the San Francisco earthquake in 1906.

"BEST KNOWN" TITLE WENT TO WALDORF

The Waldorf-Astoria Hotel is probably the best known hotel in the world. The original Waldorf, completed in 1893, was also probably the best known hotel in the world in its day. When the addition was built in 1897, making it the Waldorf-Astoria, the hotel had 1,000 rooms —the largest hotel in the world at that time. It was estimated that the hotel cost $5 million, a huge sum of money in the 1890s; in addition, 765 of the rooms had private baths, a major innovation in hotelkeeping.

11. Doris Elizabeth King, "Early Hotel Entrepreneurs and Promoters, 1793–1860," *Explanations in Entrepreneurial History* (Harvard Research Center in Entrepreneurial History, VIII, February 1956).

formation is essential, the on-line arrangement is called for. Otherwise, the cost of on-line is excessive.

Several of the companies that have installed EDP have declared that the total cost of EDP is as great as the hand system it replaced, but that information is almost instantaneously available. The availability of information when needed provides the plus factor for the computer installation. Some experts in 1977 maintained that a computer was not feasible for hotels under 500 rooms in size. With mini-computers and time-sharing, smaller hotels have found computers feasible.

Simulated Decision-Making

To familiarize future managers with EDP, several of the hotel schools require each student to complete at least one course in data processing. Several schools arrange for students to play management simulation games. The games compress several years of decision-making into the space of a few hours. The use of a computer permits the use of a number of variables. In the games the computer produces the results of the various decisions within a few seconds.

The use of EDP to develop a menu has been worked out for hospital menus. The work was done at Tulane University under a government grant. Hospital menus that reflect nutritional balance, color, and cost are being selected by computer. Such menu selection must also reflect the effect of monotony in a diet and regional food preferences as well. As of 1969, menu planning for commercial restaurants has not yet been accomplished by computer.

The Century Plaza Hotel of Los Angeles puts the computer to work in a way that should please the guest. When a guest has been to the hotel three times, the computer automatically pre-registers him and recalls his room preferences. He need only pick up his key when he arrives.

Undoubtedly, many more uses will be found for the computer. As the cost comes down, wider application can be expected. Time-sharing is likely to be the favorite method of use since banks, insurance companies, and other large companies have sizable amounts of computer time which can be made available for hotels and restaurants on a time-sharing basis at relatively low cost.

Identifying Significant Market Factors by Computer

It is now possible, by using the computer, to identify more precisely those factors that bear on the sales volume of a particular hotel or motel. This is done by subjecting occupancy data to analysis. Factors that are thought to be important for sales are correlated with sales figures over a period of time. Correlations between factors are also made. Without the use of the computer, the arithmetic would be too time-consuming to be feasible.

With sufficient information based on past experience, it is possible to identify and weigh each factor which bears on the sales of a particular hotel or motel. It will be possible to predict that if a certain amount of money is spent on advertising, a certain increase can be expected, or that affiliation with a particular chain will result in a predictable increase in occupancy, and so on.

In keeping with the shifting emphasis on the systems approach and the use of the computer, the larger companies are adding new divisions which are responsible for management information systems and computer applications. Saga Food Administration, one of the most progressive foodservice operations, has reorganized top management to include an administrative division headed by an executive vice-president of administration.

Administration is responsible for the broad areas of planning and forecasting. Within the administration division are the departments of personnel, finance, marketing, technical services, and information services. Indicative of the thrust of the Saga Company has been the establishment of a separate division, New Ventures.

The magic words in management today are computerization, management information systems, linear programming, data processing, input-output analysis, progress evaluation review technique, queuing theory, econometric model, multiple regression analysis, and a few others. With time these terms may become a regular part of every manager's jargon.

High Technology Spreading

Until the early 1970s high technology had not reached the hotel business to any great extent. By the middle 1970s this was changing. Hotel managers in larger properties were called upon to familiarize themselves with certain computer applications and related technology. Computerized reservations services were widely used, especially among the chains. By 1976 the inter-hotel reservations systems of fourteen of the twenty largest hotel chains were computerized. Eighteen of the 20 used data processing for at least part of their corporate accounting.

The "Star" computerized reservations terminal used by Best Western hotels/motels, for example, consists of three elements, a Cathode Ray Tube (CRT) display screen, a computerized keyboard for sending reservations, and a hard-copy printer for receiving reservations and messages from other Best Western properties and the chain's marketing and Reservations Center in Phoenix. The Star computer is programmed so that if no rooms are available at a given property, a display automatically appears showing availabilities at the nearest alternate Best Westerns. Time required: thirty seconds. The Star terminal is seen below.

The preparation of financial and operating reports was the most prevalent in-house application of computers. Centralized accounts payable was also computerized widely. Other applications included handling of payroll, budget projections, the consolidation of daily operating reports, and return on investment analysis.

Rather than rush out and learn data processing in depth, the usual hotel manager might take a course in data processing and then learn a particular computer application as he is confronted with it. Computers are now being used in a variety of combinations, including the following:

Reservations

Room management, including communication links between front desk and housekeeping

Guest accounting, including both front-office cashiering and night audit

Guest history

Point-of-sale data collection from the hotels and motels, restaurants, bars, and other revenue centers

Telephone circuit board

Marketing analyses

Convention and other function records

Travel agency accounting

Travel agency business analysis

Back-office accounting, or interface with the back office

Data processing is predicted to be widely used in hotels of more than 200 rooms, especially mini-computers as their cost comes down and they are installed on the premises.

LOW VOLTAGE SYSTEMS

As new hotels are constructed a number of low-voltage systems can be installed in the same conduits. These systems include equipment that will control the peak power demand, room status systems, automatic wake-up systems, electronically controlled guest room access and electronically controlled storeroom access.

The automatic turn-off or turn-down of heating, ventilation and air conditioning equipment, and lighting when the guest checks out, and the automatic turn-on when the guest checks in, is likely to become widely used. Energy controlled equipment has a fast pay-off, energy savings equalling the investment within six months or two years.

Room status systems remove the need for constant phone calls between the front desk and housekeeping.

Figure 4–3   St*r. Best Western's new computerized reservation system. It features a sophisticated but easy-to-use keyboard and display screen terminal.

If security continues to be a problem, electronic security systems are likely to be installed with "forced entry" alarms, motion detectors, and metal detectors, for example. Comprehensive security systems have been in use in Las Vegas, Reno, and a few of the larger hotels elsewhere.

Telephone systems owned or leased by the hotel gained wider acceptance. Automatic transfer of the guest's local charges is made to the appropriate guest folio. This speeds guest check-out and eliminates the manual meters, which count guest's calls.

Larger convention hotels are likely to use other types of low-voltage technology including:

Large-screen TV projection

Paging—audio and visual

Closed-circuit TV

Video recording equipment

Front and rear screen projection equipment

Automatic wake-up systems.[5]

THE SALES FUNCTION

Hotels have been changing the title of the person in charge of sales to Director of Marketing, a change which implies a much broader role for the individual holding the title. Marketing is concerned not only with selling but with learning more about the product to be sold, the competitor's product, the customer, the customer's motivation and wants, and how the product can best be produced and presented to meet the customer's needs. Marketing implies research. In the case of the hotel it is folio research, carefully identifying who the present customers are, where they come from, what they earn, and what they want in the way of hotel and services. A Los Angeles Hotel may find that its principal "market," its source of customers, is Western Canada, San Francisco and Chicago, or other areas. Promotion and advertising would then be concentrated in those areas.

A motor hotel manager may be surprised to learn that 70 percent of the guests are pleasure travelers, not business travelers. A member of a referral organization may find that less than 30 percent of its customers come as referrals from within their referral system. The Group Marketing Research and Development section of Holiday Inns found Holiday Inns was not as successful as some other chains in attracting families traveling with teenagers simply because the other chains did not charge for teens. As a result a "Teens Free" policy was instituted in 1,300 inns. The same company wondered how business travelers felt about their holidomes (covered courtyards with pools and games). The business traveler thought that they were innovative and impressive, adding to the appeal of the inn. The question was raised among business travelers concerning the chain's policy of "Kids Eat Free." The program was perceived as positive and has influenced the business traveler to stay at a Holiday Inn when traveling with his or her family.

Market analysis can determine where new investment is needed. Should it be spent in redesigning the lobby or improving the restaurant operation? Ask the customer. What effect will a severe winter have on summer business? In Harrisburg, Pennsylvania, for example, a severe winter caused the schools to close three weeks late, a condition which affected the June business for a number of inns that depended upon Harrisburg as a summer feeder market. Knowing this the inns could accept group or meeting business, which they normally would have turned away in June.

Much of hotel market research is not done "in-house" but farmed out to local market research organizations and to business departments in nearby universities.

The Sales Staff

The sales staff of hotels and motels varies in size. In a small motel the manager performs the sales function. In a megahotel a Director of Sales may have a staff of eight or ten persons plus the assistance of the corporate office sales staff.

The Radisson South hotel, a 408-room hotel in Minneapolis, has a staff of five in the sales department with a game plan drawn to determine how to sell, when to sell, and where to sell. Its staff is representative of a medium-sized hotel.

5. For further information see "The State of Information Processing and Related Technology in the Hotel/Motel Industry," American Hotel and Motel Association, 1976.

The director of sales is primarily concerned with game planning, setting goals, budgeting, forecasting and supervision. He also spends 20 percent of his time on the road. With the general manager and executive assistant manager, he develops annually a "Rooms Sales Forecast" for every day in the year for group bookings. Day-to-day forecasting is done by the executive assistant manager.[6]

The assistant director of sales spends 20 percent of his time outside primarily on national conventions and assists the director of sales in reporting and record-keeping and in performing analysis and evaluation.

The sales manager spends 35 percent of his time outside and works on convention sales with emphasis on state and regional meetings. A second salesperson spends 70 percent of her time outside promoting corporate bookings of meetings and other multiple reservations. One salesperson spends 90 percent of her time outside visiting corporate offices.

PUBLIC RELATIONS

The larger hotels and hotel chains and theme parks employ public relations personnel whose primary job is to create a favorable image for their properties. This is done by cultivating editors, travel writers, and other media personnel and encouraging them to write about the property concerned. They are encouraged also to send out a series of news releases designed to keep the hotel, theme park, or other attraction in the public eye. The public relations people are usually excellent writers, likable and often highly imaginative. When the theme park Six Flags Over Texas introduced its new high-speed thrill ride called the "Runaway Mine Train" the ride broke down with a dozen newspaper writers and photographers and four television cameramen on board. The train ground to a screeching halt on the high loops and the whole thing could have been a disaster from a public relations viewpoint. The quick-thinking public relations person at Six Flags suggested that the press, TV and news people treat the incident from a different angle: "Safety Systems on New Run-Away Train Works Perfectly."

Sometimes it takes months to cultivate a good magazine—interesting a good writer by providing accommodations and meals, information, photographs, and background information. The payoff may be an article in a name magazine that would have the effect of tens of thousands of dollars worth of advertising. A giveaway guide book for an area may increase the average stay for a hotel one to three days, the guest having available a number of suggestions of new options for things to do.

NEW SECURITY MEASURES

The Courts and the general public have rising expectations as to what a hotel-motel should provide in the way of security. Or perhaps with the rising crime the general public is more conscious of criminal activity and are becoming more wary and demanding.[7]

No doubt guest security has been a problem in hotels since their beginning. In 1974 a well-known singer, Connie Francis, was raped while staying at the Howard Johnson Motor Lodge in Westbury, Long Island. She sued the restaurant and motel chain for $6 million in June, 1975 charging that the company had failed to provide her with a safe and secure room. The singer was awarded $2.5 million and her husband an additional $25,000 by a Federal District Court in Brooklyn. Howard Johnson's insurance company filed a motion, asking that the award be set aside as excessive. The parties settled out of court in 1977 for $1,475,000. The case alarmed hotel and motel keepers and focused attention on the necessity for providing greater guest security.

Larger hotels have long had security men in plain clothes, often off-duty policemen, working the hotel lobby and around the hotel since before the turn of the century. Now hotel operators are strengthening their security forces and looking for new ways of insuring guest security within the room. A number of "security systems" have been introduced.

A system called Lok-a-Wat works in this way: After a hard day a guest unlocks the door, walks into his hotel room, turns on the light and the television and flops down on the bed to relax. Two and a half minutes later the television goes off, the light goes off and the air-con-

6. "The Radisson South, A Case Study in Hotel Operation," *Lodging*, November 1977.

7. *New York Times*, March 20, 1977, p. 13.

ditioner shuts down. To activate the electrical system again, the guest must throw a deadbolt in the lock on his door. The guest must secure himself. Control for the system is operated from a metal box, eighteen inches by three inches by three inches, fitted under the desk in each room. Wires connect the box to the lock and to the electrical appliances.

Other systems require plastic cards as substitutes for keys. Peepholes are being installed in guest rooms, and stronger locks are being installed. Chain locks have been used in many properties for a number of years; now closed circuit television focuses on corridors and are monitored by security personnel.

Regardless of deadbolts and other systems it is necessary for hotel personnel to enter the room in case of fire, illness, and other emergencies in which the guest cannot open it himself.

Security experts state that a principle ingredient in the security programs effectiveness is the ability to respond promptly to a security problem. To this end, one-way beeper systems and two-way walkie talkie systems are widely used in the larger properties. Maintenance personnel can also be equipped with beeper systems and can become a prominent part of the security system if instructed in ways to handle security problems. In a large hotel the security force headquarters itself in a guest room and changes rooms from time to time.

A large hotel like the 1,000 room Marriott at the Los Angeles airport may have a security force of sixteen or more persons plus a number of off-duty regular policemen who shift on an hourly basis. None of the security people wear uniforms and only the regular police officers may make police arrests; the others must make do with a citizen's arrest. Even so they use handcuffs when necessary. This happens sometimes when people are engaged in fights or are drunk and disorderly. By far the largest arrests in downtown hotels are of obvious prostitutes. Guests are also apprehended in carrying off hotel property—although items like stolen towels are overlooked.

One of the most successful security programs utilize television monitors in all areas where large amounts of money are located. One person can monitor a number of places from one location, and if a problem arises can beep security personnel quickly.

WELL-PAID MANAGEMENT

Management personnel are a group apart, almost a caste. Over the years they have been comparatively well paid. The first manager of The Palace in San Francisco received $12,000 a year in gold, an exorbitant salary for 1875. Even during the depression Ralph Hitz demanded and got a salary of $35,000 a year as manager of The New Yorker. A first-class hotel needs two highly specialized, highly trained executives, the manager and the food and beverage director or the executive chef. The Ritz-Escoffier team illustrates what can be done with the front-of-the-house, headed by the manager, and the back-of-the-house, headed by the executive chef, when both are exceptional people.

As the chains, with their systems, moved into the larger hotels, the importance of having an exceptional man at the helm diminished. Staff planning, operation analysts, computers, and systems have partly relieved the necessity of having a man with exceptional planning and organizational skills in the individual hotel. While an exceptional manager sets the mood and creates a tone within the hotel, the design and operational procedures devised by the home office may be even more important.

The Sheraton Company for some years had the policy of moving managers at least every three years, usually more often. Other companies have a similar policy, believing that the manager tends to become too satisfied, or gets into a rut, if he remains very long at the same hotel. With enough system and control imposed upon a manager, the manager acts more as a man who makes the system work than as an innovator or a boniface in the traditional sense.

ACCOUNTING AND CONTROL SEPARATED FROM UNIT MANAGEMENT

In larger hotels the accounting and control function is divorced from every day management by making the comptroller or finance officer, as the comptroller is sometimes called, separate from line management. In the Hilton Hotels, for example, the finance officer within a large hotel, reports directly to the home office rather than being directly responsible to the General Manager of the property. Such an arrangement has advantages and disadvantages. The General Manager of the hotel may resent having the control function removed from his direct responsibility. In some cases the comptroller and the general manager may clash, and one or the other may have to be moved to another property. The primary advantage is that a specialist is in charge of the cash and accounting within a property, which lessens the possibility of ineffective accounting procedures and speculation on the point of the general manager or his immediate staff. The general manager is also freed from day to day concern over accounting and control procedures giving him more time to concentrate on guest relations, hotel operations, and the marketing function.

MANY DEMANDS ON MANAGER

Regardless of chain affiliation, the manager's job is extremely demanding, and the operation tends to reflect his motivation and attitudes. Like the captain of the ship with a structured organization backing him up, he must remain in command at all times and be responsible for everything that goes on within his domain.

A perceptive guest can sense something of the personality of the manager without ever seeing him. Does he run a taut ship? How does he feel about cleanliness? About courtesy? About attention to detail? What kinds of persons does he surround himself with? Well-managed hotels have an ambience that is not based on furnishings and design alone. The operation is articulated; things happen when they should; employees are alert and courteous; bedspreads are clean; the blankets have been laundered, at least during the past month; the carpets have no cigarette burns in them.

In a few deluxe hotels, room diagrams are kept for special guests, showing the way they like their suites laid out, the color of draperies they prefer, the kind of beverage they like to have waiting for them. The repeat guest is addressed by name. An assistant manager may call the newly-arrived guest in his room to inquire if everything is all right. The guest need not check out by standing in line at the cashier's desk. His bill is sent later.

In the typical 100- to 250-room hotel or motor hotel, only two to four people receive salaries of any size, the manager and the chef or food and beverage director. Between them, they are responsible for the complete operation of the hotel, and supposedly their expertise is sufficient to make the property go.

The innkeeper at a Holiday Inn operated by the Holiday Inn Company would typically make between $12,000 and $30,000 a year in salary plus receiving food and beverage while on the job. If the innkeeper lives in then that person and his wife and family receive full maintenance, all meals, room service, laundry, and other benefits. The assistant innkeeper of a Holiday Inn-style operation is the restaurant manager, and his salary approximates that of the innkeeper.

In the independent hotel or motel, the salary is usually higher and the manager would have considerably more responsibility. As the hotel or motel increases in size and complexity, the manager's salary increases so that in a few of the major hotels, the salary exceeds $50,000 a year plus a number of fringe benefits. Department head salaries also move up. Chefs at some of the prestige hotels may receive a salary of $35,000 a year. Department heads, such as the housekeeper and the engineer, might receive salaries in excess of $20,000 annually.

WAGES

The reputation of the hotel and restaurant business for the comparatively low wages paid is widespread and of long standing. The reputation is well deserved when applied to the entry and semiskilled positions, but is not true in reference to wages and salaries paid to technical specialists, supervisory and management personnel.

Since a large number of hotels, motels, and restaurants are small, they are likely to be family enterprises. In 1963, for example, there were almost 4,000 hotels and 16,000 motels and tourist courts that had no paid employees. In the small motel, the owner acts as manager and front desk clerk while the wife is housekeeper and chambermaid. Wages and salaries in such instances are, in large part, the profit generated by the business. These can be relatively high.

In the larger establishments 50 to 60 percent of all nonsupervisory personnel are low paid, unskilled, untipped employees. These include chambermaids, dishmachine operators, housemen, washroom attendants, laundry workers, porters, and utility personnel.

Characteristically, such people are from disadvantaged groups who have few other employment options. In New York City, for example, something like 40 to 60 percent of the hotel and restaurant employees are Puerto Ricans. In a twelve-city study, blacks made up 31.6 percent of the hotel labor force, with the great majority in low paying, back-of-the house positions. Median age of the hotel employees in 1975 was forty-four, four years older than that for the nation's labor force. Women constitute 53 percent of the employees.

In the South, nearly all nonsupervisory personnel in the kitchen are black. Along the Texas, New Mexico, and Arizona borders, they are of Mexican heritage. In South Florida, they are likely to be Cubans.

Area differences in hotel wages are large, twice as much being paid in San Francisco, for example, as in Kansas City or the Deep South. With the minimum wage laws, the spread between North and South has narrowed slightly, but it is still great. The wage differentials only partly reflect living costs; union pressures are important.

Skilled and semiskilled workers, such as bartenders, cooks, desk clerks, pantrymen and women, account for about 10 percent of nonsupervisory hotel employees. Their wages are high relative to those in the unskilled groups.

Productivity and wages are rising together as ways and products are found that reduce labor. No-iron linens, convenience foods, and direct dial phones eliminate people. So, too, do self-service elevators, vending machines, and shoeshining equipment in guest rooms.

Tip Employees Often Relatively Overpaid

About 15 percent of hotel employees receive tips. Tipped employees—doormen, bellmen, waiting personnel—are a group unto themselves and are in many cases highly overpaid in relation to their contribution to the enterprise. For the tip employee, the wage may be a relatively small part of his total income. The class of restaurant, seat turnover, and average check determine to a large extent the income of the tip employee. It is not unusual for waiting personnel to make as much as $80 a night in tips. A Bureau of Labor Statistics study showed that tipped employees average income was 61 percent higher than their non-tipped counterparts.

Tipping practices vary widely throughout the country. Highest rate is in New York City and cities on the West Coast. Tips are less in the Midwest and the South and are nonexistent in some rural communities. Tipping is reputed to be highest among certain segments of metropolitan New York residents. Well-to-do people are not necessarily big tippers whereas, generally speaking, the nouveaux riches have a reputation for being big spenders, and this includes tipping.

Office personnel account for about 15 percent of the nonsupervisory employment and their wages are usually determined by the prevailing wage in the community for similar jobs. Front desk clerks have traditionally been low-paid employees, especially in resort areas. Many people are eager for such jobs since the position has a certain status and is relatively interesting. The job offers psychic income as well as salary.

About 5 percent of the hotel employees are maintenance employees—engineers, firemen, upholsterers, electricians, painters—who are paid at competitive rates for the area. Maintenance people are usually well organized and receive a union scale.

Minimum Wage Controversy

The hotel and restaurant industry officially proclaims that it is the largest employer of marginal labor in the world. Spokesmen for the National Restaurant Association and the American Hotel and Motel Association have appeared before congressional committees several times to state that large numbers of employees cannot be paid the Federal minimum wage because productivity is too low. If, said the spokesmen, the minimum wage laws were applied to the restaurant business across the board, employers would have to discharge large numbers of employees. They argued that raising the minimum wage would force the employer to pass the cost on to the consumer. Many consumers will refuse to pay the added cost and business will suffer.

The arguments are fallacious, as has been proved in states like California and Massachusetts where high minimum wage laws for hotels and restaurants have been in effect for a num-

ber of years. Some added costs have been passed on to the consumer and some have been absorbed by tighter operations and the use of
labor saving equipment. Sales volume has not
dropped appreciably.

IMPACT OF THE UNION

Unionization has played an important part in
hotel management only in the large cities outside the South.

The Hotel and Restaurant Employees and
Bartenders Union is the major union in the
hotel and restaurant business. Uniformed personnel, such as bellmen and elevator operators, may be members of the Building Service
Employees International Union, and other
unions also represent some of the technical
personnel.

The Hotel and Restaurant Employees
Union goes back to 1891 when the Waiters and
Bartenders National Union was formed. Even
earlier, societies of European national groups
were organized to provide mutual financial
protection against the hazards of illness, old
age, and death. These societies manned the
skilled occupations: Germans cooking the food,
Italians serving it, the Irish tending bar.[8]

Growth of union membership was slow until about 1937. Between 1940 and 1947, membership doubled to a little over 400,000. The
chief barriers to the unionization of service
workers in the United States, say Professor
Henderson, are employer opposition and
worker apathy. Since so many people in the
industry are unskilled and constitute a
"floating" population, it is difficult for union-
ism to gain a stable membership base.

Membership in the union is high in northern cities and in the Far West. In Boston,
Chicago, Detroit, New York, St. Louis, and San
Francisco, 90 percent or more of nonsupervisory employees, except front desk and office
workers, are in establishments with union
agreements. In New Orleans, Atlanta, and
Memphis, however, the percentage is 20 or
below.[9]

As a region, the West is the most strongly
unionized with 37 percent of the total union
membership; California alone has 25 percent of
the total membership in the continental United
States. Washington, D.C. and Florida are the
only places in the South that have much union
representation. Of the total membership, somewhat over 63,000 are found in New York City,
another 20,000 in San Francisco.

San Francisco has had one of the strongest
union leaderships since the 1930s. In 1934, the
separate craft unions joined together into a
joint board and began demanding the union
shop in all hotels "from the roof down."[10] On
May 1, 1937, all of the hotels in the city were
struck. "Bartenders took off their coats and
aprons; waiters and busboys put down their
trays; stenographers left their desks; clerks put
on their hats; in fact, every worker just simply
walked off."[11] In all, about 10,000 employees
were affected.

The strike occurred at a time when San
Francisco's famous hotels, such as the Fairmont and Mark Hopkins on Nob Hill, the
Palace, and St. Francis were expecting floods
of tourists for the Golden Gate Fiesta. Some
4,700 union members, who had been hotel
employees, were out on strike. They were
helped by 4,000 fellow members in the city restaurants who paid assessments each week so
that the strikers might be fed. The prettiest
waitresses appeared in costume, on floats
mounted on trucks, advertising the strike.

Business losses for the hotels were estimated at $6.5 million for the summer. The
strike won the preferential union shop, the
8-hour day, and an elaborate set of work rules.
A joint arbitration committee was set up to ad-
just grievances and wage disputes. In the 10
years that followed, membership in the union in
San Francisco increased to over 20,000, and
wage scales were set which have remained the
highest for the country.

The Labor Management and Relations Act,
1947, otherwise known as the Taft-Hartley Act,
encouraged unions to increase organization efforts. In 1955, the union moved in on Miami
Beach. In favor of the union was the fact that
Miami Beach is one of the most intensely

8. John P. Henderson, *Labor Market Institutions and Wages
in the Lodging Industry* (East Lansing, Mich.: Michigan
State University, Bureau of Business and Economic
Research).

9. U.S. Dept. of Labor, *Employment Outlook for Hotels*,
Bulletin No. 1550-107, 1968.

10. Matthew Josephson, *Union House, Union Bar* (New
York, N.Y.: Random House, 1956).

11. Ibid.

competitive hotel areas anywhere. At the time, it had 350 hotels, with 30,000 hotel and motel rooms, on a strip of land covering only seven square miles. Hotels were being sold, resold, and often operated by men without previous experience in the industry. Also, many of the Miami Beach employees were loyal union members when they worked in their northern home cities during the off season.

The union spent over $1.5 million on the Miami Beach effort for legal fees, soup kitchens, and other strike costs.[12] The union published ads in other cities warning members that they would be subject to fine and expulsion if they took jobs in struck hotels. Recruiting efforts on lower Manhattan's employment agency row were effectively stymied by pickets placed in front of the employment agencies. Pickets also marched at Idlewild Airport where replacement employees were taken for the flight to Miami. The union was also successful in getting the three television networks—NBC, ABC, and CBS—to stop originating shows in Miami Beach as long as the labor dispute in the hotels continued. An advertising campaign was launched in the North to dissuade travelers from coming to Miami Beach at all.

In 1957, the Hotel Association, represented by only a few hotels, signed an associationwide, master contract bringing to an end the strike which had lasted twenty-one months, the longest and costliest strike in hotel history.

Prior to 1955, the Hotel and Restaurant Employees Union opposed the National Labor Relations Board in taking jurisdiction over hotels and restaurants. Then the union changed its position and favored NLRB jurisdiction. In 1959, the National Labor Relations Board supervised its first election to determine if the union was to be the bargaining representative of the employees (the Hotel Floridan in Tampa).

Restrictive Union Practices

Several restrictive practices imposed by a number of union contracts push up the cost of labor unnecessarily in hotels and restaurants. For example, a contract at the Condado Beach Hotel in San Juan, Puerto Rico, specified that the hotel may never employ fewer than 75 per-

cent of the number of employees employed at the time the contract was negotiated.

Although the unemployment rate in Puerto Rico is above 15 percent and living costs considerably below those in U.S. mainland cities, wages paid hotel employees are about the same. Labor efficiency is low, 1.5 to two employees being needed to accomplish the work done by one employee on the mainland.

Job classifications are zealously guarded by union representatives in many places. A glass washer may not wash dishes. Do not ask a bellman to clean anything, if the union contract does not permit it. A roast cook may not prepare soups, and so it goes.

The ultimate weapon in any union's arsenal, the one weapon that gives any employer or group of employers real pause, is the strike or the threat of a strike.

The union gathers muscle when other nonhotel or restaurant unions back strikes against hospitality businesses. In 1969, in a strike against Seattle restaurants, members of the Teamsters Union refused to deliver supplies.

Learner-Controlled Instruction

Programmed instruction has been developed for a number of jobs in the industry. The first sizable textbook in the hospitality business which was programmed was *Understanding Cooking*, an attempt to explain the rationale of the cooking processes and the chemistry and physics involved in those processes.[13] The book has been widely accepted by schools offering courses in food preparation and by a few food-service companies that emphasize employee training. An Anglicized version of the book was published in 1970 in London. The "Holiday Inn University" uses most of the lecture time for discussion and motivation; students are expected to learn the technical material via the programmed instruction materials provided.

The use of the programmed instruction technique is being employed for management education as well as for employee training. J. W. Bottell, a director of Fortes Holdings, Ltd., a British hotel and restaurant chain, has programmed the company's financial control sys-

12. Edwin B. Dean, "The Miami Beach Hotel Strike," *Cornell Hotel Administration Quarterly*, May, 1962.

13. D. E. Lundberg and Lendal Kotschevar, *Understanding Cooking* (Holyoke, Mass.: Marcus Printing Company, Revised 1976).

tem. The program is considered so valuable that only one copy has been printed. The program has been assembled in one large notebook and is carried personally by a representative of the home office to each of the company's hotels. At the hotel, the manager is asked to go through the program within the next two days. The program is then carried back to the home office and locked in a safe.

EMPLOYEE STOCK OWNERSHIP PLAN

The federal government has encouraged the spreading of ownership via an Employee Stock Ownership Plan (ESOP), under which a company may contribute a percentage of its earnings to a trust, which then buys stock in the company; in effect, a retirement plan funded with the employer's stock. A big appeal of the plan is that the earnings contributed by the company to the trust are not taxed. The maximum that a company can contribute each year is 15 percent of the compensation of the participants in the plan. That amount is treated as a tax deduction for the company. Since a corporation normally pays 50 or more percent of its profits in corporation taxes, the company in effect contributes nothing. The federal government subsidizes the plan. Further encouragement for such plans come since companies having them are allowed an additional 1 percent investment credit on any new investment, for example, equipment. A 10 percent investment credit is allowed any corporation. Those with ESOPs get an added 1 percent tax credit. The ESOP is designed on the assumption that employees once they are part owners of the company have added incentive to make it profitable and have a different feeling about the capitalistic system than if they are employees working for wages.

Briefly, when a company establishes an ESOP it creates a trust that borrows from outside sources to buy stock from the company at the market price. As the company pays off the loan the stock is allocated to employees in proportion to their salaries. The employee becomes a stockholder and when he leaves collects his ESOP stock from a trust fund which has been established. He receives a tax break in that he can use "forward averaging," approved by the IRS and which has the effect of spreading the income over ten years. If the

stock has appreciated it is taxed as a capital gain rather than as straight income—another tax break.

The Company itself gets an additional tax break when it establishes an ESOP. A company is allowed to claim an additional 1 percent credit for money used to pay off an ESOP loan.

Each year the company contributes to the trust that continues to buy the company stock at a price determined by outside experts or by the stock market. If the plan continues, ownership of much of the stock passes to the trust, and from the trust to the employees. The amount of stock distributed to an employee is based on a percentage of his earnings and his time with the company. The employee is "vested" in ownership at the rate of 10 percent a year. After ten years, he is fully vested and has 100 percent ownership of the stock accumulated for him by the trust.

As stock is distributed to employees —usually treasury stock—the stock of old stockholders is diluted, and eventually control of the company can pass to the employee stockholders.

The International Restaurant Supply Company of Los Angeles which introduced an ESOP program in 1973, has found it very effective in stimulating efficiency, cost control, and pride in the company.

Profits that ordinarily would have been paid to the federal government in the form of corporation taxes have been used to purchase company stock. In their experience, earnings have risen sharply since the inception of the ESOP. Ownership which had been closely held is now being shared with employees according to each employee's wage or salary and his length of service with the company. The old stockholders expect to pass control of the company to the employees, but since the old owners are also active in management, they, too, receive shares of the stock and have seen the value of their stock increase.

HOSPITALITY BUSINESS AS LABOR INTENSIVE

Obviously the hospitality business is labor intensive and as industrialized societies raise wages and salaries, the cost of service climbs. In the past industrially advanced societies have attracted less advantaged groups who are more than willing to work for relatively low wages—groups such as blacks, Mexican-Americans, and Mexicans in the United States and Middle Easterners, Italians, and Spaniards in West Germany and England. As long as these labor streams are available the costs of hospitality have been kept relatively low. This is a changing condition in the advanced nations.

Consider the fact that one or two persons are needed to service a full-service hotel room, and it is easy to see why the cost of the room has increased so fast. Add to this the fact that the cost of the room itself, the capital investment of a downtown hotel, is anywhere from $20,000 to $70,000 per room; and it is understandable why room rates climb to $50 or $60 a day.

In the restaurant business, low cost labor has been and hopefully will continue to be available in the form of young folks, teenagers and students in their twenties, who are quite ready to work at the minimum wage.

As labor costs and capital costs increase in the industrially advanced countries, vacations to those countries are likely to be shortened. Destinations where cheap labor is available increase in appeal because of low cost and the fact that the cost of transportation via air for the pleasure traveler is going down relative to other costs. It is quite possible that with the 747 being redesigned, it will be cheaper to fly 1,000 persons per plane to Portugal or Spain, Mexico or Cuba and to live more cheaply than at home. The British have been doing so for years in Spain.

THE RIGHT ROOM RATE

How to determine the room rates has been the subject of much discussion and dispute. The idea, of course, is to "optimize" profits by charging a rate that will bring the most profit but is not high enough to discourage the guest from coming or returning in the future. The starting point is to settle on a rate which will cover all costs and still provide a reasonable profit. Once this figure has been determined, the rate can be increased as much "as the traffic will bear," without antagonizing or driving off the guest.

In computing the room rates for a seasonal operation, it must be remembered that about three-fourths of the total revenue of the resort is usually taken in during the peak season which may last only three or four months. The high season rates must be set accordingly.

Rates Based on Projection of Expenses and Anticipated Profit

One way to determine a room rate is to work backwards: find the total revenue that is needed to break even; add the profit that is expected, and divide by the number of rooms that will be sold in the upcoming year. The Hubbart Formula, developed by the two national accounting firms and named in honor of Roy Hubbart of Chicago, who was the major proponent of the plan, is the best known plan for arriving at a room rate.[14]

It is a formula for estimating the number of rooms that will be sold in the coming year. This number is divided into the amount of money that will be needed for the total operating expenses plus a fair profit. The resulting figure is the room rate that is needed to meet expenses and to make the profit.

As an example, suppose that in a 100-room house the total income needed for expenses and profit is $200,000. On a predicted occupancy of 70 percent, the number of rooms that will be sold in the year is 25,550. Suppose the house costs $2 million and that the owner expects to make 15 percent profit on the investment, or $300,000. The owner needs to take in $700,000 in the course of the year to meet his costs and to make his profit. Dividing $700,000 by 25,550 gives him an average room rate of about $27.40.

Recognizing that other factors may be more important than a mathematical computation, the computation is still worthwhile as a guide.

At one time, much attention was paid to developing a proper room mix, the right number of singles, doubles, twins, and suites, that would make it possible to offer a range of room sizes, quality of furnishings, and rates to the hotel guest. It has been found that in the usual transient hotel the suites are the last rooms to be sold. Suites also return the least revenue per square foot.

In convention hotels, however, suites are usually in demand by companies wishing to use

14. *The Hubbart Formula,* American Hotel and Motel Association.

them as hospitality suites. The newer convention hotels have a number of suites with rates starting at about $100 a day.

The motels offer a one-size room with two double beds and have demonstrated the value of such an arrangement. Unless a motor hotel is certain that its market will be largely for the single traveling man, most of the rooms will be doubles. A double room can be rented at a single rate to the single traveler and is also available for the couple or for the family.

Rate Cutting

The inclination of the motel or hotel owner when business is slow is to reduce room rates. Mom and Pop in their motel feel that any business is better than no business. "There's no business like slow business." A sign goes up outside the motel, "$10 or $12 Monday through Thursday," or some other rate cut. Resorts have always cut rates drastically during their off-season, and transient hotels have a number of special rates: for groups, for commercial men, for students, weekend packages, and so on.

No less a person than Ernest Henderson believed that reducing rates was one way to increase occupancy. In the early 1960s he did just that for all the Sheraton Hotels. Some of the less desirable hotels and blocks of rooms in some of the better Sheraton Hotels were labeled "Sherwyn," and their rates were drastically reduced. He reasoned that by increasing total occupancy the extra profits from increased food and beverage sales would more than compensate for the loss in rates. Later, Sheraton rates were quietly increased.

The accountants have likened the results of rate cutting to the wages of sin and can draw up charts to prove it. For example, if a motel or hotel owner has a 60 percent occupancy at a $10 rate and decides to reduce his rate to $8, his occupancy would have to increase to 81.8 percent to make up for the $2 loss in rate. The charts do not consider the effect of increased food and beverage sales. Another example: if a house has a present occupancy of 70 percent and the rate is reduced by 20 percent, occupancy would have to increase to 95.5 percent to equal the same room revenue as received at the former rate. The accountants may make believers out of the big hotelmen, but it is doubtful if their charts have much effect on the small operator who would rather see something than nothing. A hotel or motel is very quiet without guests.

For a theoretical discussion of supply and demand as related to hotel sales, see chapter 9 of *The Art and Science of Modern Innkeeping.*[15]

The $1 per $1,000 Rule

A rule of thumb for determining room rates which has been in existence for a number of years is that $1 should be charged for each $1,000 invested per room. If a 100-room hotel costs $1 million, the cost per room is $10,000 —and the room rate necessary for a fair return on the investment would be $10.

The usual Holiday Inn Motel costs $12,000 to $20,000 a unit, so the rate based on this formula would be $12 to $20. Of course, the actual rate is much higher. So much the better for the owner if he can get the rate. The dollar per thousand rule of thumb would be difficult to apply in the case of the Mauna Kea Hotel, which is said to have cost $100,000 per room. The room rate would have to be $100 per day.

Calculation of the $1 rate per $1,000 building cost assumes a 70 percent occupancy over the life of the hotel and management good enough to show a 55 percent house profit on room sales. House profit is defined as all profits except income from store rentals, and before deduction of insurance, real estate taxes, depreciation, and other capital expenses. It assumes that store rentals are enough to offset real estate taxes and interest charges on the land. Calculation further assumes that the hotel will show a 6 percent return on the total investment.

The average rate being discussed is not the rate advertised by the hotel. Average rate includes double occupancy. As percentage of occupancy increases, so does the average rate. Less expensive rooms sell first and as they are sold out, higher priced rooms are sold, raising the average rate.

By the 1970s, hotel costs—at least in the big city downtown areas—had risen to the extent that the $1 per $1,000 rule no longer ap-

---

15. Jerome J. Vallen, *The Art and Science of Modern Innkeeping* (Rochelle Park, N.J.: Ahrens Publishing Company, 1968).

plied. When the hotel room cost from $40,000 and up to construct, it was impossible to charge the $40 or more average room rate. A profitable room rate depended upon a number of factors: contributions from sub-rentals, the assumption that the food and beverage operations would be profitable (and many were), and the cost of money used to construct them. Several of the large city hotels built in the middle-1970s were part of the urban redevelopment plans of various cities, and the developers were able to secure money at less than the going rate through the Economic Development Administration from the cities involved and elsewhere. In some cases, the land cost them nothing: feasibility studies and the determination of a room rate had to be tailored to the particular property, and the $1 per $1,000 rule of thumb was not relevant. That rule probably still applied to the motor hotels, which could still be constructed at somewhat reasonable cost on the outskirts of cities and towns.

In the last analysis the room rate is what the market will bear, a combination of a number of factors, including general economic conditions, competitive rates, and what is necessary to sustain an acceptable rate of return. If a property continues to lose, the owner has the choice of upgrading, selling, or in a few cases changing the product or seeking a different market.

The rule of thumb of trying to attain a room rate of $1 per $1,000 invested has been modified to include the cost of land, building, and equipment; and a return of 10 percent on invested capital has been selected as a minimum goal by the firm of Laventhol and Horwath.[16]

A rule of thumb is only a rule of thumb since occupancy rate and the ratio of food and beverage sales to room sales vary widely from one hotel to another. Generally speaking, the greater the ratio of restaurant sales to room sales the higher the occupancy or room rate needed to achieve a desirable return on the investment. The reason for this is that food and beverage sales do not produce the high percentage of profit generated by room sales.

Room Rates Up

Room rates, like taxes, have a history of going up and will probably continue to do so. The average room rate has increased year after year since 1936. In that year the average room rate was $3.03; by 1940 it had increased to $3.29; in 1945 it was $4.00; in 1950, $5.71. Rate increases have occurred month after month until, by 1978, the average room rate as reported by Harris, Kerr, and Forster was $31.83.

The traveler may well ask, "Where can I find a $20.00 room?" Certainly not in the major cities or in the leading hotels. In the new budget motels, yes. Rates are much higher in the convention cities of the north, lower in the south and in the small towns. The lowest rate for a single person at the Plaza Hotel in New York City is $50.00, and the average rate for the "name" or expense-account hotel is probably well over $50.00 for a single person. Many resort hotels have even higher rates but usually include some meals and services in the rate. The rate for two persons at the beautiful Rockresorts, Dorado Beach in Puerto Rico and the Caneel Bay Plantation on St. Thomas, U.S. Virgin Islands, was $150 per day in 1978.

The so-called budget motel appeared on the American highway in 1962. Arbitrarily defined as a fairly new property which has room rates 30 to 50 percent lower than the established nation-wide chains—and part of a chain organization, it is either a franchise or owned by a chain.[17] The definition excludes older or less expensive independents that have low rates because of obsolescence. Growth of the budget motel was slow until about 1970 when it mushroomed across the southern United States, so that by 1974 more than 65,000 rooms existed in such chains as Motel 6, Days Inns, Scottish Inns of America, and Econo-Motor Hotels.[18] The first of such chains, Motel 6, was started in Santa Barbara, is now a subsidiary of City Investment, Inc. of New York City, and is headquartered in Los Angeles.

What starts out to be a spartan, limited operation often is added to with time. The hamburger chains of the 1960s began to add sand-

---

16. "An Updated Formula for Rating Guest Rooms," Lodging, January 1977.

17. Hart and Erickson, "Economy Motels—Threat or Opportunity?" The Cornell Hotel and Restaurant Administration Quarterly, November 1973.

18. H. Robert Rosenbrough, "A Prospectus on Budget Motels," The Cornell Hotel and Restaurant Administration Quarterly, November 1973.

wiches, and the budget inns began to add conveniences and facilities in the 1970s. Days Inns of America, Inc., Atlanta, now offer gasoline stations, a restaurant, gift shop, swimming pool, children's playground, and coin-operated laundries. Of some 250 properties in 1976, 90 percent contained a Tasty World Restaurant, offering a low-priced menu made up of items pre-portioned and vacuum-packed. Purchases are made company-wide and on future contracts, signed months in advance.

The budget properties are usually located near one of the established national chains, such as Holiday Inns, Ramada Inns, or Howard Johnsons, where the budget property attracts the price-sensitive traveler. The lower room rate is possible because of lower construction costs, and in some cases the complete absence of public space and restaurants, and a minimum of land and landscaping. Management is often a man and wife team, the husband having retired from the military or other business in many cases. Management salary is usually supplemented by a bonus plan.

The rooms are quite adequate and well-furnished in most cases. Carpeting is likely to be shag rug; there is pay television and sometimes a small pool to attract the family trade. Most of the chains are regional in character and have not developed the more costly reservation systems using computers.

Typically, 10 percent of the motel investment is in the land. Television is leased. Cost of furniture, fixtures, and equipment runs from $750 to $1,000 per room. Modular or prefabricated construction techniques are often used in building the motel, and most of the rooms are slightly smaller than the typical new hotel room of the national chains. Using the modular construction permits quick entry into a market and avoids the cost of interim financing. Total investment is said to be between $7,000 and $12,000 per room, up to 20 percent higher in the Northeast than in the South and Southeast because of the need in the North for interior corridors and additional insulation. Savings and loan associations have provided most of the long-term financing for budget motels.

Occupancy rates up to 1976 ran considerably higher than the conventional motel and, because of the absence of services, operating expenses were lower.

There is little doubt that the budget motel has intruded upon the established motor hotel and motel scene and will force a leveling or even decrease in room rates in those areas where there are a number of budget properties. One national motel chain has tried to hold rates in the face of economy motel competition by offering a family rate for the price of a double room.

Special Rates

The price-insensitive traveler prefers the established multiple-serviced motor hotel or motel and is not concerned with the room rate. The same person, though, traveling at his own expense, will often pick a budget property, especially if it is new, clean, and reputable. It is interesting to note the number of expensive automobiles, including Cadillacs, parked in the budget motel parking lot.

The international chains—mostly air line-owned have also found it necessary to provide less expensive rooms. Room rates in such cities as Tokyo, Paris, and London skyrocketed during the early 1970s and even the affluent traveler began cutting back his travel plans or changed to a less expensive destination.

Inter-Continental Hotels introduced their version of a budget hotel—Forum Hotels: self-service is emphasized with vending machines on each floor, buffet breakfasts, and self-service restaurants. Registration and baggage handling is expected to be automated.

European Hotel Corporation—owned by Alitalia, British Airways, Lufthansa, Swissair, and TAP—is a similar chain of moderately-priced hotels called Pentas. Room rates of about 30 percent less than that of first-class international are made possible by the absence of bellmen, automated room service, and other cost-cutting practices.

The commercial rate—a reduced rate for regular guests—started sometime before 1915. The traveling man, usually a salesman—more commonly called a drummer—began asking for the lower rate and usually got one a little lower than was charged the few tourists or other travelers who were in the hotel. The idea prevailed, and still does, that the commercial man, since he is a regular patron of the hotel, is entitled to a lower rate than the occasional visitor. Later, during the great depression, many hotels permitted the commercial man to bring his wife along at no extra charge. As is the case with the family plan presently in vogue, cries of "rate-cutting" were heard by those hotelmen not engaging in the practice.

Hotels in resort areas that cater to both commercial men and vacationers have a real problem of separating the sheep from the goats. The goats are those experienced travelers who ask for the commercial rate while traveling as tourists during the peak seasons. Arthur Feenan, manager of The Columbus Hotel in Miami, solved the problem by requiring the person asking for the special rate to have stayed in the hotel at least 3 times during the off-season.

When the motel first appeared, the practice was to rent the room at a price regardless of the number of people who occupied it. Hotels characteristically rented a room on the basis of the number of people occupying it. The so-called family rate was so popular in the motel that eventually most hotels began offering special rates for family groups. The hotel is more likely to charge a double rate for each room occupied, adding a small charge for setting up roll-away beds.

It is also customary to offer reduced rates to groups and to provide a certain percentage of the rooms on a complimentary basis. Such "comp" rooms are usually occupied by the executive secretary of the group and some of the officers. Seasonal resorts have an off-season rate that may be only half or less than half of the high-season rate.

Hilton, Sheraton, and a number of other chains offer reduced rates to students and faculty and on many campuses employ a student representative to publicize the availability of such rates. The Sheraton-Student-Faculty Plan, for example, allows a slight reduction to faculty, administrative personnel, athletic teams, and students during the summer, weekends, and the low period between December 15 and January 1.

Package plan rates, which usually include transportation and lodging, and sometimes meals, are likely to be arranged by a travel agent in cooperation with an airline and hotel or a group of hotels. The rate often is the same as the guest would pay if he had no package plan, but the guest does not know this.

Guaranteed Maximum Rate Plan

Rates for hotel rooms listed in the *Hotel Red Book* range from low to high. But how many rooms are available at the minimum rate? Often, the minimum rate room is an oversized broom closet located next to the elevators or in some other unlikely spot.

One of the biggest headaches of innkeeping is to maximize room sales without "going overboard." Going overboard is selling more rooms than are available in the house. The operator wants to get as close to 100 percent occupancy as possible, and when hotel rooms are in short supply, hotels have operated at 100 plus occupancy, beds being turned over more than once in a twenty-four-hour period. Consequently, the typical hotel manager is likely to take more reservations than he has space, anticipating that a certain percentage of the people reserving will be "no-shows."

Many regular travelers, aware of the problem of overbooking, reserve at more than one hotel to be certain of getting into at least one of their choices. Certain reservations are less likely to show than others, for example, MDs are an unsure bet. Weather plays a part. But what happens when a guest with a confirmed reservation appears and has no room at the inn? Quite naturally, the guest is furious; one sure reaction is ill will toward the house.

Various systems have been devised to take care of this emergency. The usual policy is to arrange to get the confirmed guest to another hostelry. Some companies pay his cab fare to the other hotel. The Sheraton, for a long time, issued the guest a certificate worth $20 in any Sheraton property.

To assure the guest that he will receive the rate which he requested, several chains have established a Guaranteed Maximum Rate Plan. This program guarantees business travelers who qualify a preset maximum rate for accommodations. TraveLodge, for example, has such a plan in effect for more than 1,000 companies.

A flurry of complaints published in the press in the middle 1970s, coming from consumer groups, placed greater emphasis on taking care of the guest with a reservation who appears and finds no room available. Holiday Inns assure such people that if 6 P.M. reservations are not honored the Inn must secure comparable accommodations, pay any difference in room rate, pay for transportation to the substitute property, and pay for phone calls to family or business to notify them of the change. If the guest has a guaranteed all-night reservation and there is no room, the Inn also pays the full cost of the first night's lodging. The guest must cancel by 6 P.M. to avoid being billed through his or her credit card companies. Those Inns which require advance deposits but accept guaranteed reservations by credit card in lieu of a deposit require seventy-two-hour cancellation notice. Quality Inns International has a similar plan. When a guaranteed reservation is not honored, the Inn must provide and pay for an alternate room elsewhere, pick up the transportation costs to the new location, and pay for one phone call.

When the traveler guarantees his room through a credit card and does not show, the credit card company pays the hotel for the first night's lodging regardless of whether or not the guest recognizes his responsibility to pay.

THE BREAK-EVEN POINT

Every hotel and motel has a break-even point, the percentage of occupancy necessary to pay all operating expenses including interest on indebtedness. Since the national average on occupancy for hotels and motels is between 60 and 70 percent, the break-even point for the average hotel and motel is obviously lower than 60 percent. The break-even point, of course, changes with wage rates, efficiency of operation, and rise in costs. It also changes with the room rates charged.

A 100-unit motel might have a break-even point as computed here:

Total operating expense	$120,000
Real estate taxes	15,000
Insurance	3,000
Depreciation	20,000
Interest	27,000
Total annual expenses	$185,000
Total daily expenses = $185,000 ÷ 365 days =	$506.85

In other words, the motel must take in $506.85 each day to break even. If the motel's average room rate is $10, it must sell at least fifty rooms a day to break even. Its break-even point is 50 percent. The illustration does not consider the food and beverage operation and other revenue departments.

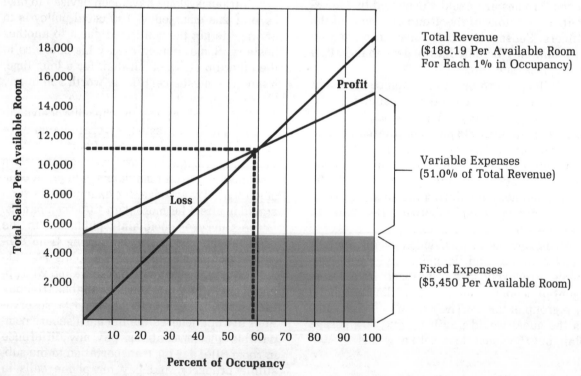

Figure 4–4   Break-Even Analysis of All Hotels and Motels.
Source: US Lodging Industry, 1977, Laventhol and Horwath.

The break-even point is that point at which the income covers both fixed and variable expenses, where no profit is made. Break-even points are difficult to compute, but the concept is valuable. According to the firm of Laventhol and Horwath, the break-even point in 1976 for all hotels and motels in their nationwide sample was a room occupancy of 59.1 percent. The break-even analysis chart for the hotels and motels in the Laventhol and Horwath sample shows that the fixed expenses for that year for the median hotel or motel was $5,450 per available room. In other words the usual hotel or motel in this country for the year 1975 had some $5,500 in expenses, which were fixed for each room, regardless of occupancy level. Total revenue was $188.19 per available room for each 1 percent in occupancy. Variable expenses amount to 51 percent of total revenue. The chart shows that a little over $10,000 in sales were needed per available room per year just to break-even.

The break-even point analysis is a graphic way of pointing up the fact that once the break-even point is reached profit rises sharply (the distance between total revenue line and the line representing fixed and variable expenses). In the chart, for example, on a 60.5 percent occupancy there is no profit; but at 100 percent occupancy the profit per available room would rise to almost $4,000 a room.[19]

HOTEL MONOPOLY

Can a hotel or group of hotels develop a monopoly and fix prices? A large majority of people staying in first-class hotels are expense-account travelers, many with unlimited expense accounts as regards hotel bills. Such people will not go to any great effort to stay outside of the area, nor will they stop at a less desirable class of hotel.

Monopoly in the classical sense is not possible in the hotel business over a wide area because of the relative ease of entry into the business by individual corporations. Within a city or small area, and among first-class hotels, however, monopoly or oligopoly (an industry characterized by few sellers) would be possible. In the country as a whole, Thomas Powers has pointed out, only 2 percent of the

properties and 4 percent of the rooms are controlled by the eight largest chains.[20] However, in local markets, chains control a very sizable portion of the market. Chains may also have competitive advantages not possessed by independent or smaller operations in their reservation systems, credit arrangements, national advertising programs, and extensive guest services.

According to Horwath and Horwath, "When hotel guests start to economize, first they reduce the amount they spend for cocktails and other alcoholic beverages, then they begin spending less for meals, and their last step is to take more moderately-priced rooms than in the recent past."[21] In effect, if there is a shortage of hotel rooms within a particular trade area, a group of first-class hotels could exercise a limited monopoly. People who are not on expense accounts or unlimited expense accounts—or those who are naturally frugal or parsimonious—will not be affected by the monopoly. They simply stay outside of town or in less expensive hotels or motels.

Indeed hotels have been convicted of price fixing. In 1977 four hotel companies and the Hawaii Hotel Association pleaded "No Contest" to criminal charges of conspiring to fix Hawaii hotel room rates. The Sheraton Hawaii Corporation and the Hilton Hotel Corporation were each fined the maximum $50,000. Cinerama Hawaii Hotels and Flagship International were each fined $25,000, and the Hotel Association was fined $10,000. The price fixing took place during 1971–1972 when visitor totals to Hawaii dropped and many new hotels had opened. Room rates had been cut to below breakeven points, while tour operators and travel agents had pitted hotels against each other and had obtained net room rates that were often 15 percent below rack rates (and lower) for groups. The hotel operators felt some kind of price fixing necessary to survive.[22]

CORRELATES WITH HOTEL/MOTEL DEMAND

An analysis of Input-Output Tables prepared for the U.S. Department of Commerce by W. L.

19. Laventhol and Horwath, The U.S. Lodging Industry, 1976.

20. Thomas F. Powers, "The Competitive Structure of the Hotel/Motel Market," paper presented to the Council on Hotel, Restaurant, and Institutional Education, 1969.

21. The Accountant, LKH&H, Vol. 42, No. 11, 1962.

22. Travel Weekly, May 1977.

Sommer, a member of Laventhal and Horwath, showed that the demand for overnight accommodations by tourist and vacationers tends to follow changes in the employment picture. Business travel, on the other hand, seems to be most sensitive to changes in new construction, wholesale trade, food processing, retail trade, and finance and insurance. The table below is taken from the report and ranks these five sectors of the economy as they affect lodging demand. The table also ranks them as a purchaser of lodging services. In first place as a purchaser of lodging services is wholesale trade. This is followed by finance and insurance, miscellaneous professional services, new construction, and retail trade.

As a stimulator of lodging demand, new construction is number one followed by wholesale trade.[23]

_____
23. William L. Sommer, "The Lodging Industry: On the Road to Recovery," _L & H Perspective,_ Spring/Summer, 1977.

THE LODGING DOLLAR, INCOME AND OUTGO

Each year two international accounting firms, Laventhol, Horwath and the firm of Harris, Kerr, Forster, publish an annual survey of the financial results of the lodging business in the United States, providing the most reliable financial statistics for the industry for the preceding year. These studies have been conducted for many years and give a running account of the financial health of the business. Data are collected from the client hotels and motels of the two companies. Therefore, they do not represent the entire industry and are probably biased in favor of the more successful enterprises. The chart below shows the source of the lodging income and the manner in which most of it was spent. The percentage of income produced by each department is shown below:

Guest room rentals	56.4
Food sales	26.5
Beverage sales	11.2

Where It Came From*

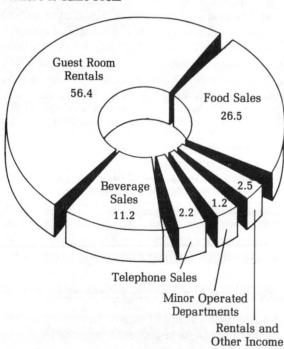

Where It Went*

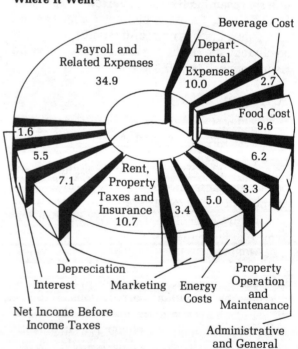

Based on the arithmetic mean; expressed as percentages.

Figure 4–5   The United States Lodging Industry Dollar.
Source: US Lodging Industry, 1977, Laventhol and Horwath, Philadelphia, PA.

Rentals and other income	2.5
Telephone sales	2.2
Minor operated departments	1.2

For the typical property, then, food and beverage sales constituted about 38 percent of the total income; the other departments contributed about 6 percent of the income. Of course, any individual hotel may have a widely different breakdown of income.

Percentages of the income dollar that were spent by each department were as follows:

Payroll and related expense	34.9
Rent, property, taxes and insurance	10.7
Departmental expenses	10
Food costs	9.6
Depreciation	7.1
Administrative and general	6.2
Interest	5.5
Energy	5
Marketing	3.4
Property operation and maintenance	3.3
Beverage cost	2.7

With these costs net income before taxes was only 1.6 percent of sales.

According to the accountants then, net income before income taxes constituted only 1.6 percent of revenue. It should be remembered that the depreciation, 7.1 percent of the income, was part of the cash flow. Energy costs have almost doubled since about 1972. Marketing costs, constituting 3.4 percent of the income, would be more representative of the larger property than of the smaller one.

The fact that the depreciation rate is 7.1 percent suggests that most hotels are being depreciated as quickly as possible. If the average hotel took a depreciation of 7.1 percent of its total income, the property would be completely depreciated in about fourteen years. At that time or before, the property would probably change hands so that a new owner could start with a new tax base of 100 percent of the market value of the property.

NEW MANAGEMENT AND PLANNING TECHNIQUES

An emphasis on "management style" is finding its way into the hotel and restaurant field. The style of management refers to the way management acts in motivating people. In the past, the style of management in a hotel and restaurant business has been, to a large extent, autocratic.

The manager presumably knows what should be done, how it should be done, and when. He does not hesitate to tell all concerned exactly when and how things should be done. Planning presumably is done only at the top. The boss orders; employees obey. The system works well if the employee is conditioned by his upbringing and temperament to respond to an autocrat. Many of the most successful restaurants and hotels in the world are run largely by an autocratic style of management.

The new style of management, labeled "participative management," involves much more two-way communication between boss and employee. Management is by objective, objectives that presumably are at least partly arrived at jointly by boss and employee. Participative management, however, is not democratic management. The boss must retain the full burden of responsibility for final results. He is not outvoted by the employees in his group. He involves most employees in problems and in goal-setting. But his is the final determination and the responsibility for profit.

Participative management lends itself to team building where the emphasis is on change, challenge, and group goals. Saga Food Administration, for example, asks each of its unit managers to spend at least an hour each week in group meetings with employees developing team feeling. Participative management conceivably can change the nature of innkeeping for the better.

Recently some hotel and restaurant companies have adopted advanced management training methods and policies. Management by objective, or management by results, is a management system being used by Sonesta. Under this plan each supervisor and his superior independently establish, in writing, goals for the next six months. They then meet and together determine the six-month goals for the department. At the end of the six months, the supervisor is asked to itemize—again in writing—what he thinks his work achievements have been for the previous period. The list is sent to his superior who adds any achievements to the list that the supervisor may have overlooked. The superior at this time assesses the quality of performance by the supervisor. This, too, is placed in writing and given to the supervisor to read.[24]

Sonesta has also developed an interesting management team approach to opening new properties. The team, the six to ten people involved in the opening, go off to a relaxed setting for a two- or three-day session that is led by a skilled consultant. The general manager of the new property and all department heads are asked to describe the assigned role in the new hotel as it appears to the individual. They state their broad areas of responsibility and authority and agree on who is responsible for what. After the opening of the property, follow-up meetings are held to check results and to review the various commitments made at the first meeting. With change taking place at an unprecedented rate, a growing number of companies in the hospitality business are becoming involved in strategic planning (also known as long-range planning).

Typically, companies engaging in long-range planning develop a strategy covering a five-year period. The main purposes of such a plan are to specify the overall objectives of the company, to establish the main courses of action that the company will take to achieve these objectives, and to determine the resource requirements necessary for these courses of action. A five-year horizon (as opposed to four or six years) is commonly used because many security analysts request financial information pertaining to this particular time frame.

These companies also develop short-range plans covering one- and two-year horizons. The one-year plan outlines specific tactics to be carried out during the year and summarizes anticipated financial results. A two-year plan is necessary in some cases because of the eighteen- to twenty-four-month lead time associated with the real estate and construction activities of restaurant and lodging operations. As presented by James Crownover, long-range planner for Saga, the strategic planning process consists of five major steps:[25]

24. See Lundberg and Armatas, *Management of People in Hotels, Restaurants and Clubs* (Dubuque, Iowa: William C. Brown, 1979).

25. Much of this section is based on a lecture presented by James Crownover, at California State Polytechnic University, 1976.

1 Establishing a business definition
2 Setting long-range objectives
3 Diagnosing current company operations
4 Developing strategies for meeting long-range objectives
5 Determining implications of strategies:
   a. Financial resources
   b. Top management resources
   c. Organizational structure

THE BUSINESS DEFINITION

A hotel, restaurant, or foodservice company should be able to state in one sentence the overall purpose of the company. The statement should describe the services or products to be provided and the customer group or groups to be served with these services or products.

Establishing a business definition is particularly important because it provides a foundation upon which the corporate strategy is based. The business definition should not be overly narrow: everyone is familiar with the example of the railroads defining themselves as being in the railroad business rather than the transportation business. Nor should the definition be so broad that it fails to give the company proper direction in identifying and evaluating alternative strategies.

Examples of business definitions mentioned during the the symposium were:

1 "Providing food and feeding services to people who eat away from home"
2 "Providing medium-priced, relatively speedy foodservice to the traveling public on major highways in or near cities of populations of at least 100,000"
3 "Operating major hotels that serve business people and high income travelers in major capitals around the world"

The business definition can be modified if circumstances change dramatically inside or outside the company, but should not be changed on a year-to-year basis.

More on long-range planning is covered in the last part of the chapter on restaurant operations.

Room Sales Terminology

Like all specialized businesses, the hotel and motel business has coined a number of words and terms peculiar to the business. Among those terms dealing with room rates are the following:

AP (Full American Plan): rate includes three full meals and rooms (full board or full pension).

Bermuda Plan: rate includes room with full American-style breakfast.

Commercial Rate: rate agreed upon by company and hotel for all individual room reservations. Often given to any regular guests who are known to be commercial travelers.

Comp: complimentary, no charges for room.

Confirmed Reservation: an oral or written confirmation by hotel that a reservation has been accepted (written confirmations are preferred). There is usually a 6:00 P.M. (local time) check-in deadline. If guest arrives after 6:00 P.M. and the hotel is filled, the assistant manager makes every effort to secure accommodations in another hotel. (This does not apply to guests with confirmed reservations where "late arrival" has been specified.)

Cut-off Date: designated day when buyer (upon request) must release or add to function room or bedroom commitment. On certain types of groups, rooming lists should be sent to the hotel at least two weeks prior to arrival.

Day Rate: usually one-half regular rate of room, for use by guests during a given day up to 5:00 P.M. Sometimes called a "use rate."

Demi-Pension (European Usage): rate includes room, breakfast and either lunch or dinner.

Deposit Reservation: a reservation for which hotel has received cash payment for at least first night's lodging in advance and is obligated to hold the room regardless of the guest's arrival time. Guest is preregistered.

Cancellation Procedure: can be cancelled as early as possible but a minimum of 48 hours prior to scheduled date of arrival in a commercial-type hotel. For resort hotels, guests should verify cancellation policy at time of making reservations.

EP (European Plan): no meals included in room rate.

Farm-Out (Walk): sending guests who have reservations that cannot be honored to other hotels with vacancies. This is done when there are no rooms available even though guests have reservations.

Flat Rate: specified room rate for group, agreed upon by hotel and group in advance.

Full Comp: no charges for anything taken in hotel including room, meals, telephone, and valet.

Guaranteed Payment Reservation: room set aside by hotel, at request of the customer; payment for room is guaranteed regardless of whether the guest appears unless reservation is properly cancelled.

Guaranteed Reservation: a confirmed reservation with the promise to accommodate, or, if unable, to pay for a room elsewhere, including transportation involved. Guest guarantees to pay if a no-show.

MAP (Modified American Plan): rate includes breakfast, dinner, and room.

Preregistered: no delay check-in, usually provided guests who have stayed in hotel previously; often room assignments based on guest's previous preference.

Rack Rate: current rate charge for each accommodation as established by hotel management.

Run of the House Rate: an agreed-upon rate generally priced at an average figure between minimum and maximum for group accommodations for all available rooms except suites; room assignments usually made on a "best available" basis.

SOURCE: *The Professional Housekeeper,* Georgina Tucker and Madelin Schneider (Boston: Cahners Books, 1975).

Questions

1 About how many employees do you expect would be needed in a 100-room motor inn without a restaurant?

2 Hotels-motels are often built and operated by the same individual or group. Name three other ways in which a hotel or motel is operated.

3 The large hotel chains today favor which means of operation—ownership, management contract, or franchise? Explain why.

4 The principal owners of the very large hotels in this country turn out to be members of what business?

5 Around the turn of the century the Ritz hotels were highly fashionable in several parts of the world. Were they all owned and operated by the Ritz Company or was there some other arrangement?

6 Be able to name two advantages to the franchisor and two advantages to the franchisee of a franchise arrangement.

7 Name at least two disadvantages for the franchisee and two for the franchisor.

8 By far the largest franchisor of accommodations in the world turns out to be what company?

9 Besides the Holiday Inns franchise arrangement, what other well-known franchises are available in the hotel or motel business?

10 The larger hotel or motel, something over 300 rooms, that installs EDP equipment would probably first put it to use in what two areas of operation?

11 In reservation systems, a cathode ray tube is often used in what way?

12 Explain a room status system and its advantages for a large hotel.

13 In a large hotel catering to businessmen large numbers of guests want to be awakened at 7 A.M., how can this be done without a large number of hotel personnel being used?

14 In larger hotels a sales staff of several persons are on hand largely to solicit group business. What other functions do they perform?

15 Be able to define these commonly used terms dealing with room sales: Rack rate, MAP, AP, EP, Commercial Rate, Full Comp.

16 Increased vigilance to insure guests' safety stimulated a number of new security systems including the Lok-A-Wat, plastic cards for keys, beeper systems, and television monitors. Explain the function of each.

17 What is the big advantage of hiring off-duty regular policemen as security personnel in a hotel?

18 Who are likely to be the three highest paid persons in a large hotel?

19 In some hotel chains the auditor or financial officer in each hotel does not report to the general manager of that hotel. Why?

20 About what percentage of hotel employees in major cities are black; in New York City what percentage are Puerto Ricans?

21 What is the name of the most prominent union that deals with hotel employees in the hotel and restaurant business? It is headquartered in what city?

22 What advantages are there for a hotel proprietor to establish an Employee Stock Ownership Plan?

23 As employee costs rise in the hotel and restaurant business what effect does this have on tourism in the less developed countries?

24 In establishing a room rate, the Hubbart Formula factors into the formula all the operating costs, other costs, and also one other important factor. What is that other factor?

25 An old rule of thumb for establishing a room rate is the $1.00 per $1,000 rule. Based on this rule a hotel that has cost $40,000 per room to build would charge an average rate of what amount?

26 The dollar per thousand rule of thumb for deriving a room rate can be modified in the light of certain operating experience. Name some.

27 In the light of experience over the past fifty years, what is the outlook for room rates, up, down, or sideways?

28 Besides the rack rate, hotels offer a number of other rates. Name a few of them.

29 When a guest is "walked," sent to another hotel because of no vacancy, some hotel chains are providing the guest with what to minimize the resentment?

30 How would you explain the meaning of the "break-even point" for a hotel?

31 Is it possible, or has it ever happened, that a group of hotels have exercised hotel monopoly? Explain.

32 Which sector of the economy is most closely tuned to hotel occupancy, whole-sale trade, food processing, retail trade, or finance and insurance?

33 What ranks right after guest room rentals as the source of hotel income?

34 The principal cost in operating a hotel turns out to be what?

35 If someone were to say that the net income of a hotel is at least 10 percent of sales, what would be your reply?

36 The allowance made for depreciation in a hotel runs about 7 percent of the income. Where does this 7 percent go?

37 Some of the major hotel chains are setting objectives for a long period of time. Usually the period covers about how many years?

38 Define a Budget Motel.

HOTEL FOOD AND BEVERAGE OPERATIONS

FIVE

In all except the smaller hotels and motels, food and beverage service is expected by the traveling public. For many hotel managers this service presents as much as 80 percent of the problems of managing the property. Much of the hotel's reputation centers around its food and beverage service; much of the appeal of the hotel is in decor, atmosphere and the service offered in the restaurants and lounges. F & B sales constitute 35 to 45 percent of total sales in the typical larger hotel but may exceed room revenue in some instances. F & B sales exceeded five billion dollars in hotels/motels in 1978 (hotels $3 billion; motel and motor hotels $2.4 billion). Several of the larger hotels experienced F & B income exceeding $10 million annually and the MGM Grand Hotel had F & B sales of more than $35 million.

After the housekeeping department, the food and beverage department employs the most people in the usual hotel. The department is usually headed by a food and beverage director or an executive chef. The department may be divided into restaurants and catering, the catering covering responsibility for banquet sales and service.

The tavern, predecessor of the hotel in the United States, was the center of community activity and was likely to be the only place the general public could eat away from home. Service was family-style; food, and sometimes beer or ale, were served as part of the total charge for bed and board. In the South, some of the larger taverns offered dining facilities for ladies separate from the gentlemen's dining rooms. Foodservice became definitely associated with the taverns and later with hotels so that today, by some definitions in some states, a property is not a hotel unless it offers foodservice as well as rooms to the public.

When the hotel, with its larger size, displaced the tavern, it was expected to offer foodservice, and the grander properties in the cities had several dining rooms and at least one ballroom. These "palaces of the people" were the scenes of public and civic entertainment as well as offering food and drink to the guest.

The "city ledger" was set up to account for sales to other than hotel guests, and much of the success of a larger hotel depended upon the promotional skill of the general manager in attracting food and beverage functions into his property. Ceremonial banquets quite naturally were held in the leading hotels of a community, one reason being that there were often no other suitable places to hold them. Famous hotels like the Astor and the old Waldorf-Astoria in New York City became known for their food as well as for their rooms. The hotel dining room of the usual town throughout the U.S. in the early 1900s and into the 1930s was one of the few first-class eating facilities available. Civic and fraternal clubs held their luncheon and dinner meetings in the hotels, and except for the private clubs, the hotel became the logical place to meet for entertainment and business discussion. Well-known restaurants operating independently of hotels were scarce even in the large cities.

THE RESORT BUSINESS

SIX

The vacation hotel business was originally identified with the resort hotel. The resort hotel most often was a stately, old building surrounded by broad acres of trees, or fronting on a lengthy section of beach or other natural beauty.

Name resorts like The Biltmore in Phoenix, the Boca Raton in South Florida, the Del Coronado near San Diego, the Greenbrier in West Virginia, and The Broadmoor near Colorado Springs represent the grand resort of the early part of the century. Many, including these, still flourish. They usually have broad acres, sometimes hundreds of acres, large rooms, a multitude of staff, and a bounteous table.

The vacation hotel, which encompasses the bulk of the vacation hotel business today, is more often a high rise building in an urbanized setting, a hotel found among some 400 hotels on Miami Beach, on the Strip in Las Vegas, or in crowded Waikiki. The image of the mountain or

Figure 6-1 *One of the salons of the Ritz of Paris, considered by many to be the best hotel in the world. It has no television and does little advertising. Charles Ritz, son of Cesar Ritz, says the place is not "ritzy." Rather, to its patrons, it is a place like home, a townhouse for the wealthy. It has 210 rooms, two restaurants, and three bars. Every guest room has a golden clock and is kept cozy by a wood fire.*

sea resort hotel is still around but is overlaid in color with the bright new vacation-entertainment complex: the vacation hotel.

Since World War II, business and pleasure traveling have tended to commingle. Much of the convention business takes place in the vacation hotel, in Hawaii, Las Vegas, Florida, and the Caribbean. Pleasure travel has become, or will become, bigger business than business travel.

Strangely, it was not until the middle and late 1960s that the vacation hotel business was recognized as a part of the pleasure travel business. The interlocking nature of the hotel vacation business was underscored in the 1960s when a number of oil companies and airlines bought or built hotel and restaurant chains. Pan American Airways started the pattern in 1947 by setting up International Hotels, Inc., a wholly-owned subsidiary. Until about 1960 its growth was fairly slow and restricted to Latin America and the Caribbean. Since then it has gone international, with hotels in operation in, or planned for, most of the free world.

In 1967, Trans World Airways startled the hotel world by buying Hilton International. Travel and vacationing began to be seen more clearly as two sides of the same coin. Whereas the travel agent, the hotel, and the airline had operated independently, TWA merged the three activities, selling travel and hotel space as a package. International airlines, especially, have moved into the hotel business in a big way as seen in the chart on page 39.

CONGLOMERATES BUY HOTELS

The year 1968 saw the vacation business being integrated even further when ITT bought the Sheraton Hotels, linking rent-a-car, airport parking, and the motel and hotel business together.

Another development of importance to the vacation business is the movement of some conglomerates into the hotel business. U.S. Steel, at Disney World in Florida, is building the convention complex which will eventually contain 5,000 rooms. Alcoa owns the Century-Plaza, the hotel which is part of a living-entertainment-hotel complex in Beverly Hills, Calif. MCA owns the Yosemite and Curry Company; Amfac owns the Fred Harvey Company.

In Europe several companies sell travel, carry the traveler to a destination, and accommodate him in their hotels.

The Commercial jet plane, which was introduced in the United States in 1959, brought formerly remote resort destinations to within a few hours of population centers.

Larger planes and shorter flying times made air fares less expensive. The result was that tourism surged upward in such resort areas as Hawaii, Puerto Rico, the Bahamas, and Bermuda. In 1978 about 1.9 million people visited Puerto Rico, and more than 3 million people travelled to Hawaii.

Tourism, formerly a small scale business in places such as Jamaica and the Virgin Islands, sprang to life, to be reinforced later by cruise ship visitors by the thousands. The southwest coast of Mexico, "the Mexican Riviera," developed rapidly as a resort destination. Tourism became a new major industry in such places as Portugal, Spain, the Canary Islands, and Greece.

TRAVEL ON CREDIT IS CHANGE MAKER

Air travel and travel on credit has changed the vacation business. In the past, the bulk of the airlines' market had come from the business traveler. Some airlines now report that more than 60 percent of their business is from the personal and pleasure traveler. Yet the market has a great deal of room to grow.

Whereas in 1966 only one family out of twelve had an income of $15,000 a year or more, by 1978 that was the median family income.

International tourism is said to be the second largest single item of world trade, after oil and petroleum products. Most of the international travel, however, is concentrated in Europe and North America. According to the World Tourism Organization (WTO) of the $34 billion in receipts from tourism, 90 percent of it went to fifteen countries in North America and Europe. The number of international travelers visiting Asia, Africa, and the Pacific is only about 7 percent of the total.[1]

---

1. Chib. Som N., "Measurement of Tourism," *Journal of Travel Research,* Fall, 1977, p. 22.

Estimates of travel expenditures within the United States vary widely depending upon methodology and definitions used. According to the United States Travel Data Center[2] in 1976 travelers spent $89.7 billion within the U.S., Puerto Rico, and the Virgin Islands. California alone garnered some $9.5 billion from travelers, Florida $7.2 billion, and Texas $5.3 billion. In little Rhode Island, the traveler spent $170 million and was responsible for 9,000 jobs. Nationwide travel expenditures generated some 3.6 million jobs, $20.4 billion in wages and salaries. Governments benefited handsomely with $11.7 billion in federal, state, and local tax revenues. For each dollar spent by travelers in the United States, 7.3¢ accrued to the federal government in taxes, 4.8¢ for state taxes, and .4¢ was received in local tax revenue.[3]

Who are the big vacation travelers? The people with money and those who are young enough to withstand the rigors of travel. The higher the income, the greater the propensity to travel, at least until people reach the age of sixty-five.

Travel by credit makes the whole thing easier. By 1969 there were over 300 million credit cards in the U.S., and according to the American Express Company, credit traveling is growing at a rate of 11 percent a year. In sum, more people with larger incomes are traveling by air and auto, and many of them are doing it on credit.

The vacation business is multi-dimensional, a grand mix of business in which nearly every community has a stake. *The New York Times* pointed out that more than half of our states list tourism among their top three industries. Mexico receives 40 percent of its foreign exchange income from tourists.

An amazing number of people visit the state and national parks, visits which can be considered part of the vacation business and generate millions of dollars in the sale of lodgings and in restaurants. The operation of tourist facilities within the parks is big business, sometimes under the direct operation of a governmental unit, at other times leased to a private contractor.

---

2. Travel Printout, Volume 5, #5 (Washington, D.C.: U.S. Travel Data Center, May, 1976).
3. Ibid.

THE LURE OF STATE AND NATIONAL PARKS

Visits to national parks in 1973 exceeded 215 million compared with about 33 million in 1950. Virginia ranks first in national park visits followed by Tennessee.

State parks attract other millions with New York and California leading the way in numbers of visitors to state parks. Kentucky, which has placed emphasis on increasing tourism to the state via the state park system, had over 27 million visits to their parks in 1973.

With the oil crisis in 1974, it was believed by many that travel to state and national parks would drop sharply. In 1974 there was some drop-off but in 1975 attendance at many parks jumped 50 to 60 percent.

Private campgrounds have surged since the 1960s. In 1975 there were some 800 Kampground of America campgrounds, 50 Holiday Travel Parks, 200 campgrounds in the United Safari International chain, 50 in Jellystone Parks, and 18 Ramada Camp Inns.

Another way of arriving at the magnitude of the vacation business is to examine the figures published by the various states covering the estimated visitor or tourist expenditures. The figures are suggestive only since what constitutes a tourist and the method of arriving at his expenditure varies widely from one study to another.

The tourist business is often defined to include the business traveler, as well as the pleasure traveler. The distinction between business and pleasure traveling is becoming less distinct. Much of the travel for business takes on elements of travel for pleasure. The wife may accompany the businessman on his business trip; the business trip may be extended a few days to include a vacation. Travel for business purposes is still listed as the number one reason for travel to American hotels. The Sheraton Corporation states that 71 percent of the travel to their hotels is done for business purposes, 29 percent done for pleasure. Some of the larger airlines have found that the mix is about 50–50. For purposes of this chapter, the tourist will be defined as the pleasure traveler, more specifically the person on vacation.

VULNERABILITY OF THE VACATION BUSINESS

The vacation business is particularly vulnerable to severe economic recession, but not

Figure 6-2   The Ahwahnee Hotel, Yosemite National Park, California, one of the "grand" old resort hotels.

much to minor recessions as experienced during 1972–1975. In August of 1932, during the big depression, a Michigan resort known to the author had one paying guest, and some thirty employees. In 1929 when national income was high, resort hotel receipts totaled $76,562,000. By 1932 this figure had dropped to $22,237,000.[4]

A 1969 poll, conducted by Louis Harris and Associates for *Life Magazine*, showed that when the economic pinch is on, the three areas of spending that will be cut back first are recreation, entertainment, and travel.[5] Forty-three percent of the people interviewed said that they would cut back first on recreation and entertainment. Twenty-eight percent said they would cut back on travel first.

With the recession years 1971 to 1975,

however, travel and vacation spending dropped only slightly. Longer trips were replaced by shorter ones. Travel to Europe dropped off up to 25 percent, whereas travel within the United States and to places like Canada, Mexico, and Hawaii increased.

CONCENTRATION OF RESORTS

The map on page 158 shows the concentration of resort hotel rooms within the continental United States. The map is useful in that it shows that resorts are clustered in New England, along the Jersey shore, in Florida, and the Southwest. Hawaii and Puerto Rico also have heavy concentration of resorts.

To be represented, the state must have at least 500 resort rooms, and those rooms must have been listed in *The Hotel Red Book*. In 1948 two states—New York and Florida—did 43 percent of the total seasonal hotel business. Together with New Jersey, California, and Massachusetts, they did 64 percent of the total.

4. William A. Hayes, *An Economic Analysis of the American Hotel Industry* (Dissertation, The Catholic University of America, Washington, D.C., 1952), p. 139.

5. *Life Magazine*, August 15, 1969.

Figure 6–3   Wentworth-by-the-Sea, a resort near Portsmouth, New Hampshire, is in the grand style. It opened in 1874, and various owners have spent many millions of dollars in expansion and maintenance. The Wentworth achieved international fame in 1905 when the Russians and the Japanese met there to decide the Treaty of Portsmouth. Many of the great or near-great of the world have stopped there over the years. At one time only a July to August guest season hotel, the Wentworth was restyled to take in conventions that now amount to about 60 percent of the total business. The months of July and August are still reserved for seasonal guests.

Most resort hotels have one thing in common, seasonal business. New England resorts typically open about June 20 and close on Labor Day, or soon after. Tropical and subtropical resorts have a peak season lasting from about Christmas through March and a summer season, with lower occupancies, at reduced rates.

Spring and fall are the low points (so-called "shoulder seasons") in California, Arizona, Florida, and the Caribbean. Atlantic City and the Poconos have year-round occupancy of less than 60 percent. The constant effort on the part of the resort operator is to extend his season, usually by bringing in convention groups at the beginning and the end of the seasons.

Until the 1960s, many resort operators could make a profit operating on a 90- to 110-day season. Labor and food costs were comparatively low; the fixed expenses of taxes and insurance were also comparatively low. These expenses are now high; many resorts are surrounded by towns where taxes are up. The resort operator is forced to extend his season and many have done so. October has become a popular month in the Poconos, White Sulphur Springs, and parts of New England.

RESORT MARKETS

Each resort area tends to develop a particular market or markets. New York City is a principal tourist market, and New Yorkers, by all odds, are the biggest resorters in the world. In season, perhaps 90 percent of the guests in Miami Beach are from New York and New Jersey. Long-stay New York tourists going to Jamaica in 1968 numbered over 50,000, three times more than from New Jersey and Florida (about 15,000 each). New Yorkers populate the beachfront hotels of San Juan and of most of the other Caribbean island hotels. Californians are the largest group of resorters in Hawaii, Las Vegas, and Mexico.

Figure 6–4   *Concentration of Resort Hotels in the United States.*

DIFFERENT PLACES FOR DIFFERENT PEOPLE

Obviously, travelers select destinations for different reasons such as climate, historical or cultural appeal, water sports, entertainment, and shopping facilities. The major appeal of England for Americans seems to be historical and cultural. Among a large number of travel customers of American Express to Florida, California, Mexico, Hawaii, the Bahamas, Jamaica, Puerto Rico, the Virgin Islands, and Barbados, the appeals, in descending order of importance, were:

scenic beauty

pleasant attitudes of the local people

suitable accomodations

rest and relaxation

air fare cost considerations

historical and cultural interests

cuisine

water sports

entertainment (e.g., nightlife)

shopping facilities

golfing and tennis[6]

In analyzing 230 questionnaires, which had asked respondents to rate various appeals, four basic considerations emerged: entertainment, purchase opportunities, climate for comfort, and cost. These respondents represented a definite sample of persons, a group whose annual household income was $26,000, almost half of whom were professionals, generally middle-aged, well-educated, middle-to-high income earners, many of them wealthy, and frequent vacation travelers outside the United States. Even within a group, of course, a different constellation of factors would apply. One individual selects a destination primarily because of the golf and tennis, another because he likes the local people, and another because the place offers rest and relaxation. Most people are at least somewhat influenced by air

6. Jonathan N. Goodrich, "Benefit Bundle Analysis: An Empirical Study of International Travelers" *Journal of Travel Research,* Fall, 1977.

fare cost considerations and the convenience of getting to and from the destination.

Many resorts seek to attract only a particular type of guest; others welcome just about anybody who can pay the tab. The larger resort hotels that rely on conventions may have a medical group one week and the plumbers union the next.

The manager of a resort that relies heavily on social guests is usually concerned about having a fairly homogenous guest list. He recognizes that most people enjoy being with people of their own background and social position while in a resort setting. He also recognizes that deep in the heart of most of us lies the urge to be a snob. The origin of the word "snob" explains a great deal. It comes from the Latin "sine nobilitas," a term reserved originally for students at Oxford who were "without nobility." Those without nobility, of course, would like to have it and the abbreviation of the two words, "s-nob," refers to the urge to associate with those we consider to be of a higher class and to exclude those considered to be of a lower class. Snobbery is a term to be reckoned with in the nonconvention hotel.

The terms "restricted" and "nonrestricted" have played a prominent part in the resort hotel operator's lexicon. Houses that made an effort to exclude persons of the Jewish faith were restricted; those that made no such effort were nonrestricted. Prejudice works both ways. Some resorts do not welcome gentiles. The importance of "restriction" in resort keeping has faded. Many "WASP" bastions are now open to anyone who can pay the tariff.

Whether or not a resort is predominantly Jewish or gentile affects the bar operations, the menu, and the entertainment. A few hotels maintain strictly kosher kitchens in which a great deal of effort is made to separate meat and dairy products and to insure that only kosher foods are served. In recent years, this kind of separation by religion appears to be fading, but it is still a factor in resort keeping in the resorts catering to persons from the large eastern cities.

At beach resorts, the pool is the focal point. A tan is a vital part of the experience, signal evidence that the guest has been on vacation. The tan is sought at all costs, come cold weather, sweltering sun, or sunburn. On with the lotion. Sit in the sun another hour. How else will the folks back home know you have been to Florida, or Arizona, or Nassau? The poolside is the great leveler. The isolated guest cries for friendship. Persons who in everyday life have little in common suddenly develop appreciation for each other. The pool is the body of warmth, the altar of sun worship. Here, the currents of humanity flow, revitalizing the tired, soothing anxieties, and bringing peace of mind.

VACATIONING IS A LONG-TIME URGE

The urge in man to vacation is deep-seated and expresses itself today in the weekend rush to the beach, the pell-mell trip to the mountains to ski, the ten-day junket to Miami Beach, or the European tour. Vacationing brings change, excitement, and for some, relaxation. For others, a vacation is a series of slides to show the neighbors. It may be a way of getting a prestige tan during the winter. Going to the "in place," mixing with the best people may be important. For a number of older people, it may be an escape from loneliness. For the young man or woman, it can be a flight to the mating grounds.

The urge to vacation has been around a long time. The ancient Romans who had summer villas in Herculaneum and Pompeii were vacationing when Mt. Vesuvius erupted and covered them and their towns completely in lava, hot mud, and volcanic ash. In the United States, resort history does not record just when the first resort appeared but many persons who attended the first Continental Congress of 1774 and 1775 "escaped the heat and humidity" of Philadelphia by traveling to Germantown, where they leased homes or stayed with local residents.

The first American resort advertisement, it is said, appeared as a broadside, dated May 20, 1789. It tells of the "genteel and plentiful table" of Gray's Ferry, Pennsylvania. "Guests could expect free concerts weekly and fishing tackle . . . to those who may be fond of that amusement." Transportation between Gray's Ferry and the City would be provided twice daily, announced the proprietor, by "a handsome State Waggon mounted on steel springs, with two good horses . . ."

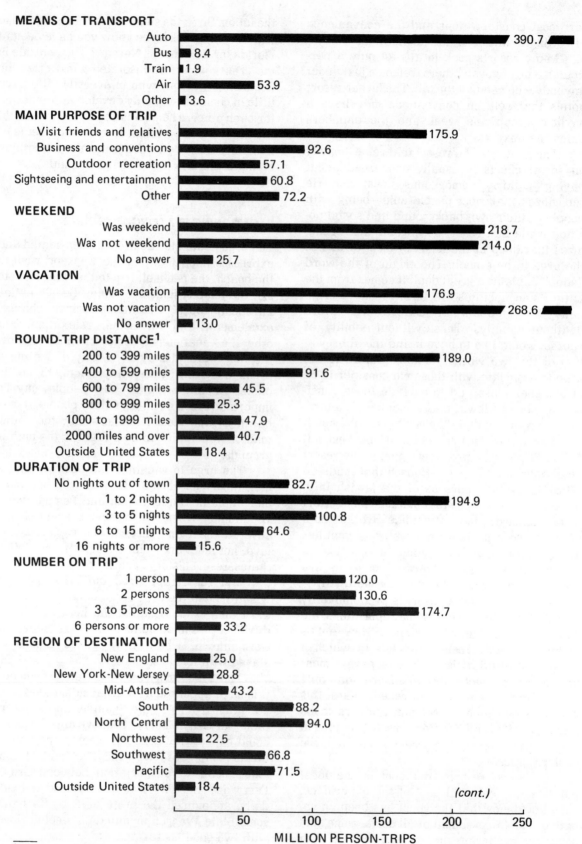

MEANS OF TRANSPORT
- Auto — 390.7
- Bus — 8.4
- Train — 1.9
- Air — 53.9
- Other — 3.6

MAIN PURPOSE OF TRIP
- Visit friends and relatives — 175.9
- Business and conventions — 92.6
- Outdoor recreation — 57.1
- Sightseeing and entertainment — 60.8
- Other — 72.2

WEEKEND
- Was weekend — 218.7
- Was not weekend — 214.0
- No answer — 25.7

VACATION
- Was vacation — 176.9
- Was not vacation — 268.6
- No answer — 13.0

ROUND-TRIP DISTANCE[1]
- 200 to 399 miles — 189.0
- 400 to 599 miles — 91.6
- 600 to 799 miles — 45.5
- 800 to 999 miles — 25.3
- 1000 to 1999 miles — 47.9
- 2000 miles and over — 40.7
- Outside United States — 18.4

DURATION OF TRIP
- No nights out of town — 82.7
- 1 to 2 nights — 194.9
- 3 to 5 nights — 100.8
- 6 to 15 nights — 64.6
- 16 nights or more — 15.6

NUMBER ON TRIP
- 1 person — 120.0
- 2 persons — 130.6
- 3 to 5 persons — 174.7
- 6 persons or more — 33.2

REGION OF DESTINATION
- New England — 25.0
- New York-New Jersey — 28.8
- Mid-Atlantic — 43.2
- South — 88.2
- North Central — 94.0
- Northwest — 22.5
- Southwest — 66.8
- Pacific — 71.5
- Outside United States — 18.4

(cont.)

50   100   150   200   250

MILLION PERSON-TRIPS

[1]Round-trip distance is route miles and includes circuitry. Miles do not include any portion of trips with destinations outside the United States.

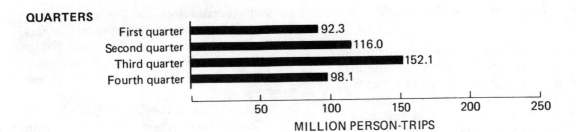

QUARTERS

First quarter   92.3
Second quarter   116.0
Third quarter   152.1
Fourth quarter   98.1

50   100   150   200   250

MILLION PERSON-TRIPS

Figure 6–5   Profiles of Travel by Trip Characteristics.
Source: National Travel Survey, *1972 Census of Transportation, Bureau of the Census.*

Resorts as vacation spots satisfy at least four basic human needs—social, recreational, health, and prestige. Different resorts have specialized in satisfying particular needs. Health and therapeutic springs were the vogue before 1850, some of them having been operated since before the Revolution. Before 1900, nearly 2,000 spas (named after a small Belgian village that has bubbling mineral springs) were attracting the health seeker in this country.

A visitor to Huntington Warm Springs, Pa. in 1775 noted that there were twenty-two persons seeking health and "barren women hoping for pregnancy." Pennsylvania had some thirty spas during this period where people went "to take the waters" and to bathe. Bathing was no small thing at the mineral springs where a bath could take all day, to the accompaniment of music, good food, and conversation. Some were quite large. A hotel accommodating 300 people was built at Fayette Springs, Pa. in 1860; a 600-guest hotel at Minnequa Springs in 1869.

At the Battle of Gettysburg, in 1863, Confederate doctors charged the Union soldiers and sympathizers with having poisoned their troops. It seems that the Confederate soldiers had partaken heavily of the mineral springs and experienced considerable intestinal disorder. The laxative powers of the springs are well known, proof enough that no germ warfare was perpetrated.

The Effect of the Railroad

The coming of the railroad was as much of a boon for the resort business as it was for the city hotel. People could travel long distances quickly and penetrate areas that formerly were relatively impassable. Where the railroad went into the mountains or other recreational areas, the resorts soon followed.

The Delaware Gap region in Pennsylvania is an example of what happened when the railroads arrived. Around the turn of the nineteenth century, summer visitors to the region braved the trip by stagecoach and canal boat and stayed in the spare rooms rented by the local residents. When the Delaware, Lackawanna, and Western railroad came in, visitors also came, in such numbers that hotels were built by the score. Today the area has about 500 hostelries of one kind or another for the summer guest.

One of the oldest tourist establishments in the Gap region, the Swiftwater Inn, took pains to reassure travelers that everything would go well with them while at the inn.

Rest ye Bones

Tickle ye Palate

and nae

Rob ye Wallet

Figure 6–6   Sign at the Swiftwater Inn.

The inscription on its sign might well serve as a motto for all good innkeepers.

Romantic Movement of the Nineteenth Century

The romantic movement of the early nineteenth century modified the Puritan tradition of utilitarianism in America. The new religion of nature, as expounded by the romanticists and abetted by Thoreau's "return to simplicity," was hardly needed to get people out of the industrial centers. "Go to the mountains," said the brochures of the time, for "deep reflections, leading to wisdom and happiness."

The Catskills became an early center of American resorting. The Catskill Mountain House opened July 4, 1823. The elite of American society began patronizing the place its very first season. By 1843 one could choose from a selection of burgundies, madeiras, French dishes, and French dances.

The Catskills, romanticized by Washington Irving as being Rip Van Winkle country, became a symbol of the American romantic movement in paintings and literature. Nature paintings by such people as Winslow Homer and Thomas Cole helped to heighten the aura of desirability of a return to nature. Before this time, Americans never thought of going to the mountains and countryside for vacations. Most of them were already there.

In the 1880s and 1890s, converted farmhouses allowed the summer visitor to enjoy the illusion of rural existence without facing its hardships. Farmhouses could accommodate 10 to 25 paying guests. By 1905 there were at least 900 hotels, farmhouses, and boardinghouses accommodating about 25,000 guests in the Catskills.

The Catskills, about 100 miles north of New York City, are easily reached by highway. The region is an exception to the poor showing of most mountain resort areas. Known as the Borscht Belt, it draws most of its 2 million guests from metropolitan New York, with a sizable proportion of the Jewish faith. They come to frolic, look for marriage partners, and, as one wit put it, seek exhaustion.

In Sullivan County, where most of the Borscht Belt hotels are located, the first resorts were ramshackle farm buildings of twenty to forty rooms. Each had a communal kitchen for workers from New York's lower East Side who were determined to capture the pleasures of rural life.

The boom 1920s brought Tudor architecture and stuccoed four- or five-story hotels. Most of the 500 Catskill hotels were built at this time. Twenty of them can accommodate 500 or more guests, and there are about 2,000 bungalow colonies, with total space for almost 450,000 people.

Grossinger's and the Concord, the largest of the Catskill hotels, have set the pace with something new, a single room with two baths. The larger hotels use big name entertainers, many of whom started their careers as employee-entertainers at the same place. Celebrities are courted, all expenses free.

Matchmaking is a big business and considered part of management responsibility at Grossinger's. Lists of single persons from the same areas are made, and arrangements made so that they can meet. A prize was once offered to the first couple who met and were engaged while at the resort. No takers. The promotion department became desperate. Finally a couple was located that seemed to be making progress. A canoe trip was arranged—and while the couple believed themselves to be alone—a crew of anxious people played soft music and watched their every move. The program was successful.

Early New England Resorts

New England's resort business had several beginnings: farmers taking in summer tourists; old inns gradually merging into the resort business, and hunting-fishing camps gradually taking on the character of resorts. Big farm families were naturals for the resort business. The big families meant plenty of cheap help, big houses that could accommodate city folks during the summer, and plenty of chickens, eggs, and vegetables to feed the visitors.

The wonderful mountain scenery was free. All that was necessary was a ledger book with a big "Guest Register" scrawled across it and a potato in which to stick a pen for use by the city folks in writing their names and home addresses. As business grew, the family added wings here and there until they finally had a moderate-sized summer resort.

The location of some of the inns made them desirable as resorts. The Crawford House at Crawford Notch, N. H. is an example. The site was first used as a combination tollhouse, workshop, and tavern. Later a resort hotel was built, only to be destroyed by fire—the fate of so many resorts. The present resort was built in 1859.

In Maine the first tourists were Indians from inland and Canada who spent their summers along the seacoast, fishing and feasting. The first white summer boarder came to Old Orchard Beach in 1837 and by 1850 Maine's tourist business was well underway, accompanied by promotion leaflets and handbills.

Maine Resort Pattern

The hundreds of sporting camps, built first for fishermen and hunters about 1870, later changed into camps and lodges for vacationers. Following the pattern of the lumber camp, these are still built with a central lodge and dining hall with a cabin colony round about. Today, Maine has over 5,000 hotels, camps, and tourist homes where visitors, mostly from the East, and from Canada, come to eat, hunt, fish, canoe, climb mountains, and just enjoy the pleasantly cool summers. Total income from tourists is over $200 million a year.

In the Alleghenies just before the Civil War resorting at the various hot springs became a necessity for both health and social prestige. A grand tour of the springs became the established summer "must" for people of means. The tour covered 170 miles and about a dozen resorts. Colonel Job Fry, proprietor of one of the springs, described the tour when he told his guests, "Go get well charged at the White, well salted at the Salt, well sweetened at the Sweet, well boiled at the Hot, and then return to me and I will Fry you."

Figure 6-7 The Greenbrier, White Sulphur Springs, West Virginia. The Greenbrier is a mountain spa located at White Sulphur Springs. Surrounded by a 6,500 acre estate, it is a perfect setting for golf, tennis, horseback riding, skeet and trap shooting, hiking, and the numerous other sports available at the resort.

Not only were numerous glasses of the usually unpleasant spring water drunk, but at some of the springs mint juleps and food were floated out on trays to the soaking resorters. The mint julep itself was created at the Old White Springs in 1858: French brandy, old-fashioned cut-loaf sugar, limestone water, crushed ice, and young, hand-grown, mountain mint. It was at the Old White that the governor of South Carolina is reported to have said to the governor of North Carolina, "It's a long time between drinks."

Today two famous resorts are left of the dozen that operated there at the turn of the century: The Homestead at Hot Springs, Virginia, and The Greenbrier in West Virginia. The Greenbrier, owned by the Chesapeake and Ohio Railroad which has invested over $25 million in the resort, is now a grand convention property, a lavish hotel with 650 rooms, no two identical in decor. The prices are in keeping with the style. As one guest reported, "Hand a bellman a quarter and he'll hand it back to you."

Mountain Resorts on the Wane

With a few exceptions, mountain resorts in this country and in Canada have not been profitable in recent years. This has not always been the case. Before air conditioning and airplane travel, spending the summer or part of it in the cool mountains was the social thing to do, and a pleasant way to escape the heat of the city. In 1891 the White Mountains of New Hampshire had some sixty resort hotels with more than 11,000 guest rooms. By 1959 the number of guest rooms had dropped to about half as many, and today the number is considerably less. In 1890 the mountain resorts were the center of the summer social season and presented a way of life unique for both the guests and the operator, an aspect of Americana overlooked by most history books.

RAILROAD RESORT OPERATION

During the resort boom beginning in the 1880s, transportation to resorts was by horse-drawn coach, ship and boat, and by railroad. Railroad management saw the logic of building and operating resorts that could be reached easily by their railroads. The relationship was clear

enough, but railroad management for resorts is almost uniformly lacking in imagination and efficiency. Consequently, the marriages between railroads and resort hotels may have been blissful but costly. The Chesapeake and Ohio railroad was originally involved in The Homestead and now completely owns The Greenbrier, both famous resorts in the Blue Ridge Mountains.

Railroads, like most public transportation, are more or less subsidized by the government and not nearly so concerned with costs as are professional hotel groups. The Glacier Park hotels of Glacier National Park, originally owned by the Great Northern Railroad, were a case in point. These hotels, representing at least a $10 million investment, regularly lost $300,000 or more a year from the time they began operations in 1910 to 1920. In 1957 the Great Northern Railroad signed a contract with the Knutson Hotels of Minneapolis under which the Knutson Company operated the hotels for a fee. Under General Manager J. B. Temple drastic changes were introduced.

At the Many Glacier Hotel, a 230-room house, the number of personnel was cut from 220 to 165 with no appreciable loss in service. Instead of separate laundries at each location, one central laundry was set up for the four hotels and two motels. A centralized bakery was set up to serve three locations. Gift shops were enlarged, cocktail lounges added, beverage sales promoted by wine carts and room cards. A cycle menu, uniform for the several Park hotels, was introduced and food and beverage costs reduced, in some instances, by one-third.

The accounting system for the hotels was left in the hands of the railroad, with the result that groups that held conventions in mid-summer were billed as late as the following February. Following typical railroad practice, the hotels had no current operating statistics; hotel managers, paid about half the usual salary appropriate for their jobs, had been content to operate the same way year after year. The old managers were replaced, and a bonus system was installed.

An innovation that proved popular with guests, and a boost for employee morale, was the use of talented college students to provide a series of shows for guest entertainment. Students from Carleton College, Grinnell College,

Figure 6–8   The Mountain View House, Whitefield, New Hampshire, one of the stately, elegant mountain inns of New England, still survives. The resort is operated by the Dodge family whose forebears began taking summer boarders in 1866. Farmer William Dodge ran the farm that supplied the milk, cream, chickens, eggs, pork, fresh fruits, and vegetables for the table. He also took the "boarders" for rides in his mountain wagon and to church on Sundays. By the 1890s the original farmhouse had disappeared and part of the present building with the cupola had been built. The resort includes some 3,000 acres with a heated swimming pool, and golf course, and an auditorium with a capacity of 450. The Mountain View House is the oldest resort in the country to be in the hands of its original owners.

and other schools were employed as waiters, waitresses, bellmen, maids, and housemen. They did an outstanding job for the nightly performances under the guidance of a college music professor. As an outlet for the creative desires of the staff, the shows were in part responsible for the high employee morale that existed in these hotels. A series of questionnaires completed by guests showed that the employee entertainment was the thing they found most enjoyable in the hotels.

The Canadian Pacific Railroad has been a hotel operator of size for a number of years. In 1913 the Banff Springs Hotel in Banff, Alberta was built for $16 million. From a distance, the 600-room structure resembles a fairy castle. Close up it is a huge pile of rock with out-of-date equipment and operations. It manages to break even with a 90 percent occupancy during its summer season.

The Chateau Lake Louise, north of Banff in Canada, has one of the most magnificent hotel settings of the world, ranking with the Las Brisas in Acapulco, Mexico, The Conquistador in Puerto Rico, and some of the Swiss locations. The Chateau is located at one end of Lake Louise, where a glacier-covered mountain serves as a backdrop for the lake. Some 60,000 oriental poppies blanket one side of the hotel's terrace. The property is owned by the Canadian Pacific Railroad.

The Canadian National Hotels, a subsidiary of the Canadian National Railroad, do better financially. The Jasper Lake Lodge makes a profit. The Lodge combines the best of the old cottage-style resort—still popular in Canada—with the modern restaurant and recreational lodge. The central building, built after the old lodge building was destroyed by fire in 1952, is one of the most beautiful resort buildings in the world. The building cost $3.5 million. The lavish use made of warm colors in furnishings, colored cove lighting reflecting on the dining room ceiling, and a view of Jasper

Lake make dining in the Lodge a unique experience.

Both Canadian railroads maintain a continuous chef's training program with each of the hotels committed to train a certain number of trainee cooks. The program provides a steady supply of cooks and precludes the necessity of large salaries for executive chefs and the usual desperate search for chefs in resort hotels. Sun Valley, a year-around resort in a spectacular setting and with incredible ski lifts, was originally owned by the Union Pacific Railroad. Like the other railroad resorts, it probably makes little or no profit after reasonable depreciation is taken.

THE ROLE OF LADY LUCK

Gambling complements vacationing in the minds of many. What would Las Vegas and Reno be without the thrill of a brush with Lady Luck? Around the turn of the century one went to Saratoga Springs, New York, for the horses. There were two hotels built and operated in the grand manner: the Grand Union and the United States Hotel.

Saratoga was as famous for its "elegant hells," the gambling casinos, as were its hotels for their "elegant belles." Even so, the Grand Union and the United States Hotel in the 1880s and 1890s locked every entrance at 11 P.M., and no one except registered guests was permitted to come in.

BUILT ALONG THE BOARDWALK

Atlantic City was off to a flying start as a "summer watering spot" when, in 1853, a railroad was built to the shores of Absecon Island. By 1870 the beach, formerly frequented only by Delaware Indians and "beach-party goers," saw about 5,000 people coming for vacations.

The first boardwalk—eight foot wide— was laid in 1870. Each fall the sections were taken up to prevent damage by winter storms. In 1896, a pretentious forty-one-foot wide Boardwalk was laid and a "Grand Rally" with fireworks was held on the lawn opposite the Hotel Brighton to celebrate the occasion. Naturally someone—in this case the mayor's wife—drove a golden spike to signalize the completion of the walk. Today, the Boardwalk has become a promenade for over 3 million hotel guests a year who can stroll for 6 continuous miles on wood and steel. Over 450 hotels (27,000 rooms or more) accommodate the 3 million.

By the 1970s Atlantic City had lost its luster and was fading fast. In 1977 the New Jersey State Legislature passed a bill that permitted gambling in the City and gave the resort a new life expectancy. Resort areas tend to pass through life cycles—infancy, maturity, and senescence. Each stage attracts a different market. The resort destination can be revived but the process is difficult, and usually very costly.

In California the traveler can still experience the "great and grand" resort by visiting that Victorian/Queen Anne hodgepodge, the Del Coronado, across the bay from San Diego. Built in 1887, it had the first electric lighting system installed in a hotel and in 1971 was listed in the National Register of Historic Places.

Colorado has its own grand resort in The Broadmoor, near Colorado Springs, now an active convention hotel.

THE TOUR AGENT ARRIVES

Thomas Cook started the travel agency business in 1841 when he arranged a railroad trip for a temperance meeting in Leicester, fifteen miles from his home in Market Harborough, England. Soon he was arranging trips for groups all over the British Isles and later into Europe, the United States, and the Near East. In the 1890s, the Pennsylvania Railroad dispatched Pullman excursion trains from New York City to Jacksonville, Fla. This was part of a package plan that included rail fare, hotel room, and meals.

Today, the tour business is said to be the fastest growing segment of air travel. The traveler gets convenience, reservations, and often arrangements for food, drinks, sightseeing, and entertainment. Package tours have had a tremendous effect on the vacation business. Eastern Airlines started the first package tours to Miami in the winter of 1951. Package tours made Miami a summer as well as a winter resort and have been responsible for filling thousands of empty seats on the airlines.

Package tours are put together by some 200 tour wholesalers in the United States, who then turn the tours over to some 15,000 travel agents who retail them to people who do not want to take the trouble, or do not know how, to arrange their own travel, accommodations, and entertainment. Package tours come in all shapes and sizes. One can travel to Mount Kenya, shoot one animal, and have it stuffed. Most tours are much more mundane, a trip to Miami, Hawaii, or Bermuda.

For his trouble, the tour operator gets about 20 percent discount on everything he packages except the airline fare. If a hotel room rate is $20 a day, the packager may get it for $16, or less. If a tourist attraction charges $2, the tour operator gets it for $1.60. The 20 percent discount is given at restaurants and night clubs as well. The packager keeps about one-half of the discount and passes the other half on to the travel agent.

Resort hotels are usually delighted to be a part of a tour package; some hotels could not survive without being on the regular itinerary of some of the tours. The airlines are pleased; the travel agent is pleased; the restaurant operator is pleased; everybody is pleased, except the traveler who, in some cases, may feel as though he is part of a nameless crowd, being herded from one attraction to another; others would not want it otherwise. The sophisticated traveler may join a tour group because of its economy and leave it for part or most of the schedule. Tours can save the traveler tremendous time and effort in making travel arrangements, and in many cases, considerable savings.

THE MARKET VALUE OF A RESORT

What is a resort worth? What is its fair market value? What price will a willing buyer pay and a willing seller sell for, both of whom have the facts, and neither of whom is under pressure to act? Much of resort keeping is tied in with psychic income, pride of ownership, the pleasure the owner or prospective buyer has or may get from owning a resort on a beautiful lake or a beach.

Tax considerations are often a major factor. Wealthy resort owners may expect operating losses which can be used as tax deductions against other income. Many resorts have been built or bought by such individuals in the past. Special circumstances—estate settle-

ment or partnership disagreement, for example—may also distort the real market value.

According to the Helmsley-Spear Company, the largest of the real estate brokers, the traditional approach to determining fair value has three aspects:

1 Value as compared with comparable properties

2 Reproduction cost, separating the value of the land from the value of the buildings

3 The capitalized value of the property, what the property will produce in profit on a free and clear basis.

The approach most commonly used is the one based on the capitalization of earnings: what the property will yield.

From the profit viewpoint, a resort is as valuable as the net income it can generate. For a new property, a *pro forma* profit and loss statement is drawn up which projects revenues, expenses, taxes, depreciation, and expected net profit. For the established property, profit and loss statements for preceding years are a guide to future profits or losses.

ESTIMATING POTENTIAL EARNINGS

The potential earnings of a property may not be the same as what has been produced in the past. The buyer, presumably, will maximize the use of the property, and may arrive at a value, based on "the highest and best use" of the property, projected over the future period of life. Most large resorts by 1975 were tied in with land development and the sale of condominiums. The hotel itself might be viewed as the activities center of the land development, profits coming from land and condominium sales, not necessarily from operations of the hotel.

Potential earnings of a property take into consideration the land value itself, its setting, environment, and such things as riparian rights, easements, and special circumstances relating to the property.

Potential earnings of many resorts are tied almost directly to the convenience of reaching the place by air or highway. The relations that an owner or prospective owner may have with tour operators and travel agents can be highly important. So, too, is the relationship of the property to present and proposed interstate highways, air routes, and air fares.

Important to the financing of a resort is whether or not the resort can be tied into a nationwide referral system or will be part of a franchise plan. Lending institutions are more favorably disposed to loaning money for a resort operation when it is part of such a referral system.

In the past, a rule of thumb used for arriving at the value of a hotel, motel, or resort has been to multiply the income of the property for one year by seven to eight times. Of course, such a figure is only a starting point to be checked against all of the factors that bear on the net profit figures for the future.

The resort business is a highly specialized business, quite separate from the commercial hotel and restaurant business. There is a body of knowledge and practice that, combined with judgment, makes for expertise. In apparent contradiction to this statement are the numerous entries into the field by outsiders such as conglomerates, airlines, and oil companies. However, the outsiders bring their own financial and managerial know-how, adding it to the specialized management knowledge of the seasoned operator.

The question of "the highest and best use" of the property should always be asked. Many resorts have been "best used" by being torn down and the land sold as building lots. Other resorts have been turned into private clubs; still others, into schools or colleges. In Las Vegas, the hotel is only a setting for the gaming rooms and restaurants to sustain the guest until he can get back to the business at hand, gambling or being entertained.

RESORT PROFITS

What about profits? They vary tremendously, depending upon management, location, investment—and, for the summer resort, weather. Some winter resorts also can suffer from weather. Florida's 1958 winter season was shot with cold blasts extending below Miami. Neither guests nor hotels were prepared for the frigid temperatures that shattered orange trees and vacation spirits alike. Guests in a leading Miami hotel slept in their clothes on some nights and paid for the privilege. There were not enough blankets to go around, as the heating system was geared for "Florida weather," not freezing winds. Other resort hotels have been fantastically profitable, among them

Figure 6-9   Jasper Lake Lodge in the Canadian Rockies is an example of the resort centered around a lodge with the guests living in cottages, taking their meals and entertainment in the lodge.

the Caribe Hilton in San Juan; and in Las Vegas, the MGM Grand and the Hilton Hotels. The Fred Harvey operations at the Grand Canyon and Yosemite Park have generated millions of dollars in profits.

Rain and cold are the bane of the summer resort manager. Guests soon complain about the food, the personnel, and the management. *Does It Always Rain Here, Mr. Hoyt?* is the title of a book recounting the miseries of a summer resort keeper during poor weather. The title is apt. Most resorts, above all else, are selling their climate and scenery. Bad weather for a season can ruin a lightly financed resort. What is one man's poison is another man's food. While cold, rainy weather may dry up business in the Poconos, the same weather may fill other resort areas to overflowing. "We'll go to the Caribbean to get warm."

Length of season is a critical factor in northern resort hotels. In some areas it gets shorter each year. The day after Labor Day finds most summer resorts everywhere deserted. The Cape Cod season does not get underway until about June 20. The Southeast and Southwest have longer seasons and are developing into year-around resort areas with lulls during May and September.

SEASONAL RESORTS FACE HIGH OPERATING COSTS

With short seasons and many fixed costs, seasonal resorts must charge rates which to old-time guests seem inordinately high. The biggest difficulty faced by resorts is the impracticability of raising rates to meet the rising costs of operation.

Labor rates are surprisingly low in many areas, since college students clamor for jobs as a pleasant way to spend the summer. The Glacier National Park Hotels, as an illustration, received 12,000 applications in one year but had only 600 positions open. College students usually turn out to be excellent employees, but by the first of August for many the romance of the resort begins to wear thin. A multitude of reasons are found why they must return home—grandmother is dying, mother's demands, necessary shopping for school clothes, and many similar situations. To guard against a mass exodus of employees, nearly all summer resorts pay bonuses to those who re-

main for the full season. The bonuses are in reality wages that are withheld to insure compliance with employment agreements.

Many summer resorts were built prior to 1930 and so are in need of constant maintenance and repair. Steam lines leak; water hammers develop in the heating system; boilers explode. Typical of what might be expected was one manager's experience on showing a newly arrived family their room in a Pennsylvania resort. First, the lock on the door to the room would not open; finally, a skeleton key did the trick. The room was cold; no heat was coming in. Just as a matter of checking, an attempt was made to flush the toilet; the float valve was stuck. The commode top was removed and an attempt was made to lift the jammed float valve. It disintegrated in the manager's hands—whereupon he beat a hasty retreat.

Resorts spend something like 6 to 8 percent of their income on repairs and maintenance. The well-kept ones may expend 10 percent. Without constant rehabilitation, resort hotels are like MacArthur's old soldiers, "They fade away."

RESORT MEAL PLANS

Food—and plenty of it—has long been the hallmark of the American Plan resort. While French wines and French cuisine were offered at a few of the resorts before 1850, and have been since, the American Plan hotel dining room has catered to the typical American appetite. Each hotel has had to have an array of fresh baked goods. The baker might be a professional from the city or, in the mountain resorts, more frequently one of the local ladies with a flair for baking. The distinctively American food style at a resort can be seen from the menu presented by the Atlantic House of Rye Beach, Rye, N.H., dated July 27, 1859.

Also shown is a breakfast menu, dated January 18, 1887. Note the wide selection of items including pigs' feet, tripe, steak, and liver. Diet be damned. Eat hearty and well.

American Plan resort operators have more or less buried the cost of food in the total daily cost. Suppose the guest pays $40 a day, the operator arbitrarily allocates part of the rate to cover the cost of meals. Many resorts offer meals to non-registered guests for a flat charge.

ATLANTIC HOUSE
Rye Beach
Rye, New Hampshire

Wednesday, July 27, 1859

Soup
Fish
Leg of Mutton with Capers
Chickens, Pork, Corned Beef, Ham, Tongue
Entrees:
Macaroni, Mutton Cutlets, Corned Veal, Lobsters, Escalloped Oysters
Croquettes of Rice, Chicken Pies
Roast of Veal, Beef, Lamb and Chicken
Vegetables:
Pastry:
Dessert: Almonds, Apples, Fruit, Pecans, Oranges, Blanc Mange
Wines:

THE RAYMOND,

SOUTH PASADENA.   CALIFORNIA.

C. H. MERRILL, MANAGER.

⊰ BREAKFAST. ⊱

FRUIT.

OOLONG TEA. ENGLISH BREAKFAST TEA. COFFEE. CHOCOLATE. MILK

OATMEAL.   FRIED INDIAN PUDDING   HOMINY.
HOT ROLLS.   GRAHAM ROLLS.   GRAHAM BREAD.
MUFFINS.   DRY TOAST.   DIPPED TOAST.
CREAM TOAST.   CORN CAKE.

FISH.

BROILED BASS.   FRIED COD.
SMOKED SALMON.   FRIED OYSTERS.

BROILED OR FRIED TO ORDER.

SIRLOIN STEAK.   LAMB CHOPS.   MUTTON CHOPS
PORK CHOPS.   HAM.   BEEF LIVER.
BREAKFAST BACON.   TRIPE.   SAUSAGES.   RUMP STEAK
VEAL CUTLETS.   PIG'S FEET.

STEWED KIDNEYS   FRICASSEE OF CHICKEN.

EGGS.

OMELETTES, PLAIN, WITH CHEESE OR ONIONS.
BOILED.   POACHED.   FRIED.   SCRAMBLED.

POTATOES.

BAKED WHITE AND SWEET.   SAUTE.   STEWED.
SARATOGA CHIPS.

BUCKWHEAT CAKES.   GRIDDLE CAKES
MAPLE SYRUP   HONEY.

TUESDAY, January 18th, 1887.

Hotels operate on several meal plans:

EP (European Plan): no meals included in the room rate

AP (American Plan): all meals as part of the room rate

MAP (Modified American Plan): breakfast and dinner as part of the room rate

Continental Plan: the room rate includes a limited breakfast

In the United Kingdom and parts of continental Europe, bed and breakfast (B & B) plans mean that breakfast is included in the rate. In parts of England, Ireland, and Scotland the breakfast is lavish, including bacon, eggs, cereal, beverage. In France and Spain, the continental breakfast is likely to be rolls, jam or honey, and a beverage.

Accommodations listed as "garni" mean only breakfast, no regular restaurant service. MAP is growing in popularity. It reduces food cost for the hotel, and more guests are becoming diet conscious. The plan permits the guest to have lunch at some other place than in the hotel, perhaps combining it with sightseeing.

EMPLOYEE SCHEDULING

A continuing problem in resort keeping is employee feeding. Chefs, eager to hold down food cost or indifferent to employee appetites, are prone to run a few menu items over and over. Few resorts account for employee meals separately. Comparisons between resorts in terms of food costs are usually meaningless because of the numbers of employees being fed and the artificiality of the figure set aside by management for food.

How much of the American Plan rate that is charged should be allocated to income from meals? Usually the prices charged on the menu are the amounts allocated from the income from American Plan rates as food income. In 1975 the MAP (breakfast and dinner) additional charge ranged from about $12 to $25 in first-class resorts.

Since employees come cheap, owners in the past tended to overhire. With analysis and tighter scheduling, the number of resort em-

ployees can often be drastically reduced. A 230-room resort reduced its employee numbers from 220 to 160. A 100-room house cut its payroll from 110 to 62. Each employee, though he may be paid little and does little, eats 3 meals a day, and requires linen and supervision. Such expenses add up fast.

Another way to reduce payroll costs in resorts is to schedule employees more closely to fit the season. Many resorts open June 15 but have only 20 to 30 percent occupancy until July 1. By contracting for something less than half of the entire crew during the June weeks, payroll is reduced, cost of employees' meals is less, and employee morale higher. A small crew is easier to train and forms a nucleus of experience on which to build when the rest of the employees arrive in July. Employees are kept busy, which for tip employees is especially important.

Combining jobs is another way of reducing payroll. Strange job combinations are possible: an eighteen-year-old at a resort acted as lifeguard in the morning, switchboard operator during the afternoon, and busboy in the evenings. The boy still found time to ring the fire bell in the wee hours of the morning, causing the guests no small alarm.

And what about advertising? Resort operators must be promoters or have an imaginative alert promoter working for them, either on the staff or in an advertising agency. The best advertising has been, and probably always will be, the enthusiasm of present guests. They, too, must be resold during each visit and between visits.

Nearly every resort has a brochure with copy that often overdoes the superlatives. If the descriptions of what the guest can expect were true, the poor guest would die from pure ecstasy. Either that or relax so much that revival would be impossible. Here is the description of the Boom Boom Room in a Miami Beach resort:

"Calypso . . . voodoo . . . the cool, cool joy of a jungle cave . . . French-Haitian darkness lit with primitive primary colors and the flickering glimmer from hammered copper oil lamps. Sip a rum and let your pulse respond to the beating drums . . . the offbeat rhythms . . . the dark, glistening movement of Calypso!"

◄ Figure 6–10 *These hearty offerings are typical of the American Plan menus featured in early resort dining rooms.*

DIRECT MAIL

Direct mail, sending letters and literature to old guests and to prospects, is a major part of resort promotion. Direct mail can be an art. A few operators rely on it completely, spending nothing on paid advertising. Personal letters, referring to the fact that Mr. James broke par on a certain hole (or says he did), or that it is hoped that little Mary's tooth has grown back in, or that the Van Highnoses were just asking about the Joneses, make wonderful reading and create friends for the resort.

Direct mail must be personalized and, even if the same letter goes to 1,000 people, should always add the cheery closing, "Mary and I are eagerly awaiting your return." Hand signatures are a must, and postage stamps rather than a franking machine help. Direct mail requires skill and knowledge. Guest mailing lists must be kept current. The experts say that mailings should be made to every guest who has been at the resort during the past three years. The value of mailing to those who have not returned after three years becomes marginal. After five years the cost is excessive for the probable return. At least three mailings must be made during the year if the mailings are to be effective for promotion.

Honeymooners are great business for a resort. If the bride is not wearing an orchid, she can still be identified, says a veteran hotelman, by the fact that all of her clothes will be spanking new, especially the shoes. Honeymooners usually keep to themselves but are grateful for any friendliness shown. Certain locations have come to be known as honeymoon spots: Acapulco, Bermuda, Hawaii. Guam is a prime honeymoon destination for the Japanese.

ECONOMIC IMPACT OF TOURISM

The vacation business has received increasing attention from local, state, and federal government officials as a spur to a sluggish economy. The federal government, for example, sees tourism as a possible means for developing the economies of such states as Kentucky and West Virginia. The Economic Development Administration, a federal agency, has underwritten millions of dollars worth of resort developments for parks in those states and other millions to foster tourism on Indian lands. States like Nevada, Colorado, Wyoming, Arizona, and Florida are well aware of the value of the tourist dollar.

Many of the Caribbean islands may have to turn to tourism as the only realistic way of raising themselves from the poverty level. The tourist dollar, it has been maintained, is more valuable to a local economy than the dollar generated and spent within the economy. Much of the tourist dollar goes to pay for services by people, both in operating, and for the construction of, vacation facilities. It is money that is brought in as fresh—money from outside the economy, triggering several "rounds of spending."

The U.S. Dept. of Commerce states that the tourist dollar "turns over" an average of 3.27 times during a year. In other words, a tourist dollar is received and spent more than three times in the course of a year. This "multiplier effect" of the tourist dollar varies with the self-sufficiency of the local economy. If food has to be imported, for example, the money that goes to pay for the food is immediately shipped out of the community and does not take part in the multiplier effect.

A 1962 study of the multiplier effect of tourism on the economy of the state of New Hampshire showed that travel-vacation expenditures accounted for $120 million in direct income to lodging establishments, restaurants, service stations, grocery stores, and other businesses that served travelers. Within a year, the $120 million was re-spent several times for a cumulative effect of $230 million. As each "round of spending" took place, additional value accrued to the people of New Hampshire. "Leakages," in the form of savings, federal tax payments, and purchases made outside the state, reduced the amount left for the next round.

In the less developed countries, the multiplier effect is less applicable. Much of the construction materials, furnishings, and equipment, and most of the food, must be imported. In the Caribbean, for example, one study showed that for every tourist dollar spent on an island only eighteen cents remained on that island.

The state of Vermont is an example of the change of heart that is taking place among some state officials. In 1969 the Chief of the Promotion and Travel Division of the state anhounced that, although tourism brought over $200 million into the state, there were dangers ahead. The state decided to place restrictions on land use and to change its advertising theme to restrict the kind and number of tourists who come to the state. The state, he said, wants quality rather than quantity in tourists. Overbuilding and unwise use of the land, say the officials, will destroy the natural beauty of the state.

The beneficial effect of the vacation business on an area can be great, as seen on the island of Bermuda which is almost completely dependent upon tourism. The side effects of tourism, what it does to the psychology of the service people, how residents not connected with tourism react, and how much of the rewards of the venture reach the people at the bottom, vary widely with the area. Several vacation places, including Hawaii, Oregon, and Cape Cod, are having second thoughts about the desirability of unlimited tourist growth in their areas.

THE CARIBBEAN—FLIGHT TO THE SUN

The Caribbean could become one grand vacation lake. It has sun, scenery, and history, the tropical vacation area most accessible to the Eastern Seaboard of the United States. In 1971, 4.5 million visitors went to the Caribbean (excluding Cuba).[7] Puerto Rico, the Virgin Islands, and the Bahamas each received about one million visitors, mostly from the United States and Canada. The remaining one million went to the other islands, including Barbados and Trinidad-Tobago. Puerto Rico received one to two million; the Virgin Islands just over one million. Jamaica had more than 400,000 tourists; Barbados, 236,000. The Bahamas, though not geographically a part of the Caribbean, are very much a part of the Caribbean tourist scene. In 1971, about 1.5 million tourists visited these islands.

---

7. The Caribbean Travel Association, *Report of Tourist Travel to the Caribbean for 1971* (New York City, NY: The Caribbean Travel Assn., 1972).

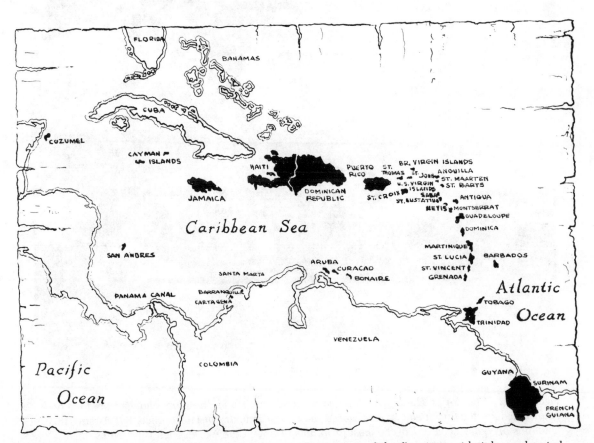

Figure 6–11   A map of the Caribbean Sea, an area where many of the finest resort hotels are located.

parts of the towns of Provincetown, Truro, Wellfleet, Eastham, Orleans, and Chatham.

The Cape Cod experience demonstrates that a sizable community should not expect high personal income for all of its residents from tourism alone. Tourism must be balanced with other sources of income. It blends well with seasonal homes, retired residents, and some "smokeless industry." Industry, however, must not be allowed to mar the charm and beauty of an area.

The Cape also illustrates the necessity of keeping markets of vacationers well defined. The Cape presently mixes its markets more than is feasible. Cottage colonies can exist alongside motels and hotels. But some of the cottage colonies on the Cape are built so close together, and of such cheap construction, that areas degenerate into vacation slums. Since there are greater profits in renting cottages than there are from other tourist businesses, efforts must be made to insure that cottages are not built too close together and are at least of minimum quality.

The construction payroll is almost three times that of the payroll for the vacation business per se. This led the chamber of commerce to favor construction since it raises considerably the per capita income of the permanent residents on the Cape.

FLORIDA

Florida's economy has been likened to a three-legged stool supported by tourism, agriculture, and industry. Tourism is, by far, the largest single business. The increase in tourists has been spectacular: five million in 1950, ten million in 1960, more than twenty-one million in 1969, 31.5 million in 1978.

Visitors to Florida in 1976 numbered about 29 million in 1977. Those traveling by auto spent about $22 a day; those traveling by air spent about $39 a day. The average visitor spent around $350 during his trip. Total spending was reported at $10 billion.[20]

Major appeals of the Florida vacation were "rest and relaxation," the beaches,

sports, and the major Florida attractions such as Disney World, Busch Gardens, Sea World, and Cypress Gardens.

Two names stand out in the growth of tourism in Florida, Henry Morrison Flagler, who was responsible for building a railroad from Jacksonville to Key West, and Henry Plant, another railroad tycoon, who pushed a railroad down the West Coast to Tampa. Both Henrys were self-made men, both were entrepreneurs of the first order, both made their fortunes prior to the time they went into Florida.

Flagler acquired great wealth as treasurer of Rockefeller's Standard Oil Company. Flagler's first wife had died, and later in life he remarried. The honeymoon trip to St. Augustine convinced him of the tourist potential of Florida. He was fifty-three.

In 1887 he built the first luxury hotel in Florida, the 450-apartment Ponce de Leon, in St. Augustine. It cost $1.25 million, at the time a large sum of money. The hotel was authentic Moorish with an imported tile roof and Spanish gardens. With the success of the Ponce de Leon, another hotel was built nearby, the Alcazar.

Flagler became the rail tycoon of Florida through the Model Land Company which he controlled. Awarded 8,000 acres of land for each mile of railroad built south of Daytona Beach, he eventually owned two million acres of Florida land. As the railroad pushed south from St. Augustine, Flagler built hotels at Ormond Beach, Palm Beach, and Miami. The "winter season" in Florida became not only healthful but a social necessity for the elite of the East.

Altogether Flagler spent $50 million in Florida, $20 million in pushing his railroad down to Key West. (It was abandoned after hurricane damage in the 1930s, but provided the base for the present U.S. Route 1 to Key West.) In 1900, $50 million was worth several times that amount today.

Flagler's empire reached full tide in 1912: he owned two hotels in Nassau, and a steamship line connecting them to Miami. The Florida East Coast Railroad connected a string of Flagler properties from Jacksonville to Miami. He lived in a marble palace, Whitehall, at Palm Beach, a home which cost $3 million, complete with gold plumbing fixtures, $35,000 worth of throw rugs, and fifty sets of dinner

20. 1976 Florida Tourist Study, State of Florida, Department of Commerce, Tallahassee, Fla. (The $10 billion figure is higher than estimated in other studies.)

service. Later, Whitehall became a hotel for a short time; it now houses the Flagler Museum.

Though Flagler was unassuming, his political influence in Florida was such that when at the age seventy-one he wanted a divorce from his mentally ill wife, he was able to convince the Florida legislature to pass a special law allowing the separation. His third wife was thirty-four. It was she who urged him to build Whitehall. Ironically, at eighty-three, Flagler died of complications resulting from a fall on the marble staircase of Whitehall.[21]

On the West Coast Henry Plant built another large Moorish style hotel, The Tampa Bay, now used as a building by the University of Tampa. Plant eventually erected seven hotels.

Through the 1920s, the Belleaire, near Clearwater, one of Plant's hotels, became the winter home of more railroad presidents and industrial tycoons than any other private resort. Private railroad cars by the dozen were parked on the Atlantic Coastline spur east of the hotel.

The Florida land boom reached its peak in the summer of 1925, with people swarming into the state in such numbers that railroad tickets were at a premium, and even food was scarce. Shortly after, the boom became bust. But dozens of hotels had been built, many of which faded from the scene during the 1930s.

Miami was opened up in 1896, when the first train chugged into the little community bringing crowds of new settlers and sightseers. Its spectacular growth came later. By 1912, it still counted only 5,000 residents. In 1913 the Collin's Bridge reached Miami Beach. Carl Fisher, one of the founders of Prestolite Company, used millions of his own money and a keen sense of ballyhoo to help make Miami Beach what it is today. One writer claimed that Fisher "rehearsed the mosquitoes so they wouldn't bite until after you bought."

Miami Beach

Miami Beach is one of a kind, the most closely packed aggregation of resort rooms in the world. Strangely, only a few of the hotels on the Beach are managed by professional hotelmen.

Figure 6–16   *The Americana, one of the Loews Hotels, on Miami Beach. Note the guest room balconies, so arranged that they all face the Atlantic Ocean. The Americana was one of the first large resort-convention complexes to be built on the Beach. It is truly a resort complex combining guest rooms, food and beverage facilities, convention facilities, and cabanas.*

Most of the hotels have been owned by a succession of New York City businessmen whose primary interests are not hotelkeeping. Probably nowhere else are there so many partnerships or so many family members involved in the operation of hotels. Each partner gets a title as an officer in the hotel. Hotels are bought and sold regularly.

Hotels are done in lavish and spectacular style. Flood-lit palm trees are standard equipment as are oversized lobbies. Swimming pools are close to Olympic size, surrounded by sundecks where guests eye other guests, drink, relax, and feel expansive. Most will not consider going into the water.

Large hotels came with the era of conventioning in the 1950s. At the end of the 1940s, a good-sized hotel on the Beach had 125 rooms. In the early 1950s a 250-room operation became standard. The Fontainbleau had 1,000 rooms, but in 1977 was in bankruptcy.

Financing Miami Beach hotels has been wild in the past. According to Ivan DeNary, a senior member of Horwath and Horwath, most

21. K. C. Tessendorf, "The Lavish Years of Flagler's Florida," *The Travel Agent*, February 15, 1973.

Figure 6-17 The Americana—another view. The swimming pool in the subtropical and tropical resort is the center of activity. The Americana's food and beverage business has moved close to the pool, the locale of a large part of the luncheon business at today's resorts.

hotels were financed by a combination of methods that represented the equivalent of a financial education at the Harvard Business School. "Interwoven with the financing are the mental gymnastics of income tax planning. It is quite impossible to explain how it is done. One has to see it—and then he probably won't believe it."

Sales promotion is highly prized on the Beach. Sales managers often make more in salary and commission than hotel managers. There are many who believe that Miami Beach exists by the grace of the travel agent and the airlines. National Airlines and Eastern Airlines have both been active promoters of Florida and especially of Miami Beach. Package plans put together by travel agents and airlines bring thousands of people to the Beach during the periods of low occupancy.

Percentages explain a great deal about Miami Beach hotelkeeping. Much of the operation is leased out at a flat rental or a percentage of gross revenue. Some places lease the valet service, shops, parking, cabanas, and even tennis courts.

Resort Concentration

When speaking of Florida as a resort state, we are really speaking of the southern half of the state. Florida is some 500 miles long; northern Florida is not winterized for the resort business. The great concentration of the resort business on the East Coast begins at about Ft. Lauderdale and extends down into the Keys. On the West Coast, Clearwater is the beginning of Florida's winter resort area.

The West Coast is comparatively quiet, largely residential, with relatively small resort hotels and thousands of motels and apartment rentals. Ft. Lauderdale is also relatively reserved and residential in character. Miami Beach is an urbanized resort area thriving on crowds, entertainment, and excitement.

Over 85 percent of Florida's visitors come from east of the Mississippi, with Miami the leading destination, followed by Datona Beach, Jacksonville, and Ft. Lauderdale. Heaviest tourist traffic comes from the Atlantic seaboard, the southeastern states, and the northern areas of the Middle West.

Various sections of Florida attract clientele from specific areas. During the winter season Miami Beach is largely peopled by persons from metropolitan New York. On the West Coast—in St. Petersburg, Sarasota, Venice, and Naples—Middle westerners predominate. The summer season at Daytona Beach brings guests mostly from states adjoining Florida. Panama City, on the north Gulf Coast, is almost entirely a summer resort peopled by guests from the southeast, as well as Alabama.

It might be said that the airlines built Florida tourism. This is partially true, but the effort has been joined by a number of agencies and people. The Florida Power and Light Company has a sizable public relations budget for the promotion of Florida. The Citrus Commission, a quasi-state agency, supported by a tax on citrus sales, ties Florida promotion into its citrus advertising. The State Advertising Commission formed in 1945 advertises Florida widely and has one of the highest state advertising budgets.

Disney World, constructed near Orlando, attracts some 112 million persons a year. The amusement area is five times as large as Disneyland in California. Disney World is expected to generate $6.6 billion in economic benefits to the state in its first ten years of

Figure 6–18   The ultra-modern Contemporary Hotel, Disneyworld, Florida. The Disneyworld monorail goes right through the lobby of the hotel.

operation. It can be predicted that Disney World will become a vast convention and entertainment center with groups vying for the opportunity of scheduling their meetings there.

Interama, a permanent international exposition, to be built north of Miami, will cover 4,700 acres, will include a marina for 300 boats, a 200-room "yachtel," an aerial tramway, and an exhibition area. It is expected to attract 6 million visitors yearly.

Apartments in Florida, to a large extent, are a part of the tourist business. Large numbers of apartments are built primarily for tourist occupancy. The condominium apartment building is set up to be occupied by the owner only during vacations and to be rented during the remainder of the year. This plan helps in financing second or vacation homes as the apartments are largely paid for out of rental fees. Rental management is frequently part of the owner's contract so he does not

have to cope with the usual landlord-tenant problems. To attract renters in some locations, foodservice is being made available on a catered basis. Florida also has hundreds of licensed trailer parks, the number increasing each year, many with swimming pools, tennis courts, and shuffleboard courts. A few have their own post offices. In effect, several are tourist communities with seasonal occupancy and the atmosphere of a resort.

Resorts Rise and Fall

Resort destinations rise and fall, Miami Beach and Atlantic City are excellent examples. Both cities were once meccas for the East Coast vacationer. In 1977 both were down at the heels, Miami Beach being supplanted by destinations as far away as Europe, Cancun, Hawaii, Acapulco, and Caribbean resorts. A major factor in the decline of Miami Beach was the bright and shiny new Disney World located in Orlando in middle Florida, cutting off the visitor from the north "at the pass." Things were so bad that the hotelmen went to Washington to seek Federal backing for low-cost refurbishment loans refused by South Florida Banks. The number of hotel rooms on the beach dropped to 27,000 in 1976 from 30,000 a decade earlier. *Time* Magazine claimed that only 3,500 of them were first class. In the same ten-year period Las Vegas added 15,000 rooms for a total of 36,000 and Hawaii's total increased to 44,000 from 16,800. The Mexican resort of Cancun, which didn't have a room in 1966, was a fast growing resort destination.

Gambling may rejuvenate Atlantic City, and Miami Beach hopes to survive by attracting as many as 50 percent or more of their visitors as part of conventions. The Fontainbleau Hotel, largest of the Beach hotels, thought it had a way out: it advertised a plan for singles that included nude sunbathing in the solarium and video-taped matchmaking services. Outraged citizens in Miami quashed that idea. The once proud Fontainbleau Hotel—largest of the Miami Beach hotels — was sold in 1977 in bankruptcy court.

Miami Beach's problems are said to stem not only from outside problems but by poor management and lack of maintenance. When profits were made the money was siphoned off without thought for the morrow. Hotels were built close together along the beach, making them invisible from the street and causing beach erosion.

THE SKI BUSINESS

Each winter some four million skiers take to the mountain slopes of New England, Pennsylvania, Colorado, California, Nevada, Washington, and wherever else snow falls or could be made for skiing. There is a ski resort at Gatlinburg, Tenn., in the Great Smoky Mountains (opened in 1961).

Nevertheless, the number of skiers grows by an estimated 20 percent annually, and the number of "camp followers" grows accordingly. Skiing offers challenging athletics and lively socializing. Skiing also offers opportunity to the resort operators of the area for a two-season operation, summer and winter.

Numerous hotels, motels, and an assortment of lodges accumulate around the ski area. The economics of the ski business are not clear-cut.[22]

Mt. Snow in Vermont, one of the largest ski areas in the world, is extremely busy on weekends with good snow. Like most ski areas, business drops sharply on weekdays. When there is no snow, the place takes on the air of a ghost town. Mt. Snow is said to be profitable.

Mt. Tom, located within the city limits of Holyoke, Massachusetts makes its own snow and, since it is available to hundreds of thousands of people within a few minutes, is quite profitable.

Heavy investments and short ski seasons help to account for the financial picture. The number of days of skiing in Wisconsin in 1959 was only 40. Aspen, Colo., on the other hand, had 147 skiable days in 1964–1965. The 1976–77 season was a disaster in the Far West for ski operators because of lack of snow.

Weekends, the areas are overrun with skiers. Weekdays find relatively few skiers on most slopes. Storms and thaws take their toll. Snow-making equipment has added many skiable days, but such equipment cannot prevail against warm weather. In many places, the state involved has helped to finance ski areas. The financing may take several forms, from building access roads to the area to completely building an area, as was done by the state of New Hampshire at Sunapee.

Skiing can bring a great deal of money into an area: construction money, payroll money for lodges, restaurants, and grocery and liquor stores. Ski facilities also stimulate the building of private lodges and year around homes. Real estate values jump and, to some extent, the community as a whole prospers.

The origins of ski business, as we know it today, are debatable, but it is known that in 1931 the Boston and Maine Railroad sent its first snow train to Warner, New Hampshire with 197 winter enthusiasts aboard. The skier at that time was regarded as a hardy eccentric who was willing to put up with cold and hardship for a day or a weekend on narrow ski trails.

In 1934 a Model T Ford engine was placed at the base of a hill in Woodstock, Vermont. At

---

22. *The Wall Street Journal,* January 7, 1969.

the end of a shaft, turned by the engine, was a wheel. Over this wheel, held in position by a flange, a rope was set going; it was the first uphill tow. In 1938 the skimobile was built at Cranmore Mountain in North Conway. Later, the aerial passenger tramway was built at Franconia, New Hampshire.

Today, enclosed gondolas travel for miles up mountains. Plush lodges with European cuisine may be scattered around the foot of the slopes. The typical skier, however, does not stop at such lodges. He travels by auto from a population center, usually for a weekend. He eats in a cafeteria line, or from a vending machine. The usual fare is hot dogs, hamburgers, beef stew, and soups. The skier is usually a younger person in his teens or twenties. As a part of the ski operation, there are usually one or two orthopedists with X-ray machines and plenty of plaster for making casts for broken legs.

The ski business is an adjunct to the hotel and restaurant business; however, for the skiing addict in the business, the lodge can be a sideline to the principal purpose in life, getting onto the slopes.

By the 1960s, skiing had moved into the realm of big business. Many ski areas now cater to the family, offering deluxe accommodations and the American Plan tied in with ski lessons and use of the slopes. Mom and Dad, in their forties, struggle into strange clothes and equipment to join ski classes with their grammar school sons and daughters. Hundreds of thousands of students and young marrieds dash off on Friday afternoon for several hours at a ski area.

The lodge and ski tow operators enjoy it while it lasts. Most are at the whim of the weather. Good snow means big crowds; storms and warm weather and the business collapses. Though snow-making equipment is becoming a must in many places, temperatures above freezing drain away the snow (made during the night), and the profits. Even so, the ski business is likely to continue its mad growth.

Lodges and restaurants in ski areas depend upon snow conditions. The lodges at Mt. Snow may be filled to capacity one weekend, have almost no guests the next. Summer resorts near ski areas have everything to gain, since they can at least do business on skiable weekends. Some of the large summer resorts, of course, do not open during the ski season because of the cost and problems of staffing.

Factors Affecting Ski Operation Profitability

In analyzing profitability—or the lack of it—in ski operations several factors become apparent: the large heavily-invested ski operation with a diversity of activities and attractions has a much greater appeal to the general public than the traditional ski operation with a few tows and a cafeteria style of food service. The large corporation with access to large sums of money can extend the season by introducing indoor tennis courts, a disco, and a variety of restaurants.

Most successful ski operations are part of a larger concept involving land development with condominium and land sales for private homes. Perhaps as much profit or more is made via the land development as in the ski operation itself. The ski operation becomes the focal point and the major appeal of the larger concept. Merely operating ski lifts and hoping for snow is not enough.

The ski operation has a much better chance of success if within an hour's travel time of a population center of 50,000 or more people.

Climate should be such that there are at least 105 days of snow. The possibility of little or no snow, even in areas where large snowfalls are normal, means that most ski areas should take out insurance in the form of snow-making equipment.

Summer ski camps are one way of extending the season. Two-week blocks can be sold to groups interested in body conditioning through hiking and skill improvement via movies, professional indoor instruction, and classroom-type lectures. Summer operations can include backpacking tours, fishing camps, health seminars, and related sports and health activities.

Installation of a convention center and emphasis on selling group business during off-peak seasons has long been a means of extending the resort season. Ski resorts enter the convention business to extend the season.

Cluster resorts seem to add to the appeal of the individual resort just as the "restaurant row" is more than the sum of its parts. The avid skier enjoys moving from one ski area to another if they are relatively close together.

Figure 6–19   A heated swimming pool in the midst of a ski resort—this one at Sun Valley, Idaho, is probably the first one to be built. The pool was installed about 1950. Though few people use such pools, they do add glamour, novelty, and decorative value.

The cluster resort can also support a greater variety of restaurants and evening entertainment than the individual property.

Larger ski resorts maintain a year-round marketing program, which includes advertising in magazines, newspapers, circulars, radio and occasional TV. Periodic mailings are made to travel agents, groups, and individuals. Sales calls, ski shows, and ski club councils are contacted and presentations made to them. Generally speaking, ski resorts do little marketing. The primary marketing is done via ski shows.

The ski resort remains a high risk business requiring heavy capital investment in ski lifts and land (some resorts are on land leased from the National Forest Service). Ski resorts represent a substantial gamble in that they may be highly profitable one year and financially disasterous the next. Generally ski resort profits are reinvested in the property rather than distributed to the owners.

A major factor in the break-even point of a resort is the uphill ski capacity available—the number of skiers that a resort can move to the top of a mountain.

Typically hotels close to a ski resort run close to 100 percent occupancy on weekends and anywhere from 50 to 80 percent during the midweek.

Ski resorts must continue to innovate, and some are doing so. For example, Squaw Valley maintains an extensive babysitting program. Other resorts sponsor races and exhibitions during slack periods of the ski season.

Skiing historically begins in most ski areas at Thanksgiving where the snow pack is suitable and continues through Easter.

A ski resort could not possibly be profitable without depending heavily upon seasonal employees. The free seasonal ski pass is a big inducement for the seasonal employees because the salary range is usually low compared to city pay standards.

VARIETY IN RESORT AREAS

It is misleading to think of the vacation business as confined to the traditional resort areas, such as the mountains of New England, the sea coast of New Jersey, or the ski slopes of Colorado. By far the largest concentrations of the vacation business are in places like New York City, London, Paris, San Francisco, Honolulu, and Las Vegas. The traditional vacation cities such as Paris, Rome, Copenhagen, Salzburg, and Vienna attract many more people than such glamour spots as the Greek Isles or the Canary Islands.

New resort destinations are developing on the southern coast of Spain, the Algarve in Portugal, and several locations in Mexico besides the better known Acapulco (Cancun on the Gulf Coast, Puerto Vallarta, Ixtapa, and Mazatlan on the West Coast of Mexico). The island of Maui is second largest in the Pacific Basin, after Oahu.

THEME PARKS AND RESORT OPERATION

Copenhagen has long had its Tivoli Gardens and Vienna its Prater Entertainment Park, but it took a Walt Disney to demonstrate what can really be done in the way of a major theme park. When well-done and well-operated a facility becomes a major draw for the area in which it is located and for millions of visitors from hundreds and even thousands of miles away. Las Vegas has its gambling, Los Angeles has its Disneyland, Santa Clara has its Great America, and Orlando Disney World. Disneyland attracts half of its customers from the Los Angeles area, the rest from "all over." Around these theme parks thousands of hotel rooms and restaurants are grouped as ancillary operations, introducing a new dimension to the hotel and restaurant business.

Since the middle fifties when Walt Disney built Disneyland near Los Angeles, theme parks have become very much a part of the hotel business, magnets for the vacationer, providing entertainment, education, food, and fun for the family. Disneyland was an unqualified financial success to be followed by Disney World, which proved even more successful. Disney World, a 27,400-acre entertainment complex near Orlando, Florida is said to be the foremost tourist destination in the world.

More than thirteen million visitors came in 1976 and the figure was forecasted to rise year after year. In that year the Disney World complex grossed almost $255 million support for some 40,000 first-class hotel rooms in the Orlando area. The three Disney Hotels within the Park ran occupancy rates of about 97 percent. A Disney World complex in Tokoyo is in the planning stage and will cost some $800 million.

Numerous other theme parks have been developed with the Marriott Corporation jumping into the field with both feet. Closely related to the theme parks are such attractions as the Polynesian Village on the Island of Oahu operated by the Mormon Church which indeed is an educational experience and adds tremendously to the appeal of Waikiki, in effect adding one more day of entertainment to the Hawaiian visit.

THE VACATION HOTEL BUSINESS OF THE FUTURE

The vacation hotel business is seen as merging with a number of other businesses or being so related that it becomes a part of them. Perhaps it is better to think of the vacation business as a part of the broader business of tourism. Traveling for pleasure has become one of the world's great businesses, involving vacation planning, the means of travel, accommodations enroute and at the destination, and entertainment during the complete process.

Economic forecasters are unanimous in predicting greater discretionary income for the average person, and more interest in travel and vacationing in the future. As airline travel becomes easier and relatively less expensive, its growth will continue.

The vacation business is often inextricably bound up with land development, with hotels adding lustre and value to newly developed communities, or in entertainment complexes such as Disney World in Florida, and projects in Hawaii, Spain, Sardinia, the Carribbean, California, and Mexico.

The rapid growth of condominiums that are also rentable as vacation apartments may have a marked effect on the economics of hotel-keeping in resort areas. By 1975 some 300 condo apartment complexes doubled as resort hotels, the owners renting while not in residence. Hawaii had the largest number, but many were in California and Florida. Some were in Idaho, Maine, Vermont, and Colorado. The condominium owner makes his apartment available for rent to a vacationer when the owner is not in residence. Fifty to 70 percent of the rental income goes to the owner, the rest to the condominium manager. Foodservice for the condominium renter is available in many areas.

In 1971, a new concept for resort keeping appeared in Hawaii in the form of time sharing. It is being used in several other resort destinations now. The concept takes several forms:

1 Time Sharing Ownership (TSO)
Units in a resort are purchased outright, but the unit is shared with other owners, and each may use the apartment, room, or cottage for a specified length of time each year. Title to each undivided interest is conveyed through a warranty deed, including an agreement of use for a particular time period each year. The buyer, in effect, becomes a part owner of a condominium and must pay his prorated share of maintenance, taxes, and utilities. The part owner can sell, transfer, or bequeath his interest as in any real property ownership.

The part owner has the pride of ownership, may participate in a rental pool together with the other owners, and has his own vacation unit for part of the year. His investment is relatively small, and if the property appreciates, he has a profit.

The original owner or developer has his money back and perhaps a management contract to operate the establishment. The cost of marketing to the large number of owners, however, is likely to be high.

Part of the resort may be kept as a traditional resort, with units rented to vacationers. TSO units may also be rented when not occupied by the owners.

2 Interval Ownership
Similar to TSO except that each unit is separate from others, and the ownership is not subject to partition or to tax liens on the interests of other owners. The deed creates an estate—usually for the useful life of the unit—after which it becomes the property of the tenants in common.

3 The Vacation License
The owner buys a leasehold interest in a resort unit for a certain period each year for a specified number of years.

Created by Carribbean International Corporation, the vacation license gives the purchaser the right to use a unit for a certain time period for the useful life of the resort, at least forty years. By 1976 some 6,000 licenses were sold by Caribbean International Corporation for use in their resorts in Ft. Lauderdale, San Juan, St. Thomas, and St. Croix. Buyers have a choice of the resorts for spending their vacations.

The Sea Pines Company, developer of the outstanding resort, Sea Pines Plantation on Hilton Head Island off South Carolina, sells vacation time segments of one or several weeks. According to a company spokesman, the plan enables an individual to invest his vacation dollars, build equity, and, at the same time, have a vacation retreat of outstanding quality in perpetuity for only the amount of time he plans to use it. Corporations can buy TSOs in a resort and use them as employee awards, incentive rewards, and vacation spots for personnel.

4 Vacation Bonds
Like other corporate bonds, the vacation bond represents an unconditional promise of the owner of a resort hotel to pay the face amount of the bond plus interest at a stated rate at maturity. The bonds are secured by either a first or second mortgage on the hotel.

Owners of the bonds may redeem them using them for payment of room rents and receive a 40 to 60 percent discount from the current rack rate.

Time for use of the hotel is specified, one week a year for from fifteen to forty years, but the bond holder must reserve sixty to ninety days in advance. Vacation bonds have been sold in California, Hawaii, the Caribbean, and Europe.

Time sharing plans permit resort developers to finance without the need of conventional long-term financing. Owners of existing properties may expand or pay off mortgages.

THE RECENT PAST

As energy prices rose sharply, beginning in 1973, the cost of travel increased as well, causing a rapid change in vacation travel patterns and in the nature of the business itself. Vacationers took shorter and fewer vacation trips and the focus was on economy. By 1978 visits to state and national parks had risen sharply. Trips to Europe and Hawaii were up. Mexican tourism had dropped as a result of political unrest, uncertainty about personal safety, and police harassment of tourists in Mexico, but by 1979 was on the rise again. Travel and tourism was booming within the United States.

Resort hotels, and others that were big enough, shifted marketing efforts to reach group business. The FITs (Foreign Independent Tour) became fewer; the various tour packages rose in popularity. To reach and motivate group travel, hotels added directors of tours to their marketing departments. The special function of these individuals, often attractive women, was to sell group business and to look after the group members while they were guests there.

The package tour took on major importance because of economies possible in selling blocks of airline seats, rooms, sightseeing, and entertainment tickets. On the off season, blocks of hotel rooms would be sold to wholesalers for 25 to 50 percent below the published rate; airlines also discounted their tickets, legally or otherwise. The package hastened what was already a firm trend toward mass travel.

Hotel management and convention and visitor bureaus began to work together much more closely, hotel and bureau representatives traveling together to sell vacations. The San Diego Convention and Visitor Bureau, for example, traveled with hotel general managers and sales personnel to major cities in the United States and Canada selling travel agents on San Diego as a destination. The trips were partly underwritten by Western Airlines and other interested airlines. Convention bureaus grew in number and importance, usually partly funded by a hotel room tax of about 6 percent.

Conglomerates such as ITT, MCA, and AMFAC may play an even larger role in the vacation business as they expand around the world. The major chains such as Hilton, Sheraton, and Western International are much involved in vacation destinations such as Hawaii, Las Vegas, San Juan, and Mexico.

The vacation hotel business, until very recently, had been the domain of the independent entrepreneur. This has now changed. It will be interesting to observe the new character of the vacation hotel business as it develops during the next several years.

Questions

1 The classic resort hotel of the turn of the century was usually a fairly remote, independently operated mountain or beach resort. How has the resort business of today changed in location and character?

2 Name three prestige resort hotels of the world.

3 Name at least one conglomerate that is active in the resort business.

4 The largest single item in world trade is petroleum and its products; what is the next largest?

5 Of each tourist dollar spent roughly how many cents are realized by federal, state, or local tax agencies?

6 Polls suggest that when there is a recession, people will cut back travel expenditures very quickly. Did this actually happen in the 1972–75 recession?

7 Name two or three major city tourist markets in this country.

8 Regarding seasonality of the resort business, define "shoulder periods."

9 In the past some resorts have been "restricted." What does "restricted" mean?

10 In the early days of the American resort what relationship existed between growth of resorting and the railroad?

11 As a resort destination Atlantic City has been fading but more recently coming back to life because of what legislative change?

12 Thomas Cook is a famous name in the travel business. For what reason?

13 What does the word "garni" signify when used with a European Hotel?

14 What significance does the "multiplier effect" have on the dollar that is spent at a tourist destination?

15 Give three reasons why some states are less enthusiastic about tourism than they have been in the past.

16 Puerto Rico has as many as one million tourists a year. How does this compare with the number of visitors to Hawaii?

17 Give three reasons why the cruise ship business has been growing in recent years.

18 Why is it that cruise and passenger ships do not fly the American flag?

19 Operating a resort in the Caribbean Islands sounds romantic; give three reasons why it may not be.

20 Besides Puerto Rico, name three other prominent tourist destinations in the Caribbean or close to it.

21 As a travel manager, what would you recommend people see and do for a two-week period in the Hawaiian Islands?

22 A large proportion of the employees in the hotel and restaurant business are drawn from the so-called disadvantaged groups. Can you explain the reason for this and its effect on society as a whole?

23 Gambling has been a significant inducement for travel. Besides Las Vegas where are citizens of the United States likely to go for casino gambling?

24 Which resort hotel is the largest and cost the most to build?

25 If you were a resident of Cape Cod how would you feel about increasing promotional efforts for tourism to the Cape?

26 Why has Miami Beach declined in popularity?

27 Generally speaking is the ski business a highly profitable one for a ski resort operator? Explain.

28 Contrast Disneyland with Disney World in size and financial objectives.

29 How does employment compare in the service sector of the economy with that of industry generally?

30 Is the service sector of our economy likely to grow in the next twenty or thirty years? Why or why not?

THE RESTAURANT BUSINESS

SEVEN

The restaurant business, says the National Restaurant Association, is the third largest of all businesses in the United States. One of every three meals eaten in this country is eaten away from home and this ratio, says the Association, will be one in two by 1980. Employees in the industry, including those who work part-time, number more than eight million.

Sales per restaurant increase year after year: average sales for restaurants with a payroll jumped from $66,281 in 1963 to $190,000 in 1975. As restaurant sales per unit increase, the necessity of professional management increases. Whereas a few years ago a restaurant with sales of $1 million annually was a rarity, by 1972 about 1,500 had such sales and included coffeeshops, cafeterias, and a number of fast food restaurants that feature the hamburger.

The commercial restaurant business prospered greatly following World War II as more people acquired the habit of eating out and had the money to do so. Many aspects of our changing lifestyle such as the fact that more women work favor restaurant growth. Eating out is tied closely to available disposable income; as disposable income increases, so too do restaurant sales. In the period 1969–1975 food and beverages consumed away from home accounted for just under 5 percent of disposable income of consumers. That percentage held almost constant, even though other costs that compete for the consumer dollar such as medical services and transportation rose during the same period.

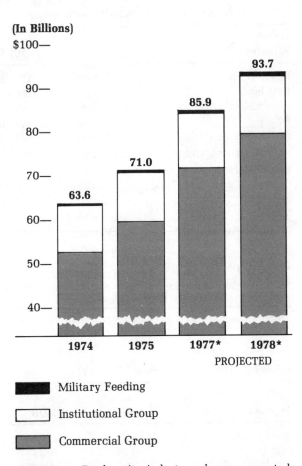

Figure 7–1 Foodservice industry sales are expected to reach $93.7 billion in 1978 and to top $100 billion by the end of 1979, says the National Restaurant Association.

More than half of the families of households in the United States in 1977 were composed of only one or two persons. The reasons:

lower fertility rates, a tendency for young people to postpone marriage, the ease and frequency of divorce, and the ability and desire of young singles and elderly to live alone. The size of households has shrunk from 4.8 persons in 1900 to 3.4 persons in 1950 to 2.9 persons in 1976. Only 65 precent of U.S. households in 1976 were maintained by married couples. What does this mean for the restaurant business? Small households probably encourage eating out in that the dining experience is a social as well as an alimentary experience.

Like hotels, restaurants are becoming fewer but larger. Seen below are two charts summarizing the number of food service units and the drinks market between 1970 and 1980. According to these figures, produced by Institutions/Volume Feeding Magazine, the number of commercial restaurants will decline in the 1970s but the volume of sales will increase markedly, a trend that began a number of years ago. Although many observers of the restaurant scene feel that the fastfood segment has leveled off, this forecast is much more optimistic and projects some 140,000 units by 1980.

In 1977 total commercial food service (restaurants, fast food, hotels/motels, retail,

Table 7-1 Number of Foodservice Units: 1970–1980

Segment	1970	1976	1977*	1980*	Growth Rate 1970-80*
Restaurants	165,000	173,150	173,000	169,690	+ 2.8%
Fast Food	66,530	104,990	112,860	140,210	+ 110.7
Hotels/Motels	41,400	43,200	43,200	43,000	+ 3.9
Retail	45,000	55,000	56,000	59,000	+ 31.1
Recreation	30,900	25,400	25,095	23,500	− 23.9
Total Commercial	348,830	401,740	410,155	435,400	+ 24.8
Health Care**	27,580	28,660	28,800	29,082	+ 5.4
Colleges/Universities**	2,525	2,830	2,886	3,060	+ 21.2
Schools**	116,300	112,700	112,136	108,000	− 6.9
Military**	260	255	251	247	− 5.0
Total Noncomm'l.**	146,665	144,445	144,073	140,389	− 4.2
TOTAL	495,495	546,185	554,228	575,789	+ 16.2%

* Estimated.

**Unit numbers represent total count of institutions, rather than actual foodservice units; no unit count included for employee foodservice and transportation.

Source: Institutions/Volume Feeding, March 15, 1977, page 145.

Table 7-2 The Drinks Market: 1970–1980

Segment	1970	1976	1977*	1980*	Growth Rate 1970-1980*
Restaurants	$1,627	$3,406	$3,747	$ 5,176	+ 218.1%
Fast Food	159	356	399	600	+ 277.4
Hotels/Motels	899	1,495	1,630	2,190	+ 143.6
Retail	19	33	36	48	+ 152.6
Recreation	878	1,418	1,602	2,228	+ 153.8
Transportation	120	186	214	253	+ 110.8
Military	579	567	592	771	+ 33.2
TOTAL	$4,281	$7,461	$8,220	$11,266	+ 163.2%

* Estimated.

Source: Institutions/Volume Feeding, March 15, 1977, page 145.

and recreation) reached $56.6 billion and was projected to reach $77.5 billion by 1980. The chart below shows the breakdown of the total foodservice market for 1970 to 1980. Keep in mind that these figures are not adjusted for inflation.

About 29 percent of the employees in the foodservice business are waiters and waitresses. Cooks and chefs account for 15 percent of the total; counter and fountain workers about 5 percent, and bartenders and clerical workers about 5 percent each. Proprietors and managers constitute about one-fifth of the total employment.[1] In 1975 teenagers occupied about 30 percent of all foodservice occupations; women held 70 percent of all foodservice occupations.[2] An NRA report (NRA News, December, 1976) stated that one-third of the employees in the foodservice business were students, 50 percent in college. The restaurant business thus provided the first job for hundreds of thousands of young people, most at minimum wages.

HISTORY OF EATING OUT

Eating out has a long history. Taverns existed as early as 1700 B.C. A record of a public dining place in Egypt in 512 B.C. showed a limited menu—only one dish was served, consisting of cereal, wild fowl, and onion. Be that as it may, the ancient Egyptians had a fair selection of foods: peas, lentils, watermelons, artichokes, lettuce, endive, radishes, onions, garlic, leeks, fats—both vegetable and animal—beef, honey, dates, and dairy products, including milk, cheese, and butter.

Women were not permitted in such places then. By 402 B.C., however, women became a part of the tavern atmosphere and little boys, too, could be served, if in company with their parents. Girls had to wait until they were married.

Eating Out in Ancient Rome

The ancient Romans were great eaters-out. Evidence can be seen even today in Herculaneum, a resort town near Naples that, in 70 A.D. was buried in some 65 ft. of mud lava

by the eruption of Mt. Vesuvius.[3] Along its streets were a number of snack bars vending bread, cheese, wine, nuts, dates, figs, and hot foods. The counters were faced with marble fragments and jugs were imbedded in them, which contained wine, kept fresh by the cool stone. Mulled and spiced wines were served, often sweetened with honey.

A number of the snack bars were identical, or nearly so, giving the impression that they were part of a chain under single ownership. Bakeries were nearby, where grain was milled in the courtyard, the mill turned by blindfolded asses. Some bakeries specialized in cakes. One of them had twenty-five bronze baking pans of various sizes from about 4 in. to 1½ ft. in diameter.

After the fall of Rome, eating out usually took place in the inn or tavern, but by 1200 there were cook houses in London, Paris, and elsewhere where cooked food could be purchased. The coffee house was also a forerunner of the restaurant of today. It appeared in Oxford in 1650 and seven years later in London.

Coffee, at the time, was considered a cure-all. As one advertisement in 1657 had it: "... coffee closes the orifices of the stomach, fortifies the heat within, helpeth digesting ... is good against eyesores, coughs, or colds ..." Lloyds of London, the international insurance company, was founded in Lloyd's Coffee House. By the late seventeenth and eighteenth century, there were about 3,000 of them in London.

Coffee houses were also popular in Colonial America. Boston had many of them as did Virginia and New York. The words cafe and cafeteria are from the word cafe, French for coffee.

The first restaurant by that name carried this inscription over the door: "Venite ad me omnes qui stomacho laboratoris et ego restaurabo vos." Few of the Parisians who saw this sign in 1765 could read French, let alone Latin, but if they could, they knew that Monsieur Boulanger, the proprietor, said, "Come to me all whose stomachs cry out in anguish and I shall restore you."

1. NRA *Washington Report*, April 23, 1973.
2. NRA *Washington Report*, November 3, 1975.
3. Joseph J. Deiss, *Herculaneum, Italy's Buried Treasure* (New York, NY: Thomas J. Crowell Co., 1969).

Monsieur Boulanger called his soup "le restaurant divin." His "divine restorative" was quite an improvement over the bitter herb and vegetable mixtures brewed by the medieval physicians as restoratives. A richly delicious bouillon, it attracted fashionable ladies and gentlemen who would not ordinarily patronize the public taverns where eating ran a poor second place to drinking.

Monsieur Boulanger's Restaurant Champs d'Oiseau also charged prices sufficiently high to make the place acceptably exclusive and a place where women who were ladies would enjoy being seen. Boulanger lost no time in enlarging his menu, and a new business was born. Soon the word restaurant was established, and chefs of repute who had worked only for private families either opened their own restaurants or were employed by a new group of small businessmen, the restaurateurs.

The Restaurant in America

The word "restaurant" came to this country in 1794, via a French refugee from the guillotine, Jean Baptiste Gilbert Paypalt. Paypalt set up what must have been the first French restaurant in this country, Julien's Restorator. Here he served truffles, cheese fondues, and soups. The French influence on American cooking was felt even earlier; both Washington and Jefferson were fond of French cuisine, and several French eating establishments were opened in Boston by French Huguenots who fled from France in the eighteenth century to escape religious persecution.

The restaurant generally credited as being the first in this country was Delmonico's in New York City, begun in 1827.[4] This claim may be disputed by the Union Oyster House in Cambridge, opened in 1826 by Messrs. Atwood and Bacon and still operating.

The story of Delmonico's and of its proprietors is a fascinating one and epitomizes much about family-operated restaurants in this country. Few family restaurants last more than a generation, but four generations of the Delmonico family were involved in nine restaurants from 1827 to 1923. The name Delmonico once stood for what was best in the French-American restaurant.

As has happened with most family restaurants, the name and the restaurants fade into history. The last of the family-owned Delmonico restaurants, at 44th Street and Fifth Avenue, closed its doors in humiliation and bankruptcy during the early prohibition years. The family gathered acclaim and a fortune, but finally the drive for success and the talent for it was missing in the family line.

John Delmonico, the founder, was a Swiss sea captain who, in 1825, retired from ship life and opened a tiny shop on the Battery in New York City. At first he sold only French and Spanish wines, but in 1827 with his brother Peter, a confectioner, he opened an establishment serving wines, fancy cakes, and ices which could be enjoyed on the spot.

New Yorkers, apparently bored with plain food, approved the petits gateaux (little cakes), chocolate, and bonbons served by the brothers Delmonico. Success led to the opening of a second-story restaurant in 1832, and brother Lorenzo Delmonico joined the enterprise. Lorenzo proved to be the restaurant genius. New Yorkers were ready to change from a roast-and-boiled bill of fare to la grande cuisine—and Lorenzo was ready for the New Yorkers.

A hard worker—the basic qualification for restaurant success—he was up at four o'clock and on his way to the public markets. By eight o'clock he appeared at the restaurant, drank a small cup of black coffee, and smoked the third or fourth of his daily thirty cigars. Then home to bed until the dinner hour when he reappeared to direct the restaurant show. He set high standards for himself, Delmonico employees, and for Delmonico patrons. No Delmonico guest could entertain behind closed doors, not even a married couple.

Lavish Banquets

Guests were encouraged, however, to be as profligate with food as they could afford. A yachtsman in the 1870s gave a banquet at Delmonico's which cost $400 a person. Before each guest was a yacht basin, 20 inches in diameter, and in each floated a perfect model of the host's yacht, complete in detail to a tiny gold bar.

At another banquet, an artificial lake 30-foot long was created and in it swam four

4. Thomas Lately, *Delmonico's, A Century of Splendor* (Boston, MA: Houghton Mifflin, 1967).

swans. Golden cages full of birds added to the decor. The most expensive of all Delmonico dinners was one given by a visiting Englishman for 100 New York tea and coffee merchants. The bill was $20,000.

Delmonico's pioneered the idea of printing the menu both in French and in English. The menu was enormous, offering twelve soups, thirty-two hors d'oeuvres, twenty-eight different beef entrees, forty-six of veal, twenty of mutton, forty-seven of poultry, twenty-two of game, forty-six of fish, shellfish, turtle, and eels, fifty-one vegetable and egg dishes, nineteen pastries and cakes, plus twenty-eight additional desserts. Some twenty-four liqueurs and sixty-four wines and champagnes were listed. The highest priced entree was canvasback duck, fed on sherry.

What restaurant today could or would offer 371 separate dishes to order? Except for a few items temporarily unobtainable, any dish could be called for at any time, and it would be served promptly, as a matter of routine.

Delmonico's expanded to four locations, each operated by one member of the family. Lorenzo did so well in handling large affairs that he was soon called upon to cater parties all over town. Delmonico's was the restaurant. In 1881 Lorenzo died, leaving a $2 million estate. Charles, a nephew, took over but in three years suffered a nervous breakdown, brought on, it was believed, by overindulgence in the stock market. Other members of the family stepped in and kept the good name of Delmonico's alive.

The senior chef, Charles Ranhofer, also acquired a reputation, one of the few chefs in this country to do so. His book, The Epicurean,[5] was considered authoritative. Oscar of the Waldorf, whose full name was Oscar Tschirky, got his start at Delmonico's in 1887 as a waiter.

Shortly before the old Waldorf opened, enterprising Oscar composed a letter of recommendation for himself on Delmonico's stationery and collected eight pages of signatures from Delmonico's regular customers. It was sufficiently impressive to win him the job of headwaiter at the Waldorf.

In the 1890s, Delmonico's was given this left-handed tribute by Richard Harding Davis,

5. Charles Ranhofer and R. Ranhofer, The Epicurean (New York, NY: 1900). The book includes a selection of Delmonico's menus from 1861 to 1894, all French.

"Another place where you can get a good square meal, well cooked and fitly served, for about seventeen dollars." In 1910 the last male member of the Delmonico family to run the restaurants died of a heart attack, and Delmonico's began a slow decline, which ended completely in 1923.

Lobster a la Newburg was invented at a Delmonico's restaurant by Mr. Wenburg. Cruelly, Mr. Wenburg was deprived of gastronomic immortality when, after an altercation with one of the Delmonicos, the first three letters in the dish were transposed.

American Style in Restaurants

Only a few cities in this country could, or would, support the kind of high cuisine and prices offered at Delmonico's. Restaurants in the same tradition, such as Le Pavillon, the Colony, Antoine's, Ernie's, and the Blue Fox exist only in sophisticated and sizable metropolitan cities. New York City, New Orleans, and San Francisco are the centers of such cookery. Boston has only three such restaurants; Chicago has perhaps the same number. Even in New York City there are only about fifteen restaurants that have fulltime sommeliers (wine stewards). These restaurants, of course, influence American cookery but constitute a minute part of the American restaurant business.

The gourmet writers are fond of disparaging the average American restaurant, calling it a vulcanizing plant, and extolling, in contrast, the expensive restaurant in the French tradition. It should be pointed out that there is also an American style in restaurants, in fact, several American adaptations.

These are the coffee shops, fast food restaurants, cafeterias, and good solid table service restaurants now being copied around the world. They meet the taste, timetable, and pocketbook of the American.

While the Delmonico restaurant is to be admired for its subtlety, grace, and service, it will probably remain more of a novelty on the American scene than the norm. While the Delmonico restaurants won the kudos of the day and were the scene of high-style entertaining, there were hundreds of more typical eating establishments carrying on their business. It has been so ever since.

Figure 7-2   The dining room of Le Pavillon in New York City, considered by many to have been the finest restaurant in this country, some say in the world. The restaurant was created by Henri Soule who came to this country to manage the French restaurant in the French exhibit area during the first World's Fair in New York City in 1938. House specialities included poached striped bass, duckling aux peches, and plume de veau. Unfortunately, the restaurant closed in 1972.

Louis Sherry was perhaps the best known caterer in the country and, in 1898, opened a fine restaurant across the street from one of the Delmonico restaurants. Rector's was the other internationally known restaurant in New York City toward the end of the century. The great and the notorious came to see and be seen. Some thought Rector's was too gay or slightly mad. Some called it Naughty Rector's, which detracted not at all from its glamour. Antoine's, in New Orleans, advertises that it has been operating continuously since 1840, one of the very few that can make such a claim.

Dining for Travelers

After about 1850 much of the fine eating in this country was found on the river boats and in railroad dining cars. Dining car service was among the most elegant and the most expensive, both to the customer and to the railroads. The writer remembers ordering the least expensive item on a cross-country train during the middle of the depression. The item was three stewed prunes priced at 50¢, very high for that time period.

Railroad dining service on some of the crack trains was indeed deluxe. Yet, on a cost accounting basis, each meal cost the railroad between $1 and $1.50 because of the high labor costs and the inefficiency of the dining car operation. As on the ocean liners, foodservice on some of the railroads was considered a prestige operation and a promotion cost.

The better known resort hotels have always set a fine table, food costs being buried in the cost of the American Plan rate. Many of the finer city hotels were also known for their excellent foodservice.

The public restaurant business grew steadily but, as late as 1919, there were still only 42,600 restaurants in this country. For the average family in the small cities and towns dining out was an occasion. The workingman's restaurant and the boarding house were strictly meat and potatoes. In 1919 the Volstead Act prohibited the sale of alcoholic beverages and forced many restaurants that depended upon their liquor sales for profit out of business. It also forced a new emphasis on food cost control and accounting.

The Early Drive-Ins

By the 1920s there were enough automobiles to provide a market for a new type of foodservice,

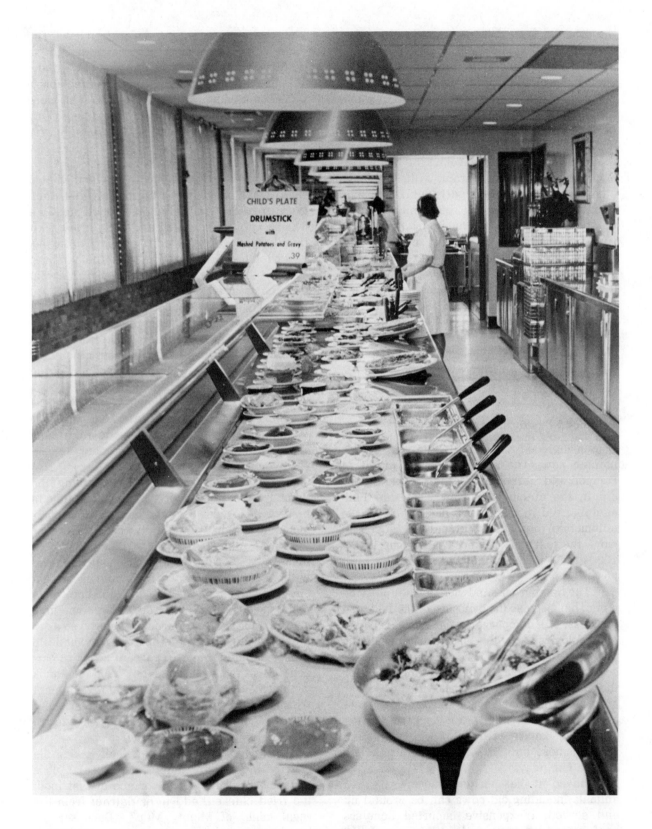

Figure 7-3 Food display is carefully designed for Pop's Cafeteria counters in the St. Louis area. A bowl of salad and whole desserts are used as highlights on the line. Special merchandising of a Child's Plate speeds selection as children often take extra time when confronted with so many choices.

the drive-in. Some drive-ins exist because they are located on major highways; others draw most of their trade from the local area. Both must have plenty of parking spaces for automobiles. The drive-in brought curb service and the carhop. Depending upon its location, the drive-in catered primarily to the young family and the teenager, although on a major highway it caters to everybody traveling the highway.

The drive-in restaurant, with its large parking lot, carhops, and garish entrance sign, is on the way out. Many communities across the country placed zoning restrictions upon such restaurants. It is easy to see why. Sections of some major highways were lined with drive-in restaurants, one next to the other. In the late evening, traffic congestion on such roads could be horrendous. Some drive-ins became gathering points for the rowdy, and sometimes destructive, teenagers. It became necessary to employ off duty policemen to direct traffic and preserve order.

Fast Food Restaurants

Dispensing food on request, fast and hot, is nothing new. The ancient Romans did it at Pompeii and Herculaneum; the roadside diner did it; the automats in New York and Philadelphia did it; but it took the franchise, the automobile, and plenty of parking space to move the fast food business to become in the 1960s the phenomenon of the restaurant business.

The hamburger sandwich, a meat patty on a bun, has become the cynosure of the fast food business. The hamburger is pattied, garnished, and eulogized by the smartest advertising people in the business. The hamburger goes to college at Whopper College, training camp for those who aspire to greatness in the Burger King chain. At Hamburger University players are drilled for wealth and status in the McDonald Empire. Little known in the restaurant business until 1930, the hamburger has come a long way.

Indeed it has virtues: most grass fed animals including old cows can be ground up and served. Inexpensive imported boneless beef, raised on grass and containing only 10 percent to 12 percent fat can be mixed with domestic beef to produce a patty containing 18

percent to 20 percent fat, the desired level. The American public has been conditioned to salivate at the thought of the Mighty Mac, the Whopper, and other anthropomophized forms of the sandwich. McDonald's chain with more than 5,000 outlets and $5 billion in sales, is king over Burger King with only 1,700 units. Burger King, owned and backed by Pillsbury's resources, is racing to catch up.

Hamburger history goes back to medieval times when merchants from the town of Hamburg traveling in Baltic areas adopted the Tartar habit of scraping and eating raw meat (Steak a la Tartar is still fancied by some). Later the meat was browned and the hamburg brought to this country by immigrants and German sailors.

In England in 1888 a physician, Dr. J. H. Salisbury, promoted a variation of the burger as wonder food, which he was certain would cure an assortment of diseases including colitis, rheumatism, gout, and hardening of the arteries. This was the Salisbury Steak.

The St. Louis Exposition in 1903 served the hamburger in a bun and later, in 1921, the White Castle chain added onions to a flattened meatball and griddled it. The hamburger sold for five cents.

Hundreds of people are examining the hamburger to improve it. No other food item in history has received such minute and enormous attention. Should it be broiled or griddled? Should it be garnished with a tomato? What kind of lettuce should be used with it, shredded or leaf? Should it contain onions, mayonnaise? Should the bun have poppy seeds, caraway seeds, or something else? Should it be prepared and stored so as to be ready to hand to the customer or made to order? Should it have 20 percent fat or 18 percent? Must the meat come only from the chuck or the whole animal? What percentage of meat trimmings are allowable? Should cheek meat be used? These and other questions have led to the fine tuning of the hamburger.

Although the hamburger itself is king, its courtly accompaniments also bear close scrutiny. Does the crown prince of fast food, the fried chicken, add to or detract from the regal might of Mighty Mac? Does serving breakfast in a hamburger restaurant detract from the King hamburger's pomp and circumstance? Fries, shakes, and in some locations even Mexican food, the burrito and the taco, are acceptable at court.

Many entrepreneurs who have flocked to the hamburger banner have been suitably rewarded with millions of dollars. Franchised chains exist within chains, hamburger barons within the hamburger realm. Those who would support king hamburger must not come empty-handed. Something like $500,000 is needed to invest in the Burger King. There are many candidates, few are chosen. To open a McDonald's requires at least $100,000 in cash; the store and property are rented from the parent company.

The fast food restaurant—with parking lots and walk-up service—surged during the 1960s and into the 1970s. McDonald's and Kentucky Fried Chicken led the way with national limited menus, national TV advertising, and good food. Sales at McDonald's in 1977 exceeded $3 billion. Some served the hamburger with tomato, lettuce, and mayonnaise; some served it plain. Patty size range from 1 to 4 ounces. The bun might be plain or with sesame seed. Patties were griddled and broiled. The advertising suggested that the hamburger was love, family, fun, pure ecstasy. Later, fish sandwiches, cheese sandwiches, and other items were added.

RESTAURANT CHAINS

Fastfood restaurants, those offering simplified menus, highly standardized service, training and decor, are dominated by chains. One source estimates that the sale of hamburgers is about 90 percent controlled by large chains. Pizza and ice cream sales are over 80 percent in the hands of the chains. Chain participation in the full menu segment of the market is much less and for a fairly obvious reason. The more complex the menu, the more difficult it is to standardize and control and the more managerial knowledge and skills are needed. It is comparatively simple to develop a fastfood concept for hamburgers or pizza, lay out the plans and the format of operation, and train relatively inexperienced managers and inexperienced teenagers to operate it. A full service restaurant is something else, more complicated, requiring a greater range of knowledge and managerial know-how.

Our first big chain operator was Fred Harvey, an Englishman. His first eating house opened in Topeka, Kansas in 1876. By 1912 he operated a dozen large hotels, sixty-five railway restaurants, and sixty dining cars.

A man of enterprise and imagination, he sent an envoy to Guaymas and Hermosillo in Mexico to get fruit, green vegetables, shellfish, and other foods. A contract was made with the chief of the Yaqui Indians to supply green turtles and sea celery. The price was right. The Indians were paid $1.50 for each turtle weighing 200 pounds and full of eggs. Turtle steaks and green turtle soup were a house specialty; the sea celery was used for salad.

The Fred Harvey restaurants were models of efficiency: train passengers were served well in minimum time. When patrons disembarked from the train they were immediately asked their choice of beverage. Waitresses used a code in placing the cup on the table and a "drink girl" followed "magically" pouring the patron's preferred beverage without even asking.

The Fred Harvey Company, serving the Santa Fe Railroad, had a major impact on the Southwest where Fred Harvey Girls, who were brought to the area as waitresses, married and settled down. The company, until recently headed by sons of the founder, is now owned by AmFac, a Hawaiian-based conglomerate. Indicative of the changes in travel, Fred Harvey severed its ties to the iron horse by canceling contracts with the Santa Fe Railroad in 1968 and acquiring contracts for airport foodservice at Palm Springs, Lansing, and Las Vegas.

Another early, large chain operator was John R. Thompson. In 1893 Thompson, a young storekeeper, and his wife left the little town of Fithian, Illinois with $800 to purchase a small restaurant in Chicago. By 1893 there were three units and Thompson, like every successful entrepreneur, cast about for a better way of doing things. He switched from the service-style restaurant to a one-arm dairy lunch, one of the first self-service restaurants. The customer walked up to a serving counter where he picked up his food and carried it back to a school-type chair, the arm being used as a tray.

He was probably the first restaurateur to use a central commissary and delivery by electric truck. Part of his success could be accounted for by the fact that the labor cost of the day was 15 percent of gross sales. By 1926 there were 126 one-armed dairy lunches in the Midwest and the South. By the 1940s the dairy luncheons were changed over to straight-line cafeterias or sold. Today, the John R. Thompson Company is a highly successful, Chicago-based restaurant chain with high-style cafeterias, luxury table service operations called Henrici's, and drive-in restaurants, The Red Balloons.

Another chain which was started before the nineteenth century, and is still active, is Horn & Hardart Restaurants in New York City and Philadelphia. The two are separate corporations. Joe Horn, with $1,000 in capital, and Tom Hardart, a luncheon waiter, started the business in 1888. In 1898 they introduced the automat, paying $30,000 for the German invention. The automats, a kind of grand vending machine operation, had their day and are now closed.

Change Constant Factor

Evidence that the restaurant business needs constant revitalization is Child's restaurants, during the 1920s the largest chain in the world. The chain pioneered food cost analysis, breaking down all food purchases into categories and developing standard ratios for each category. Centered in New York City, the chain operated 150 units and did about $28 million in sales.

Then, in the 1930s, the president became fascinated with vegetables because of their presumed health value and because of their low cost. By the 1950s the chain was almost bankrupt and was bought, largely as a tax loss investment, by A. M. Sonnabend, principal owner of Hotel Corporation of America (Sonesta).

Stouffer's, probably the best known table service restaurant chain in the country, started in 1924 as a $12,000 lunch counter in Cleveland. Mother Stouffer baked the pies that were sold. Dad and the two sons helped run the restaurant. The chain expanded steadily, going from about $2 million in sales in 1930 to $90 million in 1967.

The company operates eleven "Tops," restaurants sited on the top floor of large buildings in major cities. The company also operates motor inns and a Frozen Prepared Food Divi-

sion. Today it is a subsidiary of Nestle, a Swiss-based corporation, and the Stouffer family is no longer a part of management.

The Marriott Corporation and the Howard Johnson Company, largest of the restaurant chains, both started in the 1920s.

RESTAURANT CHAIN ORGANIZATION

Restaurant chains grow, and when successful are often acquired by conglomerates such as General Mills, W. R. Grace, and Pillsbury. Typically a restaurant owner builds a small chain, and nearing retirement-age, sells out to a larger company. Some food service chains acquire other chains, preferring to buy an established proven restaurant concept.

Saga Corporation has expanded in this way, acquiring other chains, each appealing to a different market. In this way Saga has "positioned" itself in several markets, none of their divisions competing with the other. (The Saga Organization Chart is seen at the end of this chapter.)

The Saga corporation is the parent organization (headquartered in Menlo Park, California). The Company is divided into three principal divisions: Dinner House Restaurants, Fast Food Restaurants, and Contract Food Service.

Straw Hat Pizza, The Velvet Turtle, The Refectory, and Black Angus are restaurant chains within Saga, each with its own format and market. Contract Food Service is another noncompeting division serving schools, colleges, hospitals, and business and industry.

The Mariott Corporation presents a more complicated organization, including separate divisions operating cruise ships, hotels, fast food retaurants, dinner houses, in-flight food services, and most recently, theme parks patterned after Disneyland.

A restaurant chain such as Far West Services is only one company among dozens in the W. R. Grace corporation.

Advantages of the Chain

The restaurant chain, once it has established itself, has several advantages over the independent operator, advantages that chain management often neglects to use. With its larger resources, the chain can more readily establish credit and make long-term leases on land and buildings; in addition, its management can afford to make more mistakes than can the independent. One serious mistake and the independent is likely to go bankrupt.

Nearly every chain has a few restaurants that have never succeeded or have "turned sour." Because of its resources, the chain can afford to experiment with the menu, the decor and design, experiments that the independent is reluctant to try.

Theoretically again, a chain can afford to make mistakes through trial and error, eventually developing a highly successful design and format of operation. Once the pattern has been established and is presented to the public—as a Howard Johnson Restaurant or a McDonald's—the chain can replicate the standard by the dozens. This is what has happened. The public, seeing the success of a particular style of operation, is then eager to have part of it, and there is little difficulty in selling either the franchises or stock to the public.

Theoretically at least, the chain can afford to employ at least a few men of unusual talents which cannot be afforded by the independent. The chain can have a top food and beverage director, a far-seeing president, and a few other key executives who may be paid $50,000 a year and up, plus stock options. The chain can afford to employ specialists: an experimental chef, an advertising and promotion expert. It is more likely to turn to outside consultants whose fees may be $5,000 and up for a particular analysis.

Chain Dangers

Since the chains have so many built-in advantages, why then are more than 75 percent of the restaurants in the country still independents? Part of the answer lies in the development of that insidious disease, "bureaucratitis," hardening of the corporation arteries.

Once the corporation has reached a certain stage of development, it tends to lose its forward motion. Entrepreneurs are replaced by professional managers who are more interested in turning wheels than in making the vehicle go in a particular direction.

Markets change; neighborhoods change; food preferences change; fashions change. The bureaucrat in the large chains is more interested in doing what has been done and preserv-

ing his own position than in taking risks and innovating. He has position, power, and status. Why should he exert himself unduly?

Another disease found in some chains is that of nepotism. The father, who was a driving, driven, capable man, hands over the reins of the organization to his son. The son is probably a nicer guy than his father but lacks Dad's motivation. He is secure; he has to prove very little. The organization begins to lose momentum.

Not only sons are brought into the organization, but also relatives; and then the old school tie makes its appearance. Only the graduates of elite schools are named to top positions; the club begins to form within management. Management is more interested in holding what it has than in forging ahead.

Change in Motivation

The professional manager may be as bright as or brighter than the entrepreneur who formed the chain, but his motivation and values are different. The game changes from "Let's be the biggest" to "Let's get accepted into society," "Let's devote our energies to pleasing the powerful." Perquisites of all kinds appear for management. The luncheon begins with cocktails and lasts until 3 P.M. Weekends get longer and factions appear.

The periodic introductions of "operation belt tightening," instituted by men like Ernest Henderson and Howard Johnson, are out of favor. "The company can afford it" becomes the byword. Suggestions for change get lost in committees. No one wants to take responsibility for anything. Why take a chance on something failing?

More secretaries, more assistants, more specialized departments appear to load down the payroll. The company that has been based on a strong tie-in with a particular market rolls along for several years. Profits are good. No changes are necessary, say the new managers. The company has a fine reputation; everybody is happy.

Then symptoms appear, sales hold steady or decline in some units. Really capable people leave for organizations offering more challenge. Those left are the cautious, the well paid, and the complacent. It is about this time that the company goes on the block. An outsider, sensing what is happening inside the company, makes a take-over bid. If he is successful, he cleans house; a new entrepreneur is in the saddle.

The restaurant chains actively recruit the graduates of the hotel and restaurant college programs and probably have been the largest employers of hotel and restaurant school graduates.

Some of the chains offer specialized services. Host International concentrates on serving the air traveler. At one time the predecessor company, Interstate Hosts, had contracts with sixty-three different railroad companies. During the 1950s attention was turned to turnpike and airport terminals, and by 1969 Host International had contracts for serving food in some twenty airports. It also operates airport hotels, a chain of Charlie Brown's restaurants, and a number of gift shops. In 1968 it acquired the Church's Chicken of Houston chain of thirty carry-out fried chicken outlets.

Sky Chefs, a subsidiary of American Airlines, is one of the largest of the airline caterers. In the late 1960s it added the Americana Hotels to its business.

FOOD PROCESSORS AND OTHERS ENTER THE RESTAURANT BUSINESS

Beginning in 1967 a number of large food manufacturers entered the restaurant business. It is only surprising that they had not done so before. By 1973 more than 40 major food manufacturers and processors had moved into the restaurant business. Most of the large food manufacturers have separate divisions set up especially to market their products to the institutional food trade, which includes restaurants. They are well aware of the size of the market: at least $20 billion a year is spent on food by restaurants and institutional foodservices.

United Fruit in 1967 purchased the A&W Root Beer chain. United Fruit was in turn purchased by United Brands. General Hosts bought the Uncle John's Restaurants. In 1968 General Foods entered the fast food restaurant field with the acquisition, for $15 million, of the Burger Chef Systems, Inc., an Indianapolis-based, 900-unit, nationwide chain of hamburger specialty restaurants. General Foods also operates the Rix chain of roast beef sand-

wich shops and, through a Canadian subsidiary, owns the White Spot group of restaurants in British Columbia, as well as two other restaurant chains in Canada.

The Pillsbury Company bought Burger King Corporation, which had been founded in Miami in 1954 and which owns or franchises about 2,000 restaurants in this country, Puerto Rico, and the Bahamas. By 1973 it had 854 units. Pet, Inc. bought the Schrafft's Restaurants and Motor Inns. The company also runs the Steak and Ale chains.

Consolidated Foods owns the Chicken Delight chain, with more than 700 units; the Lyons-Magnus Division, 21 restaurants in northern California, and the Manners Management Division which operates 38 Big Boy Restaurants in Ohio. General Mills owns about 100 Red Lobster Inns and York Steakhouses. Quaker Oats has a series of Magic Pan Restaurants.

Ward Foods acquired Zuider Zee Oyster, Inc., a franchise chain of seafood houses. Ralston Purina has more than 300 restaurants known as Jack-in-the-Box, Oscar's Drive-In Hamburger House, and Family Tree Restaurants in southern California. Aristo Foods, Inc. operates restaurants and motels, mostly Holiday Inns, and has opened Drummer Boy Drive-Ins.

Green Giant owns the Henricks chain of dining restaurants. W. R. Grace, originally a shipping line and now a conglomerate of some 450 companies, owns three restaurant chains, Del Taco, El Torrito, and Far West Services. In 1977 Pepsi-Cola bought Pizza Hut for $300 million in stock. TWA owns Canteen, one of the largest contract food service operators.

The food manufacturing companies' entrance into foodservice marks a decided change in the character of the restaurant business: these companies bring capital, management know-how, and computer technology with them.

The restaurant business provides these companies with controlled sales outlets for their products. Their restaurants can be used as testing stations for food products. Even more important, the food companies have access to capital for acquiring sites for new restaurants and for buying existing ones. Some of the purchases by food companies, however, have not worked out well; one was a disaster. For a time

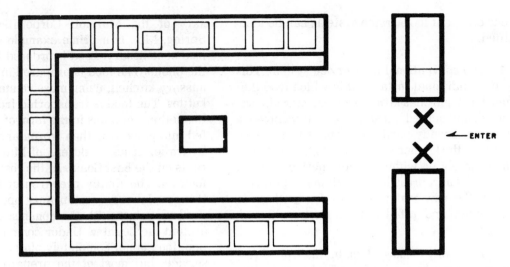

Figure 7-6   Floor plans.

about in the shopping center, going to the counter which is least crowded. Once the patron gets accustomed to the free flow, he usually likes it.

The shopping center, or open square, is like a giant U or open square. Three sides of the square are serving counters; hot foods on one side; salads and desserts on the other; and sandwiches and beverages on the third. Snack bars may be included as part of the scramble. Speed of service in a free flow system is largely determined by the number of cashiers; there should be enough to permit rapid egress of the customer from the system. Total area of the free flow system is greater than that mentioned for other systems.

The speed at which customers move through a cafeteria is also determined by the manner in which cashiering is done. In a commercial cafeteria a cashier can handle a maximum of six to eight transactions per minute, usually fewer. Adding a food checker who totals the bill before the customer arrives at the cashier station may double the number of transactions per minute. Sometimes the line must be slowed so as not to overcrowd the seating area. Free-flow service systems, with duplicate sections serving the same foods, but separated from each other, allow free flow of patrons, moving to the section least crowded, or selecting only the sections from which particular foods are desired.

Cafeterias have been particularly well-received by senior citizens who enjoy selecting only a few items from a great array of foods for a particular meal. The fact that many cafeterias avoid tipping by offering complete self-service is an attraction for the low-budget eater.

Successful commercial cafeterias usually prepare most of their food on the premises, especially when they have a volume of sales exceeding about $500,000 a year. A number of these cafeterias have sales in excess of $2 million a year. Often the cafeteria does its own baking with a baker who begins baking at 6 A.M., and has the baked goods ready for service at 11 A.M. The key to good food on the cafeteria line is for management to assure that the food is freshly cooked in relatively small quantities so that it does not have to remain in the steam pans on the line long enough to dry out and lose quality. This means that vegetables are often prepared by pressure steamers more or less continuously during the hours of service. Gelatin desserts and salads are not allowed to remain so long on the line that they become rubbery.

The use of frozen entrees has not been well-received for cafeteria service. One chain that was prominent in California withdrew from the field after trying to prepare meals in a commissary, freeze them, and serve them later in a number of their cafeterias.

FOODSERVICE SYSTEMS

The term foodservice system has been applied to the activities involved in purchasing, receiving, storing, preparing, and serving food. Some four different foodservice systems can be identified.

1 *The conventional foodservice system.* This is the traditional restaurant in which food that has been purchased is received, stored, prepared, and served. Most of the food received is raw, or already partially prepared. It is prepared in the kitchen and served to the customer immediately or within a short period of time. This system represents a small manufacturing plant, the raw material being food, which is processed and retailed to a restaurant customer.

2 *The ready foods system.* In this type of restaurant some or much of the food is prepared and frozen for later service, the rationale being that some kitchen skills may be available when food is not needed for service and that the food can be prepared in fairly large quantities and stored for use when needed. Food may be packaged in plastic pouches or prepared in quantity in pans. The system assumes that the skills are available in the kitchen to do this type of preparation, storage, and service, a dubious assumption for most kitchens.

3 *The centralized kitchen system.* Under this system, food is fully prepared and distributed for service within an area to a number of units. Sizable economies have been achieved in many school districts by preparing the food at a central kitchen and distributing it to the various school lunch rooms within the district, where it is served to the students.

4 *The central commissary foodservice system.* Under this system, food may be partially prepared and distributed within an area or over long distances. The centralized commis-

sary of the Marriott Corporation in Silver Spring, Md., is a prime example of a centralized commissary. Food is ordered by code over the phone. The food is prepared in a huge commissary kitchen, using massive steam-jacketed kettles. The food is transported from one place to another via pipes in the form of a slurry and fed into pans. It is then frozen and distributed by trailer truck to dozens of Marriott restaurants on the East Coast. At the restaurants, the food may be finally prepared or finished off. Howard Johnson restaurants operate with a similar system with the commissaries spaced around the country. Under commissary operation, food is not completely plated or ready for service, but most of the preparation is done prior to delivery to the restaurant. Many commissaries prepare only a few items, such as hamburger patties, soups, and sauces.

The "flight kitchen," where meals are prepared for service aboard airplanes, is a kind of commissary operation. Some airlines operate their own flight kitchens: others contract with airline catering companies for the purchase of meals.

5 *The convenience food system.* A convenience food system can be incorporated into any of the other systems. Much or all of the food is purchased pre-prepared and packaged in one form or another, ready for "conditioning" for service. The quality of convenience frozen foods varies widely. There are those who believe that the best of the frozen food cannot be distinguished from foods prepared from scratch on premise. Every restaurant uses a number of "convenienced" foods. It is a matter of degree as to how much of a convenience food system is incorporated into a foodservice.

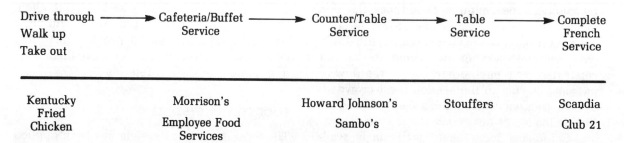

Figure 7-7 Degree of Service Offered. Minimal to Full Service is shown here, with examples of each style.

HOSPITAL FOOD SERVICE DELIVERY SYSTEMS

The larger hospitals with their several floors or wings and several hundred patients to be fed three or more times a day have special problems in preparing and delivering food to the patients in a palatable condition. A number of systems have been tried: centralized kitchens with food delivered by conveyor belts to the various floors or wings; food prepared centrally and delivered by cart, sections of which can be refrigerated and other parts heated; food prepared frozen or chilled, delivered to the floors and heated there by microwave oven.

The hospital food service system is complicated by the necessity of preparing a number of special diets—low fat, low cholesterol, low sodium, and such. When patients are given a choice of menu, the system becomes even more complicated.

Some delivery systems utilize a pellet system, the pellet heated and placed in a specially designed dish unit, to keep the food warm until served. Other units use a dish unit having a cover that when placed over the bottom part of the unit seals it, like a thermos bottle, and retains the heat. Several companies have produced food carts that become heat retainers when plugged in. One system uses an insulated cart that holds up to forty full trays. It can be hooked to a chilled air unit until heating begins within the cart. Computer-operated controls contain five heat selections and various temperatures for each tray. At the same time, refrigerated items remain cold. After thirty-five minutes that meal is cooked and ready. Panel buttons control the heating and permit holding late trays for patients who are not in their rooms when food is served. If computer controlled, it can be interfaced with existing hospital computer terminals. Carts keep food hot while being transported from kitchen to patient floor. Carts are powered by batteries, which are charged during the night.

The computer controlled hospital delivery system flow diagram seen on page 225 explains one such delivery system. Starting with the patient (1) the menu choice is placed on a memory tape (2). Using the computer entry board (3), the information is fed into the minicomputer with the memory tape (4). The memory tape is fed into a minicomputer, which is part of the food/beverage cart (5).

The food is taken from the chilled tray assemblies (7) and loaded into the cart (8) and the cart placed into a chilling/holding unit (9).

The cart is transported to the patient floor and connected to chilled/holding unit (10) and the cooking begins following instructions given by the memory tape (11). After the food is cooked the trays are delivered to the patient (14 and 15); and finally the soiled trays are placed back in a cart (16) ready to be transferred back to the scullery for washing and sanitizing.

One hospital food service that incorporated microwave reheating of food uses an oven that permits heating only half of a tray. The other half is shielded from the microwaves so that one tray, half to be heated, the other half to remain chilled, can be placed in the oven. This permits assembling the complete tray in a centralized area and avoids the necessity of adding the cold or chilled items later.

TRADE AND PROFESSIONAL RESTAURANT ORGANIZATIONS

Numerous state and local trade and professional organizations relating to the foodservice industry have been formed over the years. Some are specialized, such as The American Culinary Federation, whose members are primarily chefs. Others are more general in character, such as the Food Service Executives' Association with chapters here and abroad. Membership represents supervision, management, and ownership in the foodservice industry.

Some organizations are concerned primarily with fraternal social functions; others have been formed largely to deal with unions. Still others, such as The National Restaurant Association, and the various state associations are concerned with affecting legislation favorable to the industry and in preventing passage of unfavorable legislation. The National Restaurant Association, headquartered in Chicago, maintains a lobby in Washington, D.C., and conducts an active educational program, including seminars offered around the country and the operation of an active book department and research library.

The various state restaurant associations are not affiliated directly with The National Restaurant Association. Some are very strong

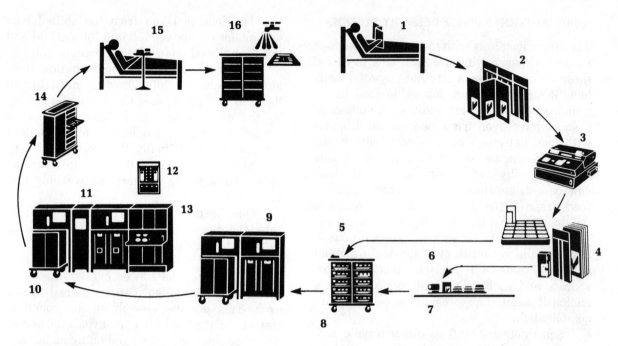

1. Patient Menu.
2. Menus and Memory Tape Worksheet.
3. Computer Entry Board (programs memory tape for cart).
4. Mini Computer with Memory Tape, Worksheet and Menus taken to chilled assembly line.
5. Mini Computer Food/Beverage Cart.
6. Menus.
7. Chilled Tray Assembly.
8. Food/Beverage Cart is loaded with Trays.
9. Food/Beverage Cart is connected to Chilling/Holding Unit.

10. After Food/Beverage Cart is transported to patient floor, it is connected to Chilled/Holding Units. There, hand-sized Mini Computer Pack is inserted into temperature unit.
11. Timed Temperature Control Unit begins scheduled cooking automatically.
12. Computer-operated Controls program non-scheduled meals individually.
13. Additional Unit for hot beverages (also stores undeliverable trays).
14. Meal Service (first time assembled trays are handled).
15. Patient is served.
16. Soiled Trays transferred for washing and sanitizing.

Figure 7–8   Computer Hospital Delivery System Flow Diagram.
Source: Volume Feeding/Institutions, December 15, 1977.

and effective, such as the California Restaurant Association, the Texas Restaurant Association, and the Indiana Restaurant Association. The strength and the effectiveness of the associations depend in a large part on their funds. Those that must rely completely on membership fees are not very effective. The National Restaurant Association with a budget of some $7 million a year receives much of its funding from profits made in conducting an annual trade show in Chicago. The California Restaurant Association receives similar funding from trade shows held in Los Angeles. The trade shows make possible the exhibition of

new food products, kitchen equipment, and a vast array of other products of interest to the foodservice operator. The fact that the expenses of attendance can be written off for tax purposes adds to the attractiveness of the shows.

MOTIVATION RELATED TO EATING OUT

In terms of motivational theory, people eat out for a variety of reasons: to satisfy hunger, to satisfy social needs, and satisfy ego and self-fulfillment needs. People select a particular restaurant because of particular psychological needs at the moment and the way they are feeling about the money they have to spend, the prices of a restaurant, its service and how the restaurant is perceived in terms of its esthetics, social status, and the kind of people that can be expected to be there, patrons, management, and employees.

Restaurants can be classified according to prices charged, the amount of service offered, and the extent of their menus. Well-known prestige restaurants like The Scandia in Los Angeles and Club 21 in New York City project an image of luxury—in price, in menu, and in service.

Moving down the scale a bit, the midpriced restaurants with full menus and "full-service" may be seen in places like Victoria Station and Trader Vics restaurants.

A step down the prestige line and into the moderately priced restaurants, we see such places as Sambos and Dennys with a full menu but moderate price and moderate service.

Limited menu restaurants like Pizza Hut and Bonanza are moderately priced with self-service. At the low end of the price spectrum are found the hamburger chains offering limited menus, low prices and self-service, restaurants such as Wendys, McDonalds, and Burger King.

Relating restaurant service, price, and menu size to physiological and psychological needs can be an interesting exercise that provides some insight into why people select particular restaurants. The most popular motivational theory, that proposed by Maslow, states that man is a wanting animal, always wanting. As soon as one need is satisfied another appears to take its place, moving from the safety or security needs up the scale through social, ego, and self-fulfillment needs. People go to restaurants to satisfy not only hunger but self-esteem, self-respect, self-confidence, and prestige needs. The chart below suggests that we may eat at a stand up snack bar to satisfy a hunger or physiological need but will select varying styles of restaurants to meet social needs and will finally go to the high-priced places for self-esteem and self-fulfillment needs.

DISPOSABLE INCOME AND RESTAURANT SALES

Aside from all of the reasons why people find pleasure in eating out or need to eat out, there is the problem of having the money to do so. Discretionary income is the key term here. It is the income that can be used as one sees fit, that left over from the sum required to meet expenses. A 1974 study of the U.S. Dept. of Labor found that families with incomes of about $19,000 or more a year spent more than a third of their food budgets eating out.

Eating out is usually pleasurable; therefore, the more discretionary income a person has, the more likely he is to eat out and to spend more in the process. The amount of disposable income in the United States was $160 billion in 1946. By 1961 the figure had more than doubled to reach $350 billion. In 1969 disposable income was close to $650 billion. In 1973 per capita disposable income was $4,195.

As disposable income increases, so, too, does the amount of money spent in eating and drinking places. Both almost doubled in the period of 1961 to 1969. In the United States the average annual increase of personal income was 6.1 percent between 1959 and 1966. For the same years, the average yearly increase in eating and drinking place sales averaged quite close to this fugure.[7] As with discretionary or disposable income, the greater the family income, the greater the proportion of it spent in restaurants.

Another interesting correlation between income and eating out: For every 1 percent increase in personal income, expressed in constant dollars, real eating place sales rose .84 percent from 1963 to 1967. Income elasticity rose to .96 percent from 1967 to 1972 and over 1 percent from 1973 to 1975.[8]

OTHER CORRELATES WITH EATING OUT

Several attempts have been made to identify other factors in the economy that correlate highly with restaurant sales. Mr. Steve Bram, a student at Claremont Men's College, did a correlation study of fair possible predictors for sales between years 1947 and 1975. He found that the growth of the percentage of families with incomes over $15,000 appeared to predict fairly accurately the true sales line during those years. Prediction errors appeared during the years 1947 and 1951, which could have

7. Washington Report, Vol. II, No. 48, November 25, 1968.
8. Economic Report, N.R.A. October 18, 1976.

been the result of the Korean War, and again in the period 1964 to 1968, probably the effects of the Vietnamese War.

Women in the labor force was a good predictor most of the time, following the actual sales line, except for the period after 1970 when women in the labor force did not increase as rapidly as did sales. Population growth turned out to be a poor predictor of restaurant sales. Disposable income was the best predictor of restaurant sales.[9]

THE SMALLER FAMILY AND THE WORKING WIFE INCREASE RESTAURANT SALES

With fewer children, smaller living spaces for the family, with less housework for the wife, the wife and other women have gone to work. The result: more disposable income, a greater desire to eat out, and the money to do so.

In 1950, about 24 percent of wives were in the labor force. This rate increased year by year so that by 1976 the rate was 45 percent. The portion of families having two or more workers rose from 36 percent in 1950 to almost 49 percent in 1976.[10] The median family income (what the middle range of families earn) in 1975 rose to more than $15,000, enough so that when the working wife came home at night she felt little guilt about insisting on eating out, or at the very least picking up prepared food from a take-out establishment.

9. "Statistical Models for the Restaurant Industry," Steve Bram, 1977.

10. Economic Report, NRA, August 8, 1977.

What's more, by 1985 half of the women in the country will be in the labor force. In the twenty- to twenty-four-age bracket 73 percent will be working, good news for the restaurant business.

Despite the massive growth of the restaurant chain the restaurant business is still a stronghold of free enterprise in the United States. Few businesses can be entered so easily with so little capital, and success or failure seen so quickly. Operators who have assessed the market correctly and put together the right menu and format of operation win big; those who are wrong, fail.

Chains and franchisors there are aplenty (31 percent of the total in 1972)—but anyone can join them with determination, know-how, and luck. The restaurateur—the small businessman—is still free to come up with a new design, a new recipe, a new market approach. And must do so periodically to win.

The advertising slogan of Jack-in-the-Box, "Watch out, McDonald's," can be applied to hundreds of restaurant owners. One thing is certain: McDonald's will one day be surpassed by a Wendy's, Carl's Jr., or someone just opening his first small restaurant. What goes well in the East may fail in the West, and vice versa. A restaurant flourishes, may proliferate into a chain, become stagnant, and be overtaken by a fresh format, a better market fix, a different sandwich, or a menu mix better tuned to a market. The restaurant business in the United States is challenging, changing, bringing wealth—and vast disappointment—to its practitioners.

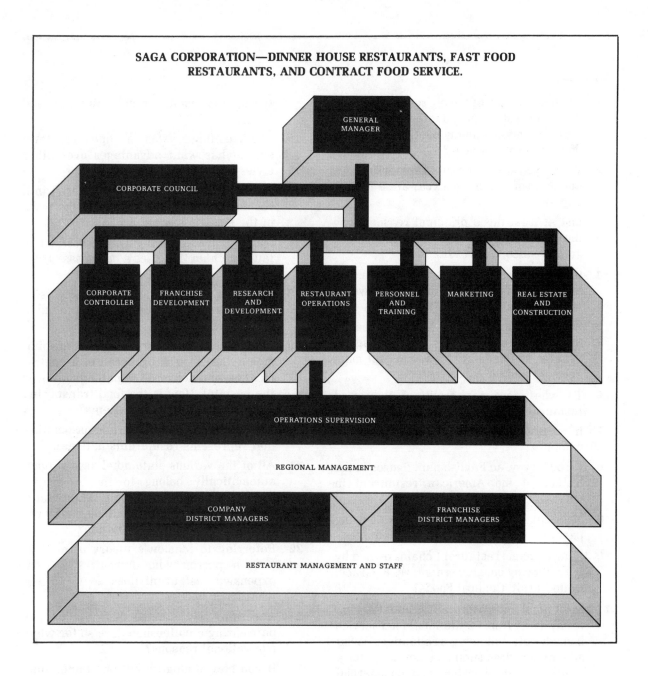

SAGA CORPORATION—DINNER HOUSE RESTAURANTS, FAST FOOD RESTAURANTS, AND CONTRACT FOOD SERVICE.

Questions

1 We tend to think of the big restaurants and the small restaurants, but the average restaurant does how many hundred thousand dollars in sales a year?

2 Would you say that restaurants with sales in excess of $1 million a year are a rarity? Explain.

3 List at least three principal reasons why the restaurant business has prospered so greatly since World War II.

4 It has been said that there are fewer restaurants today than there were twenty years ago. Is this true? Explain.

5 About 30 percent of all the employees in the restaurant business are teenagers. What does this imply for restaurant management and for labor costs?

6 To what does the origin of the word restaurant refer?

7 In what way is steak a la tartar related to hamburg?

8 Fred Harvey, an Englishman, figures in the history of the American restaurant in what way?

9 Name at least three advantages of being part of a chain and three disadvantages.

10 Can you name restaurant chains owned by the following conglomerates: W. R. Grace, United Fruit, General Foods?

11 Most hotel and restaurant graduates tend to shy away from institutional food service immediately following graduation. What advantages does such food service offer a graduate over working in a commercial restaurant unit or chain?

12 The term convenience food is often misunderstood. Would you describe sliced bread, ice cream, and canned vegetables as convenience foods? Why or why not?

13 Preprepared foods have their proponents and outspoken critics. Is there some middle ground regarding the use of such foods?

14 Food service is often divided into four types: American, French, Russian and _____.

15 The free-flow system or open cafeteria system has what advantages over other styles of cafeteria service?

16 As more complete service is offered in a restaurant what will happen to the price of the meal?

17 Name at least one highly successful restaurant chain that uses a commissary system.

18 Why is it that hospital food service is so much more complicated than that found in a restaurant?

19 Centralized food service in a hospital means that food is prepared in a central location and delivered to patients all over the hospital. How is the food transported from the kitchen to the patients?

20 What is the name of the trade association that represents restaurants nationally?

21 All of the various state hotel associations automatically belong to the American Hotel and Motel Association. Do the State Restaurant Associations automatically belong to the National Association?

22 Referring to Maslow's theory of motivation, a person who patronizes a very expensive restaurant does so to satisfy what basic needs?

23 According to the same theory, a person patronizing a coffeeshop does so for what motivational reasons?

24 If you had to identify but one factor that correlates most highly with the number of people eating out in the United States, what would that factor be, disposable income, unemployment rate, or rate of savings?

25 Which of these factors probably accounts for more of the increase in eating out than any other: the working woman, smaller family, smaller living spaces for the family, or more self-indulgence on the part of Americans?

RESTAURANT OPERATIONS

EIGHT

A person considering the restaurant business has several career and investment options:

Manage a restaurant for someone else, individual or a chain

Purchase a franchise and operate the franchise restaurant

Buy an existing restaurant

Build a new restaurant and operate it

In considering which way to go an individual can analyze the advantages and disadvantages of each style of operation and consider the potential risks and rewards of each option.

In comparing the advantages and disadvantages of buying, building, franchising, or managing, the individual should assess his own temperament, ambitions, and ability to cope with frustrations. Buying a restaurant may satisfy an aesthetic personal desire; if the restaurant is a success, the rewards can be very

high. If it fails, the financial risk is also high but usually not as high as if the investment were made in a new building. Franchising a restaurant reduces risk all along the line and may also reduce the potential reward because of franchise fees. No financial risks are ordinarily attached to being a manager, but the psychic cost of failure can be high.

Examples can be given of people who have gone into the restaurant business with almost no experience, built a restaurant, and been successful from day one. Such examples are relatively rare. In buying an existing restaurant that has failed or is for sale for some other reason, the purchaser has some information that the builder lacks. The buyer may know that the previous style of restaurant was not successful in that location or that a certain menu or style of management was unsuccessful. Such information could cut risks somewhat. On the other hand the buyer may find it diffi-

Table 8-1 Buy, Build, Franchise or Manage—Advantages and Disadvantages.

	Original Investment Needed	Experience Needed	Potential— Personal Stress	Psychic Cost— Failure	Financial Risk	Potential Reward
Buy	medium	high	high	high	high	high
Build	highest	high	high	highest	highest	high
Franchise	low to medium	low	medium	medium	medium	medium to high
Manage	none	medium to high	medium	medium	none	medium

cult to overcome a poor reputation acquired over a period of time by the previous operator.

As a general rule, it is best to learn a format of operation thoroughly before buying or building a restaurant. The franchisee is protected by the fact that he usually completes a management training course before opening a franchised restaurant. The franchise parent should be just as eager to avoid failure in any unit as is the franchisee, a plus factor for a franchisee. Of course, franchised restaurants also fail, and the prospective franchisee must be careful to select a reputable franchisor, one with an excellent track record.

RESTAURANT LOCATION

Generalizations about restaurant location are much more difficult to make than those relating to hotels and motels. Perhaps these statements are valid:

1 Restaurants catering to the luncheon trade must be reasonably convenient to the clientele. Other than the expense-account restaurants, the luncheon restaurant must be within a few minutes walk or drive of the clientele. In this country, most luncheons eaten away from home are consumed during a specified lunch time break that may last from thirty minutes to one hour. The business luncheon usually lasts much longer and includes liquor. The quickie luncheon, necessarily, must be close to the place of work, preferably in the same building. The expense-account luncheon can be farther away, but must be conveniently reached by taxi or private car.

2 The highway restaurants, on the main thoroughfares, are placed for convenience to the traveler. The restaurant catering to the highway traveler must be readily accessible. Even a five-minute drive from the highway may be disastrous for the restaurant.

3 Fast food restaurants are most successfully located adjacent to a main thoroughfare, in a busy shopping mall, or in an apartment condominium area.

4 Locations for the atmosphere, theme, or special-occasion restaurants can be less convenient. The clientele will search them out. One of the most successful in the world, in terms of

sales volume, is the Pier 4 Restaurant in Boston. It is relatively difficult to reach, but its harborside location adds glamour.

5 In a restaurant/entertainment concentration. In Marina del Rey, near Los Angeles, for example, some thirty-five restaurants are concentrated. The public comes to think of the area as a place to go for fun and eating out.

Some leading restaurants are found in highly unlikely locations. The Bakery, in Chicago, is found in a run-down part of the city. Commander's Palace in New Orleans is a long cab ride from the heart of town. This is not to say that such restaurants might not be even more successful if more conveniently and pleasantly located.

The "Tops"

Restaurants that are on the top of something have a special appeal. "Top" as a location did not become popular until the 1960s. Stouffer's now has thirteen "Tops," all of them successful. The Top of the Prudential Center in Boston, fifty-two stories in the sky, grosses more than $3 million a year in sales. The diner gets not only good food and drink but a marvelous view of Boston Harbor and metropolitan Boston. The top restaurant in the John Hancock Building in Chicago is ninety-five stories in the air; the World Trade Center in New York serves food on an even higher level.

The Germans were the first to revolve a restaurant, one built in 1959 atop a television tower in Stuttgart. La Ronde was our first revolving cocktail lounge and restaurant, perched on top of the La Moana office building in Honolulu. The Space Needle at Seattle's World's Fair brought wide publicity for the revolving restaurant. Currently, they exist around the world: in London, Brussels, Rotterdam, Frankfurt, Montreal, Cairo, Tokyo, and Hong Kong, among the many. Naturally, Russia has the highest, one called Seventh Heaven, an unexpected choice of name in an atheistic nation. It is perched on top of a television tower, 1,085 feet above the ground.

The revolving restaurants turn on donut-shaped turntables around a stationary core. Turntables may have a diameter as large as 132 feet. Believe it or not, only two ¾ horse

Figure 8–1 *Indicative of a trend to luxurious appointments in cafeterias is the Holiday House, a John R. Thompson Cafeteria in St. Louis. Note the wall to wall carpeting, the rich leather upholstered chairs, and decorative lighting fixtures. Note also the fact that the dining area has been broken up into several rooms.*

power motors are needed to revolve a restaurant weighing some 200,000 pounds and filled with over 300 diners.[1]

Obviously, revolving restaurants are expensive. However, since the supporting structure is usually built for some other reason, the restaurant itself may cost about $300,000. The restaurant in the Regency-Hyatt Hotel in Atlanta cost more than $650,000. Some problems in operating revolving restaurants exist: lingering customers, trouble finding one's seat after going to the restrooms, motion sickness.

Appeal of Revolving Restaurants

Kemmons Wilson, chairman of the board of Holiday Inns, who favors the revolving restaurant, is quoted as saying, "At a revolving res-

taurant the food is terrible, the price is high and the service low, but the people are lined up to get in." Wilson estimates that revolving restaurants attract more than twice the business ground level restaurants do.

The fact that the restaurants revolve makes them about 10 percent more attractive than the non-revolving rooftop restaurants. Most of the restaurants give the diner one complete turn around the building in the course of an hour. He can buy a drink or two, look down upon the little people, sit eye-level with a passing airplane, and become detached from it all. At the end of the hour's merry-go-round, the restaurateur hopes he will depart contented, relaxed, and minus $10 or more.

The character of the restaurant—its tempo, decor, noise level, and personnel—must fit a location. In a downtown congested area, people do not seem to mind being processed rather than served. Otherwise, how could the success of such chains as Chock Full O'Nuts

1. "Keeping the Diners Going in Circles," *Business Week*, July 13, 1968.

and the foodservice of Kresge's, Woolworth's, and Nedick's be explained?

Often the customer is required to push his way to the serving counter and stand while eating, then is expected to leave in about 10 minutes. Young people, especially, seem to relish this type of eating behavior. They will spend little more than a few minutes eating in college and university dining halls that are luxuriously equipped, carpeted, and lighted.

Dinner, however, is something else, especially for the middle-aged and older. The person who is satisfied to sit on a stool 14 inches away from somebody else at lunch wants a chair with arms on it and at least 15 square feet per customer while eating dinner.

Menu price goes with location. A luxury restaurant in a high seat-turnover location would fail, and the opposite would also be true.

THE USE OF ECONOMETRIC MODELS

The construction of mathematical models for site evaluation and diagnostic simulation, using the computer, is being done for food-service operations. Econometric (combining economics and mathematics) modeling began in the 1930s and has been used for some years in other businesses. These models have been devised for restaurants by Professor Francis R. Cella at the University of Oklahoma.

Professor Cella was given a contract in 1966 by the Oklahoma Restaurant Association for the development of models of restaurant operations. These were to be used to simulate a restaurant operation, using a computer, and to determine the potential sales of the restaurants. According to Professor Cella, his models can predict the sales of the restaurant within 5 percent, plus or minus, 95 percent of the time.

Initially, models were built for five types of foodservice operations: general, cafeteria, drive-in, specialty, and hamburger. Information used in building the models was developed from the various experiences of Oklahoma residents.

The theory behind the construction of a model is that if the importance of the various factors which determine the sales of a restaurant can be pinpointed and weighted, according to their effect on sales, then by using the computer it is a matter of a few minutes to derive a forecast of what sales should be pro-

duced by that restaurant. The more obvious factors that bear on restaurant sales are: the population in the vicinity of the proposed or operating restaurant; the income of that population; the number of competitors in the area; the volume of traffic passing the location; the ability of the manager of the restaurant; the amount of advertising that is done, and the appearance and kind of structure which houses the restaurant.

Up to Thirty Factors Affect Sales

According to Professor Cella, a minimum of sixteen factors affect sales volume, a number that rises to thirty for some kinds of restaurant operations. Subsequently, models for other restaurants have been developed and numerous models built for chain operations. Over 1,000 site evaluations were made between the period of 1966 to 1969.

In addition to being able to predict the volume of business for a potential site, the models can be used for determining whether a particular location is being put to its best use. A location on which an unsuccessful drive-in had been operating was found to be a good location for a hamburger stand. The change was made and, after a shakedown period, the business made more money in one month as a hamburger stand than it had in the previous twelve months operating as a drive-in restaurant.[2]

In addition to projecting total business, the models can be used for making management decisions. Each projected course of action can be tested by simulation. If the advertising budget is increased by 5 percent, a forecast of the additional sales it would generate can be made. How much additional business can be expected if the restaurant is refurbished? Would it be better to divide an investment among a combination of factors or to concentrate it on a single factor? How much additional business can be expected if a more experienced manager is employed?

Without the use of computers, the mathematics of correlating the effects of the factors upon the gross sales and upon each other would be very time-consuming. According to

---

2. Francis R. Cella, *Retail Site Selection*. Printed privately, 1970.

Professor Cella, without a computer it would take forty clerks six months to manually make the calculations necessary for one model. Using an IBM 360, these calculations are made in less than five minutes.

The construction of the model cannot be done by a beginner, since some of the factors involved which affect restaurant sales are negative and some are non-linear. Decisions as to whether a factor is important enough to warrant inclusion in the model requires judgment as well as reference to the experience of a number of operations.

In the past, each expert has been able to prove that his specialty is the all-important factor affecting total sales. The sales manager feels that advertising is the all-important factor; the production man feels sure that the quality of the product is most important; the designer feels that the building structure is the thing that brings people in. With an econometric model, the size of each factor's contribution can be determined with a greater degree of accuracy.

Weighing the various factors affecting sales also requires judgment, some trial and error, and reference to the experience of established restaurants. A critical factor in the location of a restaurant is the minimal size of the market needed, what size population is required to support a particular kind of restaurant.

The Kentucky Fried Chicken people say that their restaurants can do about $200,000 in sales in a community of 10,000 people. Population requirements for a McDonald's were once stated by the company at 30,000. Later the company found that in heavily urbanized communities McDonald's restaurants could be located three miles apart. A Polynesian restaurant, serving food that is relatively exotic for the average American palate, may require a market of 500,000. Fried chicken and hamburgers are considered a regular part of the diet; sweet and sour pork is not.

The factor of "competition" also requires close scrutiny. Three restaurants, side by side, may complement each other rather than compete with each other. Numerous "restaurant rows" have experienced added business for each restaurant as other restaurants are added. A fried chicken, a hamburger, and a steak house may not compete with each other if

the total market available is large enough. Three hamburger restaurants in the same block almost certainly will compete with each other. An additional hamburger restaurant will necessarily reduce the market of the established ones.

Is a Restaurant Feasible?

Making a major investment in a restaurant is a very risky proposition and requires as much planning as possible. Some of the major accounting firms stand ready to conduct feasibility studies, and the results can be used in procuring necessary loans.

The feasibility study follows this suggested pattern.

The proposed restaurant will cost $2,000 per seat.

Return on the investment should be at least 15 percent.

What projected sales would be necessary?
$200,000 × 15% = $30,000
Estimated operating profit—10%
Sales needed, $30,000 divided by 10%
= $300,000

Suppose the restaurant has 100 seats. The feasibility projection worksheet as see on page 236 (taken from a Bank of America study) gives approximations of what can be expected in the way of volume of sales, food and labor costs, and major costs encountered in the restaurant.

THE MENU

The selection of the menu and method of presentation to reach a particular market is critical. The menu, to a large extent, determines what market can be reached. The hamburger-fried chicken-milkshake menu reaches the teenagers and the young marrieds. The steak menu is for the more affluent middle-aged market. The Polynesian menu must be aimed at the "special occasion" market and those people who want to experience a different atmosphere. The meat and potatoes menu may be right for the "have-to" eating out market, the people who eat out day after day and expect to eat more or less the same things that they would have eaten at home. The French menu, indeed individual French menu items, are for

SALES VOLUME

Meals	Number of Seats		Average Turnover Per Seat		Possible Daily Volume		Average Check Per Seat		Highest Daily Sales		Vacant Seat Factor		Total Sales Per Meal		Days Open Weekly		Weekly Sales		Weeks Open Yearly		Yearly Sales
Breakfast	___	X	___	=	___	X	___	=	___	X 2/3	=	___	X	___	=	___	X	___	=	___
Lunch	___	X	___	=	___	X	___	=	___	X 2/3	=	___	X	___	=	___	X	___	=	___
Dinner	___	X	___	=	___	X	___	=	___	X 2/3	=	___	X	___	=	___	X	___	=	___

TOTAL SALES DAILY ___   WEEKLY ___   YEARLY ___

FOOD COSTS

Total Daily Sales ___ $\times \frac{1}{3}$ = DAILY FOOD COSTS ___ X Days Open Weekly ___ = Weekly Food Costs ___ X Weeks Open Yearly ___ = Yearly Food Costs ___

PAYROLL

Manager   Monthly pay ___ X 12 = ___ = Yearly Pay

Serving Staff	Average No. Workers Per Shift		Pay Per Worker		Number of Shifts		Daily Payroll		Days Per Week		Weekly Payroll		Weeks Per Year		Yearly Payroll
Waiters/Waitresses	___	X	___	X	___	=	___	X	___	=	___	X	___	=	___
Busboys/Busgirls	___	X	___	X	___	=	___	X	___	=	___	X	___	=	___
Kitchen Staff															
Chief Cook	___	X	___	X	___	=	___	X	___	=	___	X	___	=	___
Other Cooks	___	X	___	X	___	=	___	X	___	=	___	X	___	=	___
Helpers	___	X	___	X	___	=	___	X	___	=	___	X	___	=	___
Other Employees															
Bartenders	___	X	___	X	___	=	___	X	___	=	___	X	___	=	___
Cocktail Waitresses	___	X	___	X	___	=	___	X	___	=	___	X	___	=	___
Cleanup Staff	___	X	___	X	___	=	___	X	___	=	___	X	___	=	___
Others	___	X	___	X	___	=	___	X	___	=	___	X	___	=	___

DAILY PAYROLL ___   WEEKLY PAYROLL ___   YEARLY PAYROLL ___

TOTALS

	Daily	Weekly	Yearly
Sales	___	___	___
Food Costs	___	___	___
Payroll	___	___	___

Figure 8–2 Feasibility Projection Worksheet.
Source: Figures compiled by Small Business Reporter in California.

the more sophisticated markets, the more widely traveled, and the affluent. The sandwich menu apparently reaches just about everyone, at least for lunch, from the club member to the vacationer on the throughway.

The American restaurant public likes beef. Of the 600 pounds of food that the average American eats each year, more than 100 pounds will be beef. Consumption of pork is going down; chicken is rising, also turkey; cheese is going up fast; lamb and mutton consumption is down, and veal is going down. Fish and game are about holding their own.

Ham or bacon and eggs are most preferred at breakfast, but after these Gallup poll results showed that for breakfast young people would like fancy pancakes and sweet or Danish rolls.

Among foreign and specialty foods served in restaurants, the same poll found that Italian food was the leader, followed by seafood. French fried shrimp and lobster tail were the favorites among the seafood choices. Coffee is still the most popular restaurant beverage, but, especially among young people, the cold drinks are gaining.

Tampering with Tastes Unwise

The restaurant operator is not wise to try to change tastes. He may discover that a market exists for tacos and other Mexican food. If so, well and good, but he must not try to force tacos, or anything else, down anybody's throat. Liver may be an excellent item nutritionally, but it cannot be served more than about once a month in a college foodservice.

It is quite possible, however, to modify existing tastes, to add a fillip to a basic, popular food. For example, Lum's steams its hot dogs in beer. Wurst is a modified hot dog and appeals to a more sophisticated market than the usual hot dog eater.

Nearly everyone likes roast beef and steak. There seems to be a growing preference for foods that are more acid, probably because of the vast amount of carbonated drinks being consumed, most of which are on the acid side. Almost all kinds of snacks are increasing in popularity. The popularity of seafood has gone up; witness the number of successful seafood restaurants.

Some of the most popular new menu items are those that stimulate a number of senses —smell, taste, feeling—all at once.

A hot fudge sundae sets off sensory responses for hot, cold, sweet, and bitter. Add nuts and get a desirable chewiness. Even pain elicited by red pepper has a role in the favorable response to foods. One reason for the popularity of Creole cookery is the bite in the liquid hot pepper sauce used. The gas in carbonated beverages acts on the pressure senses in the mouth. Noise, in the form of the "snap, crackle, and pop" of some foods, is appreciated.

Preference for that old Italian favorite, tomato sauce, is growing, as seen in the rapid growth of the consumption of pizza, spaghetti, and other tomato-sauced foods. There are 300 pizza operators in Milwaukee alone. Kids like hamburgers, hot dogs, french fries, fried chicken, and spaghetti. They like french fries high in fat, about 18 percent fat.

A severely limited menu may be satisfactory in a new market until competition moves in. Then other items may have to be added to reach additional people. McDonald's has added the fish sandwich, the twin-patty hamburger, breakfast, and continues to add other food items in its operations.

The menu determines the kitchen equipment needed: broiled items on the menu require a broiler or a grooved griddle; fried items need a deep fat fryer. One successful group of fish and chips restaurants has no other equipment in its kitchens except deep fat fryers.

Menu Tastes Change

Fried foods are growing in popularity, especially among younger people. And why not? Most foods that are fried are low in fat to begin with—potatoes, young chickens, onions, and veal. The frying process adds about 10 to 15 percent fat to them, which brings the total fat content up to what is found in a good hamburger.

What constitutes a prestige food for a menu changes with time. Brillat-Savarin, the famous gourmet of the early nineteenth century, ranked truffles and turkeys as the twin jewels of gastronomy. Truffles and caviar are still high status, probably because of cost.

Terrapin turtle, once on nearly every important menu, disappeared almost completely when sherry and Madeira, needed for cooking it properly, were outlawed by prohibition. Canvasback duck was largely eliminated when Army Ordnance took over the bird's favorite feeding grounds in Chesapeake Bay. Not being able to eat their favorite wild celery, they lost their distinctive flavor and, thus, popularity. Hamburgers, before 1930, were low status.

High status dishes today, at least those served in the prestige restaurants in New York City, include Duck a l'Orange (duckling in an orange and wine sauce), Truffled Fresh Foie Gras (truffled goose liver pate), Veal Cordon Bleu (thin slices of veal stuffed with ham and cheese), and Chateaubriand (thick tenderloin usually served with Bordelaise sauce). Lobster and crab are other prestige items, largely because of their cost.

Wines are also judged to some extent by cost. Among the status wines today are: Romanee-Conti, considered by many to be the greatest red wine of Burgundy; Le Montrachet, usually conceded to be the greatest white wine of Burgundy; and Chateau Y'quem, the "great" sauterne. Blind taste-testing would find most Americans choosing other wines, ones much less expensive.

Food Habits Change

Food habits and food preparation methods change with time, despite the efforts of purists to sanctify certain recipes and culinary practices. A good many people still refer to Escoffier's Le Guide Culinaire as the "Bible." The "Bible," it turns out, was written in 1902 and, as Escoffier said, was merely a collection of the best culinary information then available. Before Escoffier, Careme was the culinary arbiter.

In about 1958, the Hotel and Restaurant Catering Institute of Great Britain decided to establish once and for all what was right and wrong in the culinary world. A committee of twelve top chefs in Great Britain was appointed to the task. The committee set about diligently to develop a Codex Culinaris.

After 2½ years of weekly meetings, endless debates, and much controversy, the project quietly died. The chefs, representing a number of national cuisines, found it difficult to arrive at any particular standard, since what is good food is largely a matter of what is considered good by a particular social group, at a particular point in time. "One man's meat is another man's poison."

Name almost any food eaten by almost any group and you will find that somewhere in the world another group despises it. The fact that the French are more likely to use potato starch as a thickener than cornstarch only means that potato starch is more readily available in France and that cornstarch is cheap and handy in the U.S. The wide use of veal in Europe may mean that farmers are not so likely to raise their cattle to maturity as is done in the U.S. Culinary sacrilege usually implies that whoever is committing it is not performing according to the rules or value systems held by the accuser.

WHAT MAKES FOR PRESTIGE

What is the posh food changes with time. In this country in 1870, a prestige dinner might include buffalo tongue or, in San Francisco, bear's paw. At the turn of the century, canvasback duck and terrapin were prestige foods. Madeira wine was in, hamburgers were out and remained out until the 1930s and later.

One reason lobster is acclaimed at the moment is because of its high price. Go to any area where lobster is in plentiful supply and low in cost and it is not a prestige food. Chicken is losing its culinary status because of its low price.

Much of wine snobbery has a flimsy basis; the "authority" happens to know a little more about the subject than somebody else. One thing that gives a wine a reputation as being extremely good is its price; the higher the price, the better the wine. Tests of taste preference conducted so that the taster does not know the brand name, price, and origin often produce startling results. Less expensive beverages are frequently selected as best. The same wine placed in different bottles sets off arguments as to which wine is better. Of course, much of dining is romance, and who is the nasty fellow who would destroy romance?

The menu, in large part, determines the clientele. Some restaurant chains, such as Stouffer's, carry a range of menu items that will appeal in character and price to most American families. The usual drive-in menu is designed to cater to those under thirty. The club menu is not in character unless it concentrates on the small of the back—the tender, expensive cuts from the loin of the animal.

VARIATION IN RESTAURANT COSTS BY RESTAURANT TYPE AND SALES VOLUME

Some costs vary with the style of the restaurant. The fast food restaurants typically have lower food and labor costs than table service restaurants, while occupancy costs with the fast food places are usually higher than for the table service restaurant. As might be expected as restaurant sales increase the percentage of gross profit also increases. In other words the large volume restaurants generate higher profits and a higher percentage of profit as well. Restaurant costs and profits, of course, vary around the country. Labor costs in California run higher than they do for the country as a whole. Profits in California coffee shops and dinner houses are higher than for table service restaurants generally around the country.[3]

Occupancy costs vary widely depending upon the arrangement between the operator and the owner of the land and/or restaurant. Many restaurateurs try for a five-year lease to avoid being tied to a location that could prove unsuitable. Leases are paid in several ways:

1　Minimum sum plus, or against, a specified percentage of the gross

2　Straight percentage of gross (this is usually 5 to 8 percent)

3　Percentage of gross sales that can slide up or down (the more or less the lessee makes, the more or less the landlord gets)

4　A flat monthly sum

Various other arrangements are common, such as the lease trade-off: the more improvements the landlord makes, the higher the rent. The more improvements the operator makes, the lower the rent. Trade-offs are important when the operator is beginning a new restaurant or plans extensive remodeling.

A turn-key lease is one where the restaurant, completely furnished, is turned over to an operator for a flat sum.

A restaurant grossing $1 million needs about eighty employees. These average figures mean little, however, since in very efficient restaurants the productivity per employee may exceed $30,000 a year in sales.

As sales increase, the cost of food consumed tends to go down. In one study, the cost of food and beverages, including employees' meals, ran 40.2 percent in establishments doing less than $100,000 a year in sales. Food cost was reduced as sales increased, until finally, in those restaurants doing between $500,000 and $1 million in sales, food cost dropped to 36 percent.

RESTAURANT PROFITABILITY

Handsome profits have been made in the restaurant business; also many failures have taken place over the years. Amateurs have "made it big," but not often. Even the professionals make mistakes in projecting a style of restaurant for a particular market, and most of the larger chains have had their share of losers. The chain can afford to lose on a few places; the individual cannot.

Consider the profits that are possible with a big winner. Some restaurants gross $12,000 to $16,000 per seat each year while the national average is less than $4,000 per seat. Seat turnover can be as high as seven per hour,

Table 8-2　The Restaurant Industry Dollar

Where It Came From	
Food Sales	76.2
Beverage Sales	23.2
Other Income	.6
Where It Went	
Cost of Merchandise Sold	
Food	31.6
Beverage	6.1
Total	37.7
Payroll and Related Expenses	
Payroll	26.6
Employee Benefits	3.8
Total	30.4
Direct Operating Expenses	5.4
Music and Entertainment	.7
Advertising and Promotion	1.8
Utilities	2.2
Administrative and General	4.7
Repairs and Maintenance	1.7
Occupation Costs	
Rent, Property Taxes, and Insurance	5.7
Interest	.7
Depreciation	2.2
Other Deductions	.6
Net Income Before Income Tax	6.2

3. *California Restaurant Operations, 1977*, Laventhol and Horwath, Los Angeles, California.

or sixty customers per day. In dinner houses seat turnover is more like one per hour or more while the average restaurant gets less than two or three per hour.

In the United States restaurants as a whole, if $200,000 is invested, the restaurant grosses about $500,000 in sales. Of course, such ratios, investment to sales, vary widely. In recent years many restaurants represent million dollar investments and expect $1 to $3 million in sales per year. Seats in the dining rooms of the Marriott Motor Hotels are expected to produce about $5,000 per seat per year.

At the other end of the service scale, as it runs from fast food to elegant service, were La Fonda del Sol and the Four Seasons, at that time also operated by Restaurant Associates Industries. These restaurants were known over the country as high check average, deluxe service restaurants. Yet neither of these restaurants was particularly profitable. The Four Seasons is now operated by Paul Kovi and Tom Margittai and is doing well.

Restaurant corporations seldom report net profit, as a percent of sales, exceeding 12 percent. Nationally, the figure is below 5 percent. Corporations are not eager to show high profits on which they must pay corporation taxes. Of course, many restaurant operations are pleased to show any profits.

When a restaurant is successful, it is likely to be successful in a big way. The Pier 4 Restaurant in Boston, an independent owned by Anthony Athanas, has sales exceeding $8 million a year, the largest for any independent single restaurant. With this kind of volume, net profit would probably approach somewhere around 20 percent of sales before taxes, or something like $1.6 million a year in profit before taxes.

Restaurant profits vary widely depending on a number of factors: check average, seat turnover, cost of food, labor costs, occupancy costs, costs of advertising, and other costs. The fast food outlet, such as McDonald's, has a relatively low labor cost because of employing mostly teenagers and paying minimum wages. Some table service restaurants reduce occupancy costs by remodeling old stores, barns, and houses. Food costs are considerably lower in a Mexican restaurant than in a steak house, though both may be highly successful. The coffee shop may have a check average of $1.70, as compared with one of $20 for a gourmet restaurant. Yet the coffee shop may be much more profitable because of greater seat turnover and lower food and labor costs.

The chart, Operating Ratios, compiled by the *Small Business Reporter, Bank of America*, 1975, compares expenses among various styles of restaurants: table service, drive-in, fast food/carry out, coffee shop, and cafeteria. The fast food/carry out service comes out the winner in profit because of lower food and labor costs. Other styles of service can be highly profitable. Of course, fast food units, as well as other styles of service can fail.

By contrast, in an individually owned business or partnership, the profit includes the owner's return from the operation. Corporation profits of necessity will be lower than profits of other legal forms: this is so because of the differences in accounting methods.

As an ideal, one might set up a model restaurant which costs $3,000 per seat. With 100 seats, the restaurant's total cost could be $300,000. Ideally, we would want $10,000 per seat in sales per year, or $1 million. Ideally, we would want a net profit before taxes of 20 percent or $200,000 a year.

RESTAURANT IDEAL

Capital Cost	$300,000
100 seats @ $2,000 per seat	
Sales Per Year	$1,000,000
100 seats @ $10,000 per seat	
Profit Before Taxes	
20% of sales ($1,000,000)	$200,000

Of course, only a handful of restaurants, placed in high income, high density locations, have such a record. Average sales per seat in successful restaurants in 1975 were about $4,000.[4] As might be expected, restaurants serving liquor usually have slower turnover of seats and fewer sales per seats. The higher profit on liquor tends to compensate for the lower total sales.

Sales Per Seat May Mislead

Sales per seat, of course, is only one way of measuring efficiency and can be misleading. In

4. *Tableservice Restaurants Operation Report 1976*, NRA, 1977.

Table 8-3 Operating Ratios.

	Table Service 100%	Drive-In 100%	Fast Food/ Carry Out 100%	Coffee Shop 100%	Cafeteria 100%
SALES	[food 70%-80%] [beverage 20%-30%]				
COST OF SALES	35.0 - 44.0	35.0 - 40.0	30.0 - 40.0	33.0 - 38.0	35.0 - 42.0
GROSS PROFIT	56.0 - 65.0	60.0 - 65.0	60.0 - 70.0	62.0 - 67.0	58.0 - 65.0
OPERATING EXPENSES					
Controllable Expenses					
Payroll	30.0 - 35.0	25.0 - 35.0	20.0 - 30.0	30.0 - 35.0	27.0 - 35.0
Employee Benefits	3.0 - 5.0	3.0 - 6.0	2.0 - 4.0	3.0 - 8.0	2.5 - 6.0
Employee Meals	1.0 - 2.0	1.0 - 2.0	0.5 - 1.0	1.0 - 2.0	1.0 - 2.0
Laundry, Linen, Uniforms	1.5 - 2.0	0.3 - 1.0	0.3 - 0.8	0.5 - 1.5	0.5 - 1.5
Replacements	.5 - 1.0			0.5 - 0.75	0.5 - 0.75
Supplies (guest)	1.0 - 1.5	2.0 - 6.0	4.0 - 10.0	1.0 - 0.7	1.0 - 2.0
Menus and Printing	.25 - .5			0.2 - 0.7	
Misc. Contract Expense (cleaning, garbage, extermination, equip. rental)	1.0 - 2.0	0.75 - 1.5	0.5 - 2.0	0.1 - 0.3	0.5 - 1.5
Music and Entertainment (where applicable)	.5 - 1.0			0.1 - 0.3	
Advertising and Promotion	.75 - 2.0	1.0 - 2.0	0.5 - 2.0	0.75 - 1.5	0.5 - 1.5
Utilities	1.0 - 2.0	2.0 - 4.0	1.0 - 2.0	1.5 - 3.0	1.5 - 3.0
Management Salary	2.0 - 6.0	3.0 - 10.0	5.0 - 10.0	7.0 - 15.0	3.0 - 6.0
Administrative Expense (including legal and accounting)	.75 - 2.0	0.5 - 1.0	.25 - .75	0.5 - 1.0	1.0 - 2.0
Repairs and Maintenance	1.0 - 2.0	1.0 - 2.0	0.5 - 1.5	1.0 - 2.0	1.5 - 2.5
Occupation Expense					
Rent	4.5 - 9.0	4.5 - 8.0	3.5 - 7.0	4.0 - 7.0	4.0 - 5.0
Taxes (real estate and personal property)	.5 - 1.5	2.0 - 3.0	0.5 - 1.0	1.0 - 2.0	0.5 - 1.5
Insurance	.75 - 1.0	0.5 - 1.0	0.5 - 1.0	1.0 - 2.0	0.75 - 1.0
Interest	.3 - 1.0	1.0 - 2.0	0.2 - 0.8	0.5 - 2.0	0.5 - 1.5
Depreciation	2.0 - 4.0	1.5 - 4.0	3.5 - 7.0	2.0 - 3.0	2.0 - 3.0
Franchise Royalties (where applicable)	3.0 - 6.0	3.0 - 6.0	3.0 - 6.0	3.0 - 6.0	3.0 - 6.0
TOTAL OPERATING EXPENSES	55.0 - 65.0	53.0 - 60.0	47.0 - 57.0	57.0 - 65.0	51.0 - 61.0
NET PROFIT BEFORE INCOME TAX	0.5 - 9.0	6.0 - 12.0	10.0 - 20.0	2.0 - 10.0	3.0 - 7.0

Source: Figures developed by Small Business Reporter.

Valle's Steak Houses, a New England-based chain, each seats about 1,000 persons. Each restaurant costs about $1 million, or $1,000 per seat. Income before taxes was $2.5 million, or a little over 15 percent of sales. Part of the high profit comes from liquor sales.

Chain restaurants and franchise restaurants usually gross at least $400,000 annually and to be really profitable usually gross more than $500,000 annually. These operations are growing in number each year.

If a restaurant is a winner, the return on investment can be very high. A restaurant doing sales of $1 million a year may make as much as $200,000 net profit, before taxes. Such a restaurant might cost $1 million to build. Return on investment (ROI) could be 20 percent. A good restaurant today costs between $2,000 and $5,000 per seat to build and equip, depending upon size, cost of land, and appointments. A 100-seat restaurant would run between $200,000 and $500,000 in cost. Such a restaurant should gross between $400,000 and $600,000 in sales per year. If it nets 8 percent before taxes, profits would be $32,000 to $50,000 a year.

A few years ago, a restaurant that grossed $1 million in sales a year was a phenomenon. Not so today. In 1969 a McDonald's drive-in restaurant took in $1 million; in 1976 more than 100 McDonald's in Canada grossed $1 million in sales. One McDonald's exceeds $3 million. In 1975, dozens of restaurants exceeded the $1 million figure. A number do in excess of $3 million in annual sales. The really financially successful restaurant grosses at least $500,000 a year. At this figure, food cost is likely to be about 36 percent of sales, labor cost below 30 percent of sales (not always). A winner in a restaurant is likely to be a winner indeed.

Like most businesses, profits are not a direct straight-line percentage of sales. Each restaurant has a break-even point in sales, a point at which the income just pays for all of the operating costs and fixed costs. Until the restaurant reaches the break-even point in sales, no profit at all has been made.

Once the break-even point in sales has been passed, profits may rise on an accelerated scale. For example, the break-even point for a restaurant might be $1,000 in sales a day. If the restaurant does $1,500 in sales, profit may be 10 percent on every dollar of sales beyond $1,000. The profit may jump to 20 percent as sales pass the $1,500 mark. When sales go beyond a certain figure, the operation reaches the point of diminishing returns. When sales go beyond that point, profit begins to fall off.

The break-even point for restaurants varies widely. The family-operated restaurant may have a break-even point of only $50 or so a day. If there is little business, the wife merely retires from the scene. Taxes, insurance, utilities, depreciation, and other fixed costs, however, go on. Large and expensive restaurants have high break-even points. The Four Seasons, a luxury restaurant in New York City, at one time was said to have a break-even point of $6,000 a day. The Kon Tiki and Trader Vic type of restaurant are said to need sales of about $500,000 per year to break even.

In the chart on page 243, the break-even point is $150 in sales per day.[5] If sales rise to $250 a day, profit would be the difference between S1 and P1, or about $25. If sales go $350 in one day, profit would be $50. The point of diminishing returns would be reached when a line representing cost began trending upward and paralleled the sales line.

No Magic Formula

A survey of table service restaurants done in 1976 for the National Restaurant Association showed a break-even point for the restaurants covered of $2,785 per seat. That volume of sales could have been achieved by a daily seat turnover of 1.24 and an average check (food) of $4.69.

Fixed expenses in that study ran about $560 per seat, expenses which go on whether the restaurant has any business or not. Variable expenses ran about 80 percent of sales. The chart showing the break-even point in terms of expenses per seat is on page 243.

A wide variety in menu format has been successfully merchandised in this country. The upgraded railroad diner, serving foods right off the grill, has been favored in parts of the East by the highway traveler. It is especially popular in New Jersey where most of the "dining cars" have been built. Originally, the diner was a railroad dining car that had been taken out of service or a structure patterned after such a car. New diners are lavish indeed, and expensive.

Nondescript restaurants have been known to succeed for a time, perhaps because of good location and the personality of the operator. Funky restaurants with oddly assorted themes often succeed, whereas the more traditional restaurant does not. Deluxe restaurants come and go. Fashions in decor change. The specialty restaurant, which has spread widely since World War II, has had a greater chance of success because of its specialization.

5. "Using Break-Even Analysis in Food Service Establishments," *Food Management Program Leaflet No. 13* (Amherst, MA: College of Agriculture, University of Massachusetts).

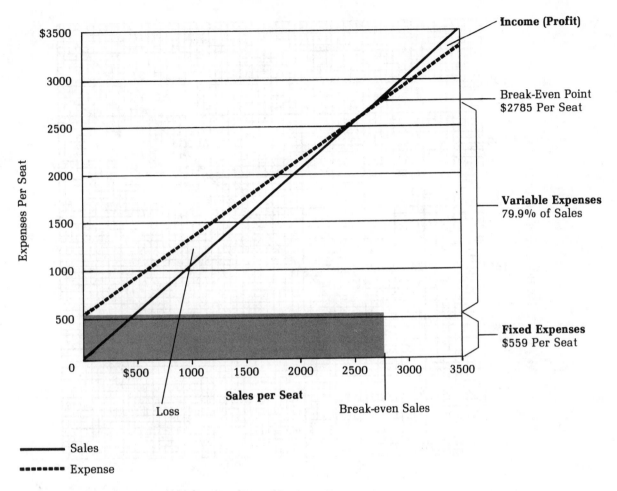

Figure 8–3 The Break-Even Point.

If a restaurant meets a need or evokes excitement, glamour, or adventure, the restaurant will succeed, if it is well managed. The big money-makers in restaurants seem to be those restaurants (1) offering a menu that is familiar to a market, or (2) that glamourize a familiar menu. The menu should be offered in an impressive, pleasing, or exciting milieu. For the teenager and patrons in their twenties, the noise level must be much higher than in the restaurant catering to older persons. Loud, rhythmic music—even noise—is pleasing to the teenager and the person in his twenties. The "tension level" must be higher for them. A buffet served in a country club will be a failure, if it has the same tension level.

The decor must be pleasing or impressive to a particular market. Something that is known to be expensive, or has status, impresses most people. Americans and Germans have stood in line to stay overnight at Woburn Abbey and breakfast with the Duke and Duchess of Bedford. The tariff was $200 per person.

Charles Creighton has put together some of the most attractive and beautiful restaurants in the world in South Florida. Instead of charging luxury prices, he caters to the great mass of people with a moderately priced menu. His profits are considerable. What is impressive or exciting changes with time. It is a format that usually wins: modestly priced food in luxury surroundings.

Food is only one aspect of a restaurant. All hamburger chains sell hamburgers, one not much different from the other. Why then are McDonald's and Burger Chef so large? The setting and the advertising account for much of the success of one hamburger operation versus another.

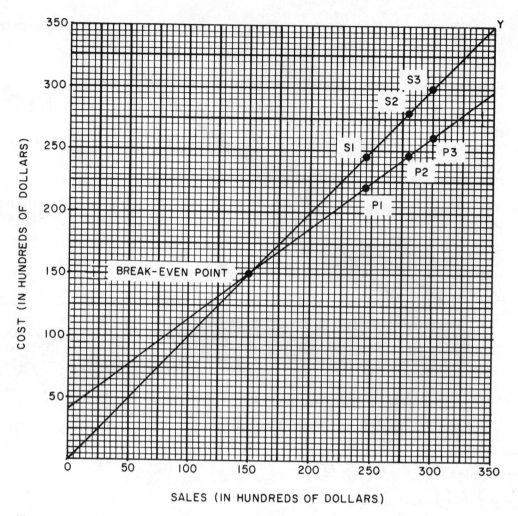

Figure 8-4   *Daily Break-Even Chart.*

If there is a formula for success in the restaurant business it goes something like this:

1   Identify a potential market

2   Develop a menu that will appeal to that market

3   Build a restaurant around the menu that will also appeal to the market

4   Locate the restaurant as conveniently to the market as possible

5   Merchandise the total restaurant to the market

6   Cater to the mass market

7   Be ready to modify the menu or the restaurant concept as the market calls for such changes

8   Design the restaurant with style, or to meet a fashion

9   Set moderate menu prices

THE RESTAURANT FAILURE RATE

The restaurant business has acquired a reputation, over the years, as having one of the highest, if not the highest, failure rates of retail businesses. The statistics are not in, but it is probable that the failure rate is not so high as believed.

Robert M. Riley, general manager of the California Restaurant Association, thinks these figures are grossly misleading. He points out that there are twelve other lines of business that have failure rates higher than restaurants, and that the rate of failure of eating and drinking places has been about the same for the past twenty-six years.

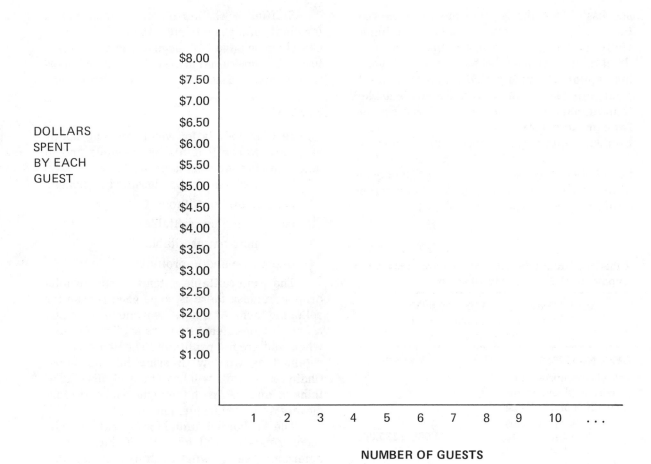

Figure 8–5   Frequency Distribution of Guest Checks.

What constitutes a failure must be defined also. The fact that a family continues to operate a restaurant even though their income is low might well be construed as failure. Hundreds, perhaps thousands, of such restaurants exist. Most of these are too small to be very profitable. Hundreds are in old homes. Some are on ferry boats, yachts, old barns, and similar unlikely locations. It would be surprising if the discontinuance rate were not high.

Unlike the European restaurant business, most restaurant operators in this country have had little or no formal training for the occupation. Behind every person who likes to cook, likes to be with people, and wants to make money lurks a would-be restaurateur. The roads all over the United States are dotted with little restaurants, or the remains of them, holding the hopes and aspirations, and sometimes fortunes, of such people.

Little Chance for Small Restaurant

Most of these places never have a chance. They are too isolated from their markets, too small, too unimpressive to compete with the established restaurants. On the other hand, most of the successful restaurant operators of today started in very modest establishments, lacked formal training, and had little financial backing. A comprehensive study of "failure" in the restaurant business would be enlightening and valuable to the industry.

Too often a would-be restaurateur allows his optimism to override his financial resources and acumen. Too little capital investment, too little working capital, too little market analysis, or too little experience make for too much disappointment when profits fail to appear.

While several millionaire restaurant operators started with small restaurants and were successful from the day they opened, most res-taurant operators have a rough time finan-cially for the first several months. Many lose all of their investment because of lack of work-ing capital. The time period required to break even in a restaurant is usually much longer than anticipated by the owners. Some restau-rants make money from day one. Others have been known to require years to break even.

The initial investment requirements of a hypothetical table service restaurant has been developed by the *Small Business Reporter* in California and are seen in Table 8-4.

Table 8-4 Initial Investment Requirements for a Hypothetical Table Service Restaurant.

Annual Gross Sales: $200,000-$350,000
Floor Space: About 3,000 sq. ft.
Seats: 100

OPENING COSTS	Range
Leasehold Improvements (wiring, plumbing, air conditioning, painting, labor and materials at $25 to $45 a sq. ft.)	$ 75,000–$135,000
Fixtures and Equipment dining area	2,400– 3,000
kitchen (500 sq. ft. at $20 to $45 a sq. ft.)	10,000– 22,500
Lease Deposit (1st and last month)	2,000– 4,200
Food Inventory (at opening)	1,000– 4,000
Subtotal	$ 90,400–$168,700
OPERATING COSTS	
(first three months)	
Payroll manager's salary	$ 3,000–$ 4,200
employees (4 servers, 2 cooking staff, 1 part-time cleanup)	11,600– 12,800
Food Supplies	26,500– 28,300
Taxes and Licenses	240– 390
Professional Services (legal and accounting)	240– 690
Insurance	290– 400
2 Months' Rent	1,000– 4,200
Cash Reserve	900– 1,500
Subtotal	$ 44,770–$ 52,480
TOTAL	$135,170–$221,180

Source: Figures compiled by Small Business Reporter *in California.*

Staffing a restaurant and conducting a feasibility study is a fairly complicated project. Our chart on page 247 suggests some of the fac-tors to be considered in arriving at three impor-tant numbers: Sales, Food Costs, and Payroll.

MENU ANALYSIS

The restaurateur is forever examining his or her menu to see if it fits his clientele and to determine if each item is profitable.

Menu items might be classified as being:

1 Popular and profitable

2 Popular and unprofitable

3 Unpopular but profitable

4 Unpopular and unprofitable

The unprofitable items are usually dropped unless there is some good reason for retaining them. At times, the menu may include a few prestige items that are seldom sold and when sold are not profitable. The items may be retained as window dressing for the menu. Chain restaurants will have none of this kind of thinking and stay with the items which are fast movers and, preferably, long profit.

The Air Force Manual for Operating Clubs recommends careful analysis of the menu to determine exactly what each item contributes in the way of profit to the enterprise. The "scatter sheet," on page 247, is the analytical device used to identify the cost of each item and the contribution it makes to the total sales of the restaurant.

In the example given, the total food cost percentage is 43 percent, but, as the menu is broken down, it is seen that different items have widely different costs:

1 percent of the menu items had a food cost of 25 percent

10 percent of the menu items had 30 per-cent food cost

10 percent of the menu items had 35 per-cent food cost

15 percent of the menu items had 40 per-cent food cost

23 percent of the menu items had 45 per-cent food cost

32 percent of the menu items had 50 per-cent food cost

9 percent of the menu items had 55 per-cent food cost

SCATTER SHEET

SALES PRICE	MENU ITEM	TIMES SOLD	TOTAL	SALES VALUE
	25% Cost			
$ .25	Hamburger	ᵗ	26	$ 6.50
.20	Cheese Sandwich		6	1.20
.30	Egg Salad Sandwich		10	3.00
.20	Jello Salad		5	1.00
	30% Cost			
.25	Pie, Cherry & Apple		13	3.25
.20	Ice Cream		15	3.00
.35	Cheeseburger		30	10.50
.40	Ham Sandwich		15	6.00
.30	Waldorf Salad		12	3.60
2.00	Baked Ham Dinner		25	50.00
1.75	Fried Chicken Dinner		20	35.00
	35% Cost			
.55	Pork Sandwich, Hot		10	5.50
.55	Beef Sandwich, Hot		20	11.00
.90	Shrimp Salad		30	27.00
1.75	Turkey Dinner		25	43.57
1.50	Pork Chop Dinner		5	7.50
.35	Ice Cream, Sundae		25	8.75
	40% Cost			
1.00	Lobster Cocktail		20	20.00
.80	Club Sandwich		35	28.00
1.50	Pork Tender, Dinner		12	18.00
2.40	Filet Mignon, Dinner		25	60.00
.40	French Pastry		15	6.00
	45% Cost			
1.00	Oyster Cocktail		20	20.00
1.25	Fruit Salad, Plate		23	28.75
1.80	Rib Steak, Dinner		10	18.00
2.75	Rainbow Trout, Dinner		31	85.25
2.50	Prime Rib, Dinner		7	17.50
.10	Coffee		46	4.60
.10	Milk		35	3.50
	50% Cost			
.40	Asparagus Tip Salad		30	12.00
1.00	Prime Rib Sandwich		19	19.00
3.50	T-Bone Steak, 16 oz.		35	122.50
3.25	New York Cut Steak, 12 oz.		17	55.25
.45	Strawberry Shortcake		35	15.75
	55% Cost			
.35	Chef's Salad Bowl		25	8.75
1.25	Calf's Liver Dinner		26	32.50
2.50	Lobster Tails		7	17.50
				$819.40

A "SCATTER-SHEET" IS A VALUABLE MANAGEMENT TOOL.

"Scatter Sheet"
RECAP

ITEMS	25% Cost	30% Cost	35% Cost	40% Cost	45% Cost	50% Cost	55% Cost	TOTALS
Cost % to Sales	0.4%	4.1%	4.4%	6.4%	9.8%	13.7%	3.9%	42.7%
% of Food Cost	1 %	10%	10%	15%	23%	32%	9 %	100%

Figure 8–6 Scatter Sheet.

Which items should be changed? Which dropped completely? Many restaurant experts urge that menus be severely limited to those items which are highly profitable and that can be done well and quickly by the restaurant. In some styles of restaurant this is not possible. Where possible and where the market exists for the limited menu, it should be used since it permits the highest profits.

What Do Items Contribute?

In the scatter sheet example, page 247, we see that T-bone steak, selling for $3.50 an order, contributes $122.50. It has a high food cost of 50 percent. Never mind the high food cost, the contribution is the thing. The T-bone steak is a star on this menu.

The chef's salad bowl is something else again. It is time-consuming to prepare and is probably a loss item when the labor cost is added to the food cost. Lobster tails might well be retained, since there is little preparation involved other than broiling them, and they can easily be stored in the frozen state.

The cherry or apple pie might look like a good item to retain or promote since it has only a 30 percent food cost. Yet, the item probably might be dropped, unless the pie has been purchased from a baker and entails little labor cost in serving. Labor cost in making such a pie would be considerable. Ice cream, on the other hand, has almost no labor cost. On the other hand cherry pie may be a menu leader and should be retained. Strawberry pie, freshly made daily, has proved to be a leader in a number of coffee shops.

Menu-making is often considered an art, but it is becoming a science. Research done at Tulane University, under a grant from the National Institute of Health, has pointed the way for menu construction using the computer. Several hospitals now plan menus using the computer. The problem is to select items which are popular, low cost, and together form a nutritious meal. The variables are staggering and cannot be handled efficiently without a computer.

The first step is to place into the computer's memory all the relevant data concerning available foodstuffs. One hospital, for example, has on file 800 recipes and 19 nutritional factors for each of 2,500 foodstuffs. The cost of these foodstuffs must be included, and the computer must be programmed so that the combinations of foods selected are eye appealing. The computer has been known to turn out menus all bland, all soft, and all white. Restraints must also be placed on the computer so that items do not appear too often on the menu.

PROPER FOOD COST?

What constitutes a proper food cost depends upon the amount of service, the cost of the atmosphere, and other factors which are offered together with the food. In an expensive, luxury style restaurant, the food cost may be only 28 percent, but the cost of labor may more than offset the low food cost, running as high as 35 percent or 40 percent depending upon what part of the country the restaurant is located in.

In city and country clubs, food costs run 40 to 55 percent. The members want it that way; dues paid make up the deficits. A drive-in restaurant might have a high food cost, 40 percent or more, but its labor cost could be 20 percent or less.

Patterned like a teeter-totter, as labor costs go up, food costs go down. In other words, the customer gets less food for his money. In atmosphere restaurants, the customer necessarily pays for the atmosphere and, in most cases, is willing to do so.

A fast-turnover steak house might run a food cost as high as 45 percent of sales and still make a good profit, if labor cost is 20 percent or less of sales.

In fast food restaurants, the cost of paper goods is often figured as part of the food cost.

One hamburger chain has a food cost of 37 percent. The reason: the chain features a roast beef sandwich, a 3-oz. portion of roasted knuckle on a roll, selling for 69 cents. Though the food cost of the sandwich is about 43 percent, the cost of labor in preparing the sandwich is low, about 15 percent. One cost balances the other.

How can a hamburger chain sell a hamburger for only 40¢? Easy. If hamburger sells for 75¢ a pound and a 1½ ounce patty is served, food cost for the patty is about 7¢. The bun costs 5¢. Garnish might add another half cent for a total cost of 13.5¢. Forty cents, the selling price, divided by 13.5¢, the cost, gives a food cost percentage on the hamburger of about 38.7 percent.

Beverages such as coke and orange drink have a food and paper cost of 20 percent or less, which, added into the overall food cost, brings it down.

An odd accounting practice in the food-service business comes in computing food cost. Usually food cost is expressed as: the cost of food consumed divided into the food sales. Cost of food consumed includes the cost of the food eaten by the employees. Other businesses would compute employee meals separately or include them as part of the cost of labor.

Food cost cannot be considered apart from labor cost. As noted previously, if one goes up, the other must inevitably come down. When labor costs rise, the food cost must come down, and the customer pays a little more for a little less. The only way to avoid raising menu prices is to become more efficient or to have the customer help in serving himself. This is what happened in the rapidly expanding fast food and cafeteria restaurants.

Combined Food and Labor Costs

It helps to look at food and labor costs as interacting variables, one necessarily affecting the other, if a profit is to be made. Ordinarily, costs other than food and labor costs do not exceed 20 percent of sales. If the combined food and labor costs can be kept below 65 percent, a 15 percent profit in sales can be made. In other words, par for the course is 65. If food and labor can be kept below 65, as is often the case, then 15 percent profit should be forthcoming.

Exceptions exist. Turnpike and airport contracts for foodservice are let to the highest bidder. The successful bidder may pay 15 percent, or even more, "off the top" to the authority operating the turnpike or airport. To meet such fees, the operator must raise food and beverage prices. Food costs come down to below 30 percent; beverage costs drop to below 25 percent.

Food costs in specialty restaurants are likely to vary widely, depending upon the menu, atmosphere, and prices offered. Polynesian restaurants—actually Chinese restaurants in a Polynesian setting—have low food costs, usually under 34 percent. The reason: lots of rice. Beverage costs are also low: lots of rum at high

prices. Mexican restaurants run food costs of about 30 percent, or less, because of the plenitude of corn, rice, and beans served.

Some rather amazing food and labor cost combinations exist, as reported by *Institutions Magazine* in 1969. The Village Inn Pizza chain had a food cost of 25 percent, a labor cost of 25 percent, for a combined total of 50 percent. The Little Red Hen, Inc., surprisingly, had a combined total of 52 percent: 43 percent food and 9 percent labor.

Lawry's, a roast beef full service restaurant chain, had a food cost of 43.3 percent, labor cost of 25.4 percent.

Ramada Inns reported food costs of 34 percent in its restaurants, labor cost of 37 percent, indicating the relative inefficiency of the usual motel dining room. Food and labor cost in the Marriott Corporation, ran 41.4 percent food cost, 31 percent labor cost.

Cost Combinations That Work

It is common practice in the restaurant business to establish food and labor cost targets that if not exceeded will ordinarily result in profit for the operation. In the old-style table service restaurant a typical cost combination might be:

Food cost as a percentage of sales:	40
Labor cost as a percentage of sales:	25
Balance	65

If other costs did not exceed about 15 percent the operation would produce a 20 percent profit before income taxes.

The combination of food cost percentage and labor cost percentage has come to be known as PRIME COST. If the PRIME COST does not exceed 70 percent the restaurant ordinarily produces a 10 to 15 percent net profit on sales.

The usual "Other Costs" would not exceed about 15 percent. There are exceptions. Occupancy costs ordinarily run 5 to 10 percent but can go as high as 15 percent in some choice locations such as found in an airport, on a choice location on a turnpike.

On the other hand occupancy cost can run as low as 2 percent of sales if in a low rent area or if the owner has taken over an old building and remodeled it himself. Sometimes also a restaurant location will have failed several times in succession and the owner is quite ready to offer a very low cost lease.

Food and labor costs can vary widely as long as the total does not exceed 70 percent. Some possible combinations in percentages:

A Steak House:
Food costs	50
Labor costs	20

A Mexican Fastfood Restaurant:
Food costs	30
Labor costs	20
Total	50

Coffee Shop:
Food costs	38
Labor costs	26
Total	64

A Dinnerhouse featuring roast beef while beef is low in cost:
Food costs	48
Labor costs	20
Total	68

Restaurants that have sizeable bar sales sometimes are less concerned about food and labor costs as long as the average of the food cost/labor cost/ and bar cost comes out to be less than 40. For example, these are the costs of a fine dinnerhouse with sales volume of 1.8 million dollars a year:

Food costs	46
Labor costs	32
Bar costs	22
Total	100
Average	33 percent

To illustrate the range of costs that can be experienced in various styles of restaurants while each of the restaurants remain profitable, four profit and loss statements from four different kinds of restaurants are seen on pages 250–252.[6]

It is interesting to note the wide differences in expenditure for advertising and promotion: fast food, almost 6 percent; pancake house 1.1 percent; the atmosphere restaurant about 4 percent.

In the examples above it is seen that the fast food shop ends up with the highest profit,

6. Taken from NRA NEWS bulletins.

Table 8-5 Operating Statement of Midwest Family Restaurant.

	January 1978
Total Sales—Food and Soft Drinks	100.0%
Cost of Sales	42.2
Gross Profit on Sales	57.8
Operating Expenses	
Salaries	22.1
Rent	5.3
Supplies	4.3
Utilities	2.2
Telephone	.1
Office Supplies	.2
Laundry	.3
Advertising	.6
Insurance	1.7
Trash Hauling	.2
Taxes and Licenses	.8
Car & Travel Expenses	.6
Repairs and Maintenance	1.1
Legal and Accounting	.8
Interest and Bank Charges	.2
Dues and Subscriptions	.3
Total Operating Expenses	40.8%
Net Profit before Depreciation	17.0
Depreciation	1.6
Net Profit	15.4

This restaurant seats 160 in the family-type dining room and three private party rooms. Serves lunch and dinner and operates daily.

largely because of food costs of 34.5 percent and labor costs of about 22.5 percent of sales. The pancake restaurant produced an exceptionally low food cost of 30.5 percent and a labor cost of close to 32 percent; administrative expenses ran 13.2, together the principal ingredients in the mix which produced an operating profit of 14.1 percent. The atmosphere restaurant showed a profit of less than 5 percent of gross sales; food cost was comparatively high (41 percent) because the place featured steaks, ribs, seafood and teriyaki, eleven points higher than that of the western pancake restaurant and about 7 percent higher than the fast food shop.

Of course, what really counts is the net profit in dollars, and it is possible that the atmosphere restaurant is the most profitable of the three restaurants because of large sales volume.

Table 8-6 Operating Statement of Midwest Fast Food Shop.

	Year to Date September 1977
Sales	100.0%
Cost of Sales	34.5
Gross Margin	65.5%
Expenses:	
Salary, Wage	20.2%
Payroll Taxes	2.3
Supplies & Service	.5
Repair & Cleaning	1.6
Advertising	5.9
Rent Expense	5.5
Utilities	2.5
Insurance & Taxes	1.1
Interest	.1
Royalties	3.5
Depreciation	1.2
Operating Margin	21.1%

Fast food restaurant open 7 days a week. Average check $1.79. 86 seats.

SERVICE SETS LABOR COST

Restaurant labor costs are largely influenced by the style of service and the amount of food preparation done on premise. The fast food restaurant, with its limited menu and minimal food preparation, has a lower labor cost than the table service restaurant. Frisch's, one of the better known drive-in groups, has a labor cost of 24.2 percent, a food cost of 34.3 percent.

Bonanza, a franchise chain, had a labor cost of only 18 percent that permits higher food cost, in this case, 42 percent. Cafeterias might be expected to have a somewhat lower labor cost than table service restaurants because the customer largely serves himself. However, in table service restaurants most of the labor cost of the serving personnel is borne by the customer in the form of tips. Forum Cafeterias, a large midwest chain, has a food cost of 33 percent and a labor cost of 35 percent, not much different than would be expected in a table service restaurant.

The food and labor equation also varies regionally. Where wages are high—in northern cities and the Far West—food costs neces-

Table 8-7 Operating Statement of a Midwestern Atmosphere Restaurant.

	Year to Date 1976
Sales and Revenues	%
Beer	4.63
Liquor	19.25
Wine	2.17
Food	72.65
Subtotal	98.70
Cigarettes	.56
Miscellaneous	.75
Total Sales and Revenues	100.00
Cost of Sales	
Beer	26.94
Liquor	18.60
Wine	46.37
Food	41.23
Subtotal	36.26
Cigarettes	81.91
Total Cost of Sales	36.52
Gross Profit	63.48
Operating Expenses	
Payroll	22.81
Employee Benefits	3.62
Direct Operating	9.47
Advertising and Promotion	3.86
Administrative and General	1.47
Repairs and Maintenance	.79
Total Operating Expenses	42.02
Net Profit Before Fixed	21.46
Less: Fixed Expenses	6.32
Net Profit Before Depreciation	15.14
Less: Depreciation	2.01
Net Profit	13.13
Less: Admin. Fees	8.20
Net Profit	4.93

* Located downtown, this restaurant is open 7 days a week, serving lunch and dinner meals. There is seating for 200 people, with parking facilities available. The guest check averages $2.95 at lunch, $9.75 at dinner. The limited menu features steaks, ribs, seafood, and teriyaki.

Source: National Restaurant Association, November 1976.

sarily must be lower. If labor costs in California average 34 percent, food cost is 34 percent or lower. In the South, with its low labor costs, food costs are higher. If labor cost in a Mississippi restaurant is 20 percent, food costs may be 40 percent or higher.

Table 8-8 Operating Statement of 150-seat Western Pancake Restaurant.

	Year to Date 1976		Year to Date 1976
Sales		Administrative expenses	
Food Sales	99.4	Bonuses & commissions	.7
Counter Sales	.6	Supervisors expenses	.5
Total Sales	**100.0**	Bonus—Manager	.9
		Insurance—General	.6
Cost of sales			
Food costs	30.1	Workman's Comp. ins.	.2
Counter costs	.4	Group insurance	.4
Total cost of sales	**30.5**	Interest expense	.4
		Other	.3
Gross profit on sales	**69.5**	Professional services—legal	—
Labor costs	27.7	Personal property and real estate	.2
Indirect labor costs	3.5	Miscellaneous business taxes	.2
		Rent	3.2
Controllable & variable expenses		Maintenance expense—home office	.5
Advertising	1.1	Royalty expense	5.0
Bad debts & short checks	—	Home office service fee	—
Bank or data proc. payroll expense	—	Home office promotion	.1
Bank service charge	—	Home office expense	—
Cash, over and short	—		
Cleaning supplies	.2	**Total administrative expense**	**13.2**
Dishwasher soap	.5		
Dues and subscriptions	—	**Total profit before fixed expenses**	**16.0**
Laundry and dry cleaning	.5		
Dry cleaning allowance	—	Fixed expenses	
Licenses and permits	—	Depreciation—kitchen equipment	.2
Menus	.1	Depreciation—dining room furniture	.1
Miscellaneous services	.5	Depreciation—auto and truck	—
Office supplies and postage	.1	Office and miscellaneous equipment	.1
Paper—sundry supplies	1.0	Depreciation—leasehold improvements	.5
Promotion and entertainment	.4	Other fixed expenses	1.0
Repairs and maintenance—Bldg.	.3	**Total fixed expenses**	**1.9**
Repairs and maintenance— Eqpt.	.3		
Replacement—china, glass & silver	.7	**Net operating profit**	**14.1**
Replacement—kitchen utensils	.1		
Sign rentals	.3		
Telephone	.1	Other income and expense	
Uniforms	.1	Vending machine—net	.3
Utilities	2.7	Interest income	—
Unclassified general expense	.1	Miscellaneous	.5
Total controllable & variable expenses	**9.1**	Controllable adjustments	(.4)
Total 4 area costs	**70.8**	**Total other income and expense**	**.4**
Total profit after labor & controllables	**29.2**	**Net profit before income taxes**	**14.5**

* Family type-sit-down restaurant, specializing in pancakes, eggs and omelets.
Average no. of employees, part time and full time: 45
Hours open: 6 A.M. to 2 A.M.
Parking spaces: 70
Average guest check: $1.85

Source: National Restaurant Association, December, 1976.

As has been pointed out, "You don't bank percentages." This means that over-emphasis on maintaining a particular food cost or labor cost percentage may divert management's attention away from its true purpose: maximizing profits.

One way to maximize profits is to sell high priced items, if patrons will buy them. Steak may have a food cost of 50 percent and sell for $8. A half-chicken might be sold for $1.50 and have a food cost of 33 percent. The profit on the steak would be $4, compared to only 53¢ for the chicken. Increasing the average check is a fast way of increasing profit because ordinarily the higher priced item will bring a disproportionately large contribution of profit, even though the food cost may be higher.

The cost of preparing any individual menu item must be considered in pricing. Those items with a high labor cost might better be omitted from the menu. Harry Pope of Pope's Cafeterias, headquartered in St. Louis, has pioneered the concept of "prime cost," the combination of labor and food cost of a menu item.

He has pointed out that many menu items may have a low food cost but a high labor cost. Ingredients for soup, for example, may cost only 3¢ a portion, but the cost of making the soup is 10 or 12¢. Most establishments today buy soup in canned or dehydrated form. Some of the canned soups are superior, those that are less affected by the high heat required for canning.

Most colleges and universities that offer hotel and restaurant management courses offer at least one quarter or a semester of work in food and beverage cost control, either as a separate course or as part of another. Restaurant menu pricing policy and the mechanics of pricing are integral parts of such courses.

Traditionally, restaurant menu pricing has been based on rules of thumb passed along from operator to operator. Pricing is a controversial subject, with various operators using different pricing systems to arrive at the selling price of their menu items. The National Restaurant Association has published a summary of three of these systems: the "good deal" philosophy, the percentage mark-up system, and the gross mark-up system. The three systems appear on page 254. Also included are explanations of three analytical tools which bear on pricing policy: average check, frequency distribution of checks, and further discussions of menu analysis.

THE "GOOD DEAL" PHILOSOPHY OF PRICING

For any foodservice establishment to be successful, the customer must believe he is receiving a fair value. The customer's concept of a value will vary with the individual. The key to success is to provide what most of your customers see as a value most of the time.

Just as the customer wants a good deal, the proprietor is entitled to at least a fair return. The proprietor has invested money and time and is taking a risk. To remain in business, he requires a fair profit.

Successful foodservice operators find ways to satisfy customers and maintain a fair profit. In any pricing work, both customer satisfaction and a fair return must be maintained.

Some methods of pricing are described in the following pages. While there will be a temptation to use one or another system, most operators will adapt one or more of the systems to fit their particular operation, customers, and competition. The concepts and systems are valid, but no concept can take the place of a foodservice professional's judgment and experience.

Percentage Markup System

The basic philosophy of this system is that a customer should pay a share of the overhead and non-food expenses based on the value of the food he buys. This is expressed by using a percentage. If we use the financial statements (see XYZ Restaurant Income Statement) as basis, we see that the Food Cost for the period was 36 percent and the Gross Profit was 64 percent. If we are satisfied with these figures, we can set future prices by dividing the cost of the food by the 36 percent figure. If we take the steak dinner example, the computation would be as follows:

$$\frac{\text{Actual Cost } \$2.26}{\substack{\text{Food Cost Percentage} \\ \text{Desired 36 percent}}} = \$6.28 \text{ Selling Price}$$

Table 8-9 Pricing Decision Guide Foodservice Proprietor.

FOODSERVICE PROPRIETOR

	LOSING MONEY	AVERAGE PROFIT	A GOOD DEAL (EXTRA MARKUP)
GOOD DEAL (SOMETHING FOR NOTHING)			
A FAIR VALUE			
RIPPED OFF			

(Left axis: C U S T O M E R)

XYZ RESTAURANT
INCOME STATEMENT FOR THE MONTH

3,000 CUSTOMERS
JANUARY 31, 1974

SALES	$15,000	100%
LESS COST OF FOOD SOLD	5,400	36%
GROSS PROFIT	$ 9,600	64%
LESS OTHER EXPENSES		
LABOR COST	$ 4,800	32%
SUPPLIES	600	4%
OCCUPATION	1,500	10%
OTHER	900	6%
PROFIT BEFORE TAX	$1,800	12%

PERCENTAGE MARKUP SYSTEM
ADVANTAGES:
1. PROVIDES A CLOSE RELATIONSHIP—OBVIOUS TO THE CUSTOMER—BETWEEN THE COST OF EACH MENU ITEM AND THE SELLING PRICE.
2. OFFERS A WIDER PRICE RANGE AND ALLOWS THE RESTAURATEUR TO SERVICE A BROADER PRICE MARKET.
3. PERIODIC FINANCIAL STATEMENTS ACCURATELY REFLECT THE EFFICIENCY OF THE OPERATION.
4. RELATIVELY SIMPLE TO ADMINISTER.
DISADVANTAGES:
1. DOES NOT REFLECT THE RISK (HIGH WASTE) INHERENT IN SOME MENU ITEMS.
2. DOES NOT REFLECT THE AMOUNT OF DIRECT LABOR INVOLVED IN PREPARATION.

Table 8-10 Price

PRICING SYSTEM	MENU ITEMS		
	CHICKEN	STEAK	LOBSTER
DINNER COST	$1.01	$2.26	$ 4.46
"GUT FEEL"	?	?	?
COMPETITOR A	?	?	?
COMPETITOR B	?	?	?
PERCENTAGE MARKUP—36%	$2.80	$6.28	$12.39
GROSS PROFIT MARKUP	$4.21	$5.46	$ 7.66
TEXAS RESTAURANT ASSN.			

STEAK DINNER		CHICKEN DINNER		LOBSTER DINNER	
		1/2 chicken—2-1/2 lb. chx @ .45/lb. = 55¢			
STEAK	$1.80	CHICKEN	$ .55	MAINE LOBSTER	$4.00
SALAD	.15	BAKED POTATO	.15	BAKED POTATO	.15
BAKED POTATO	.15	SALAD	.15	SALAD	.15
ROLLS & BUTTER	.10	ROLLS & BUTTER	.10	ROLLS & BUTTER	.10
BEVERAGE	.06	BEVERAGE	.06	BEVERAGE	.06
TOTAL MEAL COST	$2.26	TOTAL MEAL COST	$1.01	TOTAL MEAL COST	$4.46

A second method of computation is to divide the Food Cost percentage into 100, which produces a factor. Multiply the factor by the cost of the menu price to give a selling price. EXAMPLE: Divide the 36 percent into 100 = 2.8. Multiply 2.8 × $2.26 (cost of dinner) = $6.33.

GROSS MARKUP SYSTEM

Advantages

1 Recognizes that a restaurateur banks dollars, not percentages.

2 Once a price market has been determined, a restaurateur can compete very strongly in that market. Under this system, the expensive items become very attractive.

3 High costs of entertainment or other special features can be more easily passed along.

Disadvantages

1 Periodic financial statements do not accurately reflect the business's efficiency, since a change in the combination of items sold will change the potential food cost percentage.

2 If the price market is poorly identified, the restaurant can be priced out of the market more quickly, due to the narrower price range.

3 This system does not reflect any high risks inherent in some menu items.

4 This system does not reflect the direct labor involved in some menu items.

Gross Markup System

Gross Markup pricing differs substantially from the percentage markup system. The basic idea here is that each customer should share equally the cost in terms of dollars of serving a meal. The cost of serving a chicken dinner is equal to the cost of serving a steak dinner once the raw food is paid for. For example, a customer uses the same tablecloth and napkins, silverware, heat, light, and power, etc., regardless of his choice of menu items. Therefore, he should pay for what he uses.

This is computed as follows: First, we examine the Income Statement (see sample). Let us assume that you are content with the figures as presented and want to base your future prices upon them.

Calculating the Gross Markup

To calculate the Gross Markup, divide the

$$\frac{\text{Gross Profit (\$9,600)}}{\text{Number of Customers (3,000)}} = \$3.20/\text{customer}$$

This figure is added to the cost of the food to determine the selling price.

If we take a steak dinner with the following items:

Item	Cost
Steak	$1.80
Salad	.15
Baked potato	.15
Rolls and butter	.10
Beverage	.06
TOTAL meal cost	2.26
Add Markup	3.20
	$5.46 Selling Price

Three Tools to Help You Decide on Prices

How much does the average person spend in your restaurant? Three measures of this important question follow.

1 *Average check*

This is a tried and true, but only superficial, measure of what the average guest spends in a restaurant. Average check is computed by dividing Total Sales by the number of customers served.

Example from the XYZ Restaurant Financial Statement:

$$\frac{\text{Total Sales (15,000)}}{\text{Total Number of Customers (3,000)}} = \$5.00 \text{ average check}$$

Average check figures or, more importantly, changes in the average check can signal problems, such as declining sales efforts or shifting markets. This is a simple computation and offers some help in pricing. The second technique is almost as easy and offers a lot more insight into your market.

2 *Frequency Distribution of Guest Checks*

Like the average check, the frequency distribution analyzes what guests spend in a restaurant. Basically this involves a graph (see example). Each guest's charge is plotted at the appropriate place.

For example: to record a part of four with a $22.50 guest check before tip and tax, divide $22.50 by four to obtain an average check of $5.63 for the party. At the $5.50 line on the Left Scale, indicate that four guests spent in this range by marking off four places on the lower scale.

Once this is completed for all of the checks for a meal, a pattern of spending will emerge. This figure can be used as a guideline in selecting and pricing new menu items and promoting old items.

One note of caution: Frequency Distributions of Guest Checks lose some of their value if one menu item accounts for more than 33 to 44 percent of the sales, since the popularity of the item may overshadow the pricing decision.

3 *Menu Counts or Menu Tallies* are another tool to help operators decide prices. To obtain a menu tally, count the number of each item sold. Some operators identify each appetizer, entree, dessert, and beverage sold, but most identify each entree and count only the total number of appetizers, desserts, and beverages.

What can a menu count tell you? If one item attracts a major share of sales (for example, more than 20 percent of the total), it should be checked to be sure you are making your predetermined markup. If an item is attracting 40 to 50 percent of the total sales, it may be possible to raise the price. In any event, that item must meet your predetermined markup.

If a menu item sells poorly (less than 2 percent of the total, for example), why does it remain on the menu?

Some Good Reasons

1 Highly profitable

2 No waste

3 Menu variety without waste for regular customers (do they choose it?)

Some Poor Reasons

1 Menu variety

2 The manager likes it for dinner

3 The chef likes to cook it

WAGES AND SALARIES

The public image of the restaurant business is not good, or at least the leaders of the industry, as represented by the National Restaurant Association, do not believe the image is good. Part of the reason can be traced to the fact that many of the jobs in a restaurant are entry positions, those requiring little or no previous experience or training. These positions are filled by the unskilled and, very often, by people disadvantaged in one way or another. In the cities, the dishwashing jobs are often filled by alcoholics or other unstable people who may work for only a day or a few days at a time. At least 30 percent of the employees in the restaurant business work part time, a factor leading to instability in the labor force and contributing to the poor image of the industry.

Perhaps more important as a factor influencing the image are the low hourly wages paid in the industry, usually hovering near the minimum allowable by law.

Salaries paid cooks in the northern cities are largely controlled by union contract; the black chef in a southern restaurant receives much less and works longer hours. Salaries of top chefs range from about $20 to $35 thousand a year. The really experienced and knowledgeable chefs are found in private clubs; some leave the restaurant industry to work as research chefs for food manufacturers.

Management salaries, as might be expected, also show a wide range. Management trainees just out of college, in 1979 started at $11,000 a year when employed by the large restaurant chains. The salaries paid managers by unit restaurants, parts of a chain, range from about $12,000 a year to about $35,000 a year in a larger restaurant.

Wages and salaries in hotels and restaurants will increase, probably faster than in other retail trades.

The chains will continue to grow, bringing in more employees to be covered by collective bargaining agreements.

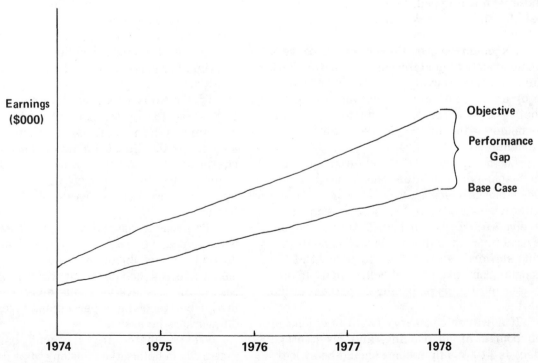

Figure 8-7

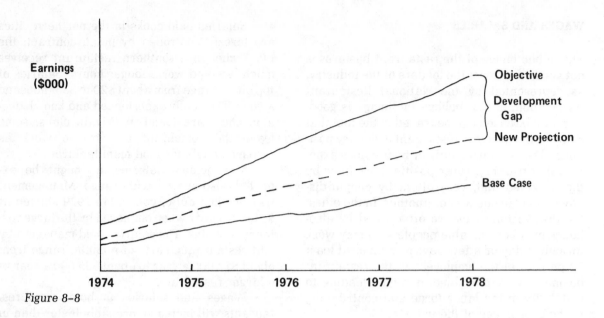

Earnings
($000)

Objective

Development
Gap

New Projection

Base Case

1974   1975   1976   1977   1978

Figure 8–8

Tipped and Non-Tipped Employees

The two-thirds of all restaurant employees who are non-tipped can be considered low paid in our society, even though they might be well paid by worldwide standards. It should be remembered that 30 percent of all foodservice employees are teenagers working in entry level jobs. The other third of the industry employees, those who are tipped, in many cases are well paid for the level of skill and training required by their jobs.

As noted before, tipping practices vary tremendously around the country. In New York City, a customer buying a 25¢ food item is likely to tip an equal amount; in the Midwest or the South—or in almost any small town or rural community—the tip would be small or non-existent.

For many jobs in the restaurant business the wages paid constitute only a small part of the employee's income. Wine stewards in some of the well-known New York City restaurants receive $100 a week or less. Their tips may be several times that. In some establishments, the wine steward receives 5 or 10 percent of the income from the sale of wine. In a luxury restaurant, the tip is usually 20 percent of the tab.

If a waiter can serve twenty persons in the course of an evening, and his average check is $10, his tip income should be at least $40 for the evening. Attractive cocktail waitresses make much more, yet girls at counter service restaurants may be lucky to make $5 to $8 a day in tips.

The practice of tipping makes waiting into "the waiting game." The waiter, in effect, sets up in business for himself as an independent entrepreneur. He tolerates the owner of the restaurant as a person providing an environment in which he can operate his own business.

Aside from the value of the tip in monetary terms, the tip is also seen as a measure of the waiter's performance, his shrewdness, or his cunning. For some waiters, the tip is a mark of gratitude freely given by the customer. To others, the tip is a form of blackmail or extortion, extracted by the shrewd waiter from a reluctant patron. Waitresses often see the amount of the tip as an evaluation of their charm or attractiveness. Among waiting personnel, competition to excel in the amount of tips received can generate jealousy and friction.

To promote teamwork, many restaurants insist that tips be pooled, all tips collected and divided equally. In other restaurants, agreements are reached between waiters or waitresses and busboys as to the division of tips, the busboy receiving a percentage taken in by the workers he assists.

Where there are frequent banquets, especially in hotels, the division of tips can be a source of contention. The food and beverage director may unilaterally decide how the 15 percent service charge should be divided; so much to the kitchen, so much to the dining room, so much to the maitre d' and head-waiters. In some cases "so much" goes to the food and beverage director, especially if he is of the European school and has been accustomed to the tronc system by which tips are divided according to seniority and position.

Private clubs usually insist that there be no tipping directly to personnel. Often a service charge of 10 or 15 percent is added to all restaurant and bar checks. In other clubs the only "tips" forthcoming are made in the form of a Christmas bonus to which all club members are expected to contribute.

As noted before, there are regional differences in tipping practices; there are also variations among individuals within the regions. Pipe smokers are usually identified as "stiffs": non-tippers. Women are usually considered poor tippers. Some wealthy persons are highly conservative in tipping; others quite generous.

A "Tippers Form Chart" was put together by a reporter who interviewed a number of Las Vegas waitresses. The chart rates various groups as to their tipping potential:

Classification	Rating
Men with their wives	Forget 'em
Men with their girl friends	Showoffs; good
Man alone	Good, but move carefully
Woman alone	Lock the door; terrible
Women in groups	Worse; move on
Touchers	Generous (if allowed)
Pinchers	Generous (if not slugged)
Craps winners	Tops
Slot winners	Fair
Keno winners	Cautious
Older men with ideas	Real good

Tips, of course, are considered part of wages by the Internal Revenue Service. As such, they are supposed to be reported by the receiver. This presents a problem for the IRS and for the receiver. The IRS has difficulty in determining the amount of tip income; the receiver must wrestle with his conscience in deciding what portion of his tips, if not all, he should report as earnings.

Each employee in the restaurant business in 1971 was able to produce $12,256 in sales. By 1975, the figure was probably $14,000, but for many restaurants productivity was $20,000, and in a few it reached $40,000 and even more each year.[7] Productivity per employee determines in large part what wage can be paid. The restaurant business is a service business; much of the work is still "two hands and the feet." If a worker produces only $15,000 in sales, the wages paid cannot exceed much over $5,000 a year, small in today's economy.

COST CONTROL

Few businesses exact the kind of attention needed for controlling costs as does a restaurant. Cost control is a never-ending, demanding, exercise in operating a restaurant. To put costs in perspective, various expenses and costs are divided into those that are controllable, those that are fixed, and those that are relatively variable.

Fixed costs include:

Taxes

Occupancy costs (Rent, lease costs, amortization)

Licenses

Insurance

Of course, no costs are immutable. Rents can be renegotiated, real estate taxes questioned, insurance policies changed.

Some expenses are semi-variable or semi-fixed:

Repairs and maintenance

Utilities (heat, light, power, water)

Telephone charges

---

7. NRA Washington Report, March 19, 1973.

Phone companies charge a fixed minimum for having a phone in operation, that part is fixed. Long distance charges are additional and variable. A certain amount of utility charges are fixed also.

Other expenses usually considered variable and controllable:

Cost of food and beverage consumed

Administrative and General

Payroll

Employee Benefits

Bookkeeping expenses

Advertising and promotion

Music and Entertainment

Laundry and linen

China, glassware, and silver

Cleaning and cleaning supplies

Paper and guest supplies

Service contracts

Even with these "controllable" costs and expenses, part of each is likely to be fixed. A cadre of key employees must remain on the payroll even though business is slow, constituting a fixed cost. Parts of most of the other costs are also fixed if the restaurant opens at all. But by separating costs into those that can be at least partially controlled, management focuses its attention on them and keeps them in line. Food and beverage costs are the perennial problem children, costs that can wreck a restaurant in a short time if not controlled. Other costs can be disastrous as well. Suppose, for example, that utility costs suddenly jump to 10 percent of gross sales when they should be running about 2 percent of sales. The eight points that are being lost could wipe out any and all profit.

Without a knowledge of what each expense item should be as a ratio of gross sales, the manager is at a distinct disadvantage. He should know, for example, that utilities ordinarily do not run more than 4 percent of sales in most restaurants; that the cost of beverage for a dinnerhouse ordinarily should not exceed 25 percent and could be much less; that occupancy cost should not exceed 6 to 8 percent of gross sales in most cases. Of course ratio analysis must be in terms of what is appropriate for a particular style of restau-

rant: coffee shop, fast food, club, or hotel. Moreover, the ratios must be appropriate for the area. Restaurant labor costs, for example, are usually comparatively low in the South, high in the northern cities, while restaurant food costs are comparatively high in the South and comparatively low in the northern cities (in other words the restaurant patron gets more food for his money in the South than he would in the North because of the lower wages paid restaurant personnel in the South).

REDUCING THEFT AND ACCIDENTAL LOSS

A number of systems have been installed to reduce theft, among them being:

Storerooms are kept under lock and key, and supplies are issued to each station only at the beginning of a watch according to a par stock needed for the day at the station.

Tight key control. All keys are signed out by name and must be returned by name. If an employee leaves, the paycheck is withheld until keys are returned. When a manager leaves all locks are changed.

Shopping reports. An independent shopping company is employed to "shop" the restaurant, to observe and report on every employee at regular intervals. Among the factors observed are whether or not all sales are recorded on sales slips. At the cash register items like candy bars are purchased by the shopper to see if the sale is rung up. Questions such as the following are completed by the shopper:

Was your guest check added correctly?

As you approached the cash stand how many patrons were ahead of you? Was payment taken in a reasonable length of time? How long?

Was the cashier working with cash drawer opened?

Were numerals on cash register window plainly visible?

Did the cashier call back the amount of sale and the amount tendered?

Was change correct?

Some restaurants are in locations where robberies have occurred repeatedly. To reduce such temptation some restaurants often have a policy that no more than $150 in cash is ever in a cash register. As cash in excess of that amount is accumulated, it is placed in an envelope and slotted into a safe, which is impossible to get into without a special key.

A record is kept of each deposit of the envelope into the safe including the day, date, time, amount, and person making the deposit.

Guest Check Accountability

A great temptation by wait personnel exists if guest checks are not strictly accounted for. If they are not, the wait person may bring in his own checks, present them to the customer, and pocket the payment. Guest checks can be altered and substitutions made if the checks are not numbered.

To avoid such temptations most restaurants require that the wait person sign for checks as received and return unused ones at the end of the shift.

Other restaurants issue checks by book, 150 to a book. For tight control every guest check is audited, additions checked, and every check accounted for by number. Guest check auditing is often done in a central office in the case of a restaurant chain, in someone's home for an independent restaurant.

Many restaurants use a duplicate check system. The second copy of the check is handed to the cook in return for the food. No check, no food. Every food item ordered is recorded on a guest check, even though the order is for only a cup of coffee.

DEPRECIATION AND CASH FLOW

As a business generates income and pays its immediate expenses, including taxes, there is money left over, all of which is not profit. In a restaurant, the building, kitchen and dining room equipment, and furnishings depreciate year after year until finally they have no value or only a salvage value. Theoretically at least, money is set aside for replacing these items, a depreciation allowance. Actually this money is seldom set aside and very often the building appreciates rather than depreciates in value. Even so, for tax purposes the depreciation allowance is a deductible item and can be used by the owner-operator. The money taken in before considering the depreciation allowance

is called "cash flow." The restaurateur is much concerned to keep his cash flow more than enough to meet current obligations.

The owner of a restaurant gets the depreciation allowance. The owner of the equipment gets a depreciation allowance. The owner of the land on which the restaurant sits gets none, for land is a nondepreciable item whereas other tangible assets that have a life span are depreciable. The matter of depreciation can be quite important in the success of a restaurant and is especially important to whoever owns the building. Restaurants are often owned by a corporation which in turn owns another corporation which owns the land. Still another corporation owns the restaurant building and equipment. The idea is to maximize depreciation so as to pay the least amount of taxes possible, especially during the first several years of operation. Some successful restaurant chains buy land, build a building on it, and sell the restaurant and the land to an investor. Then the chain leases it back from him, a sales-lease arrangement which has tax advantages for the investor and permits the operator to expand rapidly with a minimal amount of capital investment.

TAX CONSIDERATIONS

Everyone in business has a partner, Uncle Sam. That gentlemen is represented by the tax collector, the Internal Revenue Service, who is interested in every dollar transaction, interested in waiting to skim off a portion of the transaction for the good of the nation. The businessman operates knowing that the Internal Revenue Service is looking over his shoulder. Being a good citizen the businessman wants to pay his fair share of the taxes collected. What is fair is interpreted differently by the way the business is set up. Some pay a great deal more than their fair share; others pay little or nothing because they have been shrewd enough to have a tax consultant structure the business so as to avoid much or all of the taxes.

Tax laws and their interpretation continually change so that what is said here can only be suggestive. Tax experts recommend putting all real estate and equipment into an asset company. This company should be retained. It owns the building and the land and the operating equipment.

Another company is the operating company, which has as few assets in it as possible. The tax experts recommend always keeping the real estate separate from the operating company. Machinery and equipment can be depreciated and so can the building. In buying a business, buy the building and allocate as much as possible to any item which can be legally depreciated: carpets, trees, fences, roses, garbage cans, dust pans, brooms, vacuum cleaners, dishmachines, stoves. The idea is to build as big a tax base, a depreciable tax base, as possible. Then say the experts, depreciate it all as fast as possible. Those depreciation dollars are essentially tax free dollars.

The operating company, quite distinct from the asset company, can carry a great load of expenses, which again are tax free, a company automobile, a medical/dental plan for the officers, travel expenses, life insurance, entertainment expenses. Costs often borne by the individual become tax free.

Restaurant owners with families should seriously consider setting up trusts for their children. Each trust has a tax exemption. In one instance a restaurant owner has twenty-seven legal exemptions, including twelve children.

Always consider that eventually the business will do one of three things: fail, be sold, or merged. Consider the tax consequences when forming the business. Here is another tax avoidance plan:

A corporation owned by you and maybe one or two others leases a piece of land to you, the principal owner. You in turn erect a restaurant on the leased land, then lease the building back to the corporation (of which you are the principal owner). This makes you in effect both a lessee and a lessor. You, the individual, have leased the land from the corporation. You, the individual, have then erected the building and leased it back to the corporation. And you, the individual, own the restaurant and are able to take advantage of the depreciation on the building and to draw money from the corporation in the form of lease payments.

LONG-RANGE OBJECTIVES*

In setting long-range objectives, companies should consider both financial and non-financial objectives, as well as risk constraints. The most common types of financial objectives are those that deal with profitability, growth, and shareholder well-being.

Hospitality companies typically use return on equity or capital as their profitability measure and annual earnings per share increase as their growth measure. An objective of a 10 to 15 percent annual growth in earnings per share has been a fairly common target for companies involved in lodging, restaurants, and institutional foodservice—and many have achieved this target over a number of years.

As a measure of shareholder well-being, companies traditionally have used the market value of their common stock. Gyrations in the stock market and the overall downward price

* Much of this section is courtesy of James Crownover, formerly corporate planner, Saga Corporation.

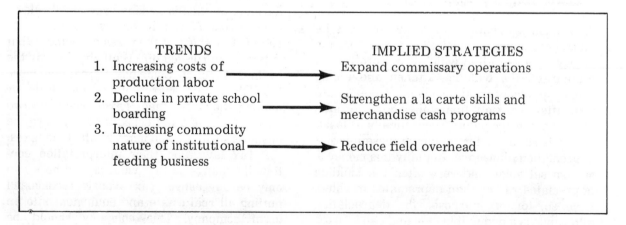

Figure 8-9

trends have raised questions in the minds of many as to the practicality of this measure.

Some believe that dividend pay-out could be used as a measure of shareholder well-being and as a financial objective together with profitability and growth targets.

Two types of nonfinancial objectives are increasingly being used. First, companies are making specific statements regarding their role with respect to employees. Saga, for example, has a bill of rights for employees. Other companies state objectives in the area of maximizing personal development for employees.

Companies are also establishing objectives regarding their role with respect to society. In recent years, manufacturing companies have been closely examining the area of pollution. Some hospitality companies have begun to define their role with respect to the conservation of resources.

Companies should consider risk at the same time they are establishing financial objectives. Typically, a company may be able to achieve higher financial objectives if it were willing to assume greater risk. For example, by borrowing larger sums of money or by acquiring greater numbers of businesses, a company might achieve relatively higher financial objectives. However, greater risk is involved.

Setting Risk Limits

Some companies set specific risk limits beyond which they will not go to achieve financial objectives. In limiting the dependence on borrowed funds, a company sometimes uses a debt ceiling based on a minimum ratio between after-tax earnings and fixed interest requirements. For example, if a company required that fixed interest requirements would remain less than one-half of current after-tax earnings, this would insure that a 50 percent drop in company earnings would not leave the company unable to meet its debt requirements.

Some companies specify maximum numbers of new businesses that they can become involved in during the year. This limitation is based on the belief that the top management structure of a company can handle only so many new businesses per year before the current business suffers from a lack of management attention.

Guidelines for Business Mix

Finally, a company may set guidelines on the mix of businesses in which they will be involved. For example, a company with institutional foodservice and restaurant foodservice businesses may set a limit on the size of the restaurant foodservice business as a percentage of the total business.

Little Capital Required

The institutional foodservice business requires little capital and, consequently, has little risk associated with it, but its growth rate is relatively slow. In contrast, restaurants require considerable financial exposure as a result of long-term lease commitments, but the potential growth is large. By setting a limit on the overall size of the restaurant foodservice business as a percent of the total, a company can limit its overall risks. Most of the larger hotel chains are limiting risk by foregoing investment and seeking management contracts.

The third step in the strategic planning process is to estimate the long-range financial results that a company can produce, assuming "business as usual." In developing this "base case" financial projection, a company should make a thorough evaluation of each market currently served by the company and should analyze trends in each aspect of the profitability equation: volume, price, cost, and investment.

The company then makes its base case projection, assuming current levels of efficiency and the continuation of current market trends. The difference between the base case projection and the objective in each financial area is called the performance gap. For example, the earnings performance gap is a measure of those additional earnings that will have to be produced, either through better performance in current businesses or through entry into new business areas in order to meet the long-range earnings objectives.

At this stage of the strategic planning process, a check should be made to be sure that the risk constraints developed in conjunction with long-range objectives have not been violated by our base case projection.

Table 8-11

MARKETS	VOLUME	X PRICE	– COST	÷ INVESTMENT
College Feeding	1% annual enrollment decline 20 net new accounts per year	No increase due to competitive pressures	5% increase per year More extensive unionization	Minimal
Hospital Feeding	2% annual increase in hospital census 15 net new accounts per year	etc.	etc.	etc.
B. & I. Feeding	4% annual increase in HQ populations 15 net new accounts per year	etc.	etc.	$100 K per year for vending

Product/Market Strategies

Product/market strategies are brief statements indicating overall courses of action that a company will take in various product and market areas. A company probably should not have more than four or five long-range strategies per business. Strategies should first be developed for improving the results of current businesses. In general, these strategies grow directly from the trends developed earlier and an assessment of the company's strengths and weaknesses.

After these strategies have been developed, another financial projection is made that is based on the likely results of these strategies. Again, the new financial projection is compared with the company's financial objectives.

A company will typically have to evaluate several different sets of strategies for the current business before becoming satisfied with the projected results. If a gap still remains between financial projections and objectives, the companies must look to new business development as a means of reaching these objectives.

In Saga's institutional foodservice business, a number of development strategies were evaluated. Saga considered selling new products in current markets (for example, selling vended products to B and I customers in order to complement the existing manual foodservice). They also examined selling the current line of products (for example, manual foodservice) into new markets (for example, public secondary schools). Finally, they evaluated entirely new product/market combinations

Table 8-12 California Restaurants.

Where It Came From	Coffee Shops	Dinner Houses	Table-Service Restaurants, United States
Food sales	94.4¢	65.3¢	75.7¢
Beverage sales	5.4	33.3	23.5
Other income	.2	1.4	.8
Where It Went			
Food cost	29.4¢	28.1¢	31.2¢
Beverage cost	1.4	9.7	6.4
Payroll and related expenses	34.0	28.8	30.6
Direct operating expenses	4.3	6.3	5.5
Music and entertainment	.1	.7	.8
Advertising and promotion	.7	1.2	1.7
Utilities	2.9	1.5	2.3
Administrative and general	4.7	5.4	5.4
Repairs and maintenance	1.4	1.4	1.6
Rent, property taxes, and insurance	9.0	6.3	5.8
Interest	.3	.3	.8
Depreciation	1.7	2.4	2.2
Other deductions	1.3	.1	.3
Net income before income taxes	8.8	7.8	5.4

Source: California Restaurant Operations 1977, *Laventhol and Horwath, Los Angeles, CA, 1978.*

such as wilderness feeding (for example, feeding workers in construction camps and on offshore drilling rigs).

If, after evaluating a number of its strategies for current and new business, a company still cannot close the gap without violating its risk constraints, the financial objectives would have to be lowered, and the process repeated.

Implications of Strategies

The product/market strategies selected will undoubtedly have a number of implications for the company as a whole. These implications generally fall into three categories: financial, organizational, and administrative. A restaurant or lodging company with an aggressive expansion strategy will require considerable thinking about alternatives for financing its growth. Another hospitality company that chooses to pursue a strategy of actively acquiring companies in different industries may need to hire a top-flight acquisition specialist and redefine organizational responsibilities among top executives to make sure the newly acquired companies obtain sufficient management attention. Finally, a fast-food company that is pursuing a strategy of re-orienting its product line away from mature dishes may need to develop special controls to determine in which location a particular dish is slipping and why.

These are all very good examples of the important financial, organizational, and administrative implications that a set of long range strategies might have. This is the final step of the strategic planning process. In some cases, if the implications identified above are undesirable to the planners, the planning process may have to be carried out again.

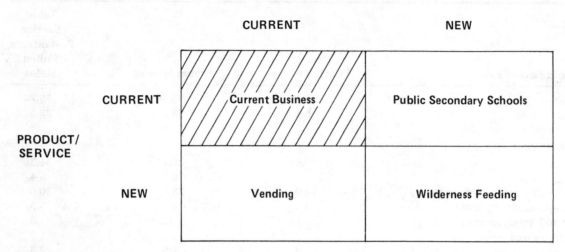

Figure 8–10

Questions

1 According to the textbook, which kind of operation represents the highest financial risk: buying an existing restaurant, building one, franchising one or managing one?

2 Of the various kinds of restaurants, which one of these could be less conveniently located to the clientele: luncheon, restaurant, highway restaurant, fastfood restaurant, or atmosphere/theme restaurant?

3 The econometric model, one combining economics and mathematics, can be used in picking the location for a particular style of restaurant. Can you explain what is involved?

4 Restaurants of the same chain and type should not be too closely located together; management of the McDonald Company feels that there needs to be how many miles between each McDonald's Restaurant?

5 Suppose someone says that there are universal food preferences; some foods will always be liked. What kind of a response do you have to that statement?

6 Give three reasons why certain foods are prestigious at a given time in history.

7 About how many thousand dollars can be expected in sales per seat in a successful restaurant during the course of a year?

8 In what way does seat turnover affect sales and profit? (Consider the seat turnover ratio in relation to average check.)

9 Some cost ratios are worth memorizing as bench marks. About what percentage of sales are these costs in a tableservice restaurant:

Payroll

Utilities

Advertising and promotion

Occupation costs

Food costs

Beverage costs

10 Although the usual restaurant probably makes a profit as percentage of sales of about 5 percent, how high can profitability go in terms of percentage of sales?

11 Why is it important to know the break-even point of sales per day?

12 In terms of a break-even chart, profit is measured by the distance between what two lines?

13 Which is better to sell, a steak at $4.00 with a food cost of 40 percent or chicken at $2.00 with a food cost of 33⅓ percent?

14 Why is it that the prices are so high at an airport restaurant?

15 Why is it that menu prices are likely to be lower in Alabama than they are in California or New York?

16 Which of these food services would you expect to spend the most for advertising and promotion: fastfood, pancake house, atmosphere restaurant, coffeeshop?

17 Which of these restaurants would you expect to have the lowest food cost as a percentage of sales: Mexican, coffeeshop, dining restaurant, fastfood?

18 The term prime costs as related to a restaurant include what two costs?

19 Can you think of some good reasons to retain an item on the menu even though its sales account for less than 2 percent of the total?

20 Part-time employees in the restaurant business are in a large part responsible for keeping labor costs down. Of the total number of employees what percentage constitute part-timers?

21 Give two reasons why making a frequency distribution of guest checks is valuable?

22 The tronc system of dividing tips used in Europe has certain advantages and disadvantages. Can you name two of each?

23 Are tips considered a part of income by the Internal Revenue Service?

24 Give three examples of fixed costs in a restaurant and three expenses that are usually considered to be variable and controllable.

25 In setting a restaurant you note that the occupancy cost will run 10 percent of sales. Is this about right?

26 Labor costs are likely to run less in the Deep South than in other parts of the country. What way will this affect the food cost?

27 List at least five items that would be observed by a "shopper" in a restaurant.

28 Why is it so important to issue guest checks by number and to control the number given to a wait person at any one time?

29 Theoretically the depreciation allowance is set aside to replace a building as it decreases in value with age. In actuality what usually happens to the depreciation allowance?

30 According to the tax experts the restaurant should be split up so that there are at least two companies, one that owns the buildings and the equipment, and the other that operates it. Why is this?

31 In buying a business, separate the land value from anything that can be depreciated such as the building and equipment, the trees, fences, roses, even garbage cans and dust pans. Why is this desirable?

32 Suppose you have three children. Tax experts suggest a separate trust for each. Why?

33 Is it possible for a person to own a piece of land on which a restaurant sits and lease the restaurant on that land from himself? Explain.

34 Larger companies are likely to set up long-range plans; a typical one to establish a plan for how many years in the future?

35 In considering an investment the higher the risk, the higher the _____ that should be expected.

36 Diversify the corporation. Is it possible to diversify too much within a given period of time? What are the factors involved?

37 Some food service companies diversified widely, others almost none at all. In looking at companies like Saga and McDonalds what are your thoughts regarding the merits of diversification in the food service field?

38 Strategic planning permits a company to envision a number of projects and to evaluate their results organizationally, administratively and _____.

dishwasher. The machines have been available for several years but were relatively unnoticed until energy and water costs increased.

KITCHEN ORGANIZATION AND PLANNING

The old prints of kitchens in the royal palaces show huge, high-ceilinged rooms, unpartitioned or sectioned. Some organization was essential. The chef during the time of Napoleon in France was seen wearing a long, floppy cap, on the order of a nightcap, as a symbol of his authority. At the other end of the status spectrum came the lowly scullion. Careme is credited with the tall starched chef hat that identified the chef or chief. The height of the "toque blanc" is supposed to correlate with his rank in the kitchen.

Though the large French kitchen had been departmentalized into sections (partis) Auguste Escoffier is credited with syncronizing their operation.

Under the old system, Eggs Meyerbeer, a dish consisting of eggs, lamb, kidneys, and truffle sauce, required fifteen minutes to prepare. With a chef at each station, the dish was prepared in a fraction of the time. An entremetier baked eggs in butter. A rotisseur grilled the kidney while a saucier prepared the truffle sauce. The work of the three specialists was combined and the eggs were hurried to the table.

At the turn of the century, and for some time after that, most hotel builders placed their kitchens in the basement where space was considered less valuable. Kitchens were large. The Astor Hotel of New York City opened in 1904 and had a kitchen 231 feet long with an average width of 150 feet.

Of course, the planners had not reckoned with the cost of operating the kitchens, of moving people, food, and ware from one level to another and within a kitchen. These are built-in costs that continue for the life of the building.

Ellsworth Statler was one of the first to see the merits of placing the hotel kitchen on the same level as the dining areas. In 1917 the St. Louis Statler was built with the kitchen placed on the same floor as all of the dining facilities, which were built around three sides of the kitchen. This layout made it possible for one kitchen to serve the dining room, the coffee shop, and a cafe. The plan has been used several times since, one of the most dramatic examples being the Beverly Hilton Hotel where the kitchen is round with the various dining facilities surrounding it.

Many high-rise buildings, especially where land is a major cost, cannot afford to place kitchen and serving areas on the same level. At the New York Hilton, for example, the kitchen and warewashing facilities are located in a central core of the building, on several floors, connected by elevator to each other and to the restaurants.

The practice of placing a number of preparation stations side-by-side behind a pick-up counter is used by most commercial kitchens preparing food for a large and complicated menu. The Waldorf-Astoria kitchen, for example, stretches a long distance with station after station placed side-by-side. The waiter enters the kitchen and drops off his order at each station, returning later to pick up the prepared food.

Some kitchens in the larger hotels are immense, the distances walked by the waiters in placing and picking up orders prodigious. Waiters and waitresses in huge American Plan resort hotels before the end of the season develop into track athletes from the constant running and walking required, and the distances involved.

Space Controls Planning

In most cases, kitchen planning revolves around the amount of space allocated or available for the kitchen. In downtown, expensive locations, the kitchens are often miniscule, one kitchen employee working almost on the back of another. Surprisingly, small kitchens turn out to be more efficient than the large ones because of the necessity of planning each work station in detail and the elimination of steps formerly required as foodservice workers moved from station to station, station to storeroom, and within a station. Reducing the size of the menu, in most cases, also improves efficiency.

Where the kitchen is the shape of a square, the kitchen equipment is frequently placed around three walls forming an open

EDDYS' RESTAURANT   KANSAS CITY, MISSOURI
ARCHITECTS: GENTRY & VOSKAMP
FABRICATED & INSTALLATION:
GREENWOOD'S, INC.   SOUTHERN EQUIPMENT CO.

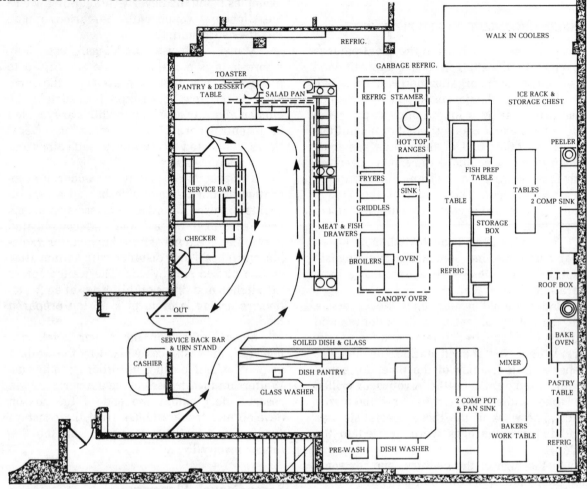

*Courtesy Institutions Magazine.

Figure 9–5   A "Custom-built by Southern" Award of Merit Winning Installation.
Source: Institutions/Volume Feeding *magazine.*

square or U. The first station, as the waiter enters the kitchen, is apt to be the dish room, the last station before entering the dining room, the pantry, or coffee and dessert station.

An example of a restaurant kitchen designed for function and speed of operation is the prize-winning kitchen of Eddy's Restaurant in Kansas City.

Waitress flow is a loop that starts with the dish pantry just six steps inside the door from the dining room.

The loop continues past the meat and fish station, vegetable station, salad station, and on to the pantry station. From there it passes the service bar and the food checker. No cross-traffic, no long distances between stations.

Preparation units buttress the serving stations and are so set up that food passes from one department to the next on its way to the serving line. Each employee is trained in two jobs, as work runs out at one station, he moves to another point of service.

Multicolored lights signal waiters when orders are ready.

Refrigerated drawers directly opposite the broilers and ranges keep food at the chef's elbow.

All equipment including ranges is elevated eight inches above the floor for easy cleaning. Interiors and shelves are removable for complete cleaning. Self leveling plate coolers and warmers are used. Ledges that accommodate two tiers of trays facilitate the assembling of orders.

Here is a case where the kitchen was planned, the building put up around it. Most kitchens must conform to the building with resulting poor layout, making process flow analysis all the more needed.

Institutional kitchens are often larger than necessary and have more cooking and other equipment than needed. Institutional kitchen planners are prone to specify extra equipment recognizing that, once money has been allocated for a kitchen, additional budgets may be hard to come by. It is better to have standby equipment on hand. Another explanation for excessive equipment is that most professional kitchen planners are paid a percentage of the total cost of the kitchen; for the unscrupulous, the higher the cost, the greater the fee.

Professional kitchen planners in the past have tended to be associated with restaurant equipment houses. The larger equipment firms employ layout specialists who are called upon to plan new kitchens, their services being included in the contract for the purchase of the kitchen equipment.

Following World War II, a few foodservice consultants set themselves up in business, offering their kitchen planning skills for a fee. In the 1950s a group of the independent consultants formed the Food Facilities Engineering Society. Another group, including both independent consultants and kitchen planners employed by equipment houses, formed the International Society of Food Service Consultants. The two groups are now merged into one.

Because the number of possible arrangements in any given kitchen is astronomical, no two kitchen consultants plan a kitchen alike. Each has developed patterns which he prefers and which he has observed as working satisfactorily over the years.

The Scientific Approach

The attempt to make kitchen planning more scientific and exact goes back to Count Rumford and Alexis Soyer. In 1945 the book, *Kitchen Planning for Quantity Food Service,* by Arthur W. Dana was published, the first systematic attempt to state principles of kitchen design and to describe kinds of problems encountered and types of equipment available for kitchen use.[2]

In 1962 the American Gas Association published *Commercial Kitchens.*[3] The book is a general statement of kitchen planning and quite naturally emphasizes the use of gas cooking equipment. The competitive situation being what it is between the electric and gas utility companies, the kitchen planner is beset by claims of superiority for gas on the one hand and electricity on the other.

Since most chefs have learned the trade using gas equipment, the tendency is for them to favor gas as a cooking fuel. Gas, they feel, as used for top-of-the-stove cooking is more con-

Figure 9-6   The layout of the McDonald's kitchens has evolved over the years. The kitchen necessarily is compact and highly efficient. Hamburger patties are grilled on the large griddle and garnished on the rotary table that is across the aisle from the griddle.

2. Arthur W. Dana, *Kitchen Planning for Quantity Food Service* (New York, NY.: Harper's, 1945).

3. *Commercial Kitchens* (Arlington, VA.: American Gas Assn., 1962).

Figure 9–7   *Another section of the McDonald's kitchen showing how the paper service is arranged for most efficient use. Hamburgers are bagged and held up to ten minutes. If after ten minutes they are not sold, they are discarded. Paper cups are separated by size and held upside-down for use.*

trollable than the electric heating element. The gas flame responds instantaneously to a turn of the knob and can be seen.

The electric utility companies point out that burning gas consumes oxygen from a kitchen, and if there is not a constant source of fresh air, the carbon monoxide level in a kitchen can rise dangerously. The electric people contend that the use of electric fuel in a kitchen results in a cleaner kitchen, a debatable contention. Proportionately more institutional kitchens use electric cooking equipment than commercial eating places.

The cost of cooking fuel is a major consideration for the operator. The American Gas Association readily admits that one Btu of electricity is equivalent to 1.6 Btu of gas for cooking. The reason is that much of the heat produced by gas is carried out the ventilation system along with the noxious fumes produced by gas combustion. But, say the gas people, even applying the appropriate gas and electric rate to this ratio, electric cooking costs in typical cities in the United States are from two to ten times as much as gas. (In a few areas where hydroelectric power is cheap, electricity for cooking is cheaper than gas.) The gas people also argue that their product is more

fail-safe in that the gas supply is not likely to break down, as happens periodically with an electric supply.

The gas versus electricity decision need not be made in favor of one or the other but in terms of specific pieces of cooking equipment. Either gas or electricity can be used to produce the hot air needed in ovens, stove top temperatures of 3000°F. or more, steam, and infrared energy.

Electricity must be used for the microwave ovens. Gas broilers seem to be more effective than electric ones; electric deep fryers, in which the heating units are immersed in the fat, seem to be more effective than gas fryers, where the heat is concentrated on the bottom of the kettle; some electric equipment in the past has been more attractive in appearance and better insulated than comparable gas equipment. Gas, in the author's opinion, is more hazardous than electric fuel because of its combustibility. As regards the fail-safe feature, the kitchen operator can protect himself by having a combination of gas and electric equipment.

The arrangement of all the cooking equipment in an island in the center of the room is used in some institutional kitchens. Institutional kitchens are not likely to be as departmentalized as are commercial kitchens. Placing the equipment in the island permits all of it to be placed under one exhaust hood, which can draw off the hot air and vapors created by the equipment.

The tendency in recent years has been to place the dishwashing section away from the kitchen or to entirely close it off from the kitchen. The scullery is a noisy, hot, and humid area. It belongs near a kitchen only because in the past waiters or busboys have had to drop off soiled ware and pick up clean ware there.

Conveyors and subveyors can deliver soiled ware to a dishroom in almost any location and also deliver the washed ware to the point of use. In some large installations, the dishroom is placed on a lower level, on a floor separate from the kitchen.

Debatable Areas in Kitchen Planning

Points of debate in planning a kitchen revolve around whether serving personnel should enter the kitchen, and what they should do if they do enter. Some operators require waiting personnel to make salads and toast and do other pantry work. Other operators believe that the less time the waiting personnel are in the kitchen, the better. They arrange for soiled ware to be carried into the kitchen via conveyor belt. Another way to move soiled ware is to install a merry-go-round type of dishmachine with part of the rotary rack system extended into the dining room where soiled ware can be directly loaded onto the dishmachine racks.

The answer to the question of how much time waiting personnel should spend in the kitchen is partly determined by the speed of the dining room. If breakfast and lunch are relatively slow, waiting personnel might well be used in the pantry and elsewhere in the kitchen. If there is a fast turnover in the dining room, waiting personnel can be more efficiently used in the dining room than in the kitchen when they are supported by specialized personnel in the kitchen.

Kitchen floors are characteristically covered with quarry tile, tile that is easy to clean, relatively impervious to water, and durable. Quarry tile is also extremely slippery when wet, probably the greatest cause of accidents in the hospitality business. Whoever has experienced a fall on tile, head hitting the floor, will never forget it—or perhaps he will.

A few kitchens have installed carpets. A Washington, D.C. cafeteria operator provides each woman employee with a small rag rug for her station and finds both safety and cleanliness increased. Quarry tile is efficient, varicose vein-forming, and tiring; it should be replaced with mats or carpets.

Duckboards are often laid behind cooking equipment. They can be taken up and cleaned in the dishmachine, and refuse can collect between the slats without interfering with the cooks' work. On the other hand, the cook may feel as though he has been working out on a trampoline after a day on the slats.

The Display Kitchen

Many of the theme or specialty restaurants that have been developed since the 1950s incorporate display kitchens in the dining room. In the Charlie Brown restaurants, the chef and his supporting equipment are installed in the dining room. Display kitchens either must be supported by an auxiliary kitchen elsewhere or must use an extremely limited menu. The Rib Rooms are built around a limited menu featuring roast beef, baked potatoes, and tossed salads. Some of the Japanese-style restaurants operate with the guests sitting around a large griddle, the waitress acting as both cook and server.

Among the most efficient restaurant operations are the Friendly Ice Cream Shops located in New England. All food preparation is done on an island surrounded by counters and stools. The menu is limited to sandwiches, soup, and ice cream so that every employee may be a grill operator as well as a waiter or waitress. The Chock Full O' Nuts, headquartered in New York City, has a similar style of operation with minimal need for preparation skills and personnel training time. The distance between preparation area and serving area is a matter of a few steps. Most of the food is pre-prepared. The waitress merely hands it to the customer across a counter.

The value of color in a kitchen is becoming recognized. Instead of the customary antiseptic white, walls and ceilings can be painted peach and yellow, colors that have been found to be "appetizing." Adequate lighting is especially

Figure 9–8 *Locke-Ober's long a noted Boston restaurant, has retained the same style over several decades, maintaining the atmosphere characteristic of fine restaurants in this country at the turn of the century. Note the weighted covers that are suspended over the silver holding dishes.*

needed at the pick-up area of the dishmachine and at food preparation work stations. Lighting must be bright enough so that the employee can see whether the dishes are clean and in the case of the cook, see the results of his handiwork in garnishment and plate arrangement.

According to Arthur Avery, a well-known foodservice consultant, the dishroom should have twenty to thirty footcandles. At the clean end of the dishwasher, lighting should be raised to forty to fifty footcandles. Egg white and white cereal residues are hard to see without enough light. The dishroom can be "cooled," from a psychological standpoint, by the use of cool blue and blue green colors on the wall.

The kitchen is usually much too noisy, especially the dishroom. Plastic racks reduce clatter. Coating the underside of dish tables with a mastic material or the use of plastic or rubber mats on the tables decreases decibels. Acoustic tile on the walls and ceilings helps. Acoustic paint can be used, or a honeycomb system of baffles hung from the ceiling. Air conditioning a kitchen or sink room increases human productivity by 10 to 15 percent. It also reduces accidents and improves quality control.

Sinks in kitchens are almost always too low for the worker; he is breaking his back by having to bend too low to work in the sink. Someday sinks will be adjustable to fit the height of the worker. Aisles are often too narrow or too wide. The industrial engineer tells us that aisle space should be at least 30 inches; 36 to 38 inches when the person has to get something from under a counter; 45 inches if he must kneel at work. When two men work on either side of an aisle, 48 inches should be allowed. Dials should be at eye level so that they can be read easily.

More Precision in Cooking

Cooking is growing more precise as more technical knowledge about the cooking process becomes known. The fisherman's platter, combining a fillet of fish, scallops, oysters, and french fries, is not likely to be cooked all at once, as it has been in the past. Each item requires a different cooking time; if they are all dumped into the deep fryer at once, some are overcooked, some underdone.

Richard Keating of Chicago tells us that though all parts of a chicken are usually cooked at 350°F., actual cooking time and temperature should be something different. At 350°F. the leg and wing require ten minutes to be cooked to complete doneness; the breast of the same chicken, a 2¾ pounder, requires twelve minutes; the thigh, thirteen minutes. This means that if the chicken parts are all placed in a fry basket at the same time, the leg and wing will be 30 percent overcooked. Shrinkage and flavor loss is the result. The next time you order fried chicken, see if the leg does not look as though it came from a smaller chicken.

With microwave cooking, timing is even more exact; seconds count. The cook today needs more than skill with the french knife to cook well. His forte, slicing onions, may not be needed at all, if he uses dehydrated onions —lower in cost, requiring less labor, and, for many dishes, just as tasty as the fresh onion.

The quality of instant potatoes varies widely, and the cook must be somewhat of an analyst to determine which are best from a cost and quality standpoint. The cook will take on some of the character of a food technologist. He must understand a little food chemistry and a little physics as related to cooking. As a specialty, his job will be easier and more rewarding.

Computer Assistance in Kitchen Planning

It had to come—computer-assisted kitchen planning. The optimal arrangement of equipment in a kitchen may appear to be a fairly simple problem. The mathematics of the problem, however, are formidable. A kitchen can be thought of as a system, a collection of interacting components.

A major problem in kitchen design is to arrange the work stations so as to minimize the steps taken between stations, equipment, and storage areas. George Conrade has estimated that if there were ten stations in a kitchen, the calculations required to arrive at the best possible layout would require three years. With a computer, the calculations can be made in a matter of minutes.

TO PRODUCE FOOD BY COMMISSARY?

Instead of operating a number of kitchens, some managements centralize food preparation into one or several central foodservice commissaries. Under such an arrangement

much or all of the food preparation for a multi-unit foodservice is done in a central production kitchen rather than in each foodservice establishment. The objective is to systematize and industrialize the food preparation, thereby reducing costs and increasing quality control.

By centralization, economies of scale are made possible. Serving units require no food preparation equipment. All purchases are made by a specialized food purchaser. Warehousing can be made more efficient with the use of forklifts and conveyor belts. Jobs can be specialized and simplified. Heavy-duty and more productive food preparation equipment can be purchased. A better qualified, more highly paid supervisor can be employed as a commissary manager, and better supervision and quality control can be effected.

Over the years some commissaries have been highly effective, others have not. Foodservice specialists disagree as to the merits of centralization. Some ardently favor it; others are vehemently opposed. Those who favor the commissary point to the value of operating the kitchen like a factory, using standardized recipes, utilizing labor-saving equipment. They recommend operating the commissary very much like a food processing plant.

Those who oppose the commissary maintain that the intricacies of relating the commissary to the unit are overly complicated. Food produced in the commissary and finally delivered to the unit foodservice, they say, is of a less desirable quality than can be produced in the unit itself.

It should be kept in mind that whenever food is prepared in one location and delivered to another energy costs are involved, and there is a strong possibility of quality loss in the food. Inflight food service is a good example. The food must be refrigerated (chilled), kept heated at relatively low temperatures, or frozen. In the plane the food must be brought up to serving temperature. Almost everyone concerned with inflight food service agrees that under the circumstances it is most difficult to produce on the passenger's tray a meal that measures up to the quality of a meal produced from scratch in a restaurant and served immediately. Food experts if they are honest with themselves almost unanimously agree that the best food is that prepared from scratch and served at once. Quality inevitably declines the longer food is held from its fresh state. Of course it is quite possible to become accustomed to any type of food, preferring margarine over butter, chicory over coffee, skim milk over whole milk, and perhaps frozen entrees over food prepared and served at once.

In holding food in any form after it is cooked, energy is required—energy to chill it or freeze it and energy to "reconstitute" (reheat) the food. Convenience food can be of top quality, for example, powdered potatoes, frozen rolls, and few other prepared foods. Once heat is applied to finish cooking these items and the item is cooked, quality usually declines thereafter the longer it is held.

The debate over using commissaries is particularly relevant to college and university foodservices since most of the larger schools have a number of houses or dining commons and have the option of centralizing part or all of the foodservice preparation. Smith College, a well-known women's college, has some thirty houses, each with its own kitchen and preparation team. The college administration recognizes that centralization would reduce costs. They are willing to pay extra for food prepared in each kitchen. Michigan State University operates from a central commissary as do a number of other universities.

CENTRALIZATION IN SCHOOL LUNCH

Centralization of the school lunch program was begun in the late 1950s, and in the 1960s many school systems centralized school food preparation. Food is prepared by industrial methods and machinery, then distributed by truck to the individual school for service. With a centralized kitchen, fewer employees are needed than when each school operates its own kitchen. Part of the savings in labor, however, is offset by the cost of transporting the food from the centralized kitchen to the individual schools.

Centralized commissaries for commercial restaurants go back at least to the 1890s when the John R. Thompson Company of Chicago operated a central commissary for three restaurants and later distributed prepared food to the individual units by electrically driven vans. The Marriott Corporation began commissary operation in the early 1930s by centralizing some of the food preparation in one store, distributing the prepared food to the other stores.

In 1941 a large centralized commissary building designed especially as a commissary and headquarters for the company was built. This has been enlarged several times and in 1967, a completely new commissary building was completed. The new commissary in Prince Georges County, Maryland, covered 285,000 square feet. It is one of the largest in operation today for serving restaurants. Food is sent as far west as Chicago and Texas, north to Albany. The Marriott operations in California are served by a separate commissary.

The Marriott operation is one of the most automated of any in the business. Purchase orders from the individual stores are telephoned into the commissary via data-phone. This system does not use words as the language of ordering but relies upon a communication code. The order is relayed by long distance phone by inserting a properly punched card; the order is transmitted via a code. A computer at the receiving end compiles the orders and prints them out.

The Howard Johnson Company is another of the large companies to make extensive use of the commissary. As early as 1952 much of the Howard Johnson menu was prepared in Miami and in a location near Boston, for freezing and delivery by trailer van trucks. Miami serviced Howard Johnson stores as far away as Texas with frozen entrees. In 1969 there were 22 central commissaries and distribution centers that prepared 700 items.

A number of companies have elected to produce foods selectively in their commissaries, producing only those foods where economies of scale are involved and foods produced are as good or better in quality than produced on premise or purchased from a supplier. Far West Services, for example, has its own meat plant that ages and cuts steaks for national distribution and grinds beef for their Southern California restaurants. A separate bakery produces breads, rolls, cakes, pies, fillings and biscuits on a regional basis, commissaries produce salad dressings, soups, sauces, chopped vegetables and fish on a regional basis. Another commissary produces breaded shrimp, fish and deviled crabs for distribution nationally. Items like soups, chili, terriyaki sauce, barbecue sauce can be made in a commissary and distributed without any loss in quality, so too can dressings.

FACTOR OF GEOGRAPHICAL SPREAD

Whether or not the central commissary is economical and effective depends upon its design, the menu it produces, the number of units it serves, and the geographical spread of the units. If an individual unit has a high enough volume of sales, it can, in effect, operate its own food processing plant on premise. If the individual unit is large enough to achieve the economy of scale, there is no need to turn to another commissary to produce the same thing and transport it to the unit.

A large dining commons in a university serving 5,000 meals a day can probably produce some of its food on the premises as economically as can a commissary. Even so, in the future the "economies of scale" of any individual unit—no matter how large—will be compared with the economies of scale of the large industrial "meal" manufacturer, companies like Swift, Sexton, Armour, and Campbell Soup Company.

The commissary style of operation is well suited to the large multiunit organization which has a fairly small range of menu items. These items can be produced in quantities of thousands on a production line basis. For example, the coconut cake served by the Howard Johnson Company is mass-produced day after day, using the same equipment and the same personnel.

The question arises as to whether or not the food for the individual unit should be purchased from a mass producer of food such as Campbell Soup Company or Armour and Company. The answer must be in terms of cost accounting, a comparison of the cost of the item produced by the individual organization versus what it costs from a food manufacturer. Also important, of course, is the comparative quality of the products available. Most food experts agree that food prepared and served at once is superior in flavor and texture than that cooked and held in any way, chilled, frozen, or warm.

According to Mr. Woodrow Marriott, Marriott's canned foods are necessarily less desirable in quality than frozen foods because of the high temperature and long cooking time used in canning foods by conventional methods. A few foods, such as baked beans and cream of tomato soup, are as good or better in the can than the same product commissary-prepared and frozen. The new high-temperature-short-time method of canning may overcome some of the objections raised by Mr. Marriott's study.

Another factor in the operation of a commissary is the distance involved in transporting the food from the commissary to the individual unit. At some point it becomes necessary to introduce another commissary or to produce locally because of transportation costs.

When food is produced centrally and distributed, there is the problem of maintaining the quality of the food from the time it is prepared until the time it is served. Freezing has been one answer; heated containers provide another.

Nearly every large hospital, in effect, has a centralized commissary. Food is prepared in a central kitchen and distributed throughout the building or buildings.

Commissaries have not always been successful. It is reported that the Horn and Hardart Baking Company of Philadelphia installed a multimillion dollar commissary only to find that its capacity was much too great for the volume of food that could be sold in the individual units. Other companies have tried commissaries and abandoned them.

Many small chains of restaurants have compromised on the commissary concept by having a central bakery and doing the heavy meat roasting, the sauce making, and soup making at a central kitchen. Salad making and all frying is done on the premises of the unit store.

HOW TO HOLD PREPARED FOOD?

In setting up a centralized commissary, the administrator has several alternatives among the methods of food preparation, the amount of preparation done at the commissary, and the amount to be prepared at the unit where the food is served. A tough administrative decision relates to whether the food should be held and transported frozen, refrigerated, or hot. This is a major decision that if unwisely made can bankrupt a company.

A pioneering effort in a commercial restaurant in New York City had the food being prepared in the basement of the restaurant, frozen, and carried to the street level where it was heated and served to the customer. Obviously, there was no need to freeze the food since it was being served on the next level. There was also no need to refrigerate it; it could have been carried hot to the next level.

An industrial foodservice operation in Long Island made a similar dramatic mistake; they prepared food in a central kitchen, froze it, and then carried it to a nearby outlet where it was reheated and served.

Chilling Rather Than Freezing

It costs money to freeze and to reheat, and it is not necessary to freeze if the food does not have to be held over extended periods. Ford Motor Company refrigerates much of its food for service in its employee foodservices. The more solid foods can be refrigerated to as low as 28°F. which is not freezing for them. The food holds for several days.

A large, hospital contract foodservice company refrigerates cooked food in five-portion quantities in vacuum sealed bags. Their system is based on the Swedish Nacka food system, named after the Nacka hospitals in Stockholm where it originated. The food is packaged and processed at various stages of doneness. Stewed items, such as meat or chicken pot pie are completely cooked. Broiled items, such as chopped sirloin steak, are grilled just long enough to give surface color. Other foods are packaged raw and completely cooked within the pouch.

The food is portioned and packaged under vacuum. It is then cooked to doneness in a water bath. Quick chilling is done in cold water, and the food is stored in the refrigerator. Shelf life, it is said, is at least sixty days for such foods. When the food is to be heated for serving, it is placed in a hot water bath for 30 to 40 min., until it reaches an internal temperature of 160°F. It is then plated and placed briefly in a microwave oven before service.

Using this low temperature cooking, meat shrinkage is reduced as much as 20 percent. An advantage of the system is that seven-day requirements can be produced in a five-day, forty-hour week. Batching of production, producing a number of the same items at one time, permits greater efficiency in foodservice.

Many times food need not be refrigerated at all if the temperature can be held at 140°F. or higher without damaging the quality of the food. A chain of cafeterias in Georgia transports round ribs of beef from a central commissary some fifty miles to various service cafeterias. Some cooking takes place during transportation, but the food is undercooked initially, and the holding merely finishes off the cooking process.

Items like soups, sauces, gravies, and heavy roasts can be held for forty-eight hours or longer at temperatures that will not permit bacterial growth. A few items actually improve with holding but most lose quality in terms of flavor. It is true that some people prefer cold chicken to hot, but they usually add mayonnaise or other condiment to increase flavor.

A flat statement can be made about fried items: their quality falls off rapidly, and none should be held for more than about fifteen minutes before serving. Salad greens can be prepared and held for several hours, if held in a moist, cool environment. Salad dressings, however, cannot be added until just before serving without severe quality loss. Salads, with or without dressings, cannot be held on the cafeteria line for more than a few minutes without quality deterioration.

ENERGY CONSERVATION

Energy costs in the kitchen have been important, but little attention was given to them until the energy crisis, beginning in 1973, when those costs doubled in some areas. Since the typical kitchen consumes 40 percent or more of the total energy used in the restaurant, the National Restaurant Association, The American Hotel and Motel Association, and several hospitality chains began to examine ways to reduce the costs of heating water for dishwashing, pot and pan washing, cooking, and heating and cooling the kitchen. Among the more intensive studies conducted was that by Sambo's Restaurants, a leading chain of coffee shops, in cooperation with Elster's, a kitchen planning and equipment firm. The Sambo's restaurant in Calabasas, California, was used as a research unit, and several energy-saving systems were installed and studied. The exhaust ducts over the cooking equipment were lined with tubes carrying water that collected heat being exhausted from the cooking equipment. The heated water was carried to a heat exchanger, a 3,000-gallon water tank outside the building. Here the heat, collected from the cooking equipment and carried through the tubing, heats the tap water.

In the usual kitchen, a large flow of air moves from the dining room into the kitchen and out the exhaust ducts over the cooking equipment, all of which costs money. In the Sambo's research unit only a small, negative pressure was maintained in the ducts, so that only about 20 percent of the make-up air from the kitchen was exhausted.

Heat generated by the compressors operating air conditioning units and refrigeration units is usually exhausted into the building or to the outside. In the Calabasas unit that heat was also captured and transferred to the 3,000 gallon tank where it was absorbed by the water. The water in the tank was further heated by the sun, through solar radiation picked up by a glycol solution in the tubing on the roof and carried to the water tank. If more heat input is needed for the stored water, it is provided by gas. With study, it was found that a 1,000-gallon heat exchanger would supply the needs of the restaurant. With these and other energy-saving devices the use of natural gas for cooking, heating water, and the building, was reduced 59 percent, electricity consumption by about 80 percent.

Other ideas for conserving energy include: constructing thick walls on the western and southern exposures of a restaurant, planning windows for 20 percent or less of the floor space, using flourescent lighting in areas other than in dining spaces, installing devices to control electrical equipment to reduce peak electricity load at any one time (rates for electricity are based on maximum consumption for a fifteen-minute period plus the total amount consumed), and installing heat recovery devices as wrap-arounds on incinerator stacks and using the hot air generated for heating purposes.

The Heating, Ventilation and Air-Conditioning System (HVAC) in a Restaurant

The workings of the HVAC system in a restaurant is usually not well understood by the restaurant operator. Understandably, his efforts are directed more to operation and seldom does he have much interest in engineering. Nevertheless, it is helpful to know in a general way how the restaurant is heated and cooled so that the system can be maintained and repaired or modified if necessary.

Ordinarily the kitchen HVAC system should operate independently of the other rooms. Exhaust fumes and odors must be exhausted through separate filters and by means of exhaust fans directly to the outdoors. Fans draw air through filters that trap grease and fumes and force it to the outside. The kitchen is kept under a slight negative pressure so that air will not move from the kitchen into the dining room. As a result there is a slight air movement from the dining and other rooms into the kitchen and out the exhaust ducts over the cooking and dishwashing equipment.

Since air is continually being exhausted out of the ducts, "make-up" air is often pumped directly into the kitchen, which helps to cool the kitchen in the summer. If necessary the make-up air can be heated during cold periods.

Air pressure for the entire restaurant must be slightly positive, meaning that the amount of fresh or make-up air should be slightly greater than the amount exhausted. When doors and windows are opened, air gently flows out; outside air does not rush in.

Some HVAC systems for restaurants distribute air through the ducts at the temperature needed by the room with the greatest cooling requirement, the main dining room. For other rooms small heaters inside the ducts reheat the air as required. The duct heaters are operated by thermostats within each room. During the winter, air is distributed through the ducts at an intermediate temperature. The duct heaters then heat the air as needed for each individual room. These systems are known as *Terminal Reheat Systems.*

Variable Volume Systems deliver the same temperature air to each room where dampers inside the ducts, operated by room thermostats, regulate the amount of air delivered in the room.

While the usual operator will never engineer an HVAC system he should look into how the system he has works, by following out the ducts from where the air is taken in to where it is exhausted. He should know the location of each blower, heater, and chiller.

The Federal Energy Administration in its *Guide to Energy Conservation for Foodservice* includes a number of simplified drawings

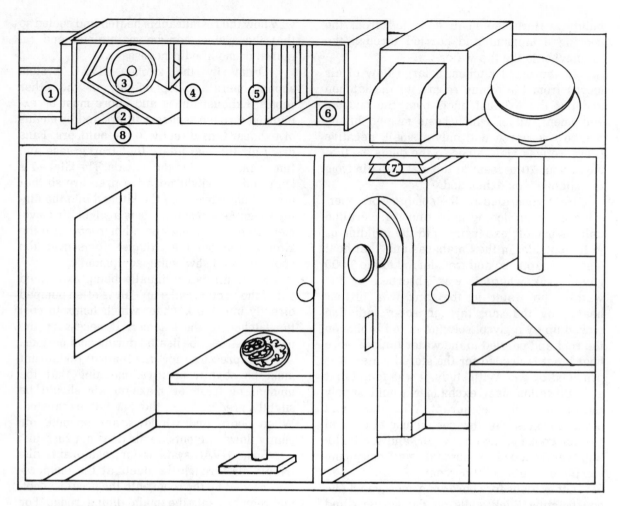

Air enters the system in two ways:
1. from outdoors, through a fresh air intake;
2. through the return ducts as stale, "return" air from within the restaurant.
The fresh air intake is covered with a screen to prevent birds from getting into the system.

A blower, run by an electric motor, draws the entering air through filters that trap particles such as dust, insects, and pollen. It then blows the clean air through

a heater in cold weather;

a chiller containing a refrigerant in hot weather.

The "conditioned"—that is, heated or cooled—air enters the ducts, which carry it to various parts of the restaurant: to dining rooms, rest rooms, corridors, kitchens.

The air passes into the rooms through diffusers or grilles. In a variable volume HVAC system the flow of air, and therefore the temperature in each room, is regulated by *dampers* inside the ducts. A damper is a plate or set of flaps, controlled automatically by room thermostats, that can narrow or close off a duct. Thus, the temperature of each room is determined by the *amount* of conditioned air entering the room, rather than by the temperature of the conditioned air, as is the case in a terminal-reheat system.

Air leaves the various rooms and returns to the unit through a second duct system, where, mixed with outside air, it is drawn again through the filters by the blower.

Figure 9-9   A "typical" central HVAC System and Kitchen Make-up Unit.

showing how kitchen equipment and HVAC systems operate. This diagram is taken from that publication.

THE EVOLVING KITCHEN

The hotel and restaurant kitchen has been changing for some time from a production "from scratch" processing plant to a finish-and-assembly station. Griddling, broiling, and frying processes will probably remain a part of most kitchens for some time. So, too, with the salad station. Most pre-preparation has already left the kitchen and is being done in the industrialized food processing plant. The romantic image of the kitchen with its gleaming copper pans and kettles is already a part of nostalgia for the past.

As research finally comes to the kitchen, specific pieces of cooking equipment will be seen to be effective for special use. The microwave oven, for example, begins to be seen as a limited heating device, one essentially for boiling the water found within food materials.

The kitchen becomes cooler, cleaner, and more technically precise. Much of the mystique and expertise has already been moved back to the food manufacturing plant. The traditional kitchen is likely to remain much longer in Europe and in a few expensive restaurants and clubs here. The fastfood restaurant has defrocked the high priest of cooking and replaced him with food warmers and miniwage, teenage assemblers. Who is to say if this is progress?

Questions

1 Name three pieces of kitchen equipment used in an ancient Roman kitchen and the colonial kitchen of the United States.

2 What is the name of a prestige restaurant that operated before 1900 in New York City?

3 Count Rumford, a gentleman who was born in Massachusetts, achieved some fame as a kitchen inventor. Can you name one of his inventions?

4 Who is the famous chef given credit for first organizing the kitchen into departments?

5 Why is a kitchen called a food processing plant?

6 The tilting skillet (or braising pan) can be used to cook several ways. Name three such ways.

7 Fires in the kitchen before about 1950 were frequently caused by overheated fat used in frying. What device has helped to limit such fires?

8 How is a forced convection oven different than the conventional oven?

9 What is the advantage of pulsing the heat source in an oven?

10 Define a magnetron and its use in the kitchen.

11 Name three advantages and the three disadvantages of microwave cooking.

12 Define a salamander.

13 What is the advantage of using a grooved griddle over the flat griddle?

14 Define bain marie.

15 Dishmachines that use a rotary table have what advantage over a flight-type machine?

16 Is it necessary to place a dishwashing room close to the dining room? Explain.

17 Why is it necessary to use 1.6 British thermal units (Btu) of gas to accomplish the same cooking action as 1 British thermal unit of electricity?

18 What is the great disadvantage of using gas over electricity?

19 Is there one best way to plan a kitchen? Explain.

20 Kitchen floors are normally covered with quarry tile. What is the advantage of quarry tile and what is a big disadvantage?

21 Define convenience food and describe its origin.

22 Why is it not a good idea to fry all parts of the chicken at the same time in a deep fry kettle?

23 Name three advantages of using a central commissary to prepare school lunches for a number of schools. Name a major disadvantage.

24 Name three or four items that can be easily prepared in a commissary and distributed without loss of quality.

25 Name two food items that are difficult to prepare in a commissary and distribute without loss of quality.

26 Name a major disadvantage of freezing preparing food before distributing it.

27 Energy management is being considered by a number of restaurant operators. Name three ideas that can be incorporated into a restaurant to reduce energy demand.

28 Air pressure in a restaurant dining room must be slightly positive. Why?

29 Which uses less energy, flourescent lighting or incandescent lighting?

30 Why not use flourescent lighting throughout a restaurant?

31 Why is it so important to spread out the demand for electricity as much as possible throughout a day?

32 Suppose you installed solar collectors on the roof of your restaurant. How would the heat collected in them be transferred and used in the restaurant?

FAST FOOD AND FRANCHISING

TEN

What single factor created the greatest change in the hotel and restaurant business in the 1960s? The answer is undoubtedly the franchise. It is a method of operation that has permitted hundreds of small businessmen to enter the hotel and restaurant business equipped with a prepackaged product, a format, an image, a system of operation, a market plan, and a scheme of finance.

It has greatly reduced the chances of failure in the hotel and restaurant business. It has produced products and services which are generally superior to what would have been produced by the businessman on his own. It has excited the imagination of: (1) persons producing the franchise, (2) the franchisor, (3) the individual buying it, the franchisee, and (4) the general public.

From the individual investor's viewpoint, the fast food franchise boom of the 1960s had faded somewhat by the middle 1970s. The reason is that several of the really successful franchise companies that had accumulated capital had shifted policy sharply. Several had stopped selling franchises and were busy buying back the properties that were successful. Also, a large number of franchisees have failed as have several franchisors.

In 1976, according to the U.S. Dept. of Commerce, franchised restaurants totaled 47,167. Total sales were about $14 billion. Those selling hamburgers, frankfurters, and roast beef had the most sales. Chicken franchised restaurants were next. Other franchised restaurants sold pizza, tacos, seafood, pancakes and waffles, steaks, and other types of sandwiches. McDonald's sales in 1979 exceeded $5 billion, Kentucky Fried Chicken $2 billion, and a number of similar fast food companies had sales exceeding $100 million annually.

The word "franchise" comes from the old French "francer," meaning "to free." The word was used during the Middle Ages in connection with franchises granted by the Catholic Church to friendly persons who served as tax collectors taking a sizeable cut for themselves and sending the rest to the Pope. Franchising appeared in the United States just after the Civil War, franchises being offered to Singer Sewing Machine dealers. Towards the end of the century auto makers, soft drink manufacturers, brewers, and the oil people spread the franchise concept. Following World War II soft ice cream outlets numbered about a hundred, but by 1969 "Frostee Freeze" alone had 2,600 franchise stands. In 1945 a total of 3,500 fast food outlets existed.[1]

Fast food franchising goes back to the late 1920s and 1930s when A & W Root Beer and Howard Johnson's franchised some of their units, but the field had little momentum until hundreds of soft ice cream stores appeared in the 1950s. The number of franchisors expanded rapidly in the 1960s, cashing in on general prosperity and the opportunity for an individual to own his own business with a relatively small investment.

---

1. Big Mac, Boas and Chain, (New York, NY: E. P. Dutton, 1976), p. 147.

In the later 1960s, fast food franchising took a new turn, with major food manufacturing companies buying established chains or building their own. Between 1967 and 1969 Pillsbury Company acquired Burger King; General Foods, Burger Chef; Consolidated Foods Corporation, Chicken Delight and Big Boy Restaurants; Ralston-Purina, the Jack-in-the-Box chain; Pet Milk Company, Stuckeys; and AMK Corporation's United Fruit Company, the A & W Root Beer chain. Others that have entered the picture include Pepsi Cola Co., General Mills, and Green Giant. These companies with their access to large capital and people resources give the franchise business a new stability.

According to a Commerce Department survey franchise restaurants employed close to 900,000 people in 1976, about 27 percent of the total number of eating and drinking place employees. About half of them featured hamburgers, the frank, or roast beef with seafood outlets growing rapidly. Seven companies each having 1,000 or more outlets did almost half of this business.

Figure 10–1   One section of the dining room of the Wedgwood Inn, St. Petersburg, Florida. Charles Creighton, the owner, was one of the first to create atmosphere restaurants in Florida. Note the green palm and other tropical plantings, and the large amount of window space that looks out on a beautiful garden. A cage on the right contains exotic birds. The name of the room comes from the fact that many pieces of Wedgwood china are permanently displayed.

In 1975 California led the states in numbers of franchise restaurants followed by Texas, Ohio, Illinois, and Michigan. Outside of the United States, Canada had 940 such units, the United Kingdom 408, and Japan 311.[2]

By the mid 1960s, the franchise had affected the entire hotel and restaurant business, stimulating it, upsetting old ways of doing business, and accelerating change. Coincidentally, it was in part responsible for making millionaires of a number of franchisors and at least small fortunes for hundreds of small entrepreneurs.

Technically, a franchise as used in the hotel and restaurant business is an agreement between one party, the franchisor, and another party, the franchisee. The franchisor grants the franchisee the right to market certain goods and services under prescribed conditions and within a certain territory. What those goods and services are can be seen on every highway: Howard Johnson Restaurants, McDonald's, A & W Restaurants, Holiday Inns and Hilton Inns.

Through franchising, small businessmen acquire an instant image, extend their economic power, and gain relative assurance of success. The franchise combines the managerial knowhow of big business with the personal incentive of the individual owner. Cost controls, promotional plans, buying advice, and, usually, tested operating methods are sold as part of the package.

Most motel franchise agreements require that the franchisee construct a building to certain specifications. Usually he also agrees to buy and erect a particular sign and to follow a list of operational practices. In many cases the restaurant franchisee has been expected to buy certain foods and kitchen equipment from the franchisor and follow particular procedures. Under some agreements the franchisee can buy foods where he likes but must follow purchase specifications laid down by the franchisor.

THE FAST FOOD FRANCHISE

Fast food franchisees may expect to pay:

1   An initial franchise fee

2. Franchising in the Economy, 1975–77, U.S. Department of Commerce.

2 Continuing royalty fees ranging from 5 percent to 7 percent of the unit's gross sales; advertising assessments of about 1.3 percent to 4 percent of gross sales

3 Equipment purchase price or rental cost

4 Rent

Cash requirements to launch a franchise restaurant run from $10,000 to $15,000 for a small pizza or seafood place up to more than $100,000 for the more profitable hamburger or chicken outlets.

The chart on the facing page lists representative foodservice franchises, gives an idea of the investment needed and the kind of advertising required by the franchisor.

The majority of the chains are categorized as fast food establishments and have these characteristics:

High speed service, mostly to walk-up customers

Immediate service of food or assignment of an in-turn number for pick-up

High customer turnover per hour

Limited menu

Low check average

Assembly line food production

Strict purchasing and portion control

Throw-away plates, cups, and utensils

Special training programs for managers and workers

Franchise operators know the value of market research and promotion and spend up to 4 percent of their gross sales on TV and other media ads and promotional gimmicks. The McDonald Corporation has the record for an advertising budget, more than $200 million a year. One chain spent a million dollars on an eight-week ad to publicize only its french fried potatoes.

WHAT FRANCHISEES GET

For his fees, the franchisee can expect from a reputable and established franchisor, an image and an established brand name, maintained by advertising, and generally a complete promotion package including roadside pylons, a logo or a signature on take-out boxes, bags, coffee cups, napkins, match books, and just about everything else that the customer sees.

The franchisee can also expect quality control in purchasing and operations, a control which he sometimes resents and resists. Perhaps most important of all, if the franchisor is not overly hungry for new franchisees, the franchisee gets careful location analysis and a certain amount of financial advice. In some cases he gets help in financing as well. Eventually it can be expected that many franchise plans will include central accounting as part of the service offered.

Nearly all franchisors provide some kind of initial training at a Hamburger University, a Mr. Donut College, or similar training center. Following his initial training the franchisee and his operation are watched over by an area supervisor or field coordinator. His books are set up for him and audited by the franchisor in one way or another to assure that the correct franchise fee is paid. Most franchise fees are based on sales together with other fees.

A prospective franchise buyer has a wide range of choices in either lodging or restaurant franchises, according to the cash he can raise and the style and size of operation he would like to be in. A relatively small amount of cash is needed for some of the smaller restaurants; several hundred thousand dollars in cash is necessary for franchising one of the larger motor lodges or inns. Among franchised restaurants, he has a choice ranging from a relatively small and simple operation like Burger Chef to a large, relatively complicated restaurant coffee shop.

The franchisor is the big winner in that he can expand his business straight across the country by merely signing up hundreds of franchisees. The franchisee is then almost always largely or totally responsible for raising the necessary capital to start the business. The franchisor can expand as rapidly as he gets franchisees. The two principal problems of the franchisor are (1) to maintain the quality and the standard of the product and services he franchises, and (2) see to it that few if any of the franchisees fail.

COMPARATIVE COSTS AND SALES

Each fast food franchise has developed its own menu and unit layout so that food and labor costs vary widely. Capital costs per stores and sales also vary widely. A Harvard Business

Table 10-1 Top Twenty-five Franchise Restaurant Chains, 1976.

Franchise System	System-wide Sales (In Millions of Dollars) 1976	Total Units 1976
McDonald's	$3,030.0	4,000
Kentucky Fried Chicken	1,600.0	3,989
Burger King	750.9	1,603
International Dairy Queen	684.0	4,792
Big Boy	550.0	937
Pizza Hut	375.0	2,321
Tasti-Freez	328.5	2,190
Hardee's (includes Sandy's)	324.0	953
Burger Chef	300.0	925
A & W	289.0	1,803
Ponderosa	250.0	550
Bonanza International	239.7	645
Arby's	209.0	568
Dunkin' Donuts	203.4	830
Wendy's	**168.0**	**520**
Long John Silver's	156.3	621
International House of Pancakes	148.0	386
Sonic Industries	136.8	567
Shakey's Pizza	124.7	528
Sizzler Steak House	120.8	287
Taco Bell	120.0	732
Pizza Inn	113.0	525
Mr. Steak	110.1	258
Western Sizzling	108.6	175
Arthur Treacher's	105.2	455

Source: Restaurant Business, *March, 1977.*

Table 10-2 Franchise Chains.

	Sales/Unit	Capital Cost Per Store	Food & Paper Cost %Sales	Labor Cost %Sales
Burger King	$463,000	$347,000	40%	21%
Chart House	665,000	750,000	43	18
Cork 'n Cleaver	517,000	550,000	44	17
Denny's	594,000	600,000	33	34
Friendly	312,000	290,500	47	20
Jerrico (LJS)	299,000	200,000	38	14
McDonald's	727,000	502,000	40	22
Pizza Hut	179,000	240,000	30	24
Sambo's	505,000	450,000	35	23
Victoria Station	1,560,000	925,000	43	19
Wendy's	463,000	280,000	42	15

Source: Harvard Business School, 1976.

School study published in 1976 suggests these wide differences:

In the chart on page 302, the fast food figures—Burger King, Friendly's, Jerrico, McDonald's, and Wendy's—can be compared with dinner house figures—Chart House, Cork n' Cleaver, and Victoria Station. Compare also the coffee shops (Sambo's and Denny's) with the numbers involved with the other two restaurant formats, and with the pizza chain, Pizza Hut.

The dollar numbers are out-of-date but the ratios remain valid. Wendy's had a prime cost (food and labor costs) of 57 percent of sales due largely to the utter simplicity of its menu and operation. Burger Chef and McDonald's run about the same prime costs. The coffee shops experience lower food costs and higher labor costs because of counter and booth service. The dinner houses have the highest food costs.

FRANCHISE SUCCESS

McDonald's, the most successful of the restaurant franchisors, has had a failure rate of less than 2 percent, failure being defined as a unit producing less than $200,000 a year in sales. For those franchised units that do fail, the franchise company either works with the franchisee to make the unit successful after negotiation or buys it back However, by 1969 some franchised units were being allowed to lapse.

The Howard Johnson Company and Denny's have decided to buy back a number of their franchised stores with the thought that standards can be more easily maintained if stores are company operated (or that the parent company can make greater profits operating than franchising). Where the franchise involves primarily the use of a name, as is the case with the Sheraton Hotel franchise, the parent company may quietly nullify the agreement, take back its sign, and remove the hotel or motel from the list of Sheraton Hotels that take part in the Sheraton referral system.

From the viewpoint of the franchisee, the agreement is generally restrictive as regards the style of operation, the product, and services offered. No room is left for imagination or for changes in menu, decor, furnishings, or equipment. Neither is there room for regional differences in taste or other customer preference. Some of the franchise fees add up to 15 percent of the gross sales, and more; this can be a burden especially during slow periods.

The franchise favors the franchisor. The terms of a franchise agreement are drawn up by the franchisor; the franchisee is free to buy the franchise or reject it. Ordinarily the agreement is fixed. Most franchise agreements contain clauses which permit the franchisor to buy back the franchise, or to cancel it, should the franchisee fail to live up to the terms of the agreement.

When the franchisor acquires capital or when the franchised units are particularly profitable, the franchisor is tempted to buy it back. Chock Full O'Nuts, a New York City restaurant and franchise company, apparently faced such a temptation. In May of 1969, ten franchisees picketed the headquarters of Chock Full O' Nuts, stormed the building, and threatened to stay all night unless they could see William Black, the company president. The franchisees protested what they called company harassment of those who did not want to sell their franchises back to the company. Moreover, they stated that they received no supervision, and that the prices of frankfurters, hamburgers, and soups charged to the franchisee by the parent company had been raised arbitrarily.[3]

The franchised restaurant was first seen when A & W Root Beer opened a stand in Lodi, California in 1919. In the 1920s, an A & W franchise was sold to J. Willard Marriott. Bill Marriott had been a student at the University of Utah and had observed another early franchisee A & W Root Beer stand doing an exceptionally large business across the street from the campus. This was in 1926.

In 1927 Howard D. Johnson began franchising his stores and the name Howard Johnson was to become a household word on the East Coast. Later, the company expanded its operation into the Midwest and, in the middle 1960s, into California. In 1973 the Howard Johnson Company included more than

---

3. Chock Full O'Nuts has about forty-five franchisees, some fifty-five company-owned stores. The fee for a Chock Full O'Nuts franchise is $7,500 plus 3 percent of the gross sales. The franchisee is required to buy all of his merchandise from the company. Total cost of building and equipping a typical store is about $100,000.

900 restaurants and more than 450 motor lodges.

The most colorful of the franchise stories involves the originator of Kentucky Fried Chicken, "Colonel" Harland Sanders. He had been a farm hand, carriage painter, soldier, railroad fireman, blacksmith, streetcar conductor, Justice of the Peace, salesman, and service station operator. At the age of sixty-five, he was operating his own restaurant-motel in Kentucky but found himself without business because a new interstate highway had by-passed his establishment seven miles away. His only income was a social security check of $105 per month.

While in the restaurant business he had experimented with frying chicken and found that cooking it in a home-size pressure cooker produced an especially tender product. He had also assembled a zesty coating for the chicken. He set off on a trip around the country selling restaurant operators a franchise to produce Kentucky Fried Chicken (KFC). Since it was a promotion package and a procedure for cooking chicken, the franchise could be used in any existing restaurant. The initial investment was low, only enough to buy a few needed pieces of cooking equipment.

With his first franchisee, Pete Harmon, he put on a television cooking show in Salt Lake City. To add some color he decided to change into a full-fledged Kentucky Colonel with a pure white suit and Kentucky colonel goatee. "You got to remember," he said, "I didn't have no money for advertising and promoting, so I had to do the best I could." The Colonel's thoughts on marketing: "If you have something good a certain number of people will beat a path to your doorstep; the rest you have to go and get."[4]

The franchisee paid the Colonel 5¢ for every order of fried chicken served. According to Sanders, he would stop at a restaurant, demonstrate his frying process, stay on a few days without pay until the customers began to react to the chicken, then move on. He traveled from city to city, often sleeping rolled up in a blanket in his car.

Within three years, restaurant operators were coming to him to procure a franchise. But

it was a twenty-nine-year old lawyer/promoter who put KFC on the map and incidentally made multimillions for himself. John Brown, Jr., was the kind of person who made $500 a weekend selling encyclopedias while attending the University of Kentucky. He and an associate changed the chicken shop into a standard red-and-white building and streamlined the operations. A $5,000 investment in KFC stock in 1964 was worth $3.5 million five years later.

The Colonel who had received $2 million in cash and KFC franchises in Canada was hired as a public relations imagebuilder under contract. His finger-lickin' good recipes were changed so that in the Colonel's words they became "slop." KFC was bought by Heublein, a liquor company, in 1971 for a reported $267 million. In 1974 Sanders filed a $222 million suit against Heublein for trying to interfere with his plans to develop a new franchise operation. An out of court settlement resulted. For his talk shows and TV commercials the Colonel receives about $100,000 a year.

Kentucky Fried Chicken is the number one chicken franchisor. By 1977 sales exceeded $2 billion. Two buildings were offered, the more popular being a 24- by 65-foot unit. The recommended location is a 126- by 125-foot lot, preferably on a corner or on a "going home" side of the road. Traffic that goes by the site should total at least 16,000 cars a day, according to their estimates.

Unlike many of the franchisors who insist that their units be in sizable population centers, KFC executives state that their operations can gross up to $250,000 in communities of 10,000 population.

As for the Colonel in 1978 he was eighty-eight and still going strong. As a representative for Heublein, the current owner of KFC, the Colonel, dressed all in white with the country Colonel black-string tie, white mustache and goatee, continued to make television and other appearances.

Always a tither the Colonel became a devout Christian after conversion at an evangelistic meeting when he was 79. In trying to live up to his new standards his hardest problem he says was to give up cussing, a practice at which he had a few peers. God, he says, was responsible for curing him of what looked on x-rays like malignant cancer of the colon. Always generous he became a philanthropist.

---

4. Colonel Harland D. Sanders, *Finger Lickin' Good* (Carol Stream, Ill.: Creation House, 1974).

One of his gifts was unusual, all of his stock in Colonel Sanders Kentucky Fried Chicken of Canada, Ltd., was given to a foundation established in Toronto. After expenses of operation all profit goes to charity. Each Canadian franchisee is allocated a portion of the profit for which he names the charities that shall receive his share. As for the Colonel his personal charities include churches, the Salvation Army, a city Mission, and a number of schools.

Of all the people who have received the Horatio Alger Award, few deserve it more than the Colonel. Few people have experienced more vicissitudes in a lifetime and overcome more circumstances. His pressure fried chicken seasoned with eleven secret herbs and spices is seen in almost every community in this country and in dozens of other countries around the world. Like Ellsworth Statler, Mr. Sanders was forced to drop out of school at an early age to help support his family. Like Statler he had the indominable will to succeed and luckily the stamina, perseverance, and ability to do so. He happens to be a good friend of Ray Kroc, the founder of McDonald's, and it is easy to see why.

"NAME" FRANCHISORS

In the late 1960s, a number of franchisors assembled a restaurant franchise package, gave it the name of a prominent sports or entertainment figure, made a public offering of stock, and sailed off into business with little or no practical restaurant experience represented in the organization. The general public, at that time eager for any stock with a franchise restaurant label, gobbled up the stock offering the day it was offered.

It has been relatively easy to offer stock to the general public through an underwriter, especially if the stock offering amounts to $300,000 or less. The Securities Exchange Commission permits such an offering, without a proven record of experience, if the offering does not exceed the $300,000 figure. Much larger stock offerings are possible, but the application for approval from the SEC is more detailed and requires a longer time for approval.

New stock issues had two fertile seasons in the 1960s. Large numbers were offered in 1960–1961, but the number fell following the 1962 stock market recession. The really big growth came in 1968 and extended through the summer of 1969. Over 200 restaurant companies went public or filed to do so in 1968.

Typically, a franchisor would offer 100,000 shares of stock to the general public at $3.00 per share. The stock offering would represent perhaps 15 or 20 percent of the total voting stock of the newly formed company. The nationally known sports or entertainment personality who was affiliated with the company might be given as much as 20 percent of the total stock for the use of his name. Of course, the personality involved knew little or nothing about the restaurant business and probably never did anything more than sample food in a few of the franchise operations.

Restaurant franchises during this period were being aggressively sold. The July 10, 1969 *Wall Street Journal* carried ads for Chefs International, Sea Host, Li'l Abner (owned by Longchamps), London Beef House, Hardee's, Mr. Pizza, Circus Wagon (burgers, hotdogs, roast beef, chicken, shakes, soda, cotton candy, peanuts, popcorn), and Zuider Zee Fish'n Puppies.

Capital required for these franchises, according to the ads, ranged from $16,000 to $35,000.

By August, 1969, the stock of most of the fast food franchisors had suffered sharp losses. Broadway Joe's, Inc. stock plunged from 17 to 1. According to *New York Magazine*, Broadway Joe's lost $243,978 on revenues of $667,952 in the 8 months ending July 31, 1970, something of a record. Namath, who obviously knows more about football than food, having performed at openings of new stores and posing for photographs, got out fast. Al Hirt's, which came out at 10½, was at 5. Mickey Mantle's dropped from 15 to 9. Minnie Pearl's Chicken system, which reached 70 at one time, had dropped to 7 and, by 1974, was no longer in operation.

CONTROLS HAVE BEEN INTRODUCED

Franchisors in the past have promised prospective franchisees the moon and it was a case of "caveat emptor," let the buyer beware.

Controls began to be introduced. In June of 1969, the Attorney General of the State of New

York ordered Dutch Inns of America Incorporated to stop selling franchises within the state without first complying with the state's Real Estate Syndicate Act, part of the securities laws.[5] Dutch Inns, based in Miami, was selling motel franchises and, according to the Attorney General's office, had "extended financial commitments, inadequate funds to meet these commitments, and, in fact was using the franchise fees for its own working capital." Since then other states have acted to restrict what franchisors can demand of the franchisee.

Franchising offers one of the safest and easiest routes for a hotel or restaurant chain to go international. Special problems found in any particular area can be better solved by the franchise owner on the scene who is wise socially and politically. In many instances the franchise holder is already a foodservice or lodging operator who knows the ropes locally and has an established organization.

FRANCHISING INTERNATIONAL

Intercontinental Hotels Corporation led the way in operating hotels abroad and was soon followed by Hilton International. The soft ice cream franchisors, Tastee Freez and International Dairy Queen, have the largest number of units abroad, 460 and 386 respectively (1969). In 1977 Holiday Inns had franchised some 200 inns around the world. A number of other restaurant and lodging franchisors are abroad in a small way, and a great many more are considering such a move. It is no longer surprising to see Kentucky Fried Chicken in Acapulco.

DANGERS OF OVER-FRANCHISING

Franchising makes it easy for a man and wife to get into the restaurant business, perhaps too easy. In some areas too many franchised food outlets have appeared, so many, in fact, that few can achieve a satisfactory sales volume. In Nashville, home of Kentucky Fried Chicken, when Minnie Pearl Chicken was also in operation, there were nineteen fried chicken stores.

Another reason for caution in rapid expansion of franchising is the rise in land values. A site that might have leased for $8,000 a year in 1963 cost $12,000 to $20,000 in 1969. Many of the franchisors lacked food experience and have failed. General Foods, parent company for Burger Chef for a time, "was shutting down Burger Chefs all over the country."[6]

FRANCHISING HERE TO STAY

Currently, among the franchisors who are successful, there is a trend toward increasing the number of company-owned units. The management of Denny's, for example, no longer franchise their stores, and are buying back units so as to better control menus, prices, and operations. Reason: if the chain is successful, more profits for the parent company.

While the franchised food outlets showed hamburgers the favorite specialty at 35 percent of total dollar values, followed by fried chicken and ice cream (20 percent each), many of the franchisors were elaborating the menu and decor to tantalize the public into eating more, and to eating out more often. Food companies like Pillsbury's (Burger King), General Foods (Burger Chef and Rix Roast Beef), and Green Giant have deeply involved themselves in the franchise business. Nor is the little man shut out. Another Colonel Sanders may be putting together a chicken package or another Ray Kroc assembling the successor to the hamburger franchise.

By 1979 it was clear that single units of a franchise operation located some distance from similar franchised units were at a disadvantage in promotion and advertising. Franchise restaurants were growing more like the retail grocery market business, highly standardized, and highly competitive. The single unit did not have enough A & P (Advertising and Promotion) money to compete with chain units advertising as a group. As a consequence, some franchise companies would not sell less than five units, clustering units so that mass newspaper advertising and television time could be purchased. Franchisees, unless family operations, needed three or more units to be competitive, competitive in profits and in promotion and advertising.

5. *The Wall Street Journal*, June 5, 1969.

6. *Barrons*, September, 15, 1969.

Another trend in franchising appeared that could be called "standardized flexibility," a concept that permits some flexibility in menu building and operations. The Lums restaurant corporation offered franchisees optional packages A, B, and C, or combinations of the three options. The franchisee could use the exterior of Plan A with the interior of the B plan or of the C plan. Standardized flexibility had to be controlled to maintain the overall image that the franchisor needed to maintain identity and quality.

Another trend became apparent when a major franchise company such as McDonalds introduced a new concept and the others were quick to follow suit or at least to take advantage of the change. When McDonald's began promoting breakfast sales, breakfast sales increased in other restaurants as well because the consumer was conditioned by the advertising and the experience of eating breakfast out.

Federal and state legislation has been enacted to supervise more closely the sale and franchise and the post-contract relationship between franchisor and franchisee. Several states regulate the conditions under which a franchisee may terminate or fail to renew a franchise, and a number of states can more closely regulate registration and disclosure of information pertinent to the purchase of franchises.

Typical Restaurant Franchise Companies

BONANZA INTERNATIONAL, INC., Dallas, TX
Volume of Sales: $165 million.
Appeals to 30 to 50 year olds. Steak house menu, also has fish and sandwiches; beer and wine in some stores.
Franchise Fee: $10,000: minimum cash required $25 to $100,000; $90,000 equipment package; 3% of sales for local advertising; 4.8% royalty.

BURGER CHEF SYSTEMS, INC., Tarrytown, N.Y.
Volume of Sales: $270 million.
Appeals to young families: 18 to 35 year olds. Limited menu features hamburgers.
Minimum Franchise Requirements: $25,000 franchise fee; $50,000 to $75,000 cash; $65,000 equipment package; $130,000 for building (plus site development); 4% royalty; 4% for advertising (includes national, regional, and local).

BURGER KING CORPORATION, Miami, FLA
Dollar Volume: $614 million.
Appeals to 18 to 49 year olds. Fast food menu: hamburgers, fish sandwich, fries, shakes.
Minimum Franchise Requirements: $150,000 net worth (including $75,000 liquid assets).
Franchise Fee: $30,500.

CHURCHES FRIED CHICKEN, San Antonio, TX
Volume of Sales: $155 million.
Appeals to 20 to 38 year olds. Limited menu: chicken, french fries, cole slaw.
Minimum Franchise Requirements: $175,000 total per store.
Franchise Fee: $7,500; royalty: 4% of sales; 2% advertising program.

DUNKIN' DONUTS OF AMERICA, Randolph, MA
Volume of Sales: $200 million.
Appeals to 18 to 55 year olds. Limited menu features donuts and coffee.
Minimum Franchise Requirements: $20,000 to $30,000 cash; good health and financial history.
Franchise Fee: $27,000 in east, $22,000 southeast and west. One-third discount if franchisee develops own realty.

INTERNATIONAL DAIRY QUEEN, INC., Minneapolis, MINN
Dollar Volume 1974: $590 million.
Appeals to young families; fast food menu combines sandwiches and soft ice creams.
Minimum Franchise Requirements: $35,000 cash.
Franchise Fee: $15,000.

KFC CORPORATION, Louisville, KY
Estimated Sales 1975: $1.5 billion.
Appeals to all age groups. Menu limited to: fried chicken and related products. Also ribs.
Minimum Franchise Requirements: initial equity. This includes franchise fee, working capital of $25,000, and 20% down payment on equipment. Franchisee must personally participate in the business.
Franchise Fee: $4,000.

LONG JOHN SILVER'S, Lexington, KY
Dollar Volume 1976: $195 million.
Appeals to all ages. Seafood menus; also chicken, hush puppies, corn on the cob, pecan tarts. Beer where available. Prospective franchisee needs financial ability for development of 5 or more stores.
Franchise Fee: $10,000 plus royalty of 5% of sales.

(continued)

MCDONALD'S SYSTEMS, INC., Oakbrook, ILL
Appeals to young families. Expanded menu includes some breakfast items, hamburgers, fries, shakes.
Minimum Franchise Requirements: Vary from $85,000 to $100,000; includes $20,000 equipment package.
Franchise Fee: $10,000.

THE PIZZA INN, INC., Dallas, TX
Volume of Sales: $85 million.
Appeals to 14 to 35 year olds. Menu is limited: pizza, spaghetti, Italian sandwiches. Beer and wine ok.
Minimum Franchise Requirements: initial unit: $40,000 cash plus ability to finance (mortgage or lease) approximately $200,000 for land, building, equipment package.
Franchise Fee: $10,000 for first unit; $5,000 for additional unit.

PONDEROSA SYSTEM, INC., Dayton, OH
Volume of Sales: $236 million.
Menu is "full meal" oriented and includes meat, potatoes, salad, and desserts.
Franchise Fee: $20,000, capital needed for franchise investment is $75,000 to $80,000.

SIZZLER FAMILY STEAKHOUSES, INC.,
Los Angeles, CA
Volume of Sales: $110 million.
Appeals to 18 to 39 year olds. Limited menu: steak, seafood, and fish sandwiches; beer and wine in some stores.
Franchise Requirements: minimum $80,000 cash.
Franchise Fee: $20,000. National advertising program requires 5% of sales; local advertising 3%. No equipment package.

Source: Food and Lodging Hospitality, Dec., 1975.

Questions

1 Someone states that fastfood restaurants have never grossed as much as a million dollars in sales in one particular unit. What is your reply?

2 As a franchisee of McDonald's you would be paying what percentage of your gross revenue for rent?

3 Who originated the McDonald's concept of restaurant operation?

4 One of the keys to the success of the fastfood franchise is to have a standardized format. Looking at the development of McDonald's design, would you say that design should be fixed and never changed?

5 As an owner of McDonald's Company stock would you expect much in the way of a yield on your investment?

6 Someone says "With a franchise you completely avoid a chance of failure in a fastfood restaurant." What is your response?

7 Name at least three of the top ten fastfood franchisors in this country.

8 Give at least three advantages for an individual in buying a franchise over operating from a private format.

9 Give at least three disadvantages of franchised operation as compared with independent operation.

10 Restaurants generally spend less than 2 percent of their sales for advertising; fastfood restaurants, however, spend about what percent of sales for advertising and promotion?

11 One of the more colorful characters in the fastfood business is Colonel Harland Sanders who put together what franchising chain?

12 Two individuals who have been highly successful in the fastfood franchising did not get into the business until they were over fifty. Can you name them?

13 Some of the franchisors sell only groups of franchises—a state or a large area. What does this have to do with advertising and promotion?

THE PRIVATE CLUB

ELEVEN

The urge to join a club probably goes back to the days of primitive man or his predecessors, the hunting apes. When the upright apes left the forest they found it necessary to band together to survive. Mutual protection, common interests, social and economic advantages were and are still reasons for people gathering together to form clubs. We feel safer, more secure, and comfortable being with people of similar background, social status, and interests. Membership in some clubs brings prestige and perhaps a sense of accomplishment.

Practical reasons for the existence of clubs are several. A family of middle income can belong to a luxurious country club with part ownership in an olympic-sized pool, an eighteen-hole golf course, tennis courts, a fine restaurant, and bar. A chemist can join a club whose members are also chemists. The sports-minded can join an athletic club, a tennis club, even a curling club. The man with the yacht, and no place to park it, can dock at a yacht club slip paying by the foot for the privilege. There are fraternal clubs, religious clubs, and service clubs.

Country clubs are given several concessions, concessions without which they probably could not exist. In many states the nonprofit club is granted a liquor license at no cost. Clubs without liquor licenses are few and far between. The real property of the golf club is taxed at a much lower rate than similar, privately owned land. In California the rate is about one quarter that of comparable private land. A third concession is seen in that clubs are charged a much lower water rate than, for

example, industry. Usually the rate is regressive, the more used, the less cost per unit. And golf clubs in most parts of the United States require heavy sprinkling.

If the club is large enough or has enough facilities, employees and a manager are needed. Food and drink are the common denominators of most clubs, and this makes them a part of the hospitality business.

Starting a golf course club house for a country club is not cheap. About 160 acres of land are required for the course. The National Golf Foundation notes that there were 4,770 private club courses and 1,586 municipal courses in 1976. Graduates of hotel and restaurant schools don't rush into the club field immediately following graduation even though starting salaries tend to be higher than for trainee positions in motels and restaurant chains. Later in their careers, however, many do shift over to the club field, finding it less stressful and in many instances more lucrative.

CLUB MANAGERS' ASSOCIATION OF AMERICA

The term "club" is broadly defined and could refer to a stamp club, a bowling club, a bridge club, or the Cosa Nostra. What is usually referred to by the club business are those clubs known as private city, country, and military clubs. The Club Managers' Association of America, CMAA, the professional organization of club managers, has about 3,000 members who manage most of the important city and country clubs in the United States and Canada A number of CMAA members manage military clubs. The CMAA defines the private club as a made-up group of people who select their fellow members, pay annual dues, and usually have permanent facilities for serving food and beverages to their members.

In 1977 The Club Managers' Association of America estimated that nineteen million Americans belonged to 12,000 private clubs in the United States paying initiation fees ranging from $50 to $25,000 and annual and family dues of $10 to $200 per month. The club industry, said the Association, employed almost 600,000 persons with an annual payroll of $2.5 billion. Beverage sales alone exceeded $1 billion dollars in that year.[1]

Since the late nineteenth century, city and country clubs have been a sizable part of the hospitality business in the United States. Clubs probably employ more top chefs than do hotels and restaurants. Few restaurants serve food in the style and of the quality found in the better clubs. A majority both of the managers and the food and beverage managers in clubs have been a part of the hotel and restaurant field, as students, employees, or managers.

Let us trace the development of clubs through the years and then examine club management as a specialized area of management within the hospitality business.

Our clubs are mostly developments of English city and sporting clubs. The Royal and Ancient Golf Club of St. Andrews, Scotland, founded in 1758, is known as the home of golf and is the ancestor of our country clubs. The precursor of the city club dates back to the early fifteenth century when a club called "La Court de Bonne Campagne," or Club of Good Companions, was formed. Sir Walter Raleigh is credited with founding the Mermaid Club, which made its headquarters at the Mermaid Tavern in London and included such notables as Shakespeare and Kit Marlowe among its membership. Ben Jonson founded a club that held forth at The Devil, another of the Fleet Street taverns in London in the early seventeenth century. These early clubs were vehicles for people of like interest to associate together, sharing food, drink, and expenses. This is how the word club probably came to have its present meaning, "to share," or divide, expenses.

One of the quips about the British comes in the answer to the question, "What is the first thing two Britishers do in a foreign country?" The answer: "They form a club."

EARLY ENGLISH CLUBS

The early English club, especially those that flourished in the late seventeenth and early eighteenth centuries, usually met in one of the taverns or coffee houses of the day. White's Club, one of the most exclusive of today's London clubs, was originally a coffee house. The owner, Francesco Bianco, an Italian immigrant who anglicized his name to White, raised the admission fee from an English penny to a sixpence, which assured him an exclusive clientele.

Gambling was also a part of the appeal and many of the English clubs retain that appeal. Play ran high. Lord Carlisle lost $10,000 at a cast of hazard. The members could bet on anything. Horace Walpole records that when a man fell down, apparently dead, at the door of the club, he was carried inside, and the members at once made bets on whether he was dead or not; "and when they were going to bleed him, the wagerers for his death interfered and said it would affect the fairness of the bet." Quarrels at gaming tables frequently resulted in duels. In 1751 the gambling salons employed a captain, "who is to fight any gentleman who is peevish at losing his money."[2] In 1736, the customers took over from White and established the practice of admitting no one except those who had been voted on by an admissions committee. Membership became a "social credential of definite significance and practical value," and many clubs still offer prestige as a primary appeal. The practice of black-balling, the right of any member to drop a black ball into a box thus excluding an applicant from membership, has long been a source of snobbery in clubs, making them especially attractive to the social climber.

Some of the early clubs accepted only members of a particular political stamp. The

1. *Club Management*, Club Managers Association of America, Washington, D.C., 1977.

2. James Laver, *Age of Illusion* (New York, NY: McKay, 1972).

Reform Club is perhaps the best known of the English political clubs. Our own political clubs have had less stability.

One reason for the fame of the Reform Club was its chef, Alexis Soyer, who was with the club during the 1830s and 1840s. Soyer, a flamboyant genius, ranks with Careme and Escoffier in things culinary. As an innovator, he devised a 40- by 110-foot kitchen which included a cold meat larder, a sauce larder, a pastry room, a butler's pantry, and a game larder. He equipped the kitchen with pickling tubs, slate wells for soaking ham, marbel slabs, tin-lined drawers, steam drawers, steam boilers, gas stoves, and bain-maries.

The word club, especially as used in England, connotes exclusiveness and snobbishness as revealed in the comment of a French nobleman about a century ago. He said, "The club will ever remain a resort—tranquil, elegant, and exclusive—forbidden to the humble and insignificant." Snob appeal is a great attraction—perhaps the strongest—for members in many clubs. By the end of the nineteenth century, there were about 100 clubs in Britain with a membership of only 80,000—but this exclusiveness was not to last.

The YMCA was formed in Britain as a place for people to enjoy recreation without the necessity of drink. The Rev. Henry Solly, a Unitarian, founded the first "workingman's" club in 1862. Today, there are more than 3,700 workingmen's clubs in Britain "providing food, drink, entertainment, gaming, and, incidentally, camaraderie—women included."

MILITARY CLUBS

Military clubs had their antecedents in the Spartan messes of 200 B.C., and earlier, and in the "sodalitas" of Roman soldiers. The Battle of Waterloo was the immediate predecessor of the present military club and was responsible for some of the character of city clubs today. The London club, as an institution with a large and elaborate clubhouse of its own, did not really arrive until about 1815. The Guards Club and the Royal Navy Club already existed, but officers in Wellington's Army, accustomed to eating "in the mess," founded the United Service Club in 1815. "With the exception of a sleeping room, he may live at his club with a

degree of state and profuse luxury that nothing but a princely fortune could otherwise command, not to mention the enjoyment without the expense of constant society."[3]

After Napoleon was defeated, many unemployed British officers lived on slender pensions and "clubbed" together for purposes of association and economy in housing and eating. Professional people and members of the clergy soon followed suit and established their own clubs.

In 1975 London had some forty-two gentlemen's clubs. Many are still snobbish, still stuffy, many nearly empty except for a few senior citizens. Many are fading because of the squeeze between declining membership and the necessary money to maintain the old spit and polish. Typical is the United Service Club. Built by John Nash in 1823, its huge building is mostly quiet. Opened originally only to senior army officers, it has necessarily "lowered its standards."

About twenty-five years ago, a high ranking army officer strolled through the palatial rooms on Pall Mall and paused beneath the portrait of a marshal of the Royal Air Force, resplendent in a bemedaled dress uniform. "When you start letting chaps like that in," grumbled the general to the club secretary, "it's the beginning of the end." Dues are still minimal, $118 a year in 1974.

White's, one of the most famous gentlemen's clubs, still has a seven-year waiting list, mainly of sons of present members. Their dues are $188 a year.

A good reason for maintaining membership is the fact that members at most clubs can get meals at about 50 percent or less than they would in a quality restaurant, and wine by the bottle is especially inexpensive.[4]

Military clubs today are operated much like private city clubs, divided into those for officers and those for enlisted personnel. According to the *Wall Street Journal*, the volume of sales in the United States military clubs in 1969 exceeded $1 billion a year.

In the past most of these 5,000 or more clubs were managed by officers (officers' clubs) or by noncommissioned officers (enlisted

3. Laver, *Age of Illusion.*
4. *Los Angeles Times,* December 15, 1974.

men's clubs). Today, the larger ones—both "O" clubs and "EM" clubs—are likely to be managed by civilians who report to a military man designated as club officer. Military club managers who are in the service are eligible for membership in CMAA after four years of experience as manager.

EARLY CLUBS IN THE UNITED STATES

The earliest clubs in the United States date from before 1800. The Hoboken Turtle Club was founded in 1792. Boston had a Sans Souci (without a care) club in 1785. The Somerset Club was formed in 1817 (but under a different name). The Chilton (ladies only) came along about a decade later.

The Bread and Cheese Club, noted by James Fenimore Cooper, was said to be the first private membership club with rooms of its own in New York City. Founded in 1836, it met in The City Hotel. New York City had a Union Club in 1836. The need to support the Civil War led to the founding of Union League Clubs in New York, Philadelphia, and San Francisco (later the Pacific-Union Club). Some of the finest food in the country is today served at the Union League Club of Philadelphia.

The first country clubs in the United States appeared outside Philadelphia, the Foxborough (1887) and the St. Andrews Country Club of Westchester (1888).

FRATERNAL CLUBS

In this country almost anyone can be a club member. If a veteran, he has only to join the local post of the American Legion or the Veterans of Foreign Wars. He can be an Elk, an Eagle, or an Odd Fellow, a Knight of Columbus, or a Son of Italy. He can be one of the more than a million Moose in this country. He can join the local branch of the American Polish Club, the YWCA, or the YMCA.

A bit further up the social ladder, he may be a Mason, wear his fez and regalia, and proudly display his Shriner ring or lapel pin. It is often a distinction of sorts to belong to the local Women's Club, and one must have the right ancestors to be a Daughter of the American Revolution or a member of the Cincinnatus Club.

SERVICE CLUBS

Service clubs are slightly different in appeal and activity. Rotarians, Kiwanis, Optimists, or one of several other such clubs are made up of business and professional men who support one or more charities. They usually own no property but meet for lunch once a week at a local hotel or restaurant.

COUNTRY CLUBS

According to some commentators, the prime motive in joining a club is status-seeking. No doubt this is true for some prestige clubs. Status-seeking, however, accounts for only part of the fact that clubs are growing at the rate of more than 200 a year.

Most of these new clubs are a part of land developments. The developer well knows that the presence of a fine country club increases the value of the land nearby, and in many developments club membership comes with the purchase of the building lot or a condominium. Several of the old clubs, such as the Dallas Country Club and the Chevy Chase Country Club in Washington, D.C., are now surrounded by city. Their land is extremely valuable.

In suburbia, the country club offers a relatively inexpensive way of gaining access to a fine golf course, a swimming pool, and a higher type of cuisine than can otherwise be had in the community. In the 1970s tennis courts, indoors and out, became a major draw for club membership. In the mid-1970s racquetball clubs became popular, one reason being the relatively small amount of land required. Most country club members are athletically and socially minded, but in the prestige city clubs the average age of the membership exceeds forty-five years, and the athletic facilities are more symbolic than used.

UNIVERSITY CLUBS

The larger cities have University clubs which anyone who has been to college may join. Yale, Harvard, Cornell, and a few other universities have their own clubs in a few cities. The Oxford Club in London may not be representative of the prosperity of such clubs; its furniture is becoming unglued, and the place has the musty smell of an enterprise that is not doing well. The University Club of Philadelphia has passed away. It may be that attendance at a university no longer stamps one as a member of the elite.

COMPANY CLUBS

Some of the most thriving clubs are subsidized by companies for their own employees; IBM has its own club. In England, the most vigorous of the new clubs may not have a former guards sergeant as a doorman or claim a few dukes as members, but they are more in tune with the times. Probably the most dynamic of the London clubs is the Managing Directors Club —any managing director (president) of a business, no matter how large or small, can be a member.

PROFESSIONAL CLUBS

Engineers, parachutists, chemists, and a variety of other groups with the same professional interests have formed clubs in major cities, some of the club facilities being impressive and well done. The Washington Press Club and the Petroleum Club of Houston are examples of such clubs.

KEY CLUBS

A new type of drink-and-sex club has appeared; typical are the Playboy and Gaslight clubs. These are operated for profit. Whereas the snobbish English club excluded women, the key club counts them and supplies nubile maidens as waitresses with something more than Maidenform bras to whet the appetite.

They are not bona fide clubs in the usually accepted sense. The Playboy clubs are part of the Hugh Hefner enterprises, which are tied together with a bright red ribbon of sophisticated sex and a fast-stepping style of life. Of the nineteen Playboy clubs in 1969, fifteen were owned by Playboy International; the other were franchised.

The average age of the Playboy Club keyholder is forty-two. He is a businessman in management or in one of the professions. Eighty-five percent are college graduates. The some 500,000 playboys apparently like to be close to beautiful, undraped females, ounce-

and-a-half drinks, and sprightly shows. Some playboys are more equal than others, for there are VIP rooms where the meal cost is higher per person, drinks extra. Little difficulty is experienced in securing the bunny waitresses, for their average income is said to be well above $15,000 a year.

CLUB STATISTICS

A 1977 study of clubs by Harris, Kerr, and Forster showed that the usual country club took in about $830 in dues and guest fees from each member and another $780 in food and beverage sales for a total of about $1,900 per member. The cost of food consumed in a club runs much higher than in the usual commercial restaurant for the simple reason that the member expects lower menu prices, a loss that is made up in the form of dues. The cost of food runs about 54 percent of sales, allowing about 6.5 percent for employees meals. Beverage cost was also higher than found in a commercial restaurant, close to 30 percent of sales. Payroll ran about 41 percent of sales, much higher than in the usual hotel and restaurant.

In the city clubs surveyed, each member paid about $350 dues and guest fees and spent another $450 in food and beverage in the club. Food costs ran about the same as for country clubs. Membership declined somewhat in clubs in the northeast and increased in the sun belt in the south and west.[5]

THE CLUB MANAGER AND HIS JOB

What about the job of club manager? It is somewhat different from that of a hotel or restaurant manager. The primary purpose of the club manager is to satisfy the club member; the hotel and restaurant is operated primarily for profit. The club manager usually reports to a house committee or the club president; a hotel or restaurant manager usually reports to a corporation executive or an owner.

The job of club manager is more demanding in the area of human relations. The hotel or restaurant manager tries to satisfy the patron

5. "Clubs in Town and Country," 1976, Harris, Kerr, Forster and Co., 420 Lexington Avenue, New York, NY, 1977.

or the guest; the club manager's reason for existence is to please the member, and, in the smaller clubs, he has much more face-to-face contact with the member than the hotel or restaurant manager usually has with his guest.

As the club grows in size, the manager tends to be more of an executive; where there are thousands of members, he may not see many of them from one year to the next.

In the hotel and restaurant business, ownership or top executives change from time to time. In the club, the change is more frequent; at least some of the officers and committee members change annually. A major responsibility for the club manager is to orient himself to the new officers and at the same time orient them to their new responsibilities.

Because club members often think of themselves as part of the social elite (this may be even more true of the women), and because they may pay an initiation fee of as high as $25,000 plus annual dues, they may expect the same deference from the manager as from a servant. This the wise manager rejects.

He tries instead to maintain a social relationship which is somewhere between that of a business manager reporting to a board of directors, a friend of the family, and a professional hotel or restaurant manager dealing with his patrons. To make life more interesting for the manager, many members expect to pay less for the food and beverages they buy at the club, expect a higher quality than they would find in a first-class restaurant or hotel, and expect service at odd hours.

The club manager is a technical expert, or should be. He is better informed and experienced in the operation of the club than any of the members, no matter how rich or expert they may be in other fields. If he is tactful and has ability, he can shape the nature of the club, help in great part to set a proper tone, and act as a leader for the governing board, the members, and the employees.

Club managers' hours are dictated by the peak periods of activity at the club—weekends in the country club, luncheon periods in the city clubs being the busiest. Many club managers work long hours at a stretch, particularly in the busy season, and then go for weeks or even months with little to do.

Starting and average salaries for club managers are considerably higher than for comparable positions in restaurants and hotels. Salaries go as high as $50,000 a year, plus food and, often, bonuses and other fringe benefits. In 1975 the average member of the Club Managers' Association received about $30,000 a year (including fringe benefits such as meals, car allowances, travel, etc.). According to a study conducted by the Club Managers' Association (from which many of the statistics in this section are drawn), the average manager received a salary of 3.2 percent of his club's annual revenue from all sources.

The club manager must dress well and appropriately and drive a respectable car. It helps if his wife is socially attractive. He is usually a highly intelligent individual with more than his share of social poise and ability. He should be "au courant" on manners and social niceties. Good health, being well informed, and possessing an interest in people are assets. He cannot be a ladies' man, for obvious reasons. He must be discreet and above suspicion if he is to survive among the various factions that abound in the club atmosphere.

A few club managers retire from the same club where they started. Typically, however, the manager moves every three to five years, having grown tired of the same old faces, or perhaps his personality having palled on the club members. The job can call for a great amount of imagination or for hidebound routine, depending upon the age and attitudes of the club members.

Food Skills Paramount

Among the many skills required on the job, those connected with planning and producing interesting and varied food and parties are paramount. He himself need not be a skilled cook, but he should be aware of what is fashionable and impressive in this way of hors d'oeuvre, buffets, and foodservice generally. Some club experts recommend that food and beverage experience be acquired before entering the club field.

He should belong to the professional Club Managers' Association of America, the CMAA. The average club manager is likely to be married with two or three children. He probably carries life insurance, owns two or more cars, owns or is buying a house, and invests in stocks and bonds. About a third of the managers speak a language in addition to English, and, among city club managers, 23 percent were European-born. Through the CMAA, the average member constantly upgrades himself. A five-year certificate program is offered by CMAA that enables the member to attend seminars and other activities each year.

The club manager must "fit" his membership. A club manager who is highly successful in a middle class club, where aggressiveness might stand him in good stead, could find this trait completely out of place in an old, quiet, prestigious club. His appearance, too, must fit and his manners must be what the members feel to be acceptable. A new, growing club needs one kind of manager; an old, established club prefers another, more subtle type. The dynamic manager of a new club may find that he is developing himself right out of a job after the club has reached a certain level of style and size.

The manager may be confronted with divided loyalties on the part of some of his employees. Older employees are likely to have developed personal relationships with influential club members and to relate themselves directly to the particular members than to the manager. One fine Southwestern club had a porter who reputedly was worth $2 million and received about $300 a day in tips. It can be seen that such an employee might not be too responsive to the wishes of the manager. Once in a while the manager finds that he is in the position of throwing down the gauntlet over whether *he* goes or one of the employees who refuses to cooperate is discharged.

The manager is well advised to find a powerful sponsor or sponsors within the club membership who will stand by him when the inevitable storms appear and the boat begins to rock. Of course, he cannot openly favor one member over another. If he is knowledgeable, honest, and reasonably diplomatic, he can survive for at least a few years. The job is no place for an alcoholic, a woman chaser, or a gambler—even though he may be charming, socially acceptable, and carry the cachet of a prestige school on his college diploma. The odds will be against him.

A source of friction between private clubs and hotels and restaurants has been the practice of many nonprofit clubs of soliciting parties. Restaurant and hotel owners feel this is unfair competition because the nonprofit clubs pay no income tax.

The problem has apparently been settled by the Internal Revenue Service, which has ruled that private clubs may do no more than 5 percent of their total food and beverage business with patrons other than club members.

Alcohol Creates Problems

Another major problem in clubs centers around alcohol. Most clubs cannot survive without it, and many owe their existence to the fact that the club has a special political concession for serving liquor in a "dry" community. When for some reason liquor is not permitted in the club, the club is likely to die, as was recently the case of a British club in the Moslem community of Kuwait where liquor privileges suddenly ended. Overnight the club was deserted.

Many clubs in dry communities, as in parts of the deep South, rely heavily on the fact that they can serve liquor in a social setting. The same is true of many of the American Legion and Veterans of Foreign Wars clubs around the country.

It is no easy problem to handle the member who has had that extra martini and is criticizing the food, a waitress, or the manager. Evidence that the job of club manager is no bed of roses is the fact that each year, according to the CMAA, one of every six managers changes jobs, and 25 percent of these leave the field permanently. Yet few club managers want long-term job contracts; apparently they want to be free to change jobs at short notice. One manager put it pointedly, "I live very closely with my members—too close. I want no strings attached. I want to be able to move quickly whenever I get sick of them, or they of me."

It was not long ago that the club manager was considered a high-class servant or, as he was called, a steward. As recently as 1914, the manager of the Harvard Club in Boston had to insist that his title remain club manager and not steward. It was not until 1927 that the Club Managers, Association of America was formed. In 1946 there were only 623 members. By 1956 the number had increased only to 916. Today, CMAA has several thousand members managing clubs in the United States, Canada,

and abroad. The official journal of CMAA is
Club Management.

Challenge of Management

Club management is a particularly challenging
field, one that calls for social skills, poise,
leadership, and good taste. In addition to being
a manager and all that term implies, the club
manager must also be respected by members
and be a person with whom they enjoy dealing.
Clubs, both nonprofit and operated-for-a-profit,
are growing in number and sophistication.
They are part of our English heritage, offering
millions of Americans amenities and associations that would be difficult to enjoy without
the club.

The exclusive clubs are centers of wealth
and influence, according to Ferdinand Lundberg in the book *The Rich and the SuperRich.*[6]
Private clubs, he avers, are societal control
centers of the elite. Each major city has at least
one club for the wealthy, either an imitation or
extension of earlier clubs in Boston, New York,
Philadelphia, and Baltimore. Those, in turn,
were imitations of English clubs. The most
important, he says, are in New York City,
where the greatest fortunes are centered. The
leading New York clubs include among their
members the wealthiest of the out-of-towners
and many foreigners.

The Chicago Club, the Cleveland Club, The
Jonathan Club of Los Angeles, the Houston
Petroleum Club, and the Duquesne Club of
Pittsburgh are such centers of wealth and
influence. At the top of the social rating, says
Lundberg, is the Links in New York, followed
closely by the Knickerbocker, the Metropolitan,
the Racquet and Tennis Club, the Brook, the
Union, and the Union League.

Some of the other prestige clubs include
the Philadelphia Club and Union League club in
Philadelphia, the Somerset Club in Boston
(naturally, the oldest), the Algonquin in Boston,
the Houston Club and Petroleum Club in Houston, the Lake Shore, Standard, and Chicago
Clubs of Chicago, The California Club of Los
Angeles, and the Bohemian Club of San
Francisco. Yacht clubs tend to be exclusive
since not everyone owns a yacht.

Figure 11–1   *The Jonathan Club of Los Angeles,
one of the prestige city clubs on the West Coast.*

Figure 11–2

---

6. Ferdinand Lundberg and Lyle Stuart, *The Rich and the
Super-Rich* (New York, NY: Bantam, 1969).

Figure 11-3

Cleveland Amory, another commentator on the American social scene, writing in the book, *Who Killed Society?* rates clubs by quoting a club man who says, "At the Metropolitan or the Union League or the University, you might do a ten thousand deal but you'd use a Knickerbocker or the Union or the Racquet for a hundred thousand dollars, and then for one million dollars you would move on to the Brook or the Links." The Chevy Chase Club in Washington, D.C. is another well-known club.

CLUBS INFLUENCE POLITICS

There is little doubt that many of the clubs are aristocratic and privileged. No doubt many great financial deals are concocted "at the club." The author believes that the more important clubs also greatly influence politics. Once a party line has been reached, the clubs present a solid front. Views are invariably expressed in the light of property interest. They are the most intense partisans of freedom—their freedom—in the world today. To control or influence public policy, one is better placed if he has a strong voice in an important club than if he has a strong voice in the Senate of the United States. Amory writes that the leading freedom of the top clubs is the freedom to be anti-democratic and pro-aristocratic. In the earlier days, he says, they would have been Federalist. Clubs were no partisans of the New Deal. They feared and hated Franklin D. Roosevelt. Their heroes were Harding, Coolidge, and Hoover. They showed little enthusiasm for Eisenhower, much less for Kennedy, but were inclined to favor Lyndon B. Johnson who was a big depletion allowance man after their own hearts.

Many clubs are pretty boring places; nevertheless, membership in some of them is the ultimate mark of status for most businessmen of the area. The exclusive clubs want to remain that way. An applicant for the Racquet and Tennis club in New York, for example,

Figure 11-2, 11-3, and 11-4   Lake Arrowhead Country Club offers this area as a focal point for guest activity. Overlooking a magnificent wood area, the lobby soars to forty feet and is flooded with light from the continuous skylight at the apex of the A-frame. The Country Club, with an eighteen-hole golf course, was the first of the supporting facilities constructed at Bella Vista Village, north of Fayetteville, Arkansas. Membership is made up primarily of home owners in the Village. The majority are senior citizens, and furnishings for the lounge are selected with their requirements in mind. The clubhouse is built on the side of a hill and arranged so that the large public spaces face the golf course and the view across the valley.

must be proposed in writing by a member, procure a seconding letter and six supporting letters, then meet individually with at least eight members of the Board of Managers. Club waiting lists can run as long as ten years, and some clubs even have waiting lists for their waiting lists.[7]

Members of the Jewish faith are excluded from many of the prestige clubs. A 450-page report in 1969, published by the American Jewish Committee, concluded that Jewish executives are deprived of opportunities because of exclusion from important clubs.[8] Of some 1,800 downtown men's clubs, roughly 80 percent have no Jewish members, according to a survey made by the same committee.[9] In most cities the Jewish community has countered such exclusion by building clubs of its own, often the most lavish in the area.

The importance of the private country and city club in social and political power has not been explored in any depth. That the club is a focal center of such power is highly likely. If some clubs are suspicious of ethnic or religious groups dissimilar to themselves, many have also been suspicious of women, forbidding them entrance to parts of the club or allowing them in only at certain times of the day, or even the year. This is no longer legal.

The Yale Club of New York City, which for seventy-two years had prided itself on its all-male tradition, in 1969 met to decide if female graduates of the University would be admitted. The decision was whether or not they would be admitted on the same basis as wives of members and lady guests of members. They would not be allowed in many of the twenty-two story building's rooms, nor allowed to use any athletic facilities, or eat in three of the club's dining rooms. They would, however, be allowed to eat in the roof dining room, to stay in boarding rooms, and to walk in the especially designated "women's lobby" on the ground floor. Such restrictions can no longer be enforced.

At first the Harvard Club allowed Radcliffe College graduates to sign for food and beverages but denied them most other privileges. However, most Harvard Clubs are now fully open to Radcliffe College alumnae. Cornell

University's club allowed women graduates to be associate members, which meant they could not vote. The women countered by establishing exclusive clubs of their own in some cities.

Pressure for pushing open the doors to clubs always existed and is increasing. In Maine a club dispensing food and liquor legally cannot exclude anyone on the basis of race or religion. The Union League Club of Chicago admitted its first black member in 1969, and the eighty-seven-year-old Detroit Club accepted a Jewish businessman.

PROFIT-MAKING CLUBS

As noted previously, the word "club" originally meant to divide expenses; most were not in any way concerned with operating for a profit. It is true, however, that some of the early clubs operated in conjunction with a coffee house, and the owner, of course, did operate for a profit.

Some of the gambling clubs of Britain and elsewhere are profit-making organizations, to be sure, and about 10 percent of the town and country clubs in the United States are operated for profit. The Hathaway family of Los Angeles are prominent among clubs-for-profit operators, owning and operating the Los Angeles Athletic Club with some 6,000 members, a country club, and a yacht club. The La Jolla Beach and Tennis Club is another well-known club, presently owned by the Kellog family. The other 90 percent are nonprofit in nature and are so treated by the Internal Revenue Service. Any surplus that they might build is not distributed to members but is plowed back into the club, usually in the form of improvements and additions.

The IRS states that a club qualifies for federal income tax exemption as a club organized exclusively for pleasure, recreation, and other nonprofitable purposes. No part of the net earnings may go to private shareholders. May a club get most of its revenue from the gambling of its members and their guests? Yes, says the IRS, since gambling supplies those elements of diversion that are commonly accepted as pleasure and recreation. Oddly enough, illegality of gaming devices under local law has no effect on the club's exempt status.[10]

7. "The Blooming Clubs of Business," *Dun's Review*, July, 1969.

8. Ibid.

9. *The Wall Street Journal*, September 10, 1969.

10. *Washington Report*, National Restaurant Association, March 24, 1969.

Privately owned clubs must offer food, beverage and facilities at prices to compete with nonprofit clubs and restaurants in the area. Sometimes the profit comes mainly from land appreciation. For example, Riviera Country Club in Pacific Palisades, California, sits on 150 acres of prime residential land, which in 1977 was worth about $10 million and continues to appreciate.

Slot machines in a club can make the financial life of the club easy. For many years, the officers' clubs in the military took in huge sums of money from slot machines. This enabled many military clubs to build luxurious quarters and provide food and beverages at prices only a little above cost.

A PART OF MIDDLE CLASS AND UPPER CLASS AMERICANA

The club, which started in this country on the East Coast, patterned after the English golf and city club, has spread across the country and is a part of suburban and town life. Some of the older downtown clubs will fade, to be replaced by new ones.

Retirement communities, "new" towns, resort communities, and the ever-expanding suburbs will continue to create clubs as a part of the American way of life. Many clubs will be forced to lower their membership bars; others will no doubt arrange to raise theirs even higher. Social segregation will probably continue because most of us feel more comfortable associating with people whose values, beliefs—and prejudices—support our own. Regardless of social segregation there will continue to be economic segregation. The job of the club manager will continue to be one of challenge, calling for tact, diplomacy, and a considerable amount of specialized expertise.

Questions

1 Approximately how many private clubs are there in this country?

2 Would you say that a large percentage of graduates of hotel and restaurant management degree programs move directly into club management?

3 Our clubs have as their origin clubs located in what country?

4 Clubs often restrict membership by blackballing, or by other means. What is the origin of the term "blackballing?"

5 The military clubs of today date from what period in what country?

6 Can you name four different kinds of clubs?

7 The cost of food as a percentage of sales runs much higher in private clubs than is true in commercial restaurants. Explain why.

8 Name three advantages of being a club manager as compared with being a hotel manager; and name three disadvantages.

9 Would you say that the job of club manager has high job security; in other words do club managers tend to stay at the same club for long periods of time?

10 It is often said that a manager can manage anything. Is this true for different kinds of clubs?

11 Why in some cases are restaurant managers and owners antagonistic to private clubs?

12 Do some private clubs wield political influence? Explain.

13 In your opinion will clubs ever be completely democratic in their membership selection?

14 Is it possible to set up a club as a private enterprise and run it as any other business, paying income taxes and operating for a profit? Explain.

15 The fact that clubs are often part of land development schemes will have what impact on the club business in the future?

PEOPLE WHO SHAPED THE INDUSTRY

TWELVE

If, as Emerson said, "The institution is the shadow of the man," we in the hotel and restaurant business owe much to a few men, men who changed, innovated, and created the nature of the hospitality business.

Throughout this book, many men have been named who have introduced a system, invented a device, or acquired recognition from their confreres. Hundreds of imaginative men and women have dreamed and acted to change hotel and restaurant keeping. Unfortunately, they join the rest of humanity who also lived and were forgotten.

There are a few names, however, that stand out, and it is instructive to look at them more closely, to itemize their major contributions, and examine, as much as is possible from a distance, something of their personalities, motivations, and values.

PERIOD OF GREAT CHANGES

The period of great changes in hotel and restaurant keeping began about 1890. Cesar Ritz was the creator of the maximum in luxury and quiet, complete service. Ellsworth Statler, who followed soon after Ritz, was most active beginning about 1900 and extending until his death in 1928. Statler was perhaps the most creative of all hotelmen, bringing what had been luxury accommodations to the middle class. Ralph Hitz, a name almost completely forgotten today, had a meteoric rise during the 1930s and was then forgotten when he died in 1940. His forte was promotion and systematic operations.

The big growth in the Hilton companies came with World War II and has extended to the present day. Ernest Henderson was not really a hotelman, in the sense of being a career and knowledgeable hotel operator, but he was able to put together the largest hotel chain. Kemmons Wilson, starting in 1952, forged the largest of all of the accommodation chains, Holiday Inns.

GIANTS IN HISTORY

J. Willard Marriott and Howard Johnson are the only restaurant men, in the true sense of the word, among the giants in the history of the hotel and restaurant business. Beginning in 1928 with a tiny Hot Shoppe, the Marriott Corporation is now the largest of all of the commercial foodservices and, in more recent years, has entered the motor hotel field. Howard Johnson started with an ice cream store and built it into a huge chain of roadside restaurants and motor lodges.

Dozens of other names should be mentioned, names like Boldt of the old Waldorf, Boomer of the new Waldorf-Astoria, Eppley of the Eppley Chain, Vernon Stouffer of Stouffer's, Donald Clinton of Clinton's Cafeterias in Los Angeles, Harry Pope of Pope's Cafeterias, Edward Carlson of Western International Hotels and United Airlines, and a multitude of other executives in the larger companies. Without question some of the educators like H. B. Meek of Cornell, and Lendal Kotschevar, once with Michigan state, industry magazine editors passed off the reply. If the reply was "Yes," a floor manager was called and informed. "It is Mr. Jones' first stay," whereupon the floor manager extended a warm welcome. The room clerk then called a bellman and, being careful to use the guest's name, announced "Show Mr. Jones to room 1012." Then the inevitable, "Thank you, Mr. Jones."

During the registration procedure the word loved most by the guest, his name, was used at least three times. The bellman continued to use it. "Are you expecting mail or telegrams, Mr. Jones?" Later, on the elevator, the bellman passed the good news on to the elevator operator that Mr. Jones was stopping at the house. "Tenth floor for Mr. Jones." And when the correct floor was reached, the bellman explained, "This floor, please, Mr. Jones."

This "strange music" of one's name did not stop until the guest was cozily settled in his room. On the way to the room the floor clerk was also let in on the fact that Mr. Jones had arrived. The bellman picked up the key with "Number 12 for Mr. Jones."

Once in the room, the bellman hurried about putting away the guest's coat and hat, unpacking his luggage if he so desired, explaining the Servidor, the laundry, and valet facilities. Finally: "Mr. Jones, may I be of further service?" By this time, Mr. Jones was feeling quite friendly toward Mr. Hitz and the hotel.

A first-stay guest could expect even more of the red-carpet treatment: a few moments after having settled down in his room, he was called by the "Hospitality Desk" and solicitous inquiry made to see if "anything further can be done to make your stay comfortable."

Red Carpet for Repeaters

A guest who stopped at a Hitz hotel 100 times became a member of the Century Club, his name engraved in gold on a gift notebook.

Statler started the idea of slipping the daily newspaper under the guest room door, "compliments of the management." Hitz went a step further and provided a hometown newspaper for the guest (provided he came from one of the cities from which most of the hotel's business was derived).

Tall people were given rooms with seven-foot beds. Parents with children were sent a special children's letter soon after registering. Sick patrons were personally visited by the floor managers. Guests leaving on an ocean trip were sent bon voyage messages. While most hotels were requiring guests without luggage to pay in advance, a no-luggage guest at a Hitz hotel was provided with an overnight kit containing pajamas, toothbrush, toothpaste, and shaving gear.

Everyone in the Hitz hotels was trained and expected to be a supersalesman. Room clerks were sent out over the country for one or more months each year to pick up business and get acquainted with their customers firsthand. A Hitz man was supposed to give his all for the hotel, and room clerks were expected to make calls within their own city during their off-hours. To insure compliance, each salesman kept a file card on each prospect and noted the time of the contact. Hitz hired a seven-passenger plane to sales-blitz all cities of 100,000 and more in population.

Selling went on all the time the guest was in the hotel. If he opened a closet door, there staring him in the face was a placard advertising one of the hotel services or a dining room. Even the mirrors in the bathroom medicine cabinets held advertisements. Should the guest settle down on the bed to listen to the radio he was still within the master-seller's voice range. The radio was interrupted at set intervals so that the hotel services might be extolled and called to the guest's attention.

At 8:00 A.M. the radio system started with a breakfast announcement; at noon the day's luncheon and prices were quoted; at 6:00 P.M. the radio was cut off, and the guest learned about the wonderful dance band currently playing in the dining room; at 7:00 P.M. three minutes were given over to a little talk made by the publicity manager who told about the interesting guests and events of the day. Finally, at midnight, the valet service, or candy store, laundry, or some other hotel service was featured, and the guest could drift off to sleep assured by the words, "Good night on the behalf of the management and entire staff."

Development of Guest History

Hitz is credited with being the first to develop and exploit a guest history. Ritz, before the turn of the century, had sent private letters to his hotels describing the idiosyncracies, and special likes and dislikes of his guests. Hitz systematically collected the information he wanted on each guest and set up a guest history department. This department, manned by a separate staff, kept guest records and followed the Hitz system of bringing the guest back to the hotel.

The system made routine the collecting of each guest's birthday and wedding anniversary date, his credit standing, and other information of value to the hotel. Routine also was the sending of a letter to all first-time guests, to each guest who had stopped with the hotel twenty-five times, fifty times and one hundred times.

On the fiftieth visit the guest received a complimentary suite. With the hundredth visit an appropriate gift with a letter was sent. Birthday greetings and wedding anniversary felicitations went to all regular guests. Color signals on the record showed if there was to be no publicity, if the person was undesirable and not to be welcomed, or if the address given was questionable.

Any complaints made were also recorded, and personal explanations were made by one of the hotel's traveling representatives. When a guest returned, he would be given the same room he occupied on his last visit, another personal touch to increase one's ego.

Special credit cards for people important to the hotel were developed by Hitz management. Statler had given gold-fringed cards to his friends that entitled them to the ultimate in service and accommodations. Hitz also gave a Gold Credit card to persons who might influence convention or other group business.

Anytime a Gold Card holder checked into the hotel he was extended special courtesies, and he was at liberty to bedazzle wife and clients with virtually unlimited credit. So, too, were "Star" reservations, people who for any reason the management thought important.

Hitz had a system for nearly everything. If one of his employees had a baby, he got a bank deposit book with a $5 deposit in it. For twins, the employees received $25 and, just in case there were triplets, $100.

Waiters were instructed never to ask guests, "Do you wish more butter?" but always, "Do you wish butter?" Beer was served at 45°F. in the winter, 42°F. in the summer. Should an undesirable person attempt to register at a Hitz hotel, this little contingency was handled with adroitness and business acumen: he was offered only the highest-priced rooms.

To insure that guest rooms were really clean and in immaculate order, a full-time room inspector went from room to room checking on everything in the room. His inspection was over and above the O.K. placed on the room by the regular inspector.

"Setups" Controlled Hotel Operation

Hitz preached service, service implemented by system. From his days as a busboy and waiter, every system was a "setup." He had a setup for each hotel practice. A Hitz hotel operated by the numbers. Bellmen were uniformed and drilled by a former trainer of Roxy Theatre ushers. On checking in, the guest was ushered to his room and on checking out, led to the cashier with ceremony.

To emphasize cleanliness on staircases, the corners of each step were painted white and kept white by the staff.

Hitz demanded much from his employees, and, because he was a leader and because it was a time of economic depression, he got superior performance. He also paid higher wages. The prevailing wage was $85 a month for a room clerk; Hitz paid $135. His department heads were the highest paid in the business because he knew it was through them that his systems would be effected.

Successful Operator in Great Demand

Promotion was a part of the Hitz personality, and he used it to promote himself as well as hotels. In 1927 he was offered the management of the Cincinnati Gibson Hotel, which was having financial difficulties. No one was more surprised than the board of directors when Hitz promised to earn $150,000 in profit during his first year of operation. The directors were more astounded than surprised when his first year's profits were $158,389.17.

Hitz, not one to hide his light, publicized his methods and cost accounting system to the entire hotel industry. In 1929 the Hotel New Yorker made its debut, along with the great depression. Hitz, undismayed, went on as its manager, to use the New Yorker as a laboratory where all operations were done by the book. His "setups" became standard practice in the other properties which Hitz managed.

Because he gave the man or woman paying $3 to $5 deluxe service of a type usually associated only with deluxe rates, his hotels ran high occupancies. During the depression, when hotel occupancies over the nation were at 50 percent and lower, such an operator was in great demand. Bankers and insurance company officials, who reluctantly got into the hotel business via closed mortgages, were eager for his services.

Hitz played his new role like a true dramatist. He would let it be known that he would be in a certain town on a particular day. The new owners would assemble at his suite to discuss his taking over the management of their properties. Hitz would appear briefly, then give the excuse of being very busy and retire. Hitz would then go into a back room and play pinochle with some old waiter friend while his lieutenants, who were polished diplomats, would close the deal.

Hitz did more than promote; he introduced all-out standardization to hotelkeeping. His kitchens were fine examples of efficiency and uniformity. Controls of all kinds were installed and thorough-going accounting practices followed. Hitz memorized standard operating ratios, then set about to excel them. The income from his restaurants, and such services as valet and guest laundry, were so high as to confound his contemporaries. What others had done, he could do better.

Like others before him, he could make money for other people—but not for himself. With friends, he bought The Belmont Plaza, across the street from the Waldorf-Astoria, ran out the prostitutes, and put in the Hitz systems. Nothing seemed to work. According to his son, if an idea failed, he would not admit failure, as he would have done if spending other people's money. Instead, if an ice show failed to bring in the crowds, Hitz would spend another $50,000 for promotion of the show. This did not prove to be the answer. The Belmont Plaza was one of the causes of his death. He died leaving only a small estate.

A hard-driving man, he was also known for quick thinking and a well-developed sense of humor. It is said that he craved friendship and had a genius for hospitality. To get a true picture of him, one had to see him making daily tours of his house, busily taking copious notes, and later, during the check-in hours, to see him in the lobby, a short, ebullient man, personally greeting new arrivals in an almost incomprehensible Viennese accent. He also had his failings; drinking and gambling were problems. He died in 1940 at the age of forty-nine.

Because he was the driving force of the company that operated ten of the country's largest hotels, his death brought quick disintegration of the system. Hitz owned no hotels and left no institutions as his shadow. Surprisingly, his name is scarcely known to the younger generation, his memory almost lost.

He did leave a number of practices and a new emphasis on system in hotelkeeping. He added a flair to promotion that has not since been emulated.

ERNEST HENDERSON (1897-1967)[6]

The person who built the largest chain in the world never took any real interest in designing a hotel or building one, never managed a hotel, and probably never thought of himself as a hotelman. As his son, Ernest Henderson III, put it, "My father had been bumping around from one industry to another. He got interested in buying common stocks in companies which had more bonds outstanding than the value of the property, and in doing so, acquired four hotels: the Lee, Wayland Manor, the Stonehaven, and the Sheraton. So in 1941, he had four hotels. The Statler was the great company at that time in the hotel industry. It had the same name on all of its properties. My father felt that he should have the same name on all of his hotels. On the roof of the Sheraton in Boston was a big sign saying 'Sheraton,' so he selected this as the name for the hotel chain."[7]

Ritz came into the hotel business via the restaurant business as a waiter and later a manager. Statler moved into the industry at an early age as a bellboy and later as a restaurant owner. Hitz started as a waiter, and Hil-

ton received his first experience in innkeeping at an early age helping his mother in taking in roomers and boarders. Henderson was forty-four years old before he really took the hotel business seriously. Twenty-six years later at his death, the Sheraton name was on 154 hotels, and Sheraton Corporation grossed about $300 million in sales annually.

Hilton Hotels was no longer the major competitor; this place had been taken by Holiday Inns with close to 900 motor inns around the country, and with plans to go international The Hilton Company had lost its thrust for growth; in fact, it had sold Hilton International Hotels to Trans World Airlines.

How did an investor from Boston create the largest hotel system the world has known in the space of about twenty-six years? Was it because Mr. Henderson had some special intuitive sense about hotelkeeping not possessed by the professional? Was he able to out-Ritz the Ritz in anticipating the guest's every wish? Could he out-Statler Statler in bringing luxury to the middle class market? Was he able to out-glamorize Hilton in promoting, beautifying, and operating hotels? Was he like Hitz in having an inexhaustible supply of energy in building a chain, making everything else secondary to the success of Sheraton?

Organizational and Financial Skill

The answer relates to none of these practices and qualities, but rather to organizational and financial skill, hard-bitten New England common sense about investments, operations, and profits. As a person, Mr. Henderson had a strong sense of duty and self-discipline. He gloried not in the display of wealth or the pleasures it might bring, but rather in the accumulation of wealth and the exercise of imagination and enterprise.

He was a capitalist in the best sense of the word, believing that there were few virtues greater than those found in ownership and creation of new wealth. Energy, hard work, keen analysis were combined with skepticism and shrewdness. He was an opportunist in the best sense of the word, ready to buy or sell a hotel if the right deal could be worked out.

While Hilton would stalk the Waldorf-Astoria for years, Henderson was quite happy to buy and sell many lesser hotels. With Hen-

6. Information adapted from *The World of Mr. Sheraton* by Ernest Henderson, David McKay Company.

7. *Guest Lecture Series*, University of Massachusetts, November, 1967.

derson, sentiment played little part in whether a hotel was bought or sold; the tax base against which depreciation could be taken was much more important. Some hotels were bought and sold as many as four times by the Sheraton Corporation.

Money and property were things to acquire, to use to build more wealth. Let Hilton live in ducal splendor in Beverly Hills while others administered the Hilton Hotels. Henderson maintained modest offices in the Sheraton Building in Boston. He was on hand to see to it that regular "belt-tightening" programs were instituted to keep Sheraton lean and, if not hungry, at least not overweight.

Let Mr. Hilton appear at a meeting with a fashion-plate entourage. Mr. Henderson appeared alone, conservatively dressed, and with a speech he had written himself. Let Mr. Hilton charter a plane for movie stars and other luminaries of the entertainment world to open his hotel in Madrid. Mr. Henderson would open his hotels in Dallas and Philadelphia with a guest list made up principally of local businessmen and persons who would be apt to send business to the hotel. Let Mr. Hilton dance the bossa nova at the opening of his new hotels. Mr. Henderson would more enjoy having the orchestra play "Come With Me," one of his own compositions.

Few people have accomplished much in the hotel business without a superabundance of physical energy. Hilton is amazing in his vitality at the age of ninety. Statler slept only a few hours a night. Hitz was the go-go type before his time, and Ritz apparently drove himself to the point of exhaustion at the age of forty-nine. Henderson was no exception.

In his book, *The World of Mr. Sheraton*, he tells about being dared to walk from Chestnut Hill (Boston), his home, to the family summer home in Dublin, New Hampshire. The distance was seventy-three miles, which Henderson negotiated in spite of several blisters and an unseasonably cold night.

Few hotel people have time for hobbies. Henderson collected coins, was an avid ham radio operator, a song writer, a dabbler at poetry, a story-teller, a staunch family man, and still found time for being a director of Northeastern University, Boston College, and Boston University. He served as a director of the Boston and U.S. Chambers of Commerce,

founding member of the World Affairs Council, and Chairman of the World Trade Center in New England. No other hotelman has so extended himself in civic commitments.

Unusual Interest in Outside Activities

In light of his tremendous range of activity, it would be easy to picture a man who was trying to overcome serious social or financial drawbacks: such was not the case. His family was not wealthy, but was well enough off for his father to acquire a Ph.D. in Berlin, to maintain a home in Cambridge, and a summer home in New Hampshire.

Mr. Henderson was proud enough of his ancestry to include a chapter about it in his biography and to name his middle daughter, Penny, after a distant relative who was the wife of Lord Llanover. Grandfather Henderson founded Henderson and Company, a New York Stock Exchange firm, and left "something of a nest egg for the surviving children." Real estate and investing were part of a family tradition which Ernest enthusiastically continued.

The name Ernest itself tells something of the family's attitude toward work, wealth, and ethics. One of Henderson's ancestors was an active Quaker, and apparently his father and mother believed strongly in imparting a sense of morality and honesty to their children, sent them to bed early, and helped to form Henderson's beliefs about hard work, fair play, honesty, and self-control. Henderson tells how he never smoked because his father insisted upon his smoking a long, cheap, very black cigar at the age of fourteen. He felt that money saved in not smoking was more profitably invested.

If we are to believe that people show evidences of their later careers in early life, Henderson is a case in point. He tells how at the age of twelve he raised a few chickens in his room so that he could sell them for a profit.

Yankee shrewdness is tempered by a sense of what is right and wrong. "A principal objective is to operate Sheraton Hotels as efficiently as possible to produce maximum earning consistent with higher standards of business ethics. This means giving recognition to the rights of workers who make success possible, as well as the obligation to render outstanding service to the public."

Probably no one has ever bought and sold hotels with the same calculated shrewdness as Ernest Henderson. Yet one of his ten commandments reads: "Thou shalt not demand the last drop of blood when effecting a business transaction."

Decalogue for Sheraton Corporation

The decalogue that he drew up for the Sheraton Corporation tells something about Henderson. He urged that decisions be made on the basis of facts and knowledge; he commended the merits of self-control, the virtues of probity, and insisted on employees keeping their word. Here is a paraphrase of the Sheraton Ten Commandments:

1 Do not throw thy weight around, however irresistible may be the urge to do so.
2 Thou shalt not take presents from those seeking thy favors; gifts so received must be passed on to a specified vice president for auction and the proceeds used for the employee fund.
3 Suffer not thy wife to gratify a yen to decorate a Sheraton Hotel.
4 Thou shalt not dishonor a confirmed reservation.
5 Thou shalt not give orders to an underling without fully making clear the exact purpose thereof.
6 Thou shalt duly recall that the virtues of those running small hotels may be the vices of those guarding larger establishments (for example, the desirability of delegation of authority and responsibility).
7 Thou shalt not demand the last drop of blood when effecting a business transaction.
8 Thou shalt not permit food to be served cold.
9 Thou shalt make decisions based on facts, calculation, and knowledge, not on a vague feeling.
10 Thou shalt not explode like a firecracker when an underling falleth into error (it may be your fault).

What lasting contributions did Henderson make to the hotel industry? Henderson brought no new standards of comfort or luxury to hotelkeeping, no innovations in design or operation. Although Sheraton Corporation operates in ten countries, the company was tardy in expanding internationally. Hilton International and Intercontinental Hotels were far ahead of Sheraton in this respect.

The Sheraton Corporation was also late in developing any large-scale motel interests. It was not until 1962 that Sheraton began "motorizing." Neither was the Sheraton Corporation out in front in making applications of the computer to the hotel, except perhaps its development of Reservatron, the Sheraton guest reservation system, which is computer controlled.

Showed Way to Rapid Acquisitions

Henderson did make contributions to hotelkeeping. As an expert in real estate and the use of leveraged money, he demonstrated how a hotel organization can rapidly acquire numbers of hotels, rapidly expand its equity ownership in hotels and motels, and yet show only a modest profit for tax purposes. Chain hotelkeeping, as conducted by the Sheraton Corporation, is as much a real estate venture as it is bedmaking, salad making, foodservice, and advertising.

There is a time to buy a hotel and a time to sell it, the timing dependent upon the tax base which is left for depreciation in a property, general business conditions, and whether or not the cash might not be put to better use in another property. Henderson put into practice a theory of minimaxing—minimizing costs and maximizing return on one's investment. He felt that he himself should earn at least $10,000 a day for the Sheraton Corporation.

Undoubtedly he did not feel that he could earn this sum by being a corporate manager. Rather his contribution lay in recognizing opportunities, investment and otherwise. He quoted H. L. Mencken as saying, "It is not the things we do but rather what we don't do that we eventually regret." Opportunities for Henderson as an expert in real estate were the purchase and sale of properties at the right moment.

Bought Using Minimum of Cash

He believed in the use of leveraged money whenever possible and perhaps used it more successfully in the hotel business than anyone else. Ernest Henderson III, his son, cited an example of how far Mr. Henderson would go in leveraging his cash position. Suppose the Sheraton Corporation was interested in buying a motel that had a $100,000 income each year. The Corporation might be willing to buy at eight times the income, or $800,000.

Mr. Henderson's objective was to get the property using a minimum amount of cash. He knew that he would borrow half of the $800,000 from a bank or insurance company at 6 percent interest. If the owner would agree to take a second mortgage for $500,000, Sheraton Corporation might raise the offer for the hotel from $800,000 to $1 million.

With a first mortgage of $400,000 and a second mortgage of $500,000, Sheraton could take possession of the property for a cash outlay of only $100,000. This is an extreme example of how to gain control of an $800,000 property with only $100,000 in cash.

Mr. Henderson was well aware of the "Discounted Dollar," the fact that $1 borrowed today is paid back with $1 worth something less than $1. Inflation has become a way of life in America. Inflation works to the advantage of the debtor. A certain amount of inflation is countenanced by the federal government and thought necessary for the continued growth of the economy.

A price rise at 1.5 percent a year means that in 10 years a debt of $1 can be paid off with money worth only 86.2 cents. If the price rise is 2.75 percent a year, the same $1 can be paid off with $1 worth only 76.2 cents. Real property, such as hotels and motels, tends to grow in value, especially if well located and maintained. Even if the hotel itself does not gain in value, the land it occupies may well appreciate more than enough to compensate for a loss in the value of the hotel building. Of course, there are many instances to the contrary.

Leveraging money requires courage, confidence, and judgment. Mr. Henderson apparently had these qualities in abundance. One of the most daring major policies ever set in the hotel business was Mr. Henderson's decision in 1962 to reduce room rates drastically. Net income in that year for the Sheraton Company dropped from sixty cents to seventeen cents per share.

The idea of reducing room rates has been anathema to hotelmen but especially to accountants. Tables have been drawn up showing the impossibility of making a profit when rates are reduced, yet Mr. Henderson, probably over the objection of his advisors, reduced rates in all the Sheraton hotels as much as one-third or more. Reduced rates did increase Sheraton occupany to about 73 percent (slightly higher than the occupancy rate for Hilton Hotels but much lower than for such chains as Holiday Inns and the Howard Johnson Motor Lodges).

Mr. Henderson reasoned that if a person could be brought into the hotel as a guest, he would spend considerable money on food and beverage. Profit from these sales would compensate for the reduced room rate. Some of the older Sheraton properties and some rooms in other hotels were given the label "Sherwyn Rooms" and priced at about $7 to $10 a night.

First for Free Parking

Perhaps equally daring was Henderson's decision to provide free parking at all Sheraton Hotels. The decision was necessary, Mr. Henderson believed, to compete with the free parking of the motor inn. It cost Sheraton Corporation millions of dollars a year. The free parking plan is still in effect, but rates have gradually increased in most Sheraton Hotels so that they are not too different from those charged by competing hotels. Even with the philosophy that life is full of opportunities and that our biggest regrets come from failure to grasp opportunities, some mistakes are inevitably made.

One mistake made by the Sheraton Corporation, according to Ernest Henderson III, was the failure to institute tight controls, budgetary and otherwise, over Sheraton managers during the period of 1961 to 1964. Sheraton earnings fell off sharply in the period 1962 to 1965, and much of the loss was attributed to a loss of control over budgets and operations. Managers are now required to forecast sales and profits for each department for a year in advance. Centralized management with area supervisors is part of Sheraton management policy.

What about Mr. Henderson's feeling about the guest? Was he in the tradition of Cesar Ritz and Ellsworth Statler, both of whom used the slogan, "The Guest is always right?" Was he with Statler who liked to use the phrase, "Life Is Service?" Did Mr. Henderson look upon the guest as a friend to be invited into a substitute home to be pampered, catered to, petted?

The hotel-guest relationship in a Sheraton Hotel is more likely to be something like that between a business firm and a customer. The customer is not necessarily right. He may be entirely unreasonable in his expectations. He may want more than he is entitled to.

In the New England tradition, a customer is someone who buys something for a price. The customer wants to get his money's worth; the honest seller tries to provide service or goods worthy of the price. If the seller does not live up to his bargain, he makes good in some way. In a Sheraton Hotel, a customer who has a confirmed reservation has a claim on the hotel. The customer gets a $20 gift certificate that can be spent in any Sheraton property. Also, the Sheraton tries to get the customer a room in another hotel and sends him to that hotel in a cab, at Sheraton's expense.

There is little thought of trying to greet the guest by his name, or to reserve for him the room that he had during his last visit, or of attempting to escort him to his car when he checks out. Efficiency is the watchword. The guest is likely to wait in line to check in and to check out. Few, if any, assistant managers in striped pants are on hand to coddle anybody.

Found Guest Questionnaires Effective

Mr. Henderson felt that one of the most effective management tools was the guest questionnaire. Letters sent to Sheraton headquarters are answered promptly, compliments and complaints are passed on to the manager concerned. The traveler, said Mr. Henderson, can run hotels better than the management. When the voluntary flow of complaints to the head office ran low, questionnaires were left in hotel bedrooms.

All complaints were classified: failure to honor confirmed reservations; delay in the appearance of a breakfast tray; ringing the wrong room for morning call. Mr. Henderson felt that when the proportion of complaints to compliments was more than 50 percent, management was slipping. If the complaint ratio rose to 60 percent, drastic action was necessary. On the other hand, if there were too many

compliments concerning a particular manager, the suspicion rose that the manager might be giving away the profits.

Henderson was actively engaged in operations. His office in the Sheraton Building was very much the nerve center of the Sheraton Corporation, and he took an active interest in day-to-day operation problems. He believed in a lean organization. In naval terms, he ran a taut ship. Belt-tightening programs could be expected every year to clear away unnecessary people and programs.

He was no friend of bureaucracy and did not believe in a large headquarters staff. The training department was one man, the personnel department hardly much larger. Every Sheraton employee—but especially staff and executive-level personnel—was expected to contribute, and every day; no prima donnas, please, and no juicy stock options for executives. The top salary before 1967 was $52,000 a year.

"Sales Blitz" Idea

Mr. Henderson was definitely sales-minded. Though the "sales blitz" idea originated with the advertising department, Henderson strongly favored and encouraged the plan. The sales blitz was a campaign to saturate a city with the promotion of Sheraton Hotels. Sales people from a wide area converged on a city and in a team effort called upon hundreds of potential Sheraton customers. Sheraton credit cards were distributed in quantity and group business solicited.

Henderson believed in national advertising. Franchising the Sheraton name brought in additional revenue, but of more importance to Henderson was the fact that each franchise added another unit to the Sheraton referral system.

Mr. Henderson will probably be remembered largely for his ability to increase the equity value of the Sheraton Corporation from an estimated value of about $50 million in 1947 to close to $400 million in 1967. The increase was brought about with very little speculation in the usual sense of the word. Constant attention was given to avoiding the danger of financial over-extension.

Unlike several of the real estate holding companies of the 1950s and 1960s, Sheraton

Corporation never experienced any serious financial uncertainty. Yet, some of his methods of financing and accounting were unorthodox to the point that the stock market took little notice of the company's real worth. Henderson did not hesitate to offer capital income debenture bonds carrying a 7.5 percent interest rate when the going rate was 6 percent.

The Sheraton guest might be a little surprised to find an announcement on his bedside table telling him of the merits of buying Sheraton bonds. Mr. Henderson explained why in his biography. Interest payments on the debentures were tax deductible to the company; it actually cost Sheraton less in interest payments than if preferred stock had been issued paying 3¾ percent interest. Unlike the bond, interest on preferred stock interest is not tax deductible.

Building Equity

Because the Sheraton Corporation took the maximum depreciation allowable, the equity value of the company increased rapidly while earnings appeared comparatively small. The annual reports to the Sheraton Corporation devoted some space to explaining the true financial picture to stockholders. In addition to reporting net income, profits, depreciation, and cash flow, the company reported an "estimated value" of each common share. Also reported were an estimated net asset value and "adjusted earnings."

These were theoretical estimates based on the judgment of the Sheraton officers and were presented to show stockholders their real holdings and the value of their stock. Sheraton had the highest cash flow of any hotel chain, taking the maximum allowable depreciation. This practice, of course, made the net profit figure smaller but built equity.

Henderson invested for profit, not prestige. One of his investment rules was that for every dollar added in improving a hotel, the hotel should be expected to increase in value by $2.00. Indicative of the financial orientation of the company is the practice of posting in the corporation office the latest market value of Sheraton stock. What other hotel company would do this?

The financial community never really accepted the financial figures. Although it was obvious that the equity value of a share of Sheraton stock increased year after year, the market value of Sheraton dropped steadily from a high of $22 a share in 1962 to less than $9 in early 1967. The fact that International Telephone and Telegraph Company offered to buy control of the Sheraton Corporation at $35 a share came as a surprise to the "smart money" crowd.

The offer from ITT was consummated shortly after Mr. Henderson's death on September 6, 1967. The decision to sell to ITT was made by Ernest Henderson III, who had been president of the company since 1963. He remained as president for a short time under ITT, but by late 1969, most of the former officers and Mr. Henderson had left the company.

How can Henderson's career be summarized? He introduced no major innovations into hotel-keeping as a profession. He bought and sold; he built; he operated well. He gave the public fair value for its money. He was more civic-minded than any major hotel operator before him. His goal was to create a billion dollar organization, and he worked to that end diligently, quietly, and with amazing insight into the economics of hotelkeeping.

Perhaps it is more than enough to say, "He built the world's largest hotel chain."

In 1978 ITT owned Sheraton Corporation, by far the largest hotel empire—400 hotels of 99,285 rooms—and planned to add 182 more hotels within the succeeding five years. Total sales were about $1.25 billion; $450 million of it in food and beverage sales.[1]

---

1. *Restaurant-Hospitality*, June 1978.

CONRAD N. HILTON (1887-1979)

Conrad Hilton was the best known hotelman in the world, the first truly international hotel-keeper. Also the most durable. In 1978 at 90 he was still nominally active as Chairman of the Board of Hilton Hotels Corporation, which owned, managed, or franchised 105 hotels with 46,746 rooms. Of these, 45 were owned or partly owned; the rest were under management contract. The Waldorf-Astoria and the New York Hilton were 50 percent owned. The Hilton family in 1975 controlled the company by owning 29.5 percent of the stock.

What has Hilton brought to the hotel business? A concept of efficiency even more developed than that of Statler. If efficiency is defined as getting the most for the least, making every dollar of investment produce, making every square foot of space profitable, then Hilton is efficient.

According to a Hilton Hotels' release, efficiency in Hilton Hotels is predicated on six factors: time and method studies, job analysis, job standards, safety programs, budgetary control, and pricing programs. Hilton believes that costs must be controlled every day, every week, every month.

A Hilton manager knows exactly how many maids, bellmen, elevator operators, cooks, and waiters he needs for the upcoming day. Budgeting applies to the purchase of food, the right amount for the number of guests expected. The daily amount of steam, hot water, electricity, and comparable services are also computed.

New Methods of Forecasting, Control

With the help of the leading accounting firms, Hilton introduced industrial methods of forecasting and control not previously used in the hotel business.[9] A forecasting committee predicts the number of rooms and covers that will be sold a month in advance, a week in advance, and three days in advance. Forecasts are based on the reservations on hand and the experience for the same month in previous years.

Employees are then scheduled to fit the volume of business forecasted. Deviations from the number of employees allowed under the system must be approved in advance. Department heads are informed if they are over or under in number of employees needed according to the forecast.

Each of the larger Hilton Hotels set up a new position, an operations analyst, a person charged with coordinating the forecasting system. Payroll costs were reduced dramatically because only the number of employees were on hand to service the number of guests in the hotel and in the restaurants that had been forecast. The hotel business fluctuates widely from day to day and between seasons; the forecasting system correlated sales demand and labor needed.

Each hotel prepares a detailed daily report summarizing revenues, expenses, profit and loss for the day; the month to date and a comparison of these figures for the preceding month and for the preceding year. Hilton also employs corporate forecasting control. The annual forecast is prepared well before the first of the year.

Though the Hilton organization is decentralized, in the sense that pride is taken in developing a personality for each hotel, accounting and control is highly centralized.

9. Donald E. Lundberg and James P. Armatas, *The Management of People in Hotels, Restaurants and Clubs,* see chapter entitled "The Harris, Kerr, and Forster Payroll Cost Control System" (Dubuque, Iowa: William C. Brown, 1978).

Reports reach the Beverly Hills office each day from every hotel and are also funneled into the divisional offices daily so that the top operating executives know exactly what transpires every day.

Centralized purchasing for some twenty-one groups of items is done in the corporation's central purchasing department in Los Angeles. There are also branches in New York and Chicago. Among the items contracted for are linen, silver, china, glassware, carpeting, TV sets, matches, light bulbs, and bar soap. Some fifty million books of matches are purchased annually at a cost of $250,000. In an average year, Hilton purchases some three million or more towels, bedsheets, napkins, and tablecloths at a cost of $2 million, as well as china and glassware at a cost which exceeds a million dollars a year.

The Hilton Reservation Service is computerized, with the heart of the system located at the Statler-Hilton Hotel in New York City. The telephone setup and ACD (Automatic Call Distributor) was an innovation in the industry and was designed to accommodate up to 200 incoming lines. In 1972 a computerized communications system—CCS, with private line circuits, linked the office with 160 Hilton and associated hotels around the world. Reservationists handled more than 150,000 reservations monthly.

Making Maximum Use of Space

"Digging for gold" is another Hilton idea. The gold referred to is unused space. Hilton became a master at identifying areas that could be made revenue-producing. He could walk through a hotel and within a few minutes locate new restaurants and bars in the lobby area or project the installation of a lower ceiling in the lobby so that a new floor could be added.

The Waldorf-Astoria is a case in point. The hotel was under the management of Lucius Boomer from the day it opened until Boomer's death. Boomer, a highly respected and knowledgeable hotelman, could never make the Waldorf-Astoria very profitable, even during the war years.

Hilton extracted a million dollars in profit from the Waldorf-Astoria the first year that Hilton Hotels operated it. By renting small

areas and cases in the lobby, he got $42,000 a year. The laundry was moved from Manhattan to New Jersey, and his "digging for gold" operation produced a number of new revenue-producing bars and restaurants.

The Palmer House in Chicago had always been a money-maker. When Hilton bought it for $19 million, it became a gold mine. The sub-rentals in the basement of the Palmer House plus the revenue from food and beverage sales are said to pay all the operating expenses of the entire 2,200-room hotel—the first time in history that a bona fide hotel has had a break-even point of zero.

His goal for the Palmer House when he bought it was to increase operating profit by $50,000 a month over the preceding year. Actual increase during the first year was $1,450,000. All restaurants were converted to seven-day operations; locker room space was converted into sixty additional guest rooms; night clubs added photographic departments that yielded $20,000 in profit the first year.

Store rentals at the Palmer House brought in $950,000 per year. Hilton noted that some 4,000 persons passed through the lower arcade every day, with no bar facilities to serve them. He converted a book store, rental $250 a month, into the successful Town and Country Room, which produced $490,000 in revenue its first year.

When Hilton bought the Statler Hotels, they were among the most efficient of hotel operations. Hilton was able to produce an additional $3 million in profit each year. One way was to remove a million dollars a year in payroll from central office.

Buying Bargains

One thing most Hilton Hotels have in common—they were bought at bargain prices. The Palmer House cost $25,837,000 to build in 1929. Hilton paid $19,385,000 in 1945. The Stevens was built in 1925 at a cost of $30 million; he got it for $7,500,000. It had been a white elephant, yet Hilton got a net profit from it of $1,730,242 the first year. Since then profits have increased even more.

Perhaps his background explains his character. Hilton was born in San Antonio, New Mexico in 1887, a time when New Mexico was a bona fide frontier with Indians and red-blooded frontiersmen. Conrad's father, Gus, was a plunger, well-fixed part of the time, in bad financial condition at other times.

During one of Gus's lean periods, following the financial panic of 1907, Conrad jumped into the breach and began as a hotel operator. Conrad was up at 3:00 A.M. to meet the train and to rent some of the family rooms in the back of his father's store to traveling salesmen. The tariff was $2.50 for a room and three bountiful meals served by Hilton's mother and sisters.

It was not unitl 1919, after being a state legislator, a banker in a small way, and having served in the Army during World War I, that Hilton bought his first hotel, almost by chance. It was the Mobley in Cisco, Texas, one of the first of several mints converted into hotels. Hilton went to Cisco intending to buy a bank; he backed out of the deal when the price was raised abruptly. Instead, he bought a hotel when the owner caught the oil fever. Cisco was a boom town short of hotel rooms, and Hilton found himself many nights with the dubious gratification of sleeping in a leather chair in his office, having rented all of his hotel's rooms. Hilton's investment was $5,000.

The Mobley was the first of a Texas chain, which by 1929 included seven properties. Hilton expanded as fast as his profits and credit would allow. His first reverse came during the construction of the Dallas Hotel when he ran out of money. He ended by operating it on a lease.

The depression struck him hard. At one point he was so short of funds that $300 was pressed on him by one of his bellmen for "eatin' money." At one point he was $500,000 in debt. Despite everything that could be done—taking out room telephones, renting out entire floors as storage space, saving on lights and heat, he still could not meet his obligations.

Economic Operation—A Depression Lesson

During this phase of his career he learned to operate economically, one of the keys to his future success. He managed to hold on to five of his eight hotels. It was not until 1937 that he was again able to relax, hold up his head, and begin buying hotels again.

With an unshakable faith in the American economy, he acquired the famed Sir Francis Drake and for the first time attracted national attention. Hilton was fifty-one years of age. From this time on, his progress has been steadily up and up. Three times he had had temporary setbacks, but they were minor.

Once, in San Francisco, he withdrew from the city's hotel association and signed a union agreement that caused the Hotel Employers Association to denounce him for "betrayal" and for "selling out to union bossism." The Sir Francis Drake Hotel was open while the others operated with picket lines outside their doors. Finally, the pressure mounted to the point where a local group bought the Drake for a price that gave Hilton a profit of half a million. Two jousts with seasonal properties were likewise unsatisfactory, and Hilton has since stayed strictly with year-around operations.

When Los Angeles hotel owners expected a Japanese invasion force at any moment, Hilton picked up the Town House for $850,000. The Rosslyn Hotel he got for $400,000. Soon afterwards, with the West Coast a beehive of activity, the Rosslyn netted him $1,000 a day.

In 1946 Hilton Hotels Corporation was formed. In 1949 controlling interest in the Waldorf-Astoria was acquired, and in 1954 all of the Statler Hotels were purchased in a grand acquisition representing $111 million.

Financing the Statler Purchase

An indication of Hilton's daring and skill was seen in the Statler Hotel purchase. Hilton Hotel Corporation obligated itself to raise about $110 million by a certain date or forfeit $8 million. The $8 million was payable as damages pro rata to each Statler stockholder in case the deal was not closed. The $77.5 million necessary in cash was raised by organizing a new company and offering securities to the stockholders of the existing Hilton Hotels Corporation.

The new company, Statler Hotels Delaware Corporation, was organized, and it was this corporation that raised the money to purchase the Statler Hotels. More than 100 lawyers in all parts of the country worked on the deal, plus many people in banks, insurance companies, and investment banking houses. The Equitable Life Assurance Society of the United States loaned $49.5 million, and the First National Bank of Boston, $20 million.

With the new company, there was a stepped-up base for the depreciation of the fixed assets, both building and equipment. By adopting a plan of complete liquidation of the old company and distribution of the assets to the stockholders, a capital gains tax was avoided. By using the new corporation, the benefits of the sale-and-lease-back plan were also exploited. After the sale was completed, securities of the Hilton Hotels Corporation in the form of convertible debentures were offered to the stockholders of the Statler Company. Some of the debentures carried a 4½ percent interest rate, others a 4¾ percent rate, and were convertible into Hilton common stock. The warrants for the convertible debentures were oversubscribed.

Simple Organization Chart

The organization chart for the company is simple. Central offices for Barron Hilton, the company president, are in Beverly Hills, Calif. Chicago is headquarters for the senior vice-president in charge of the Central Division, the executive vice-president for franchise operations, and the financial senior vice-president and corporate treasurer. Chicago also has the main purchasing and accounting departments, as well as the directors of food and beverage, personnel, and vice-president for sales and his staff. The Eastern Division Headquarters is in New York City, and another division is centered in Hawaii.

Hilton International began in 1949 when Hilton was given the contract to operate a hotel that eventually became known as the Caribe Hilton. When the Puerto Rico Industrial Development Company was looking for an operator of the hotel they planned, letters were written to seven hotel executives in the United States asking them if they were interested in the project. Only Hilton was gracious enough to reply in Spanish, starting "Mi estimade amigo."

Hilton knew Spanish well from his early days in Mexico and Texas. The Caribe Hilton is one of the most successful ventures of all time and has for a number of years made a profit of something like $3 million a year, one-third of it going to the Hilton organization.

The contract between Hilton and the Puerto Rican government set a pattern for later international hotels. The land, buildings, and usually the furnishings and equipment are financed in each country by local capital (government or private), while Hilton International operates the hotels under a long-term percentage rental agreement, with renewal options. Generally two-thirds of the gross operating profits go to the owners, the remaining one-third to Hilton International.

The Hilton International Company cannot lose; the owners are usually pleased because they get the advantage of the Hilton know-how plus becoming a part of the huge international referral and promotion system. The other large U.S. international company, Intercontinental Hotels corporation, has not been so fortunate. In many cases the Company has had to invest at least part of the money for the construction of the hotel.

In 1967 Hilton International Company, owner of thirty-eight hotels, was purchased by Trans World Airlines and merged into the TWA corporate structure as a subsidiary. Hilton International shares were exchanged for TWA securities. As of 1975, Hilton International operated sixty-seven hotels outside the continental United States, including one in Hawaii, the Kahala Hilton. Sales in that year were $143 million. A partly owned reservation system channels business to both hotel empires.

In 1975 Hilton sold a 50 percent interest in 6 of its larger hotels to the Prudential Insurance Company for $83.3 million, retaining a management contract by which the company receives 3 percent of the gross revenues and one-half of their profits.

The move made Hilton less vulnerable to falling occupancies and enabled the company to reduce its long-term debt to $150 million. By using $26 million of the sum to buy one million shares of its own stock, eighty-seven-year-old Conrad Hilton was left with 29.5 percent of the ownership. Prudential liked the deal because hotel properties tend to be more inflation-proof than other investment properties with long-term leases.

What kind of a man was Hilton? Energetic, capable, an incurable optimist. Not one to hide his light under a bushel, Hilton was said to carry around in his pocket a roll of newspaper clippings concerning his own activities. Two biographies have been written about him—*The*

Man Who Bought the Waldorf[10] and *Silver Spade*[11]. In addition, he has written an autobiography, *Be My Guest*.[12]

A *Time* article on Hilton noted that he was very conscious of his appearance.[13] The fact that he is 6 ft. 2 in. tall and has the outdoor look makes him a handsome man by most standards. He abhored fat men, says *Time*, to the point where he did not even like to do business with them.

His ego, *Time* comments, was as big as his house, a sixty-one room mansion in Bel Air, California, called Casa Encantada, where he used to live alone with nineteen servants. (Attesting to his durability was his remarriage in 1976 at the age of eighty-nine to a woman of sixty-three.) He was indifferent to fancy foods, preferring to dine on corned beef hash, tuna casserole, and tea served in plastic cups ("It's more sanitary"). Concern over sanitation was shared with an earlier famous hotelman, Cesar Ritz.

Hilton "on Stage"

Hilton liked to be with beautiful women and smart-looking men. In public he was always "on stage." Appearing at a national hotel meeting in the mid-fifties, he breezed in with an entourage of his top executives who solicitously helped him off with his coat. They were careful satellites, regardless of their $50,000 salaries. When Hilton rose to make his address, they stood as a body and at the close of the talk gave him a standing ovation.

At one time Hilton's public relations were not of the best. His marriage to the actress Zsa Zsa Gabor and the fast life he led with the Hollywood set got him some unfavorable publicity. This was soon remedied with the aid of a public relations counselor.

His biographer explains that the night life of which he was fond was undertaken upon a prescription of his doctor. Hilton could not forget his work even after working hours. He was told that at six o'clock he should squire a beautiful woman to a fine restaurant and dance the evening away. This, together with swinging a golf club during office hours, may partly account for his longevity.

Hilton preached the value of God and country. According to his biographer, he prayed regularly and before and after acquiring another property. One public relations ad in *Time* magazine cost $50,000 and was built around the idea of Uncle Sam down on his knees in prayer. Over two million copies of the prayer were distributed. Like most hotel people, Hilton was slow to recognize the value of franchising and only in the middle 1960s began franchising the Hilton name.

The *Time* article had this to say about Hilton's philosophy of innkeeping: "Hiltons are assembly-line hostelries with carefully metered luxuries—convenient, automatic, a bit antiseptic. Conrad Hilton's life is rooted in the belief that people are pretty much equal, and that their taste and desires are, too. His hotels have made the world safe for the middle-class travelers, who need not fear the feeling of being barely tolerated in some of the older European hotels. At a Hilton all they need is a reservation and money." If this is an indictment of Hilton, it is also a commentary on the American traveling public. Many complain about and resent Hilton but continue to patronize his hotels.

In looking ahead, Hilton predicted that rooms will have not only radio and television, but also recording attachments so that guests may receive telephone messages while they are out. Bathrooms will have ultraviolet equipment, suntan lamps, and towel warmers (towel warmers have been installed in some European hotels). Room furnishings will include plastic carpets that need no cleaning and plastic impregnated furniture so hard that you cannot bend it with an axe.

In 1969 Hilton joined Statler in having his name closely associated with a school of hotel administration. A gift of $1.5 million made by Hilton to the School of Hotel Management at the University of Houston was used to pay for part of a new Continuing Education and Hotel Administration Building; the name of the Houston School was changed to the Conrad N. Hilton School of Hotel Management.

By 1977 The Hilton Corporation comprised some 63,000 rooms, 125 of them franchised.

10. Thomas E. Dabney, *The Man Who Bought The Waldorf* (Duell, Sloan & Pearce, 1950).

11. Whitney Bolton, *Silver Spade: The Conrad Hilton Story* (Plainview, N.Y.: Books for Libraries, 1974).

12. Conrad N. Hilton, *Be My Guest* (Englewood Cliffs, N.J.: Prentice-Hall, 1957).

13. *Time Magazine*, July 19, 1963.

The star property was the Las Vegas Hilton, the 2100-room resort hotel, which in some years, created as much as 40 percent of the corporations total profits. "Each Hilton Hotel and Inn is an individual, a unique and special place, free to do what it does best." That, according to Barron Hilton, is the Hilton difference.

HOWARD DEARING JOHNSON (1898-1972)

Howard Johnson is probably the best-known name to ever appear in the restaurant business. The name appears on some 1,000 bright and shiny restaurants (including Red Coach Grill and Ground Rounds in 41 states), strategically located on most of the major highways in the United States. Over 500 motor lodges carry the name. Supermarkets display a variety of Howard Johnson frozen foods and beverages. Road signs, newspaper ads, TV commercials broadcast the name. The white brick buildings with the orange roof are one of the symbols of modern America.

Such personal prominence through the establishment of the operator's name is unusual in the foodservice business. Careme and Escoffier were widely known as chefs, not as restaurant operators. Some people are vaguely aware that, before the turn of the century, Fred Harvey gained prominence as a foodser-

vice operator by contracting to serve food in the Santa Fe railroad diners and in restaurants along the Santa Fe tracks.

The name Child's—the most prominent restaurant name in the 1920s and 1930s—has almost disappeared. Names like Bickford and John R. Thompson Company are known regionally. The Stouffer name has not been associated with any particular individual. J. Willard Marriott, is not well-known because until 1968 his name was not part of the company name.

The Howard Johnson name reflects the driving ambition of an individual, a desire for excellence of a kind, and the perception that the American public would be auto-borne, want ice cream, sandwiches, and relatively simple meals while traveling. Howard Johnson's father had told him as a boy, "You will never amount to anything because you never stick to anything." A grade school drop-out, he went to work selling cigars.

Howard decided that he would stick to something, and it happened that his "something" was a part of the most important artifact of modern America, the automobile. Prophetically, and almost alone, Johnson built his restaurants on the edge of town. He built his menu around the most popular of all desserts, ice cream, and to mix metaphors, hitched his wagon to the star of the automobile. He, more than anyone else, created the highway restaurant.

The name Howard Johnson evokes images of white buildings, orange roofs, and rich ice cream. The name is synonymous with restaurants that offer a choice of counter or table seating, quick service of hamburgers, hot dogs, fried clams, chicken, and steaks. To the traveling public, a Howard Johnson restaurant is often a respite from the superhighway—a clean restroom, a quick cup of coffee, an ice cream cone, or sandwich.

At night the Howard Johnson restaurant is a blaze of lights, a break in the monotony of high speed driving, a chance to stretch, and to change the focus of life.

It All Started with Ice Cream

Originally, Johnson was a tobacco salesman for his father, preferring business to staying in school. In 1925, after his father died, Johnson

Figure 12-1   *This Howard Johnson restaurant was built in Mineola, New York in the 1930s. It is typical of the design of that period. The distinctive orange roof and white structure has been a continuing trademark of the company.*

took over a small drug store in Wollaston, Massachusetts, borrowing $500 to start it. The principal business was a newspaper distributorship. Though it was highly profitable, Johnson feared that he might lose the newspaper franchise and decided to sell ice cream as well.

It was ice cream with a difference; at first the only flavor was chocolate. Instead of using synthetic vanilla, he used the true vanilla bean. He called upon an expert to help produce a quality ice cream, and soon he had ten hand-turned freezers of the ice and salt variety making flavors of ice cream no one had heard of before. When he got to twenty-eight flavors, he felt that he had them all and developed the trademark, "28 Flavors," something like Heinz's "57 Varieties." The "28 Flavors" is still a trademark, though fifty or sixty flavors are produced today.

At the outset, Johnson recognized the value of quality control. From his father he

learned the dangers of tampering with quality in cigars. Johnson vowed to make good quality and to control that quality. In the summer he built little shacks along the Massachusetts beaches and hired boys to sell big ice cream cones and frankfurters for a dime.

The idea was new. Customers came streaming in at all hours of the day. As Mr. Johnson put it, "If I was at all bright, it was the fact that I realized that I had an idea that worked, and I followed it and kept following it; and I follow the same pattern today, except that we have improved a lot."

A Franchise Pioneer

Later, when he had developed a style of architecture for his restaurants, he franchised the complete format of operation, mainly to people in the New England area. Franchising was not original with Johnson. A & W Root

Beer, a California company, had sold one of its first franchises to J. Willard Marriott in 1925, and to other franchisees even earlier.

Johnson was a franchise pioneer, nevertheless, who franchised many restaurants in the 1930s, legally insisting that the franchisee purchase and sell only specified food items. By 1935 there were 25 Howard Johnson restaurants; 100 by 1940. The white building with the orange roof plus Howard Johnson ice cream were the most important common denominators. Many small businessmen were Johnson franchisees. Most of them profited handsomely from the agreement.

In the 1950s and 1960s, the Company bought many of the franchises back, arguing that the franchise holders were not maintaining Howard Johnson standards. The franchise enabled Howard Johnson to expand rapidly. In effect, the franchise purchasers were his bankers, providing money to build restaurants to merchandise the Howard Johnson name and products. Highway location, cleanliness, high quality ice cream, and sandwiches served in clean, attractive, and easily identifiable buildings were keys to the Howard Johnson success story in the 1930s.

With the coming of World War II, the highway restaurant business collapsed; 90 of the 100 Howard Johnson stores were closed. The war brought gasoline and tire rationing, and, without gasoline, people would not go fifty feet from the center of town.

Undaunted by World War II

It is a tribute to Johnson's drive and ingenuity that he came out of the war in better financial condition than he had at the beginning of the war. Part of this was possible because of his prewar production of ice cream, which gave him large quotas of sugar and cream. These quotas were valuable since sugar and cream were strictly rationed and in short supply. He made ice cream for the Louis Sherry firm in New York and for a number of other companies.

He contracted to serve food in colleges that were training the military, to shipyards, and to other military units. When the war ended, he returned to the highway restaurant, refurbished the ones that he had, and built more.

In the 1950s, Johnson pioneered convenience frozen foods. Quietly and without publicity, he built companies in Boston and Miami where many of the Howard Johnson menu items were produced on a production line basis and frozen. Huge refrigerated trucks left the Miami commissary, carrying frozen turkey pies and other preportioned and precooked foods as far west as Texas and as far north as North Carolina. At the time (and even today, to some extent), it was wiser to say nothing about such commissary and frozen food operations. Frozen foods were considered by many to be inferior to freshly prepared ones.

Johnson went quietly about distributing and reheating his frozen foods, while at meetings of professional foodservice organizations debates were conducted about the merits, the economics, and the feasibility of serving frozen meals. Ironically, the most successful restaurant chain in the world was doing just what those experts were debating. He froze entrees years before the idea of the frozen entree was accepted to any degree.

Commissary freezing was a milestone in large restaurant operations. It permitted impressive economies in restaurant labor. As early as 1953, Howard Johnson supervisors were being told that it was no longer necessary to hire cooks, only food warmers. In fact, food preparation in Johnson restaurants has been restricted to griddling, frying, and baking.

Teenagers have been griddle and fry cooks. No intricate recipes need be followed for preparing food. No chef salaries, just the minimum wage is paid for a kitchen preparation staff. If a "food warmer" decides to leave, another person can be trained in a few days to take his place.

The company continually sought to simplify equipment, standardize preparation methods, and control portions. When Clyde "Sam" Weithe put together a continuous conveyor belt dishmachine in his garage in Adams, Massachusetts, he took it to the Howard Johnson Company. It was not long before all new Howard Johnson restaurants were installing the Adamation machine.

One person could operate the machine, both loading and unloading. Waitresses could rack soiled ware in the racks from the dining room. A teenager could operate the machine, keep the restrooms clean, and, if necessary, fill in on the food preparation station. In the New England Division, all of the coffee-making machines were leased from one individual who also contracted to maintain them.

American Middle Class Menu

The Howard Johnson menu was aimed directly at the American middle-class traveling public. Ice cream has been a principal appeal, also meat in the form of hamburgers, hot dogs, and steaks. No frills, just solid American food. The food is served in comparative luxury, with decor that is gay and contemporary in the fountain area, carpeted and chandeliered in the table-service area. In 1972 the usual Howard Johnson restaurant was capitalized at about $250,000.

Later in his career, Mr. Johnson developed the Red Coach Grills, designed to satisfy the American nostalgia for early America. The decor is heavy oak and substantial, reminiscent of colonial New England coach stops. The menu features Maine lobster and prime steaks. The average check in the Red Coach Grill is several times that of the Howard Johnson restaurant.

What kind of a manager of men was Mr. Johnson? What made him tick? How was he able to accomplish so much in one lifetime? As Mr. Johnson himself said, his business was his life. He had no hobbies, participated in no sports; when he was at a party he ended up talking business. He drove himself and others. His method of motivation was to needle, to constantly check, to forever urge people to greater effort.

Stores were open from seven in the morning to midnight and, at any of these hours, he might be found driving up to a store, observing it from a distance, then inspecting it closely inside. He observed everything, the smudge on the front door, the piece of paper in the parking lot, or the stain on the wall. He did not wait to send a memo telling of the discrepancies he found.

The Development Era

The Howard Johnson Company developmental stage was not one for the young graduate of hotel schools, even less for the Harvard Business School graduate. Johnson hired those people who would do what he told them, and would do it with energy, persistence, and without attention to the number of hours worked. Johnson believed in certain things, wanted certain other things, and bent all of his energies and those of the people around him to getting those things.

Few college graduates were happy in the Howard Johnson organization while Howard D. Johnson ran the show. Little stock was placed in theory or in the need for staff personnel. Every manager was his own personnel manager, and the ideas he carried out were those laid down by Mr. Johnson and by a few people close to him at the top.

The manager could not be distinguished from the worker. He wore the same little hat and white coat as the fountain personnel and could be found dishing up ice cream, unloading supplies, or operating the cash register. The press was forever on to cut labor cost. The working manager was one way to achieve a lower labor cost. Bonuses were paid on the basis of labor and food cost, little else. Managers were expected to work until the job was done; the six- and seven-day week were commonplace for them.

Salaries for Howard Johnson store managers were not particularly good as compared with salaries paid unit managers of other chains. Supervisors who had responsibility for several stores were expected to step in and relieve unit managers whenever necessary. Most of the higher echelon unabashedly stood in some fear of Mr. Johnson. All respected him. All executives knew that, regardless of rank or salary, they could expect to hear from Mr. Johnson by telephone, and frequently. When abroad, Mr. Johnson called his executives daily to check on operations, costs, and new developments.

Johnson continually worked at standardizing his operations, and he probably standardized foodservice to a greater extent than had ever been done before on a large scale. Statler standardized the foodservices of Statler Hotels long before Johnson was active, but Johnson produced a menu, commissary-prepared food, and a method of reheating and serving food, which was followed almost exactly in all Howard Johnson restaurants.

In about 1955, a hotel student at Florida State University did a study that showed the average ice cream cone being served in Howard Johnson restaurants in Florida cost the company eight an one-half cents. The fact that they were being sold for ten cents meant that the ten cent cone was a loss leader. Cone prices were raised shortly thereafter, and the dippers used were of a size that made it difficult to serve a larger-than-called-for portion.

The number of seats in a Howard Johnson restaurant varied as new stores were built. But gradually there evolved a standard building with standard seating and equipment. The method of operation became more and more standardized so that each Howard Johnson store might have rolled off an assembly line. Each could have been operated by a system of signals in which each manager was the signal caller.

The Red Coach Grills were set apart. The general public was not informed that they were part of the Howard Johnson organization. The Red Coach managers receive salaries that are more than double those of Johnson store managers and are given much more responsibility in buying and operating.

Opening Motor Lodges

In 1954 the Company opened its first motor lodge. Early ones were small but were built at strategic locations and with an architectural style that allowed for easy expansion. Mr. Johnson credits the idea of the motor lodge to his son who at the time was only twenty-one. In 1972 there were almost 500 Howard Johnson motor lodges, part company-operated, part franchise-operated.

Figure 12–2 *Today's Howard Johnson motor lodges are usually built in conjunction with a Howard Johnson restaurant, although the two operations may be under separate management. The familiar colors are still highly visible.*

In about 1953 Mr. Johnson underwent a serious operation and decided to begin phasing out of the day-to-day management of the Company. In 1959 he installed his son, Howard Brennen Johnson, as president and told him to "make it grow."

Howard B. Johnson was twenty-eight years old and in many ways the opposite of his father. Howard B. is tall, 6 ft. 2 in., and slender, while Howard D. was of average height and once was on the stocky side. The new president has surrounded himself with experts, men to whom he has given responsibility and from whom he expects expert advice. The Company has been divisionalized and a large number of people added at staff levels.

When Mr. Johnson stepped down from the presidency of the Company in 1959, sales were $89 million, profits were $3 million. The Company was located primarily on the East Coast and listed 550 restaurants and 75 motor lodges. Perhaps it is fair to say that it took a Howard D. Johnson to build and shape the Company and a Howard B. to bring it to maturity. In 1974 there were over 1,000 restaurants—and some 500 motor lodges.

Mr. Johnson died at the age of seventy-five in New York City in June, 1972. He was a pioneer in restaurant franchising, the person who saw the need for the highway restaurant and set about meeting that need so that his name became a household word.

J. WILLARD MARRIOTT (1900-   )

In the last ten years a number of innkeepers and restaurateurs have been added to the list of the 200,000 millionaires said to be in the United States. A few have been included in that even more select group of those with "over $100 million." However, only one in the latter group has also been a bishop and chairman of the inauguration of a President of the United States. He is J. Willard Marriott, chairman of the board of the Marriott Corp.

The corporation owns motor hotels and hotels, Hot Shoppes, cafeterias, and airline commissaries. It also owns the Big Boy Company, which owns and franchises hundreds of Big Boy restaurants, Farrell's Ice Cream Parlours, Great America theme parks, and cruise ships.

Horatio Alger would have liked Marriott: the American boy who makes it big with hard work, a sense of venture, and an unshakable confidence in God, self, and America. Like Hilton, Marriott came out of a pioneering West. His West was Mormon Utah, a West of sheep raising, fighting drought and storm, and, on occasion, a bout with a mountain lion or a rattlesnake.

For Bill Marriott responsibility came early. At fourteen he was sent on the long railroad trip to San Francisco with several carloads of sheep. At eighteen he had already served two years as a Mormon missionary. Higher education was at Webber College and at the University of Utah. During the summer vacations, he sold woolen underwear to miners and loggers. By his junior year, he had a territory of seven states and forty-five students working for him.

The Marriott Corporation started with root beer. Upon graduation from the University of Utah in 1926, Bill, for $2,000, bought a franchise to sell A & W root beer in Washington, D.C. The root beer had been put together by Roy Allen of Sacramento. It contained the unlikely ingredients of wintergreen leaves, wild cherry bark, dandelion root, althea root, anise seed, sarsaparilla root, angelica root, sassafras root, birchbark, and spikenard. In Salt Lake City, it sold 5,000 glasses a day.

Bill and a partner, Hugh Coulton, a college friend, looked for "drive-up" locations but, because of costs, settled on two small walk-in stores in Washington, D.C., where they installed a large orange barrel in the window and began selling root beer. Bill had figured that Washington, D.C., since it was hotter than Salt Lake City, was good for 20,000 glasses a day. The catch was that in Washington it isn't the heat, it's the humidity. Washington D.C. was hotter than Salt Lake City, but also muggier. Root beer sales were brisk in the summer, but came the fall and sales dropped sharply.

Husband and Wife Team

During the first summer in Washington, the chief root beer maker was Bill's new bride, Alice, who had just graduated from the University of Utah. It was she who put the root beer syrup into a large earthenware crock and mixed it with water. Then it was pumped into a carbonating machine. Cooling was accomplished by sending the root beer through 300 feet of tubing buried in ice.

Bill and Alice worked as a team, beginning at 8:30 A.M. and often working through until 2:00 A.M. the next morning. Alice kept the cash and the books. Bill did everything else that needed to be done for the operation.

"The restaurant business was born of desperation," says Mr. Marriott. When, in the fall, root beer sales dropped sharply, the partners tried to sublease their stores. No luck, so they added hot food: chili con carne and hot tamales. The recipes came from the Mexican Embassy. Hamburgers were not on the menu because at the time they were declasse.

The change from root beer stand to restaurant was made literally overnight. The big orange A & W barrel came out of the front window. Stools went in before the counter. A steam table was placed under the counter, and the name Hot Shoppes went on the front. The name had been suggested by a customer who had jokingly asked: "When are you going to open your hot shops?"

One of the First Drive-Ins

Bill bought out his partner the same year, and when spring came, opened one of the first drive-in restaurants in the nation. He literally built the restaurant, taking up hammer and nails himself; he had no architect. The design was a simple rectangle, the building painted orange with black trim.

Employees did not just cook or serve food. They painted, washed windows, did carpentry, and, on occasion, acted as bouncers. The employee who did not work twelve hours a day, seven days a week, was a sissy. The drive-in was built in a high density, Jewish neighborhood and turned into one of the most successful restaurants ever built. Profits from the place were used to finance other restaurants. The successor of the original drive-in is still very much of a winner, grossing close to $10,000 a seat per year. At one time as many as 150 carhops were employed.

In 1930 there were five Hot Shoppes and six years of depression ahead. Profit margins were small, but with full value given to customers the business prospered. The Marriotts began laying plans for expansion. Characteristically, they had an unshaken belief that prosperity would return.

In 1933 Bill became desperately ill with what was diagnosed as Hodgkins disease. Five doctors were unanimous in telling him that he had but one year to live. Frightened, he took a much-needed vacation trip, and, amazingly, on his return the disease was found to be gone. It was at this time, Marriott states, that he realized the importance of having an organization of people behind him, one that was not dependent upon any single individual.

Diversification came early but was introduced in measured steps. In 1934 the sandwich menu was enlarged to include full-course meals. In 1937 the company became the first airline caterer, putting up meals in cardboard boxes for American and Eastern Airlines passengers out of Washington, D.C. By 1969 Marriott Flite Services was serving fifty airlines from twenty domestic flight kitchens and nineteen overseas airports.

Tapping the Take-Out Market

Early in World War II, Marriott moved into in-plant foodservice. Lunch wagons roved around five plants and the cafeteria of the Naval Communications Annex, taken under contract. Soon after, an apartment cafeteria was signed.

After the war, the takeout market was tapped with the opening of the Pantry Houses. Their slogan: "Take home food for the family."

In 1957 lodging operations were added to the food business. A 360-room motel was built in Washington, D.C. Because of its design and location, it was an instant success. Since then, motels have been added in Dallas; Philadelphia; Atlanta; Saddlebrook, Maryland; and Boston. More are being planned and built.

To a greater extent than most hotel and restaurant chains, Marriott is family-oriented. Except for periods when her children were small, Alice Marriott continued to be active in the business, serving as an officer. In 1931 brother Paul joined the organization as general manager. Woodrow and Russell, the other two brothers, joined the company in 1933. Woodrow Marriott served as senior vice-president. Today, J. Willard Marriott, Jr., is president of the company.

The family idea, deeply rooted in the Mormon tradition, is extended even to the customer. The slogan, "Food for the Whole Family," goes back to the 1930s when a children's menu was created. The first menu, featuring three fierce bears on the cover, offered a bargain menu at thirty-five cents and was an immediate success.

The entire Marriott Company has aspects of being an extended family. Attention to employee relationships began early. An employee newspaper, *Hot Sauce*, a four-page tabloid, was published in 1937. It carried sports news, personal columns, and food tips. Significantly, printing costs for *Hot Sauce* were covered by paid advertising.

The company has the largest centralized personnel department of any in the field. Annual employee parties began in 1938. Group insurance, Christmas gifts, length of service gifts, a credit union, and a suggestion system are evidence of the interest in employee relations. Since 1953, when the company stock was offered to the public, employees have been encouraged to buy the stock. Marriott has been an industry leader with the company profit sharing plan. If success in personnel matters is measured by the lack of unionization in a company, Marriott has been eminently successful. In 1979 only a few units in all of the Marriott enterprises were unionized.

Advertising and Promotion

Marriott has been a strong believer in advertising and promotion since the days of the first Hot Shoppes. When stores opened in the 1930s, bands played on the parking lot while some of the employees danced and entertained. In the 1930s free root beer tickets were given away. The prettiest girl "Curbers" were loaded into a car and driven to the outskirts of Washington. As motorists stopped for traffic lights, they were handed a ticket for a free glass of root beer at any Hot Shoppe. Another successful merchandising practice was to give 3-oz. glasses of root beer to patrons' babies. "When these babies grew up," says Mr. Marriott, "they remained our customers."

Emphasis on system and control has marked the Marriott Company from the beginning. The first recipe system was a black book each cook carried in his back pocket. New recipes were penciled in. A test kitchen goes back to the early 1940s.

Centralized Commissary

Marriott has long believed in a centralized commissary operation. In 1930 certain food items were prepared centrally for distribution to the other stores. In 1941 production, administration, personnel, and accounting functions were all moved into a new three-story building. In the new commissary, raw food items, such as vegetables, were graded but not cooked. Meat, fish, and poultry were graded and portioned. These items were later cooked at the stores. All baked items, ice cream, and sherbets were made in the commissary. So, too, were soups, stocks, and gravies.

The pros and cons of commissary operations have been debated widely over the years. The John R. Thompson Company of Chicago successfully operated a large central commissary before the turn of the century. Companies that have widely scattered stores apparently believe that the costs of distribution more than offset savings made possible by mass-producing food in a commissary.

INDEX